Caring for the Elderly Client

Second Edition

Caring for the Elderly Client

Second Edition

Mary Ann Anderson, PhD, RN, CS, CNA
Fellow, National Gerontological Nurses Associattion
Associate Professor
College of Health Professions
Weber State University
Ogden, Utah

Judith V. Braun, PhD, RN
Executive Director
The Washington House
Alexandria, Virginia
Past President, National Gerontological Nurses Association

F. A. Davis Company • Philadelphia

F. A. Davis Company
1915 Arch Street
Philadelphia, PA 19103

Printed in the United States of America

Last digit indicates print number: 10 9 8 7 6 5 4 3

Acquisitions Editor: Alan Sorkowitz
Developmental Editor: Michele Rappoport
Production Editor: Elena Coler
Interior Design: Christine Cantera
Cover Design: Alicia Baronsky

As new scientific information becomes available through basic and clinical research, recommended treatments and drug therapies undergo changes. The authors and publisher have done everything possible to make this book accurate, up to date, and in accord with accepted standards at the time of publication. The authors, editors, and publisher are not responsible for errors or omissions or for consequences from application of the book, and make no warranty, expressed or implied, in regard to the contents of the book. Any practice described in this book should be applied by the reader in accordance with professional standards of care used in regard to the unique circumstances that may apply in each situation. The reader is advised always to check product information (package inserts) for changes and new information regarding dose and contraindications before administering any drug. Caution is especially urged when using new or infrequently ordered drugs.

Library of Congress Cataloging in Publication Data

Caring for the elderly client / [compiled by] Mary Ann Anderson,
  Judith V. Braun. — 2nd ed.
      p.   cm.
   Includes bibliographical references and index.
   Includes bibliographical references and index.
   ISBN 0-8036-0462-9 (pbk. : alk. paper)
   1. Geriatric nursing. I. Anderson, Mary Ann, 1946–   .
II. Braun, Judith V. (Judith Venglarik), 1952–   .
   [DNLM: 1. Geriatric Nursing. 2. Aging—physiology. 3. Health
Services for the Aged.   4. Nursing, Practical.   WY 152 C27722 1999]
RC954.A53   1999
610.73′65—dc21
DNLM/DLC
for Library of Congress   98-51166
                                                              CIP

This book is dedicated to our families, the people we love the most: Emily Anderson, and George, Zachary, and Hannah Braun.

Foreword

The increasing median age and total number of older adults in our society present numerous challenges for the health care system. Persons over age 65 are more frequently hospitalized than other age groups and have longer lengths of stay. More than half of the intensive care unit (ICU) beds and nearly all nursing home beds are filled by older persons. The elderly comprise most of home health caseloads.

In addition to adequate and competent health-care services in general, high-quality nursing services for the older population are and will continue to be required. Nursing is a unique discipline in its ability to address the physical, psychological, and social elements of care and to provide comprehensive, coordinated services that not only treat illness but also promote health and restore optimum function. When the health-care needs of older adults are examined, most can be identified as appropriately falling within the realm of nursing practice.

As health care has become increasingly "high tech," attention must be paid to ensuring that the importance of "high touch" (physical, emotional, and spiritual) is not overlooked. This is particularly important in the nursing care of older adults. Caring, support, and continued development, so important to the health and well-being of older adults, are best afforded through human contact.

Licensed practical nurses have long contributed to direct nursing care in a "high-touch" manner. Practicing under the direction of registered nurses (RNs) and others with statutory authority, licensed practical nurses (LPNs) bridge expanding medical and nursing technologies with the most human elements of direct care. The long tradition of direct "hands-on" care associated with practical nursing will have even greater importance in an increasingly complex, sophisticated, and technological health-care system. To effectively and competently meet present and future demands, LPNs must mesh the caring aspects of direct nursing services with new knowledge and skills.

Caring for the Elderly Client is a much-needed resource to assist LPNs in meeting the new challenges of providing high-quality services to older adults. Throughout this book, a positive view of aging and the aged is conveyed. Recognizing the individuality of each person and promoting optimal function are recurrent themes.

Many fine chapters review a wide range of clinical practice topics basic to gerontological nursing. These are well written and easy to absorb. Practical guidelines and case studies bridge theory and practice on a level appropriate for the LPN. From wellness promotion to restorative care, theory and practice skills are offered to guide LPNs in assessing, planning, delivering, and evaluating care.

In addition to the wealth of clinical information provided, this book offers insights into the managerial responsibilities assumed by LPNs. This inclusion is most refreshing and relevant. Despite the arguments by some colleagues that LPNs *should not* assume management roles, the reality is that some *do*. Fortunately, the authors recognize the actual roles LPNs must fill and review the essentials of managerial activities on a level appropriate for LPN nursing.

Great strides have been made in the educational, research, and practice components of gerontological nursing. *Caring for the Elderly Client* translates these advancements into a practical level appropriate for LPNs and offers guidance to this important group of nurses as they secure their niche in a dynamic health-care system.

Charlotte Eliopoulos, RNC, MPH
Specialist in Geriatric and Long-Term Care Nursing

Preface to the Second Edition

Welcome to the second edition of *Caring for the Elderly Client*. The response to the first edition was gratifying and prompted this writing. This text apparently meets a need for students and educators, which was the goal for writing it. With the aging population of this country increasing at an ever more rapid rate, it is critical for all nurses to be prepared to care for the aging population in a caring and knowledgeable way. That is the purpose of this text.

The opportunity to prepare a second edition has allowed for an additional effort to meet the learning needs of the student. This has been done in several ways. The size of the book has been changed. The new format leaves more margin space for students to take notes or highlight concepts that have special meaning for them. The space should be especially helpful when the student is working with the case studies. Color has been added to strengthen the visual appeal of the book and the new cover enhances the concept of caring with its pleasant visual appeal.

The second edition has retained the strong critical thinking aspect of the book with some enhancements. The case studies provide a strong component of the critical thinking aspects of the text as well. The instructor's guide is an excellent strength of this book. It provides the faculty person with learning activities as well as a diversified test bank. The second edition has retained its personality of being easily readable and immediately useful for students.

Preface to the First Edition

Most nurses in the workforce today, regardless of practice setting, are caring for older persons. With the exception of labor and delivery, the client population in health care environments is composed predominantly of persons age 65 or older. Whether they refer to themselves as gerontological nurses or not, nurses in today's health care settings must possess and use knowledge unique to caring for older clients.

Caring for an older person is not the same as caring for a middle-aged person with gray hair and wrinkles. It requires knowledge related to normal aging changes, altered responses to illness, environments of care, and a host of other topics specific to the aging individual. Thus, gerontological nursing is as specialized a field as pediatric nursing.

Many schools of nursing have recognized the need to prepare nursing students for their practice roles in caring for elderly clients. Courses on gerontological nursing are offered separately or integrated into curricula in most schools preparing licensed practical/vocational nurses (LPN) and registered nurses (RN). Continuing education courses and seminars on issues in gerontological nursing are offered widely throughout the country. Although numerous textbooks and articles on gerontological nursing are in print, few comprehensive textbooks are specifically geared to the LPN.

This book was compiled in response to the need for a clear, concise, basic text on caring for older clients that includes information pertinent to any practice setting. Although it is written at the licensed practical/vocational nurse level and makes frequent reference to LPNs throughout, its content is also relevant to registered nurses seeking basic information. It can be used as a required or supplemental text in gerontological nursing courses offered in LPN and LPN-RN ladder programs, as well as other levels of nursing education. Because of its readability and its broad focus on multiple and diverse issues, it can also be used as a refresher or reference manual for practicing nurses.

The role of the LPN varies significantly from setting to setting. Although she may provide direct patient care in the hospital, she may be the supervisor or even director of nursing in the long-term care facility. Some may question the appropriateness of this range in roles and responsibilities for the LPN. The need exists, however, to educate and prepare practical nurses for the roles they are currently asked to assume in the practice arena. This book was written to address the multifaceted roles and significant responsibilities of the LPN in various health care settings. These responsibilities range from health promotion to medication administration and evaluation of side, toxic, and desired effects; to collection of physical and psychological assessment data; to making assignments for nursing assistants.

This book includes several features that set it apart from other gerontological texts. Its overall approach is health and wellness oriented, rather than sickness oriented. It includes chapters on health promotion and restorative care that are pertinent, not only in the community and rehabilitative settings but in hospitals, nursing homes, and day-care centers.

Written with an emphasis on the humanistic aspects of caring, this book attempts to blend the gentle nurturing components of nursing with the technological knowledge necessary for caregiving. The pictures throughout the text are added to remind the reader that the information contained in the chapter pertains to human beings. Thus, it must be applied in a manner that recognizes individual differences, frailties, fears, and strengths.

The diversity of topics and the range of expertise among the contributors is another unique feature of this text. Nursing experts with sound, practical experience were chosen from all over the United States and asked to condense their knowledge on a particular topic into basic, relevant information with practical application. The result is a textbook addressing clinical topics such as lab values, pharmacology, health problems, and psychological assessment, as well as health and wellness topics and management and environmental topics. Each chapter, whether clinical, management, or otherwise, is presented in a framework that lends itself to application in the practice setting.

Case studies are included in every chapter to enhance the applicability of the chapter content. The reader is given an opportunity to review a real-life situation and answer pertinent questions. Such case studies represent practice situations that the gerontological nurse frequently faces. The questions are written in a format that gives the reader experience in answering standardized test questions similar to those on licensing exams.

As a final note, it is important to recognize the gender references throughout this text. The authors acknowledge that nurses and clients are both male and female. For ease of readability, however, nurses are referred to as female and clients as male throughout the content of this text.

Acknowledgments

The process of preparing this book has been a pleasant one. Much of that enjoyment is because of the people who assisted in its creation. Our sincere gratitude and respect go to Alan Sorkowitz, our editor at F. A. Davis. Alan has been both patient and highly skilled in leading us through the publication process.

The photographic work of Emily Anderson was invaluable to the creation of this text. Appreciation also needs to go to those who willingly allowed themselves to be photographed: the staff and residents at Wasatch Care Center, Ogden, Utah, and nursing students at Weber State University and the Community College of Philadelphia.

The knowledge and skill of the contributors to this book need to be recognized with our highest respect. There also is a great feeling of gratitude and respect for the many elderly people with whom we have worked over the time span of our careers. Each of these wonderful human beings has taught us regarding the needs and approaches of care for elderly people. We have tried to faithfully share with the reader the precious truths that have been taught to us by our clients.

Contributors

Sister Rose Therese Bahr, ASC
Provincial Councilor
Adorers of the Blood of Christ
Wichita, Kansas

Colleen Brill, RN, MSN
Mental Health Nurse Manager
Phelps County Medical Center
Rolla, Missouri

Kathleen R. Culliton, APRN, MS, GNP
Associate Professor
Weber State University
Ogden, Utah

Kay Martin Grott, RNC, MS, GNP
Vanderbilt Hospital, Intensive Care Unit
Nashville, Tennessee

Pamela E. Hugie, RN, MSN
Campus Coordinator/Assistant
    Professor
Weber State University/Utah State
    University
Logan, Utah

Mary Ann Johnson, RNC, PhD, GNP
Director, Nurse Practitioner Program
University of Utah
College of Nursing
Salt Lake City, Utah

Vivian J. Koroknay, MS, RN, CRRN
Director of Rehabilitation and
    Restorative Care Services
Asbury Methodist Village
Gaithersburg, Maryland

Mary Lou Long, RNC, MSN
Clinical Director, Nursing
St. Luke's Regional Medical Center
Boise, Idaho

Jeanne Robertson Samter, MSN, RN, CS
Assistant Professor of Nursing
North Georgia College and State
    University
Dahlonega, Georgia

Yvonne A. Sehy, RN, PhD, GNP
Nurse Practitioner, Hospital-Based
    Home Care
Veteran's Administration Medical
    Center
Salt Lake City, Utah

Mary McCarthy Slater, RNC, MSN
Long-Term Care Nurse Manager
Christian Health Center
Lexington, Kentucky

Elaine Tagliareni, RNC, MS
Associate Professor, Nursing
Community College of Philadelphia
Philadelphia, Pennsylvania

Verle Waters, RN, MA
Dean Emerita
Ohlone College
Fremont, California

Contents

Unit Two

CLINICAL PRACTICE   155

Chapter 12: Restorative Care   303

Sister Rose Therese Bahr & Kathleen R. Culliton

Chapter 13: Pharmacology and Its Significance for Elderly Clients   327

Pamela Hugie

Chapter 14: Laboratory Values and the Elderly   347

Yvonne A. Sehy

Appendices

Unit One

FOUNDATIONS OF CARE FOR THE ELDERLY CLIENT

Chapter

ELAINE TAGLIARENI and VERLE WATERS

1

The Aging Experience

Learning Objectives

After completing this chapter, the student will be able to:

1. Describe the demographics of people over 65 years of age in the United States.
2. Define the term "ageism."
3. Discuss the impact on society of stereotyping the elderly.
4. Identify age-related changes in the following body systems:
   Cardiovascular
   Respiratory
   Musculoskeletal
   Integumentary
   Gastrointestinal
   Genitourinary
   Neurological
   Special senses
5. List five physiological changes that are not normal processes of aging.

INTRODUCTION

Old age is new. The composition of the American population is different today from that of any previous generation. Of course, there were old people before, but their numbers were small compared with the number of people over age 65 today. In 1776, when the Declaration of Independence was signed, a child born in the United States had a life expectancy of 35 years. Today, the average life expectancy is 73; it will be 89 in the year 2000 according to projections by the National Institute on Aging (1990). Throughout most of human history, only 1 in 10 people could expect to live to the age of 65. Today 80% of Americans can anticipate reaching the age of 65 or older. In fact, two-thirds of all men and women who have lived beyond the age of 65 in the entire history of the world are alive today. Sometimes called "the graying of America," this dramatic change in our population has many ramifications in politics, economics, health care, recreation, and entertainment. All facets of life are affected by the fact that many more older adults are living today than just a few years ago.

DEMOGRAPHICS

People aged 65 and older comprise 12.7% of the population in this country, that is, more than one in every eight Americans. The number of older Americans has increased by 2.1 million or 7% since 1990, compared with an increase of 4% for the population under 65 years of age.

The white population will grow more slowly than before and in the next 40 years, it will begin to decline by comparison with African-Americans and other racial groups. Minority populations are projected to represent 25% of the elderly population in 2030, which is an increase from 13% in 1990. Predictions have been made that between 1990 and 2030, the white non-Hispanic population 65 and older is projected to increase by 93%, compared with 328% for older minorities, including Hispanics (555%) and non-Hispanic Blacks (160%); American Indians, Inuits, and Aleuts (231%); and Asians and Pacific Islanders (693%).

The fastest growing segment of the population in this country is composed of people over 85 years old. Projections indicate that the size of this age group will double between the years 1980 and 2000 and will double again between 2000 and 2040. The population over 85 years old (the "old-old") will benefit most from decreased mortality rates in the future.

About 2.1 million people celebrated their 65th birthdays in 1994 (5600 per day). That same year, about 1.7 million people 65 years old and older died, resulting in a net increase of 385,000 (1050 per day) people aged 65 years and older.

The increased numbers of elderly people in the United States have resulted in new definitions of aging. The term "young-old" is used for people 65–74 years old; the term "middle-old" is used for people 75–84 years old and "old-old" is used for people 85 and older. It is necessary to define the differences for each age group considering their that health needs, medication dosages, and frailness relate specifically to their age category.

IMPACT OF AGING ON NURSING

The great increase in the number of older people means that nursing practice must be very different from just a few years ago. A geriatric specialist, Dr. Robert Butler (1969), said that all graduates going into health-care work today will spend 75% of their working lives caring for older people. In today's typical hospital, unless you work in maternity or pediatrics, you are, for all practical purposes, a gerontological nurse because so many of the patients are over 65 years of age.

The greatest need for health-care services exists within the old-old population. Between the ages of 65 and 74, only about 4% of the people require any assistance in their daily lives; by age 85, the proportion of people requiring some kind of personal assistance is one in three, with 20% receiving home care. Nurses, then, will see and care for the old-old whatever the work site—hospital, home, or nursing home.

Health care has changed in various ways because of the number of people who are aging. As a group, older citizens are a very powerful political force; they have influenced the actions of Congress and the President on health-related issues and will continue to do so. A few yeas ago, Congress passed legislation providing insurance coverage for catastrophic medical events for those under Medicare, which added a relatively small amount to the cost of Medicare insurance paid by recipients. The new plan was, however, unacceptable to older citizens, and as a result of numerous calls and letters, Congress was persuaded to rescind its legislation.

Older citizens want and expect to have a say in the kind of health care they receive, where they receive it, and from whom. For instance, demand is growing for home-care services from older people who need assistance and nursing care but prefer to be cared for at home.

This population of new clients in the health-care system requires the health-care provider to consider them in a new way and requires new insights. Never before have nurses had to care for elderly people who have survived the Holocaust, two world wars, the Korean and Vietnam Wars, the Great Depression, and rock and roll! Because the survival experiences and skills of these elderly clients are new, they require society to address them in a new way.

ETHICAL CONSIDERATIONS

The increase in the number of older people in this country has raised ethical questions and dilemmas that emerge when family members, nurses, and doctors must make treatment decisions for older adults. Whether to resuscitate or institute invasive treatment of a person advanced in years, to continue life-support systems when death seems inevitable, or to prolong artificial feeding of a comatose patient are frequently encountered questions with no easy answers. Most hospitals and a growing number of nursing homes have ethics committees that assume the task of developing guidelines and providing assistance to staff members who are involved in making difficult decisions. All health-care professionals are offering broader education in the care of older people and in ethical reasoning.

ATTITUDES TOWARD AGING

The study of aging is a very important part of nursing. Many myths, stereotypes, and prejudices about old age exist in our culture, and nurses need to be able to separate myths and prejudices from fact. Modern researchers are intently studying the aging experience (another indication of the importance of this topic in today's world). This chapter draws from their findings to represent a realistic picture of the processes and effects of aging. Myths and prejudices about old age are pervasive in our society. Browsing through a greeting card display reveals some very good examples of the stereotypes and fables of aging:

"I won't say you're old," reads one greeting card, "But in horse years, you'd be glue on this envelope."

"Happy birthday, Hot Stuff! Who says people our age can't still live in the fast lane?" reads another. The inside message: "Voilà! Adult diapers with racing stripes."

As the contents of many of the cards imply, old age conjures up images of rocking chairs, dentures, memory loss, and incontinence. People laugh at the humor in the birthday cards, but a serious societal danger lurks in such negative and prejudicial images. Stereotypes, myths, and distortions concerning aging and old people lead to actions that discriminate against the aged. American culture glorifies youth. Print and television advertising, clothing fashions, and other expressions of the desirable norm all push the image of zestful youth. Because today's adults have grown up in this culture, they pick up its values and prejudices without realizing it.

One of us joined a tour group led by a sincere, well-intentioned young man. He tried to exchange a friendly word with every person in the group. He spoke to a healthy-looking man, who may have been in his late 70s, in a raised voice as though he assumed that the man was hard of hearing. "What did you used to be?" he asked. After a pause, the older man replied, "I still am."

AGEISM

The term "ageism" was coined in 1968 by Butler (1969) to describe negative attitudes and practices that were directed toward the aged. He defined ageism as a systematic stereotyping of and discrimination against people simply because they are old. Ageism is very similar to racism and sexism, which discriminate against people because of skin color and gender. Old people are categorized as senile, rigid in thought and manner, old-fashioned in morality and skills. Ageism allows the younger generation to see older people as different; thus, they subtly cease to identify with their elders as human beings (Butler, 1969).

In the decades since Dr. Butler first wrote about ageism, a steady improvement in attitudes toward the aged has been seen. This partly resulted from general public education, increased attention in the media, and broadening of education about gerontology (the study of aging) in colleges and universities. Seriously negative attitudes toward the aged still exist, however, and they appear subtly, covertly, and even unconsciously. Like racism and sexism, ageism is still persistent but remains below the surface. Negative images of "greedy geezers," criticism that the aged have had "too many advantages" and are siphoning off public money that should go to poor children, continue to find expression. The cosmetic industry thrives on the sale of products that eliminate "age spots," smooth away wrinkles, conceal gray hairs, and make one look younger than one's actual age. Growing old is represented as a calamity, and being old as having a dreaded disease. The last years of life are pictured as time spent in death's waiting room.

In reality, elderly people do not offer a panorama of doom and death. Many senior citizens live well into their 70s, 80s, and even 90s with "youthful vigor," in relative physical comfort and safety, and in good health. Many others do have chronic health problems but because the problems are well managed and well controlled, such people consider themselves "healthy" and lead active, fulfilling lives. Still others have significant limitations that affect their independence and activity, but they are able to enjoy a rich and varied existence because they live with family members or in other protected environments. The frailest and most dependent members of the older generation are cared for by dedicated caregivers either at home or in nursing homes. This text emphasizes that quality care for the weakest elderly people is directed toward enabling them to enjoy the present and look forward to the future with the same enthusiasm as the more active and healthier senior citizen.

The image of the nursing home envisioned by some people is in part an expression of ageism. It is possible that some care in some nursing homes or hospitals is substandard. Most nursing homes, however, give excellent care to a frail and vulnerable population that cannot be cared for elsewhere. Even so, the image of the nursing home as a place of terrible endings reveals an attitude of hopelessness about fraility and old age. Today's nursing home is characterized by a concept of *rehabilitative,* not *custodial* care, a perspective that calls for nursing interventions intended to support the highest possible level of independence despite compelling physical and cognitive limitations.

All people grow up shaped by their culture and by the circumstances of their existence. Today's older Americans were children during the Great Depression and young adults during an all-embracing war. Their attitudes and values are marked by such experiences. Someone who grew up in another country has been shaped by a very different life background. Immigration to the United States over the past decades of substantial numbers of Asian and Hispanic people has significant implications for the practice of gerontological nursing. In time, older people from those cultures will require hospital care, home care, and nursing home care. Gerontological nursing specialists are now studying ethnic and cultural differences and providing useful information to the caregivers who work in multicultural settings.

An important concept to remember is that of the uniqueness of the individual: just as every child or every middle-aged adult is in some way unique, so is the older adult. The mistaken belief that one old person is just like another is an expression of ageism, and this perception can lead to potentially harmful treatment. Doctors and nurses sometimes treat older patients as they might treat a child, calling them by their first names without asking how they wish to be addressed or, worse yet, calling them "honey" or "dear." Caregivers often are guilty of "infantilizing" the elderly. It is easy to see how such treatment increases dependence and frailty, rather than fostering as much independence as possible even for a person with severe limitations. Not

Not all old people are alike. They look different, are different ages, have different interests and hobbies, and think as individuals.

all old people are cranky and gloomy, although the man or woman who was cranky and gloomy at age 40 is probably more so at 80. According to a saying, people become more and more like themselves as they age.

Coming to know the special and unique qualities of every older patient is one of the nurse's most interesting and rewarding challenges. Fortunately, encouraging older people to talk about themselves is good not only because it helps the nurse come to know that person *as a person* but also because it benefits the client as well. Encouraging the older patient or nursing home resident to talk about life experiences is called *reminiscence therapy* or *life review*. Remembering and recounting memories, both painful and happy, and reviewing both the successes and failures of life help the older person to achieve and maintain a sense of integrity and self-worth, one of the developmental tasks of older adulthood.

All who work in the health-care field need to examine their own attitudes and biases about older people in general and about frail or ill older people in particular. Suggested classroom activities at the end of this chapter help students identify and examine attitudes toward aging and toward work with older people. Nurses are called on to combat the influence of ageism throughout their careers.

THE NORMAL AGING PROCESS

Since the early 1950s, much research has taken place in both Europe and the United States on identifying and classifying common physiological and psychosocial changes that occur as people grow older. These changes have been termed *normal* because they represent alterations in body structure and function that occur gradually throughout life. In this context, aging is seen as a natural process, and the changes associated with it are considered to be expected and continuous.

To fully understand the normal aging process, nurses must realize that aging is a normal developmental event and that patterns of aging vary dramatically among older adults. Although the profession studies normal age changes that are universal, every person ages in a particular, individualized way. No two individuals are alike; in fact, the number of ways people age may be seen as equal to the number of people who have lived into old age. As individuals age, they become more diverse, not more alike. Thus, the range of "normal" aging characteristics is wide, and each individual exhibits a unique interplay of physical, social, and environmental influences that define the personal aging experience.

Think of the older adults in your own life, your parents or grandparents, your neighbors, and patients for whom you have cared. All are different. They vary in their outlook on life; they may be either active or sedentary, outgoing or introverted, upbeat or sullen. Many are chronically ill. How individuals age depends on life experiences, availability of support systems, and previous coping styles. Although nurses study aging as a universal and inevitable event with specific characteristic changes, not all body systems age from the same point in time or at the same rate. Each person's experience with the normal aging process is unique.

Unfortunately, normal aging changes are not always viewed as natural or positive. In fact, because most changes are described in terms of losses, for example, loss of night vision or decrease in peristalsis, aging is seen as a series of inevitable negatives to be endured. Terms such as *helplessness, decreased ability to function,* and *loss of purpose* are often used to define the aging process. Additionally, normal age changes are often presented in textbooks and in more popular literature as associated with information about pathology and disease conditions. This approach has led to the misconception that age changes indicate illness or disease. Often older adults do have a chronic or acute illness superimposed on age-related changes, but development of disease is *not* a normal part of aging. It is essential for the nurse to understand this perspective and develop a more positive approach to normal aging. It is also important to remember that most older adults live actively and independently in the community and cope successfully with age-related changes and chronic illnesses. Health, then, for the older adults, might well be defined as the ability to function at an individual's highest potential, despite the presence of age-related changes and risk factors (Miller, 1990).

Essential facts about the normal aging process can be summarized as follows:

1. As individuals age, they become more diverse, not more alike.
2. Age-related changes develop in each individual in a unique way.
3. Normal aging and disease are separate entities.
4. Normal aging includes both gains and losses and does not necessarily indicate decline.
5. Successful adaptation to the aging process is accomplished by most older adults.

NORMAL PHYSIOLOGICAL CHANGES ACCORDING TO BODY SYSTEMS

Specific age-related changes are described in terms of the body systems with which they are associated. Common functional changes as experienced by the older adult as a result of physiological alterations are also discussed. The term *function* refers to the older adult's ability to perform activities of daily living and takes into consideration the quality of life of the individual. As the older adult experiences an increase in the number and intensity of age-related changes, functional independence is often jeopardized. Nursing approaches to prevent losses and promote self-care in light of age-related changes are also considered in this section.

The Cardiovascular System

The cardiovascular system loses its efficiency with age, but because the elderly require less oxygen both at rest and during exercise, many older adults effectively compensate for changes in circulatory function. However, the high incidence of cardiovascular disease in the older population often makes it difficult to distinguish normal age-related changes from those related to sickness.

Age-Related Changes

Heart
1. Cardiac muscle strength is diminished.
2. Heart valves become thickened and more rigid.
3. The sinoatrial (SA) node, which is responsible for conduction, is less efficient and impulses are slowed.

Blood vessels
1. Arteries become less elastic.
2. Capillary walls thicken and slow the exchange of nutrients and waste products between blood and tissues.

Blood
1. Blood volume is reduced due to an age-related decline in total body water.
2. Bone marrow activity is reduced, which leads to a slight drop in levels of red blood cells, hematocrit, and hemoglobin.

Functional Changes

Because heart contractions may be weaker, blood volume decreases and cardiac output drops at a rate of about 1% per year below the value of 5 L normally found in a younger person. In addition, the heart rate itself slows. These overall effects do not compromise the cardiovascular system under normal, nonstressful conditions, but during times of illness, anxiety, and increased stress, cardiac reserve may be compromised, inducing fatigue and tachycardia. A rapid heart rate may take longer to return to a baseline rate, so it is best to avoid taking a patient's pulse immediately after exertion or a stressful event. As a result, the nurse must assess the older adult's energy level by carefully documenting the level of fatigue and the tolerated amount of activity. The greater rigidity of the vascular walls increases both systolic and diastolic pressures. The level at which this normal change in blood pressure becomes hypertension and requires treatment is a major source of controversy (Eliopoulos, 1993). Often, if no symptoms are apparent, the older adult can tolerate such increases without medical treatment.

Decreased blood flow to body organs and peripheral tissue, including the extremities, also results from narrower lumen size. Regular exercise and a good diet can diminish the effects of these changes. In summary, with normal aging, some atherosclerosis is expected, as well as decreased cardiac output, but cardiovascular response remains adequate if cardiac disease is not present.

Respiratory System

Respiratory functioning shows minimal age-related decline in healthy older adults. The age-related changes that do affect the respiratory system are so gradual that most older adults compensate well for these changes.

Age-Related Changes

Skeletal changes
1. The rib cage becomes rigid as cartilage calcifies.
2. The thoracic spine may shorten, and osteoporosis may cause a stooped posture, thus decreasing the active lung space and limiting thoracic movement.

Accessory muscles
1. Abdominal muscles weaken, thus decreasing both inspiratory and expiratory effort.
2. The diaphragm does not appear to lose mass (Burke & Walsh, 1992).

Intrapulmonary changes
1. Lung elastic recoil is progressively lost with advancing age.
2. Alveoli enlarge and become thin, and although their number remains constant, the number of functioning alveoli decreases overall.
3. The alveolar-capillary membrane thickens, reducing the surface area for gas exchange.

Functional Changes

Structural changes in the respiratory system affect the rate of air flow into and out of the lung as well as that of gas exchange at the alveolar level. Because of limited elastic recoil, residual volume increases. This means that less ventilation occurs at the bases of the lungs, and more air and secretions remain in the lungs. In addition, the shallow breathing patterns of older adults, secondary to postural changes, contribute to this reduced air flow. For this reason, nurses must routinely encourage deep-breathing exercises and daily exercise. Decreased chest muscle strength contributes to a less effective cough response and places the older adult at greater risk of pulmonary infection. The shallow breathing pattern also affects gas exchange.

Oxygen saturation is diminished. For example, the partial pressure of oxygen in alveoli (PaO_2) is about 90 mm Hg for a healthy young adult, whereas a value of 75 mm Hg at age 70 would be acceptable. This decline may result in a decreased tolerance for exercise and a need for short rest periods during activity.

It is important to note that age-related changes external to the respiratory system have a significant impact on respiratory function. Slowed gastric motility may lead to food aspiration; reduced levels of bodily fluids can may drying of the mucosa and subsequent infection; limited mobility and inactivity may limit air volume and flow and result in pooling of secretions (Eliopoulos, 1993). To maintain respiratory health, the older adult must maintain a healthy lifestyle that includes regular exercise, adequate fluid intake, and avoidance of smoking. Efficient respiratory performance is essential to live life to the fullest. Decreased performance, with attendant fatigue and shortness of breath, limits activity, often leading to confinement, isolation, and depression.

Musculoskeletal System

Most older adults experience alterations in posture, changes in range of motion, and slowed movement. These changes account for many of the characteristics normally associated with old age.

Age-Related Changes

Bone structure
1. Loss of bone mass results in brittle, weak bones.
2. The vertebral column may compress, leading to reduction in height.

Muscle strength
1. Muscle wasting occurs and regeneration or muscle tissue slows.
2. Muscles of the arms and legs become thin and flabby.
3. Muscles lose flexibility and endurance with inactivity.

Joints
1. Range of motion may be limited.
2. Cartilage thins, so that joints may be painful, inflamed, or stiff.

Functional Changes

Loss of muscle mass is a gradual process and most older adults compensate for it well. Regular exercise has been shown to reduce bone loss and promote increased muscle strength, as well as to improve flexibility and muscle coordination. Conversely, immobility and sedentary lifestyles lead to loss of muscle size and strength. Older people who are inactive may experience weakness or tingling in the extremities, stiff or aching joints, reduced range of motion, and muscle cramps due to decreased movement.

Loss of bone mass and bone density results in osteoporosis and porous, brittle bones that are at greater risk of fracture, due to estrogen deficiencies and low serum calcium levels; therefore, calcium supplements and estrogens are often prescribed. In summary, changes caused by osteoporosis, lack of joint motion, and decreased muscle strength and endurance may affect the functional ability of the older adult; however, an effective exercise program, together with adequate diet and a healthy outlook that includes independence and an active lifestyle, can reverse or slow down musculoskeletal changes. The phrase "Use it or lose it" directly applies to the older adult's musculoskeletal functional ability.

Integumentary System

Changes involving the skin probably are emblematic of the aging process more than those of any other system. The formation of wrinkles, the development of "age spots," graying of the hair, and baldness are constant reminders of growing old. In addition, no other system is so highly influenced by previous life patterns and environmental conditions, particularly exposure to the sun.

Age-Related Changes

Skin
1. The skin loses elasticity, leading to wrinkles, folds, and dryness.
2. The skin thins, giving less protection to underlying blood vessels.
3. Subcutaneous fat diminishes.
4. Melanocytes cluster, producing the skin pigmentation known as age spots.

Hair
1. Decreased activity of hair follicles results in thinning of the hair.
2. Decreased rate of melanin production results in loss of original color, and graying.
3. Women may develop hair on the chin and upper lip.

Nails
1. Decreased blood flow to the nailbed may cause nails to become thick, dull, hard, and brittle, with longitudinal lines.

Sweat glands
1. Decreases in size and number occur.

Functional Changes

Intact skin is the first line of defense against bacterial invasion and minor physical trauma. Age-related skin dryness and decreased elasticity increase the risk of skin breakdown and skin tears, leading to increased potential for injury and infection. Body temperature regulation is impaired by decreased sweat production. Because of this, older adults may not exhibit diaphoresis with elevated body temperatures and may exhibit an intolerance for a hot environment.

Conversely, the loss of insulation in the form of a fat layer may make older adults feel cold. They often ask for extra sweaters when younger adults are quite comfortable with the ambient temperature. Nurses need to be aware of temperature discomforts when bathing, dressing, or examining the older adult, and to respond appropriately to the older adult's concern.

In summary, age-related changes in the integumentary system affect the essential mechanisms of body protection and temperature regulation and also greatly influence one's perception of aging. Earlier health practices, related to nutrition, grooming, bathing, and physical activity, as well as genetic, biochemical, and environmental factors, are powerful determinants of integumentary status. The older adult who has followed a healthy lifestyle often takes pride in the moistness and softness of aging skin, revealing a newfound beauty in gray hair and wise wrinkles.

Gastrointestinal System

Changes in the gastrointestinal (GI) system, although not life-threatening, often cause the greatest concern to the older adult. Indigestion, constipation, and anorexia are common GI problems that greatly affect functional status.

Age-Related Changes

Oral cavity
1. Reabsorption of bone in the jaw may loosen teeth and, thus, reduce the ability to chew.
2. People with dentures must have them checked regularly to maintain a proper fit.

Esophagus
1. The gag reflex weakens, causing an increased risk of food aspiration.
2. Smooth muscle weakness delays emptying time.

Stomach
1. Decreased gastric acid secretions may impair absorption of iron, vitamin B_{12}, and protein.

Intestines
1. Peristalsis decreases.
2. Weakening of the sphincter muscles leads to incompetent emptying of the bowel.

Functional Changes

The slowing of peristalsis and the loss of smooth muscle tone delay gastric emptying so that a feeling of "fullness" is present after eating only small amounts of food. In addition, delayed gastric emptying time and reduced gastric acid secretions may lead to indigestion, discomfort, and reduced appetite. Frequent small meals, rather than three large ones, may be better tolerated. Decreased peristalsis also contributes to slower transit time in the large intestine and allows more time for water reabsorption and hardening of the stool, so that the nurse must recommend a diet adequate in fiber and fluids. Fatigue, discomfort, activity intolerance, and sensory losses may make food preparation difficult for the older adult living at home. This could result in a nutritionally inadequate diet. In summary, effective GI functioning creates peace of mind for the older adult and greatly influences well-being.

Genitourinary System

Changes in the genitourinary system affect the basic bodily functions of voiding and sexual performance. These issues are often difficult for the older adult to discuss. An attendant belief holds that genitourinary problems, such as incontinence and decreased sexual response, are normal results of aging. They are not, but the belief that they are often delays the older adult from seeking treatment (Eliopoulos, 1993). Helping the older adult to maintain optimal genitourinary function is often a challenge for the nurse.

Age-Related Changes

Renal function
1. Renal blood flow decreases because of decreased cardiac output and reduced glomerular filtration rate.
2. Ability to concentrate urine may be impaired.

Bladder
1. Loss of muscle tone and incomplete emptying may occur.
2. Capacity decreases.

Micturition
1. In men, increased frequency due to enlargement of the prostate is possible.
2. In women, increased frequency may be caused by relaxation of the perineal muscle.

Female reproduction
1. The vulva may atrophy.
2. Pubic hair may fall out.
3. Vaginal secretions diminish, and vaginal walls thin and become less elastic.

Male reproduction
1. Testes decrease in size.
2. Prostate may enlarge.

Functional Changes

Despite decreased renal blood flow and the loss of kidney mass, the genitourinary system continues to function normally in the absence of disease. Functional impairments result from decreased bladder capacity and include urinary frequency, nocturia, and retention of urine. These changes may eventually cause dysfunction, leading to infection, urgency, and incontinence. Although urinary incontinence is not a normal outcome of the aging process, loss of perineal muscle mass may contribute to one of the most common forms of incontinence in women, stress incontinence. This involves leakage of urine that occurs with coughing, sneezing, laughing, or lifting. Pelvic floor exercises comprise an effective strategy to strengthen muscle tone and prevent involuntary leakage. Vaginal changes may lead to painful intercourse, vaginal infections, and intense itching.

Enlargement of the prostate, which occurs in most elderly men (Eliopoulos, 1993), is most often benign. It can, however, cause urinary retention, frequency, overflow incontinence, and eventually renal damage. Therefore, older men should have regular examinations of the prostate.

In summary, changes in voiding, particularly incontinence, and changes in sexual response may dramatically alter genitourinary function and contribute to embarrassment and general discomfort for the older adult. By demonstrating sensitivity and acceptance, the nurse can effectively intervene to improve genitourinary functional response.

Nervous System

Age-related changes in the nervous system affect all body systems and involve vascular response, mobility, coordination, visual activity, and cognitive ability. Interestingly, most misconceptions about normal age-related changes involve the nervous system: for example, the misconception that mental decline or "senility" is inevitable with aging or that intellectual capacity diminishes with age. The nurse needs to teach older adults that general decline of neurological function is not an automatic response to aging and that, in the absence of disease, the older adult's neurological system functions adequately.

Age-Related Changes

Neurons
1. Neurons are steadily lost in the brain and spinal cord.
2. Synthesis and metabolism of neurotransmitters are diminished.
3. Brain mass is lost progressively.

Movement
1. The kinesthetic sense is less efficient.
2. Balance may be impaired.
3. Reaction time decreases.

Sleep
1. Insomnia and increased night wakening may occur.
2. Deep sleep (stage IV) and rapid eye movement (REM) sleep decrease.

Functional Changes

As motor neurons work less efficiently, reaction time slows and the ability to respond quickly to stimuli decreases. Research studies indicate that although response time may be prolonged, older adults are willing to give up speed for accuracy, and tend to respond more slowly but with greater precision. There appears to be little correlation between brain atrophy and cognitive loss (Matteson, Linton & Barnes, 1996). Older adults are generally well oriented to time, place, and person, with minimal changes in memory performance, despite decreased synthesis of neurotransmitters and diminished brain size. The elderly are particularly at risk for falls, due to a slower reaction time in maintaining balance and the potential for hypotensive reactions secondary to decreased blood volume. Resulting symptoms of dizziness, lightheadedness, and vertigo contribute to impaired balance. Nurses should allow the older adult adequate time for position change; dangling at the bedside and standing briefly before ambulation may be indicated.

In general, older adults sleep less at night but take naps during the day, so that cumulative sleep time is usually adequate. These frequent awakenings may cause restless sleep and abrupt wakefulness that is often troubling to the older adult. Thorough sleep assessment is necessary to determine actual sleep time. Additionally, afternoon exercise and a decrease in stimulants at bedtime may be suggested by the nurse. Environmental changes, such as noise control and regulation of room temperature, may be helpful.

In summary, common age-related changes of the nervous system, particularly slowed reaction time, affect movement, sleep, and cognition, the functions of which are vital to optimal performance of activities of daily living.

Special Sense Organs

The sensory organs of sight, hearing, taste, touch, and smell facilitate communication with the environment. Loss of sensory function, particularly vision and hearing, severely alters the older adult's self-care abilities and quality of life. Age-related changes that result in loss of sensory function may be the most difficult for the older adult to accept and cope with effectively. The nurse must be extremely sensitive to sensory changes and their impact on each patient.

Age-Related Changes

Vision
1. Ability to focus on close objects is diminished.
2. Increased density of the lens occurs, and lipid accumulates around the iris, causing a grayish-yellow ring.
3. The eyes' production of tears decreases.
4. The pupils decrease in size and become less responsive to light.
5. Night vision decreases, and the iris loses pigment so that eye color usually becomes light blue or gray.

Hearing
1. The ability to hear high-frequency tones decreases.
2. The cerumen contains a greater amount of keratin so that it hardens and becomes more likely to become impacted.

Taste
1. Ability to perceive bitter, salt, and sour tastes diminishes.

Touch
1. Ability to feel light touch, pain, or different temperatures may decrease.

Functional Changes

Despite normal age-related changes in vision, most older adults have adequate visual function to meet self-care activities using corrective lenses. Because dark and light adaptation takes longer, simple activities, like entering or leaving a theater or

Older adults are unique individuals, who have special histories and life experiences.

going to the bathroom at night, put older people at risk for falls and injury. Yellowing of the lens makes vision for low-tone colors (violet, blue, green) difficult; use of yellow, orange, or red colors on signs or on bedroom walls increases the ease with which older adults successfully interact with their environment. Older adults have a difficult time with glare, especially glare from sunlight or from the reflection of light from an object or newly shined floor. Inability to focus due to glare may alter depth perception, and older adults might be less able to see a nurse who stands talking to a patient in front of a window.

Decreased production of tears by the eye may contribute to irritation and infection; artificial tears are often prescribed. Functional hearing changes result initially in an inability to hear high-pitched tones, so that the nurse should speak in a normal tone of voice without shouting at the client and without increasing pitch. Because it takes more sensory stimulation to trigger the taste experience, older adults may use more salt, for example, to effectively produce a salt taste on their food.

In summary, sensory changes have a profound impact on the functional ability of older adults. The nurse must always determine whether the patient uses corrective lenses or a hearing aid and ensure that the patient has these assistive devices available at all times; the older adult's ability to perceive environmental changes and protect himself or herself from harm may depend on it.

Later in this book, the reader will be able to compare abnormal physiological changes of the elderly with the normal changes explained here. The gerontological nurse should have a thorough understanding of both aspects of physiological aging.

SUMMARY

This chapter has pointed out the importance of understanding the older adult in today's society. As the number of aged individuals increases, and as more and more older adults require nursing care, the nurse must develop a strong knowledge base in gerontological nursing theory. It is equally important to explore the myths, stereotypes, and prejudices about old age to begin the process of seeing older adults as unique individuals who have special histories and life experiences. Normal aging changes each person in a unique way. We hope that as you acquire the specific knowledge and skills to be effective caregivers of older adults, you will embrace the attitude that all older adults are unique and should be encouraged to function at their full potential. With this critical understanding, we firmly believe that you will make a significant difference in the quality of their lives.

CASE STUDY

Ms. B., 76 years old, lives in a duplex with her 83-year-old sister. Last year, the sister had a mild stroke, leaving her with left-sided weakness. Ms. B. manages the household and coordinates her sister's care, including home health aides, physical and occupational therapy, and visits to the doctor's office.

Ms. B. describes herself as healthy. "Okay, I had cancer of the colon 2 years ago, but I had surgery and some chemotherapy too and now I'm okay. Oh, I sometimes get constipated but that has nothing to do with the cancer." She states that she tires more easily these days and tries to "rest every afternoon." Still, she maintains a full schedule of grocery shopping, visiting friends, cooking and cleaning, and caring for her sister's needs. She has no breathing problems, and her appetite is excellent. "I can't eat as much as I used to at each meal, but my sister and I have a snack in the afternoon and at bedtime."

She does complain about nocturnal voiding two or three times a night and has had two urinary infections this year. "Sometimes I dribble urine and I use those pads."

Both sisters are always cold; their home is kept very warm, and they always seem to be wearing sweaters and heavy stockings. Every Sunday is "beauty day" at the B.'s residence, when they apply face and hand cream to dry skin, style their thinning hair, and care for their nails, which are "getting thick and brittle." Both claim that they have become shorter in the past few years; Ms. B. often feels weary at night due to joint pain. She has learned to adjust her daily schedule to changes in endurance. "No matter where I go, I take my time, sit down, and pace myself. I know where every bench and restaurant is in South Philadelphia."

Ms. B. has noticed that she needs to wear her glasses all the time when reading or paying bills; she invested in 100-W light bulbs for every lamp because "we both need stronger light to read by these days." She is never without her sunglasses to avoid glare; in fact, every shade is always lowered at their house during the day. Ms. B. claims she does not "think as clearly lately as I used to; it takes me longer to figure things out and make decisions." But she continues to manage the household and lead an active life.

"I have my friends, my neighborhood, my home, and, of course, my sister. We have been together all our lives. We care about each other and we do pretty well, taking each day as it comes, each day expecting another good day."

CASE STUDY
DISCUSSION

1. What age-related changes has Ms. B. experienced?
2. Would you consider Ms. B. to be a healthy older adult? Explain.

CASE STUDY
SOLUTION

1. Ms. B. has experienced age-related changes in all the following body systems:

   Cardiovascular
   Decreased activity tolerance
   Fatigue with increased activity

   Musculoskeletal
   Loss of muscle strength
   Height loss
   Joint pain

   Integumentary
   Dry skin
   Brittle, thickened nails
   Thinning hair

   Gastrointestinal
   Delayed gastric emptying leading to "fullness"
   Reduced GI motility

   Genitourinary
   Urinary retention, which may contribute to infection
   Urgency and stress incontinence

   Nervous
   Delayed reaction time

   Special senses
   Diminished ability to focus on close objects
   Inability to tolerate glare
   Poor vision in reduced light

2. Ms. B. is a healthy older adult because she functions at an optimal level despite the presence of age-related changes. She feels good about her life and about her coping skills. She expects continued "good days."

Study Questions

Circle the correct choice(s).

1. Your client is 84 years old. What normal change in vital signs would you expect to assess?
   a. A higher than normal temperature
   b. A slower pulse
   c. A shallower breathing pattern
   d. A lower blood pressure

2. Immobility or sedentary lifestyles have what effect on the older adult?
   a. Loss of muscle size and strength
   b. Decreased serum sodium levels
   c. Loss of skin elasticity
   d. Thinning of cartilage in joints

3. Mrs. Jones, aged 86 years, complains of fullness after eating only small amounts of food. This is primarily due to which gastrointestinal change?
   a. Delayed gastric emptying time
   b. Increased gastric acid secretions
   c. Hypertonicity of gastric muscles
   d. Loss of ability to chew

4. Mrs. Smith, aged 79 years, is admitted to the hospital. Based on your understanding of normal age changes in the nervous system, what behavior might you expect Mrs. Smith to exhibit?
   a. Decreased intellectual function
   b. Forgetfulness and confusion
   c. Lack of orientation to time and place
   d. Longer response time to questions

5. Which of the following statements most accurately describes normal aging changes in the older adult?
   a. As individuals age, they become more diverse.
   b. Most older adults experience chronic illness and functional impairment.
   c. Age-related changes are similar in each older adult.
   d. Normal age changes most commonly describe decline and loss of function.

References

Butler, R. M. (1969). Ageism: Another form of bigotry. *Gerontologist, 9,* 243–246.

Carnavelli, D. L., & Patrick, M. (1993). *Nursing management of the elderly.* Philadelphia: Lippincott-Raven Publishers.

Ebersole, P., & Hess, P. (1990). *Toward healthy aging: Human needs and nursing response* (3rd ed.). St. Louis: C. V. Mosby.

Eliopoulos, C. (1993). *Gerontological nursing* (3rd ed.). Philadelphia: J. B. Lippincott.

Matteson, M. A., Linton, A. D., & Barnes, S. J. (1996). Cognitive developmental approach to dementia. *Image, 28*(3), 233–241.

Miller, C. (1990). *Nursing care of older adults: Theory and practice.* Glenview, IL: Scott, Foresman (Little, Brown Higher Education).

U.S. Bureau of the Census. (1989). *Population report series* (Report No. 1018). Washington, DC: U.S. Government Printing Office.

Bibliography

Breakey, B. (1990). What is a geriatric nurse? *Geriatric Nursing, 11,* 11.
   A poetic view of a day in the life of a geriatric nurse—"some really special kind of nurse."

Burke, A., Shirley, E., Baker, C., Deno, L., & Tagliareni, E. (1990). Perceptions from the nursing home: How we can make a difference. *Imprint, 37,* 62–65.
   Nursing students tell their stories about their unique experiences in the nursing home.

Hahn, A. (1970). It's tough to be old. *American Journal of Nursing, 7,* 85–88.
> *A first-person account of the feelings and concerns of a nursing home resident.*

National Institute on Aging. (1990). *Progress report on Alzheimer's disease* [for administrative use only] (PHS Publication No. 94–2418). Washington, DC: U.S. Department of Health and Human Services.

Kutschke, M. (1988). Only for the moment. *Geriatric Nursing, 9,* 296–297.
> *A student gains a new insight from her work with a 94-year-old, anxious, cognitively compromised woman.*

Nesbitt, B. (1988). Nursing diagnosis in age-related changes. *Journal of Gerontological Nursing, 14,* 6–12.
> *Students find this article helpful because it clearly relates age changes to common NANDA diagnoses.*

Qualey, T. (1989). Antigone admits her father to a nursing home. *American Journal of Nursing, 89,* 1470–1472.
> *In this lighthearted story, a conscientious daughter (Antigone) struggles with the decision to have her father (Oedipus) admitted to a nursing home.*

Rice, L. (1991). Do we discriminate against the elderly? *Nursing, 88,* 44–45.
> *Examines the negative view of old age held by many in the United States. Cites research on nurses' attitudes and notes that education and self-awareness can assist in ridding our profession of bias against the elderly.*

Tests and Activities

National Institute on Aging. (Published monthly). *Facts on aging quiz.* New York: Springer.

Waters, V. (1991). *Teaching gerontology.* (Publication No. 15–2411.) New York: National League for Nursing.

Movies on Videotape

Beresford, B. [director]. (1989). *Driving Miss Daisy* [Film].
> *Story of a long-term relationship between an older Southern widow and her chauffeur. Stars Jessica Tandy and Morgan Freeman. Deals with issues of prejudice and losses in aging. Sparks discussion about elements of a relationship (99 minutes).*

Goldberg G. D. [director]. (1989). *Dad* [Film].
> *The relationship between an elderly father (Jack Lemmon) and his adult son (Ted Danson) intensifies when the father becomes ill. Selected vignettes [i.e., the ICU (intensive care unit) scene, the funeral] useful to illustrate choices about medical care and the resolution of family conflicts (117 minutes).*

Krocker, A. [director]. (1988). *Age-old friends* [Film].
> *Vincent Gardenia and Hume Cronyn costar in this film about two retirement home tenants whose bond of friendship unites them in their daily struggle with advancing years (88 minutes).*

Marshall, P. [director]. (1990). *Awakenings.*
> *Robin Williams and Robert DeNiro in a more or less true story of residents in a mental institution suffering from a form of encephalopathy who emerge from a trance after receiving L-Dopa. Powerful film that usually sparks a discussion about quality-of-life issues and the role of medical care in a long-term, chronic illness (121 minutes).*

Masterson, P. [director]. (1985). *The trip to bountiful* [Film].
> *An aging woman (Geraldine Page) yearns to return to her childhood home in Bountiful, Texas, one more time. She lives in a cramped city apartment with her distracted son and unsympathetic daughter-in-law, with whom she feuds. She takes off for Bountiful, outwitting her pursuers—a touching, adventuresome journey. The story is a wonderful study of aging and loneliness (106 minutes).*

Nichols, M. [director]. (1984). *The gin game* [Film].
> *Jessica Tandy is a resident of a rest home and develops a stormy friendship with another resident. Facilitates discussion about use of humor in relationships, communication patterns, and losses of aging (approximately 2 hours).*

Ross, H. [director]. (1975). *The sunshine boys* [Film].
> *George Burns and Walter Matthau review a friendship that is filled with anger, humor, and caring. Very touching final scene where they come to terms with their relationship. Helps students consider the strengths in a long-term relationship that may not always be apparent. Very effective to just show the last scene, which is 14 minutes long (111 minutes).*
> *(Films mentioned should be available at most video outlets and retailers.)*

Chapter

MARY LOU LONG

2

Promoting Wellness

Learning Objectives

After completing this chapter, the student will be able to:

1. Recognize aging as a normal process of living rather than a disease process.
2. Describe the role nurses play in health promotion and disease prevention activities for older people.
3. Describe key health promotion/disease prevention activities appropriate for older people.
4. Understand the importance motivation plays in the older person's ability to participate in health promotion/disease prevention activities.

INTRODUCTION

The search for eternal youth has a long history. People have died in their search for the "Fountain of Youth," and others have killed for what they thought would give them eternal youth. The legends surrounding the "forever young" concept are taking on a new reality and meaning for this country's aging society. The modern version of the legend of the Fountain of Youth is embodied in the concept of health promotion. The focus is on living longer and healthier, an opportunity offered to today's elderly. Our society emphasizes normal age-related changes and common health problems and diseases as experienced by older people. In addition, information is shared on dealing with losses related to aging, the medical treatment of chronic disease, and the financial impact of an aging society. Not enough attention has been given to the positive side of aging and the beneficial effects of health-promotion activities to prevent disease and to slow the effects of chronic disease.

In 1991, the U.S. Department of Health and Human Services published the report *Healthy People 2000: National Health Promotion and Disease Prevention Objectives*. This report concerns older adults and ways of maintaining their independence through later years. The report outlines specific health recommendations that address improvements in health status, risk reduction, public and professional awareness, health services, and protective measures, as well as evaluation measures for each objective.

This report is written from the viewpoint that a continuum of health represents more than mere absence of disease. The objectives of *Healthy People 2000* emphasize vitality and independence for older people as a priority concern. Regardless of age, as people laugh more, walk more, eat better, relax more, and think better of themselves and their relationships, they move beyond the neutral point of good health. Many of the complaints associated with the aging process, such as joint stiffness, weight gain, fatigue, loss of bone mass, and loneliness, can be prevented or managed by basic health promotion activities. One does not have to be free of disease to experience the benefits of wellness and the positive side of living.

Most health-promotion activities focus on exercise, stress management, nutrition, and dealing with substance abuse. In addition it is important that wellness activities for older adults include relationships and self-care.

CHRONIC DISEASE

As a licensed practical nurse (LPN) giving care to elderly people, you must understand the promotion of wellness in a broader sense. This concept needs to go beyond the vision of physically well, elderly people living in their own homes independently. Over 80% of elderly people experience at least one chronic disease condition and as many as 50% report two or more (Teague & McGhee, 1992). Those over 85 years old experience increased difficulty with home management activities and are more likely to depend on assistance in their living situations. Regardless of age, living arrangement, or health condition, the goal for health promotion should be to assist older people to reach a state of optimal health—the legendary Fountain of Youth.

The most common health problems of older people are associated with chronic disease. The most frequent of these chronic conditions include arthritis, hypertension, heart conditions, hearing impairments, and dementia (AARP, 1991). Because of these conditions, older people visit physicians more, are hospitalized more frequently, take more prescription and over-the-counter (OTC) drugs, and experience more functional problems than younger people. The focus of much of this country's medical treatment interventions is *curing* acute conditions. Chronic illness cannot be cured but instead requires management with a focus on caring.

Treatment Strategies

Management of chronic conditions involves treating the symptoms and maximizing the strengths of an older person's health status to prevent further disability. For example, for an older person who suffers from arthritis and is in severe pain, it is important to treat the symptom of pain. If pain is minimized, the person will be better able to stay active and prevent the further disabling effects of immobility. Nurses are key personnel in recognizing the symptom (pain) and administering the prescribed treatment (medication). As a gerontological nurse, you must go one step further and consider the impact of the disease and its treatment on the other person's ability to carry on with activities of daily living (ADLs).

What will be the side effects of the pain medication?
What could be done to prevent the onset of pain?

As an LPN, you must recognize the importance of good health and its correlation with functional independence among older people; however, understanding is not always clear as to which kind of activities will promote health and prevent development of further secondary conditions that result in dependency.

ILLNESS/WELLNESS AS A CONTINUUM

Physicians and nurses traditionally focus on working with patients who are ill or have symptoms of disease or disability. As a person's health improves, traditional medicine becomes less involved in helping the person reach optimal well-being. In contrast, health promotion efforts have been primarily focused on the opposite or *wellness* side of the continuum.

In more recent years, nurses have begun to use health-promotion efforts even when dealing with clients on the illness side of the continuum. For example, special exercise and nutrition programs have been designed for cardiac rehabilitation, exercise and weight-lifting programs for chair-bound persons, and weight management programs for older persons. The remainder of this chapter focuses on health promotion activities on both the illness and wellness sides of the health continuum.

Motivation

If you, as a nurse, are to be successful in promoting healthy choices in individuals in their later years, you need to understand the importance of individual motivation. Desire must be present on the part of the older person to make a change. It is critical to explore what motivates an older person to eat right, exercise, and avoid unhealthy behaviors on an individual basis.

As a part of human behavior, motivation is the incentive or drive that causes a person to act. Incentives to take action are based on needs and desires that are both internal and external to the person. For example, an older person may have an incentive to exercise three times a week if it helps the person experience less discomfort or immobility from arthritis. For some people, the incentive may need to be more than physical wellness. A need may also exist for a mental wellness experience, such as that derived from socialization with others.

The nursing challenge is to assist older people to identify their own incentives for participation in health-promotion and disease prevention activities. This allows the nurse to have greater insight into ways to promote health and lessens the frustration experienced from what are often incorrectly referred to as *noncompliant patients*. Compliance occurs only if the individual personally identifies a need or desire to exercise, eat correctly, reduce stress, or make other changes necessary for improved wellness.

Society frequently hears an older person refer to the strongest hope, or modern-day Fountain of Youth, which often involves remaining independent for as long as possible. The older person must believe that awareness or a behavior change will result in helping maintain or improve independence and functional ability. In addition to being motivated by the belief that the behavior will result in change, the older person also may want to have fun and a social experience.

Incentives

Studies have disclosed some of the reasons (incentives) for older people to participate in health promotion behaviors. These include:

    A belief that activities can improve fitness and health
    Enjoying socialization
    A belief that activities will help to maintain independence
    A desire to feel good and have fun

Knowledge about why a person participates in health promotion (or the incentives for doing so) can be determined through a caring and focused interview. After personal incentives have been identified, they can be reinforced in health promotion activities.

In addition to understanding individual motivation, you will need to help individuals plan their short- and long-term goals for making health changes. At any age, making health changes can be either fun or frustrating. An analogy can be made with going on vacation. The vacationer can try to "see it all" in 2 weeks and then come home more exhausted than before leaving or can pick one adventure and enjoy it to its fullest. The secret to success in health behavior is to pick personal goals with care and learn to enjoy achieving them.

Health-Promotion Activities

After an older person has identified an area of health that he or she has an incentive to maintain or improve, the challenge is to locate a properly designed activity. Many current health-promotion activities are biased for youth and have excluded the elderly by design (Teaque & McGhee, 1992).

Four reasons underscore the reason why the current focus of health promotion activities is often inappropriate for older people. The focus frequently is on life extension or on reducing the risks of premature death. For example, if a person stops smoking, reduces fat intake, and exercises, the risk of a heart attack at an early age is reduced. For the elderly, who have already lived beyond the average life expectancy, life extension may not be as important as quality of life. Stopping smoking, reducing fat intake, and exercising are important at any age, but for different reasons. The focus must be on health-promotion benefits specific to older persons.

Emphasis is often placed on advancing "youthfulness" and preventing aging. Older people recognize that they do not fit the image of youth and have already experienced some results of aging. This does not mean self-image and appearance are not important to older people, but that the image needs to match the older persons's self-perception.

Health-promotion programs focus on preventing chronic disease. Among older people, 50% already have two or more chronic diseases. When these programs focus on management of the symptoms of the disease rather than on its prevention, more elderly people have a reason to participate.

A focus on self-responsibility for health fails to consider the limitations imposed by personal circumstances. For example, an individual who has a need and desire to walk daily for exercise may live in an unsafe neighborhood. The elderly person may have a desire to eat a healthy diet but be unable to afford the proper food. The external environment may pose barriers to older people that prevent their responding to their needs and desires. These problems need careful attention.

As you, the LPN, look at the key areas of health promotion for older people, your goal must be to design, plan, and provide activities that are sensitive to individual needs and responsibility. Properly designed health-promotion activities should be:

Accessible (transportation, time of day, location)
Enjoyable and social (mental and physical wellness)

Reasonable (focus on the right activity for the right reason)
Sensitive to older people's needs (hearing, vision, functional level)

Health-promotion strategies must be based on the belief that the individual is the only one who can choose a path to a healthy life. Consequently, the nurse must be sure health-promotion activities are individually designed so that the pathways exist.

NUTRITION

With advancing age, a person's general health is determined to a great extent by the effects of dietary patterns over the years. To many older people, it may seem that diseases, such as heart disease and cancer, are the result of old age, and, therefore, that no prevention is possible. For those who already have these chronic diseases, little value may seem to exist in changing behaviors. Studies have shown that by improving one's diet and adding some form of exercise, the onset and disabling effects of some chronic diseases can be slowed and often prevented (Teaque & McGhee, 1992). Staying physically and mentally active is important to all older adults. They need to understand the role proper nutrition plays in their lives, even in later years.

As bodies age, four changes occur that affect what a person needs to and chooses to eat:

1. The body's rate of metabolism slows and no longer needs the same amount of energy and food to do the same amount of work. Older people often comment that they are eating and exercising the same as they always have but are now gaining weight. As people age, lean body mass decreases and body fat increases. This may result in weight gain and can lead to obesity.

2. Some physical changes occur as a result of wear and tear on our bodies. The senses of taste and smell may be less keen. Some or all of an elderly person's teeth may need to be replaced by dental appliances. As a result of this, older people may find themselves eating different foods and drinking less fluid.

3. Social aspects of eating are important. As people age, they retire, families grow up and move, and spouses and friends die. This results in changes in the socialization of eating. One of the most difficult adjustments seems to be cooking for one and eating alone.

4. Environmental factors greatly influence older people's nutritional habits. Lack of transportation to food stores and restaurants, inability to manage reading labels and shopping, and insufficient money to buy healthy food can be major barriers to eating properly and even to being able to live independently.

Poor dietary habits contribute to many diseases that occur in older persons. Chronic diseases, such as heart disease and cancer, can be slowed, and for some people prevented, by avoiding obesity and decreasing the amount of fat in one's diet. Studies from the American Heart Association (1993) suggest high cholesterol levels increase the risk for atherosclerosis. The American Cancer Society (1994) found marked increases in the incidence of cancer of the uterus, gallbladder, kidney, stomach, colon, and breast associated with obesity.

Osteoporosis affects 25% of women over 60 years old. The loss of bone mass and bone strength as a result of this disease leads to broken hips, arms, legs, and back injuries. Osteoporosis is often referred to as a "silent" disease. Few signs or symptoms appear until a bone breaks. Adding calcium to the diet, regular exercise, avoidance of alcohol and smoking, and, in many cases, estrogen replacement therapy are key prevention strategies.

Other chronic problems that are a frequent complaint of older people include constipation, urinary incontinence, and arthritis. Nutrition plays a role in each of these conditions.

Although one-on-one teaching may be easier, group learning that incorporates an opportunity for socialization and fun is much more likely to result in positive outcomes. The LPN may want to organize a group of elderly people in the community to participate in learning nutrition principles. One of the principles that should be taught is that of the food pyramid (Fig. 2.1). This information, new to many people, replaced the "basic four" concept that most older people have been taught.

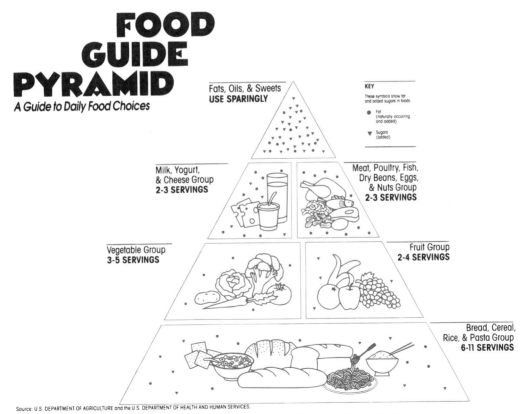

Figure 2.1   Food Guide Pyramid: A Guide to Daily Food Choices. (From U.S. Department of Agriculture and U.S. Department of Health and Human Services.)

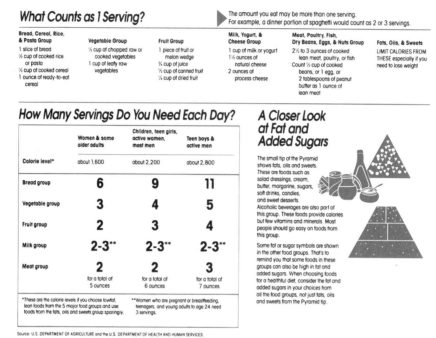

What Counts as 1 Serving?

The amount you eat may be more than one serving. For example, a dinner portion of spaghetti would count as 2 or 3 servings.

Bread, Cereal, Rice, & Pasta Group
1 slice of bread
½ cup of cooked rice or pasta
½ cup of cooked cereal
1 ounce of ready-to-eat cereal

Vegetable Group
½ cup of chopped raw or cooked vegetables
1 cup of leafy raw vegetables

Fruit Group
1 piece of fruit or melon wedge
¾ cup of juice
½ cup of canned fruit
¼ cup of dried fruit

Milk, Yogurt, & Cheese Group
1 cup of milk or yogurt
1½ ounces of natural cheese
2 ounces of process cheese

Meat, Poultry, Fish, Dry Beans, Eggs, & Nuts Group
2½ to 3 ounces of cooked lean meat, poultry, or fish
Count ½ cup of cooked beans, or 1 egg, or 2 tablespoons of peanut butter as 1 ounce of lean meat

Fats, Oils, & Sweets
LIMIT CALORIES FROM THESE especially if you need to lose weight

How Many Servings Do You Need Each Day?

	Women & some older adults	Children, teen girls, active women, most men	Teen boys & active men
Calorie level*	about 1,600	about 2,200	about 2,800
Bread group	6	9	11
Vegetable group	3	4	5
Fruit group	2	3	4
Milk group	2-3**	2-3**	2-3**
Meat group	2	2	3
	for a total of 5 ounces	for a total of 6 ounces	for a total of 7 ounces

*These are the calorie levels if you choose lowfat, lean foods from the 5 major food groups and use foods from the fats, oils and sweets group sparingly.

**Women who are pregnant or breastfeeding, teenagers, and young adults to age 24 need 3 servings.

A Closer Look at Fat and Added Sugars

The small tip of the Pyramid shows fats, oils and sweets. These are foods such as salad dressings, cream, butter, margarine, sugars, soft drinks, candies, and sweet desserts. Alcoholic beverages are also part of this group. These foods provide calories but few vitamins and minerals. Most people should go easy on foods from this group.

Some fat or sugar symbols are shown in the other food groups. That's to remind you that some foods in these groups can also be high in fat and added sugars. When choosing foods for a healthful diet, consider the fat and added sugars in your choices from all the food groups, not just fats, oils and sweets from the Pyramid tip.

Source: U.S. DEPARTMENT OF AGRICULTURE and the U.S. DEPARTMENT OF HEALTH AND HUMAN SERVICES.

Figure 2.1 *(Continued)*

Health-promotion activities aimed at altering a lifetime of eating habits must be reasonable, and the benefits need to be made apparent. Nurses must clearly understand what motivates the individual. In addition, they must be aware of the unique nutritional needs and problems that accompany later years. Some excellent resources for activities and information specifically designed for older adults are listed in Table 2.1. The success of health-promotion efforts depends on the nurse's knowledge of physical and psychosocial factors that affect the nutritional needs and practices of older adults.

EXERCISE AND FITNESS

The 1970s saw the beginning of the fitness movement in the United States. Not until the late 1970s and early 1980s did society begin to stress the importance of fitness for older adults. Studies continue to emphasize the benefits of exercise and its importance to total health for all ages. The body's responses to exercise are fundamentally the same throughout life. Exercise stimulates the mind, maintains fitness, prevents or slows progression of some diseases, helps to establish social contacts, and generally improves the quality of life.

Fatigue and lack of energy, poor sleeping habits, and poor circulation are common complaints of older adults. These complaints often result in inactivity. Inactivity

TABLE 2.1	RESOURCES FOR MATERIALS DESIGNED FOR OLDER ADULTS	

Reference	Format	Content
Healthwise for Life Healthwise, Inc. P.O. Box 1989 Boise, ID 83701	Book Program guide	Self-care
Growing Younger Healthwise, Inc. P.O. Box 1989 Boise, ID 83701	Book Program guide	Exercise Stress
Growing Wiser Healthwise, Inc. P.O. Box 1989 Boise, ID 83701	Book Program guide	Stress Relationships
Pep Up Your Life AARP 601 E St. N.W. Washington, DC 20049	Booklet	Exercises
Age Pages National Institute of Health Bethesda, MD 20892	Written information	Exercise Stress Nutrition Alcohol Drugs
Think of Your Future AARP 601 E St. N.W. Washington, DC 20049	Workbook	Stress Relationships Exercise
Over 60 and Fit Jan Mittleider College of Southern Idaho Twin Falls, ID 83301	Video	Exercise
Anybody Can Sit and Be Fit Illinois State Medical Society Auxiliary 20 N. Michigan Ave. Chicago, IL 60602	Video	Chair-bound exercises

leads to muscle wasting and weakening of the bones. This vicious cycle results in disabling conditions and functional dependency. If exercise could be packed into a pill, it would be the single most widely prescribed and beneficial medicine in the nation. Chronic conditions such as heart disease, diabetes, osteoporosis, arthritis, obesity, and depression are all shown to improve or experience a slowing of progression with regular physical activity.

Physiologically, a regular exercise program can build and maintain muscular strength and endurance and can improve the capacity of the heart, circulatory system, and lungs. The commonly heard phrase, "Use it or lose it," is the overall theme for exercise and fitness in a person's later years. Exercise programs for people over 60 years of age should emphasize a regular routine of exercise to expand and increase strength, flexibility, and endurance. This can be accomplished for individuals with a wide range of conditions, from wheelchair- or bed-bound frail elderly to the physically active. By-products of a good fitness program include increased energy, buildup of lean body mass, and increased self-esteem.

Strengthening

Strengthening exercises help to build and maintain muscle condition by moving muscles against resistance. Simple strengthening exercises are needed to promote activity without tiring a person too easily. Muscle strength is also crucial to the support of joints and can help prevent problems related to arthritis. Improving muscle strength is a primary objective in slowing the progression of osteoporosis. Patients confined to bed lose bone mass very quickly. It can be restored, however, when exercise is resumed.

As a nurse, you must be aware of the impact a short-term illness can have on an older person. Something as commonplace as the flu can cause significant weakness and inactivity. Weak muscles lead to falls, which cause hip fractures and other injuries for older people. If the older person is not aware of the importance of strengthening exercises, no incentive will be present to return to the normal level of function.

Strength-building exercises are important for the patient with diabetes because the exercises help regulate glucose metabolism by increasing muscle mass. The greater the muscle mass, the greater the glycogen level in the muscles will be and the more energy in reserve for periods of exertion.

Flexibility

Flexibility exercises involve slow stretching motions. Medical and fitness experts agree that stretching is the single most important part of an exercise program designed to prevent injuries, reduce muscle tension, and maintain range of motion.

As a result of the normal aging process, muscles tend to lose elasticity and tissues around the joints thicken. Flexibility exercises can delay or reverse this process by preventing muscles from becoming short and tight. The progression of arthritis, one of the most common and painful diseases among older people, can be slowed by an appropriate routine of flexibility exercises.

All stretching motions should be done gradually and slowly, without any sudden force or jerking motion. The LPN should encourage a variety of stretching exercises for different parts of the body including arms, shoulders, back, chest, stomach, buttocks, thighs, and calves. All exercise routines should warm up and cool down with 5–15 minutes of stretching exercises. As the older person's range of motion increases, the individual will be able to reach, turn, and move in all directions with more grace and less pain.

Endurance

Endurance-building or aerobic exercises improve the function of the heart, lungs, and blood vessels. A frequent complaint of older people is "feeling tired." Endurance-building exercises help strengthen the heart to pump blood and the lungs to exchange oxygen and also increase the elasticity of blood vessels. These functions are a vital part of fitness and feeling good. Walking, cycling, and swimming or water aerobic exercises are excellent all-around exercises.

As stated earlier, the basic components of an exercise routine for older people include strengthening, flexibility, and endurance. In addition, attention must also be given to the simple act of breathing during exercising. Breathing is a vital part of an exercise program. As a person concentrates on the exercise, it is easy to forget to breathe. The correct breathing technique is to breathe out during vigorous effort or exertion, and breathe in as the muscles relax.

Roll breathing is also a good way to reduce tension and to induce relaxation. As a result of changes related to aging, some older people experience a general loss of elasticity of the chest muscles and some postural changes. These gradual changes often affect the way they breathe. This is especially true for frail and bed-bound elderly. The roll-breathing exercises outlined in Box 2.1 encourage deep breathing and are very helpful as a relaxation technique and a component of an exercise program.

A last comment on exercise is a caution for those older people who have not been exercising on a regular basis, who are frail, or who have cardiovascular problems. Anyone with heart problems or high blood pressure, who is overweight, or who has been told to be cautious in personal activity level should have an exercise program prescribed by a physician.

Box 2.1   ROLL BREATHING

The object of roll breathing is to develop full use of your lungs. It can be practiced in any position but is best learned lying down, with your knees bent.

1. Place your left hand on your abdomen and your right hand on your chest. Notice how your hands move as you breathe in and out.
2. Practice filling your lower lungs by breathing so that your left hand goes up and down while your right hand remains still. Always inhale through your nose and exhale through your mouth.
3. When you have filled and emptied your lower lungs 8–10 times with ease, add the second step to your breathing: Inhale first into your lower lungs as before but then continue inhaling into your upper chest. As you do so, your right hand will rise and your left hand will fall a little as your stomach is drawn in.
4. As you slowly exhale through your mouth, make a quiet, relaxing whooshing sound as first your left hand and then your right hand falls. Exhale and feel the tension leaving your body as you become more and more relaxed.
5. Practice breathing in and out in this manner for 3–5 minutes. Notice that the movement of your abdomen and chest is like the rolling motion of waves rising and falling in a rhythmic motion.

Roll breathing should be practiced daily for several weeks until it can be done almost anywhere, providing you with an instant relaxation tool anytime you need one. *Caution:* Some people get dizzy the first few times they try roll breathing. Get up slowly and with support.

Source: Reprinted with permission from Kemper, D. W., Deneen, J. E., & Giuffré J. V. *Growing younger handbook* (2nd ed.). © Copyright 1992 HEALTHWISE, Incorporated, P.O. Box 1989, Boise, ID 83701. Copying of any portion of this material is not permitted without express written permission of HEALTHWISE, Incorporated.

TABLE 2.2 **GUIDELINES FOR EXERCISES BY OLDER PERSONS**

Target Group	Activity Goal	Types of Exercises
Well aging	Conditioning for cardiovascular reserve, muscular reserve, pulmonary reserve, and maintenance for central nervous system.	Flexibility, strength, endurance, aerobic—cycling, swimming, walking, water aerobics.
Limited ambulatory and wheelchair-bound aging	Independent locomotor function, gain physical stamina.	Flexibility, strength, endurance, and posture maintenance. Rhythmic activities (music) and swimming.
Frail elderly	Conditioning of cardiovascular, muscular, and pulmonary reserve, and reinforcing of basic locomotor skills for everyday living. Principal goal is functional movement activity.	Flexibility, relaxation (breathing), balance. Exercise prescribed by physician.
Bed patients	Preventing muscular atrophy, joint immobilization, and bed sores.	Low-level isometric passive-resistive exercise for flexibility. Exercise prescribed by physician.

Table 2.2 divides older persons into four groups and outlines guidelines for fitness goals and exercises. A well-balanced fitness program must consider each person's health conditions and functional limitations. No one fitness plan will work for every older adult.

Physical fitness is one component of life that enables people to live it to its fullest. Despite newfound interest in fitness in our society, certain groups noticeably lack it, one of which is composed of older adults. As a nurse, you have a responsibility to understand and teach the importance of exercise and fitness to the elderly.

Stress

Stress motivates people to act, forces them to think under pressure, and challenges them to be a creative, resourceful human beings. The key is to be able to strike a balance between too much stress and not enough, between positive stress (*eustress*) and stress that is harmful (*distress*).

As with all areas of health promotion, it is never too late to improve a technique. Failure to take a healthy approach to dealing with stress can greatly increase the risk of developing or worsening heart disease, cancer, and other chronic diseases.

For most older people, stress is related to three basic areas: environment, body, and mind. Environmental stressors are weather, crime, crowds, time pressures, and the demands of others. The human body can experience stress due to illness, accidents, drugs, lack of sleep, and the normal changes related to aging. Finally, the mind can create stress for us because of negative attitudes and perceptions, boredom, despair, and hopelessness.

Regularly occurring events such as trips to the grocery store, pain from arthritis, and fear of the unknown conditions of retirement may all create stress for older people.

Stress-related problems and symptoms include ulcers (stomach pain), high blood pressure (no symptoms), arthritis (joint pain, muscle tension), heart disease (chest

Golfing, walking, and dancing provide exercise that promotes strengthening, flexibility, and endurance.

pain, difficulty breathing), cancer (increased susceptibility), headaches (constant worry), circulatory problems (cold hands and feet), and backaches (muscle spasm/chronic pain). One of the most important strategies for health promotion is to help older people recognize their personal reactions to stress and their bodies' physiological responses. Table 2.3 can be used as a tool to help any individual recognize symptoms that are a response to stress. Other tools used to recognize stress are a stress log or journal of daily stressful situations, life change inventory, and stress control inventory.

After an individual has recognized personal stress and individual response to it, several interventions are available to help relieve it. As a nurse, you should understand and be able to recommend appropriate stress-reducing activities. These activities may be divided into the two categories of "quickie" relaxers and long-term stress management skills.

A quickie relaxer is something a person can do in 2 or 3 minutes to relax and counteract symptoms of distress. One of the most important, yet difficult, skills for some older people is learning to simply relax. Learning how to relax helps older people sleep better, control blood pressure, lower cholesterol, reduce headaches, relieve depression, reduce or eliminate use of drugs and alcohol, and smile more. Examples

TABLE 2.3   THE ART OF LISTENING TO YOUR BODY: THE SYMPTOMS OF STRESS

Circle the number that most accurately describes how often you experience each of the following symptoms or behaviors in response to stress. 1 = rarely; 2 = sometimes; 3 = frequently.

Listen to Your Body				Observe Your Actions				Listen to Your Emotions			
Change in breathing	1	2	3	Yelling	1	2	3	Worrying	1	2	3
Rapid or abnormal pulse	1	2	3	Crying	1	2	3	Depression	1	2	3
Muscle tension	1	2	3	Hostility	1	2	3	Impatience	1	2	3
Headaches	1	2	3	Decreased productivity	1	2	3	Loneliness	1	2	3
Upset or queasy stomach	1	2	3	Use of alcohol	1	2	3	Powerlessness	1	2	3
Fatigue	1	2	3	Use of drugs	1	2	3	Boredom	1	2	3
Dry throat or sweaty palms	1	2	3	Increased smoking	1	2	3	Poor self-esteem	1	2	3
Difficulty sleeping	1	2	3	Eat more/eat less	1	2	3	Frustration	1	2	3
Frequent colds or flu	1	2	3	Forgetfulness	1	2	3	Overwhelmed	1	2	3
Total _____				Total _____				Total _____			

If your total in any category is greater than 10, or your total for all categories is greater than 20, there's a good chance that your symptoms and actions are controlling you. Most of us are somewhere along a spectrum: our symptoms neither totally control us, nor do we totally control our symptoms. Because it tells us where we stand, symptom recognition is one of the most important steps in gaining control over stress.

Source: Reprinted with permission from Kemper, D. W., Deneen, J. E., & Giuffré J. V. *Growing younger handbook* (2nd ed.). © Copyright 1992 HEALTHWISE, Incorporated, P. O. Box 1989, Boise, ID 83701. Copying of any portion of this material is not permitted without express written permission of HEALTHWISE, Incorporated.

of quickie relaxers include roll breathing, progressive muscle relaxation, imagining a pleasant place or situation, eye relaxation, and exercise. The importance of exercise was discussed earlier in this chapter; however, it is worth emphasizing that exercise is the most natural way to relax. For the greatest calming effect, the elderly individual can combine fitness activities with breathing and other mental relaxation techniques.

For some older people, dealing with stress requires more than a few "stress-buster" quickie techniques. If stress causes continuous physical and mental discomfort that results in illness, learning how to deal with the source of stress needs to be a major goal. This assumes that the individual understands what is causing the stress.

Using the four stress management options listed here as a teaching tool is very helpful for many people. The four basic options are:

1. Go for symptom relief (quickie techniques).
2. Accept the stressor (change perception or attitude). *Example:* Your children frequently call you at the last minute to babysit your grandchildren. You may accept the stress and decide you really do not need much time to prepare, so say yes and enjoy! Another choice is to lovingly say "No!"
3. Alter the stressor (change or alter the source of stress so it is no longer there). *Example:* Make the decision that you will not be able to babysit unless they let you know 1 day ahead of time.

4. Avoid the stressor (remove yourself from the stressor). *Example:* Decide you will not be a babysitter for your grandchildren. After the source of stress has been pinpointed, the older person often can decide whether to accept, alter, or avoid it.

Stress management techniques may not be familiar to many older individuals, even though stress and recognition of stress have been buzz words for some time. Teaching older people stress management can be very successful through group or individual activities.

LIFESTYLES

Maintaining a healthy life at any age involves more than getting fit, eating right, and coping with stress. Other challenging issues that the elderly face are relationships, possible alcohol and drug abuse, and self-care.

Relationships

Human life is constantly defined and redefined by our ties to others. The term *relationship* means any significant bonding in which a person feels a strong sense of responsibility toward the physical and emotional welfare of others.

As people grow older, the reality is that all relationships eventually end. Whether through divorce or death of a spouse, child, family, friend, or pet, the loss redefines your life. An individual's ability to deal with the process of grief over the losses can result in significant personal and health changes, as well as changes in dealing with others. How strongly these changes affect the rest of one's life depends on how well the person, and those in the personal life of an individual, cope with the loss. How people have coped with change and crisis in younger years predicts how they will deal with stressors in later years.

As years pass, life changes can become increasingly complex. Older people must deal with changes due to retirement that have major impacts on home life, health, finances, and role changes. In addition, the loss of relationships may be frequent and numerous.

As a nurse, you have an opportunity to help the elderly person gain insight into loss and life change. You must assess the effect loss has on a person's ability to function with day-to-day activities. As an LPN, you must ask questions and allow the older person to share concerns. Health-promotion activities that focus on mental wellness can provide an excellent opportunity for older people to express the concerns they face. The American Association of Retired Persons (AARP) preretirement program offers a useful notebook that helps lead discussions about the myths, fears, and reality of change as one grows older.

Alcohol, Drugs, and Aging

Abuse of alcohol and drugs among older men and women is a more serious problem than most people realize. Until recently, older problem drinkers tended to be ignored by both health professionals and the general public. The neglect occurred for several reasons:

This country's elderly population was small and few older individuals were identified as alcoholics.

Chronic problem drinkers (those who had abused alcohol off and on for most of their lives) often died before old age.

Because they are often retired or have few social contacts, older people frequently have been able to hide drinking problems.

Some families may unknowingly accept or encourage drinking in older family members. They may have the attitude that drinking should be tolerated because older people have only a limited time left and should be allowed to "enjoy" themselves. Sometimes the alcohol consumption seems to be an insignificant amount to the family, and they blame the resulting impairment on aging.

The amount, time, and place of alcohol consumption have little significance. What alcohol does to an individual's quality of life and functional ability is the critical issue that needs to be addressed.

Older problem drinkers seem to be in two types. The first are chronic abusers, those who have used alcohol heavily throughout life. Approximately two-thirds of older alcoholics are in this group.

The second type begins excessive drinking late in life, often in response to "situational" factors such as retirement, lowered income, declining health, or the deaths of friends and loved ones. In these cases, alcohol is first used for temporary relief but later becomes a problem itself.

The physical effects of alcohol are significant for older people. Alcohol impairs mental alertness, judgment, physical coordination, and reaction time. These problems mimic and exacerbate the deleterious effects of other chronic conditions (dementia, depression, and arthritis) and increase the risks of falls and other accidents.

As people age, they appear to become less tolerant of even small amounts of alcohol, and moreover the effect of alcohol on the body may be unusual. For example, the effects of alcohol on the cardiovascular system may mask the pain of an oncoming heart attack. Older people are the greatest consumers of prescription and OTC drugs. The combined use of alcohol and drugs increases the likelihood of a toxic or lethal affect.

Treatment efforts for older alcoholic people have not been fruitful. It is easy to overlook or accept problem drinking as a device that offers enjoyment or comfort. It is much harder to create social alternatives to the life events that lie behind alcoholism.

As a health professional, you may be tempted to rush over or omit assessment questions referring to alcohol intake. The nurse often plays a key role in recognizing alcohol and drug problems. You must always ask what the impact of this problem may be on the older person's ability to function. It becomes easy to see that the physical, mental, and social impact of drinking could contribute to alcohol dependency.

The primary health-promotion goal is helping older adults and their families recognize when alcohol is a problem. Second, straightforward information must be given to seniors regarding the effects of alcohol, especially in combination with drugs. The nurse must understand the older person's reason for drinking. Health-promotion activities that create social alternatives can be made available to the older person with an alcohol problem.

Due to their critical importance, drug issues are covered extensively in another chapter; however, emphasis on the problem of drug dependency and abuse is important. Drug abuse depends on the relationship of the individual to the drug in question. Harmful drug relationships are frequently termed *overmedication, dependency, abuse, problem usage,* and *habituation.* Regardless of the reason, if an older person misuses a drug or becomes dependent on it, the effects are similar to those of problem drinking. Physical and mental impairments resulting from prescribed or OTC drugs mimic disease states and increase the risk of falls and accidents and, consequently, for dependency.

One role of health promotion is to offer education and screening regarding drug use. Promoting self-responsibility is the key component. Once again, nurses must assess the impact of drug treatment on the older person's ability to complete the ADLs. For example, if the older person cannot afford a prescribed drug, the person probably will not be taking it as ordered. If the older person does not understand what outcomes are expected from the drug treatment, misuse of a drug may ensue by taking it for too long or taking too much of it.

SELF-CARE—TAKING CHARGE

Older people are best qualified to keep themselves healthy and to know when they are ill. As a nurse, you need to respect and explore what the older person reports as the problem. Do not take charge and deny the older person responsibility for personal health and health management.

Self-care, self-help, and *self-maintenance* are terms often used interchangeably to describe various aspects of an individual's efforts to maintain optimal health and functionality (Kemper & Mettler, 1992). From a nursing perspective, the focus is frequently on ADLs, the most basic self-care activities engaged in by older persons. It is not uncommon to see dependence in at least some basic ADLs for the elderly. Surveys show as many as 18% of those over 65 years of age who live in the community are dependent in at least one ADL. Those over 85 years of age have a higher prevalence of dependence (Teaque & McGhee, 1992). In nursing homes, the prevalence is as high as 80%. In addition to ADLs, the older person faces many other self-care issues such as selecting a physician and other health-care providers, and knowing how and when to access the health-care system.

Regardless of whether the senior is attempting to overcome a functional deficit in ADLs or to make a medical decision, the same self-care skills are needed (Fig. 2.2). The art of self-care involves:

Accepting personal responsibility for your own health
Adopting healthy lifestyle habits with regard to fitness, relaxation, and nutrition
Learning how to make the changes you choose to make to do the things you want
  to do

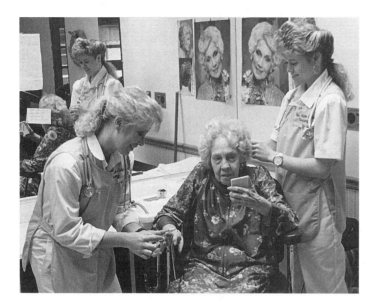

Figure 2.2 Regardless of whether the senior is attempting to overcome a deficit in activities of daily living or make a medical decision, the person needs self-care skills.

Accepting personal responsibility for health behaviors applies to the "why" of the decision more than the "what." "Self-responsibility" means that the older person does not rely solely on spouse, children, physician, or nurse to determine "what to do to be healthy." The elderly must be allowed to think through the options and make each decision. This does not mean a person should not seek the assistance of others, but rather that a need exists to work in partnership with the doctor, nurse, or family (separately or together) to make the best decision.

The self-care concept emphasizes the need for encouraging individuals to take a more active role in maintaining or improving their health. Often this process is not understood by the client, nor is it easy for older people to accomplish. Health-promotion strategies related to self-care must include helping the older person understand how to be in charge of personal health decisions. Enabling the client to be a wise medical consumer, and to know how and when to work and communicate as a partner with the health-care team, should be a focus of your efforts.

Your role as a health professional is twofold. First, you must offer activities to develop self-care skills: for example, one-on-one or group activities that teach being an informed medical consumer, or information on prevention and screening guidelines, for instance for a mammogram or a prostate examination. Then you must ensure that the environment allows for the senior to use these skills to make choices for self-responsibility. For example, if the senior wants to be a partner with the physician in a health decision and is prepared to ask questions regarding expected benefits, costs, and risks, the physician should be willing to take the time to answer the questions and ultimately let the treatment decision be made by the elderly person. This same situation applies to nursing. For example, if the senior is expected to be involved in a self-care activity program, you, as a nurse, must be prepared to explain the benefits, procedures, and risks, and then be willing to let the senior make the decision. If the person does not understand or is not committed to participate, the effort will be unsuccessful.

SUMMARY

Until recently, older people's notes have been ignored in the health-promotion movement. Health professionals mistakenly assumed elders had no interest in health-promotion programs. As this country has become more and more home to an aging society, these views have changed. The release of the *Healthy People 2000* report in 1991 clearly identified vitality in later years as a priority.

As a nurse, you must understand the importance of promoting wellness to all older adults, regardless of the presence or absence of disease. Attainment of a disease-free existence is not a realistic goal. Health-promotion efforts should be directed toward maintaining functional independence for older people.

Older Americans need information about how to lead healthy lifestyles. When such information and opportunity are provided, older people are willing to make the changes necessary to improve their health. Exercising regularly, maintaining a nutritious diet, managing stress effectively, taking medications safely, avoiding overuse of alcohol, and recognizing self-care as a choice are all behaviors that improve health and the quality of life for older people. Pursuit of high-level wellness in later years is the responsibility of both the individual and society.

CASE STUDY

Mrs. C. is a 65-year-old widow who has lived alone since the death of her husband 2 years ago. She retired 1 year ago from her job of 25 years as a secretary. She participated in a health prevention and screening clinic at the senior center. After completing a lifestyle inventory and screening, the following problems were noted in the categories of health promotion:

Nutrition:
10 lb overweight

Exercise:
Does no regular exercise

Stress:
Cries easily, often unable to sleep at night, complains of fatigue and generally low energy

Relationships:
Misses people at work, talks about missing deceased husband

Substance abuse:
Takes an over-the-counter (OTC) sleeping pill and one glass of wine before bed

Self-care:
Has not seen a physician since she had a hysterectomy 10 years ago; never had a mammogram and does not perform breast self-examination; cannot recall immunization history but is sure she has not had any in past 10 years; has never had a flu shot or pneumococcal vaccine; recently had blood pressure taken at drug store machine, when it was 150/92.

CASE STUDY
DISCUSSION

1. List additional assessment data that should be known in each of the categories of health promotion.
2. How might you determine Mrs. C.'s greatest concern?
3. What part does Mrs. C.'s motivation play in developing a wellness plan?
4. What conditions or disease states might develop if Mrs. C. continues with no changes in her life?
5. What might be the first priority for Mrs. C.?

CASE STUDY
SOLUTION

1. Additional information in each category might include:
   Nutrition:
   What are her daily eating habits? Type and amount of food and fluids? Does she eat alone?

Exercise:

What is her normal daily activity level? How does this differ from her daily activity level prior to retirement?

Stress:

What is her perception of coping with changes such as death and retirement? Any other physical complaints made, such as fatigue, headaches?

Relationships:

What family or friends are important to her? In what social activities is she involved? Any hobbies?

Substance abuse:

When did she begin drinking wine every evening? When did her sleeping problems begin? Has she always taken sleeping pills?

Self-care:

Does she have a primary care physician? Does she understand the importance of exercise, disease prevention? Does she know the danger of combining drugs and alcohol?

2. Asking Mrs. C. "What is your biggest worry or concern in your life at this time?" would be a beginning. Although the nurse may see many areas of concern, Mrs. C.'s own concerns are more critical at this time.

3. If the nurse begins by focusing on what Mrs. C. considers most important, then it is easier for Mrs. C. to understand her own motivation. Asking some of the questions about motivation listed in the Appendix would be helpful.

4. Some potential conditions include:

Excess weight, which may lead or contribute to high blood pressure and physical limitation.

Lack of exercise, which may contribute to weight gain but also worsen arthritis and its effects on mobility.

Emotional stress, which may lead to depression.

Relationship concerns, which may also contribute to depression, isolation, and abuse of drugs and alcohol.

Combination of alcohol and OTC sleeping pills, which may lead to further sleeping problems, alcohol and drug misuse, depression, injury, and further isolation.

5. If Mrs. C. has not seen a physician for 10 years, she needs at least a baseline physical assessment. She has some significant conditions that need to be addressed such as borderline high blood pressure, sleep problems, and weight gain. In addition, she should have a basic screening related to disease prevention.

Study Questions

Circle the correct choice(s) to complete each statement.

1. Incentives for older persons to participate in health-promotion behaviors include:
   a. The belief that they will find the Fountain of Youth
   b. The belief that activities will help them die well
   c. The belief that activities will help keep them independent
   d. The belief that it will please their physician

2. Health-promotion programs appropriate for older people should focus on:
   a. Maintaining functional abilities
   b. Advancing youthfulness
   c. Enhancing chronic illnesses
   d. Developing dependence on others for care

3. Basic components of an exercise routine for older people are:
   a. Strengthening, endurance, and flexibility
   b. Strengthening, dieting, and power walking
   c. Strengthening, dieting, and aerobics
   d. Strengthening, aerobics, and the food pyramid

4. Age-related changes that affect nutrition include:
   a. Increase in the ability to taste
   b. Increase in body fat
   c. Increase in lean body mass
   d. Increased metabolic rate because of aging thyroid

5. Older people with a drinking problem are often ignored because:
   a. They have many social opportunities to drink.
   b. The amount of alcohol consumed may seem small.
   c. The resulting impairment may seem to be age related.
   d. So many older people do drink.

References

AARP. (1991). *A profile of older Americans.* Washington, DC: AARP.

American Cancer Society. (1994). Recommendations on diet and cancer. *Oncology times, 6,* 1–32.

American Heart Association. (1993). Eat well but eat wisely. New York: American Heart Association.

Kemper, D. W. (1986). *Growing wiser: The older person's guide to mental wellness.* Boise, ID: Healthwise.

Kemper, D. W., Deneen, J. E., & Giuffré, J. V. (1992). *Growing younger handbook* (2nd ed.). Boise, ID: Healthwise.

Kemper, D. W., Giuffré, J. V., & Drabinski, G. (1986). *Pathways: A successful guide for a healthy life.* Boise, ID: Healthwise.

Kemper, D. W., & Mettler, M. (1992). *Medical self-care for healthy aging.* Boise, ID: Healthwise.

National Institute on Aging and Pfizer Pharmaceuticals. *Help yourself to good health: Compilation of age pages.* Clifton, NJ: Pfizer Pharmaceuticals.

Teaque, M. L., & McGhee, V. L. (1992). Health promotion. Achieving high-level wellness in the later years. Dubuque, IA: Brown & Benchmark.

U.S. Dept. of Health and Human Services, Public Health Service. (1991). *Healthy people 2000. National health promotion and disease prevention objectives* (DHHS-PHS Publication No. 91–50213). Washington, DC: U.S. Government Printing Office.

Bibliography

American Association of Retired Persons (AARP). (1986). *Think of your future.* Washington, DC: AARP.

AARP. (1990). *Pep up your life.* Washington, DC: AARP.

Burnside, I. (1988). *Nursing and the aged: A self-care approach* (3rd ed.). New York: McGraw-Hill.
   Comprehensive gerontological nursing textbook in a very readable format that combines recognition of what the older client can teach the nurse and what the nurse can bring in skill and knowledge to older clients.

Carnevali, D. L., & Patrick, M. (1993). *Nursing management for the elderly* (3rd ed.). Philadelphia: J. B. Lippincott.
   The authors effectively demonstrate that the nurse's primary area of accountability is helping clients to achieve a workable and satisfying balance between their requirements of daily living and their abilities, resources, and support system.

Matteson, M. A., & McConnell, E. S. (1988). *Gerontological nursing: Concepts and practice.* Philadelphia: W. B. Saunders.
   Excellent discussion of lifestyle modification programs in community settings.

Swinford, P. A., & Webster, J. A. (1989). *Promoting wellness: A nurses' handbook.* Rockville, MD: Aspen Publications.
   Primary focus is on wellness principles and techniques that nurses can use in their personal lives and their professional practices.

Chapter

MARY ANN ANDERSON

3

The Management Role of the Licensed Practical/Vocational Nurse

Learning Objectives

After completing this chapter, the student will be able to:

1. Identify three management styles commonly used and determine the style that is most effective in gerontological settings.
2. Express an overall understanding of communication techniques and their use.
3. Describe two methods for managing stressful communications.
4. Describe the planning hoop and its use in setting priorities.
5. Explain the purpose and basic methodology of making client care assignments to nursing assistants.
6. Identify three common errors made in doing employee evaluations.
7. Define Total Quality Management and Continuous Quality Management.

INTRODUCTION

Administering excellent care to frail and ill individuals through the mechanism of an interdisciplinary team and, frequently, a mass of bureaucratic paperwork, requires management skills of the highest level. This is the challenge of today's licensed practical nurse (LPN): successful administration of managed care to clients in all settings. Certain skills are critical for the LPN to master to function successfully in the management arena of health-care delivery. This chapter is designed to introduce such skills as they are used within the realm of gerontological nursing.

MANAGEMENT ROLES

The management role of the LPN is one that changes constantly along with changes in the health-care delivery scene. It is challenging to be an LPN prepared to assume the responsibility of management. The LPN needs to recognize that the work of a licensed nurse always involves leadership skills and that the scope of responsibility frequently changes.

In some nursing homes, LPNs are directors of nursing whereas in some hospitals, they are not allowed to administer medications. This diversity in scope of responsibility is important to understand. If a registered nurse (RN) is on the health-care team, the LPN is responsible to the RN. This is always true because of the dictates of licensure. It is possible for an RN and an LPN to have the same job description in an organization, just as it is possible for an LPN to be the director of nursing or shift supervisor.

The LPN should clarify at the time of employment the scope of responsibility and role expected to be fulfilled. Determining that the duties assigned are not in conflict with the State Nurse Practice Act is also important. As licensed nurses, all LPNs are responsible for knowing the law governing their practice. This responsibility should not be delegated to a supervisor or another nurse.

MANAGEMENT STYLES

Every individual has a personal management style. This comes from the lessons learned while maturing as a person and professional. Nevertheless, to be a successful nurse manager, it is important to understand various management styles and master those that are most effective.

Three basic styles of leadership need to be understood. In addition, other leadership styles exist beyond the basic three, and many leadership theories have been proposed. The LPN nurse manager needs to understand the basic styles and be flexible enough to incorporate other information as it becomes pertinent. The overall objective for understanding the basic styles of leadership is for the LPN to determine an effective but flexible leadership style for professional use. Professional practice requires understanding the leadership styles and integrating them into practice for maximum effectiveness.

Authoritarian Leadership Style

In the strictest sense, authoritarianism functions with a high concern for tasks done and low concern for the people who perform those tasks. People with this leadership style work well as assembly line managers in which the employees are not in a job that requires individuality, and the machinery is critical to the production of the workload. Does this description cause you to have a feeling of concern when considering an authoritarian management style for a gerontological care environment?

The authoritarian or autocratic leader tends to make all decisions in the work environment and then simply orders the employees to follow the decisions that have been made. The manager is one who has worked hard to create a power base and does not relinquish it to employees. Generally, this type of manager sees employees as irresponsible and lazy. That opinion of employees is the manager's personal justification for the control placed over the workers.

An authoritarian manager does not allow for creative thinking or new ideas. No opportunities are presented to try new concepts on a patient/resident care plan unless the idea is the manager's own. This type of manager is more interested in seeing that the work is done rather than that the patients are being lovingly cared for, and their individual needs met. As an example of this type of management, the workload plan would require baths to be completed by 11:00 A.M. instead of treating the patients as individuals and allowing them autonomy in planning their morning care.

Situations do exist in which this type of management style is critical for success, for instance, during an emergency! If a visitor or client fell to the floor in cardiac arrest, this type of manager would take over, give orders, and, in all likelihood, save the life of the person. However, the problem with this management style is that life is not a constant series of emergencies. This style does not allow for the creative and caring approaches that are necessary for effective gerontological nursing. The clients miss out on the best possible care, and the employees miss out on opportunities to learn and grow as they implement new care practices. The manager, generally not respected or esteemed by employees, feels frustrated when management is not valued by others.

Permissive or Laissez-Faire Leadership Style

The laissez-faire style of leadership is the exact opposite of the authoritarian style. Essentially, this style consists of an absence of leadership. The manager wants everyone to feel good, including self, and works hard toward that end. The basic strategy is to allow the employees to make the decisions, do the planning, set the goals, and essentially manage the organization. This manager sees employees as ambitious, responsible, intelligent, and creative. The laissez-faire manager does not require accountability from employees for their time or for the quality of work done. Initially, this may sound like an ideal leadership style.

It is important to examine this type of management style in relationship to organizations involved in gerontological health care. Most care given to the elderly depends on federal approval and on complex payment systems that go through both state and federal government organizations. It is difficult to envision the federal guidelines for safety (Occupational Safety and Health Administration [OSHA]) or for nursing home licensure carried out in a permissive or laissez-faire manner. The same is true for quality assurance programs in health-care environments. Most elder-care facilities require specific attention to the paperwork that keeps an organization's doors open. It also is necessary to have layers of responsibility that ensure every client the best possible care with, again, attention to detail.

In other environments, however, laissez-faire management is very successful. A good example is a group of highly motivated, professional people, such as a group of researchers, where independent thinking is rewarded. Conversely, it is hard to imagine an effective nursing home or hospital unit being managed with this style of leadership.

Democratic or Participative Leadership Style

This management style has a strong valuing of the people "on the team." A strong sense of a team is in existence; decisions are made through the team. The manager gathers information from the other team members and then presents it to the group. All suggestions from the group are considered before decisions are made by the group. This is a very open system of management, yet it identifies the individuals who are responsible for the various projects being managed.

The disadvantage presented by this type of management style is that it takes a great deal of time and energy. Generally the results are positive, and the employees are very satisfied. This is a style that works well in gerontological environments because it is very focused on people and includes the employee, the client, and the client's family. It is a system that considers change and improvement continuously and assigns responsibility for such ventures.

As an LPN nurse manager, you need to evaluate yourself and determine which general management style is yours. Then, consider whether it is a style that is best used in the care of elderly people. If it is not, you need to learn more about other management styles and with that knowledge make changes in yourself. You may need to find a mentor who has a management style you would like to learn more about and ask that person to assist you. This mentor could teach you, become a role model for you, and assist you in applying the management techniques you want in the real-world setting.

Being a manager is a challenging facet of your professional life. Take the time to learn the skills and patterns of thought that you will need to function at your most effective level.

This chapter discusses some critical elements that need to be learned by a nurse who manages care for elderly people in any environment. You may find that you would like more information than is given in this chapter. If that is so, please refer to the bibliography at the end of the chapter for additional readings.

COMMUNICATION

The most important skill for a manager in any situation involves communication. Nurses in geriatric care spend 85% of their time communicating with a wide variety of people who are involved in giving care to elderly clients. This makes mastering the skills of communication essential for the successful LPN. Communication involves delivering messages that will be understood, listening to messages that may or may not be confusing, and properly interpreting messages that have been misdirected or are delivered with intense emotion, such as anger.

For the LPN, the art of communication involves various groups of people. The LPN needs to be able to successfully communicate with the elderly client, the client's family or other members of the elderly person's support group, and the numerous members of the interdisciplinary health care team. Expertise in communication is demanded every day from those who manage, direct, or administer care to the elderly.

Verbal Communication

Verbal communication is the exchange of ideas and understanding that occurs through the use of spoken words and phrases. For the message to be received, the sender must use words and phrases that are appropriate for the listener. The success of all communication is measured by the question: was the message properly received?

It should be easy to remember sitting in a class and "listening" to a lecture or presentation in which the student did not "receive" the message. Perhaps the student was too tired to concentrate, or the instructor was boring or had inappropriate content to share. For communication to occur, being present is not enough. The critical measure is whether the listener actually understood or "received" the message.

Nonverbal Communication

Nonverbal communication is the ability to share messages without using words. It refers, among other things, to a person's body posture (is the person tired and slouched over or excited and alert?), the tone and speed of the voice, the kind of clothes a person wears, and hand and facial movements. Nonverbal communication is considered to be the most honest communication a person can receive. For example, someone may say, "I'm having a great day. How are things for you?" in a cheerful-sounding way, but an examination of his appearance may indicate something different. The face is not smiling, and the posture is one of fatigue. The person's hands may be clenching and unclenching as a symptom of stress. Or take another classic example: A resident in a nursing home is asked each morning, "How are you?" and each day responds verbally, "I'm fine." The person asking the question is busy with the breakfast tray or the linen and does not look at the sad and worried face of the resident who answers with the reply that is expected, rather than with the truth. This could be the resident who is found dead one morning, a victim of suicide.

The ability to recognize honest communication and respond to it is critical to a successful nurse manager. The nurse manager must learn to develop the refined skill of understanding nonverbal communication because it will convey valuable information about patients and employees. Nonverbal communication is an honest method of communication and will allow the LPN to follow through on problems and concerns that otherwise might not have been recognized.

Communicating with Clients

The decision to work with the elderly is a commitment to accept the normal physiological losses that accompany the aging process. That commitment requires knowledge of the normal changes that occur in the elderly (See Chapter 1) and the skill to work with them successfully. A tendency exists in our ageist society to negatively judge elderly citizens because of the normal aging processes they exhibit. Normal aging changes that might affect communication are slower speech, presbycusis (difficulty in discriminating sounds), presbyopia (difficulty seeing near objects), and overall slower movements or responses to what is being communicated. The knowledgeable LPN recognizes these as normal occurrences and responds to them with skill and compassion.

Some people are impatient and negative about the aging process. It is as if they were punishing people who had simply neglected to die young! This is ageist behavior and is unacceptable in any setting. The skills necessary for successful communication with elderly clients must be firmly based on respect for this group of people. If that ingredient is missing, communication is unsuccessful. Consider the following strategies (not every client will need every strategy):

It is important to move close to the patient or client so you can be seen.

Do not approach the person from the side because you may not be seen, and the client could be frightened by your sudden appearance. Approach only from the front.

Place yourself on eye level with the client so a comfortable presence occurs during the communication process.

Reach out and touch the person if it seems appropriate; this is often the bridge to a trusting relationship.

It is important to speak at a normal rate and not to shout, even if the client is having trouble hearing. Shouting does not overcome the problems of presbycusis.

If the patient is having trouble hearing you, move closer and speak in a normal tone. Moving closer often allows for lip reading or the reading of facial expressions.

Pleasantly repeat what is being said, if necessary.

Do not be impatient or judgmental.

Place yourself and the client in a setting where there is a bright light that is not glaring.

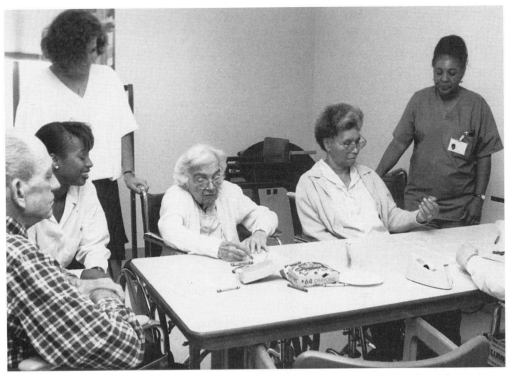

Look at the residents and staff in this picture. Nonverbal communication is shown clearly in each face.

Use a setting without disturbing or distracting noises.

If the elderly client gets confused while speaking or responding to a question, give the person time to collect personal thoughts. Do not rush the individual.

Repeat questions or comments in a different sentence structure if the client is having trouble understanding what is said. Do not keep repeating the same information in the same way.

Reflect what the client has said by repeating it back to in a different way. For example, "Do you mean that you are lonely because your wife is in the hospital and not able to visit you here in the nursing home?"

Listen carefully to the words used and verify what they mean.

"Listen" carefully to the body movements and other nonverbal communication and verify what they mean.

It is critical to keep in mind that your goal is to have the message successfully received. The use of these basic, caring strategies enhances your achievement of that goal, as well as your relationship with your clients, which is one of the rewards of being a gerontological nurse.

Communicating with Client Families

Often the family members of elderly patients or residents are worried, exhausted (if there has been extensive care given at home), and experiencing feelings of guilt over the condition of their family member or the necessity of admitting their loved one to a health-care facility. Successful communication with this varied group of people is challenging because of their emotional status. The issues involved often go beyond concern over an admission to a hospital or nursing home, to such highly charged questions as the right to die, the decision whether to do an amputation, or dealing with a diagnosis such as Alzheimer's disease.

It is critical for the LPN to recognize the emotional environment of the family members prior to entering into any communication with them. The goal is still the same. You want the message to be received by the listener. Some communication strategies for families are:

Listen to them before you attempt to impart information. It is essential that you evaluate the emotional environment prior to presenting information. Often just listening allows for the sharing of critical information that you otherwise would not learn.

Plan to spend time with the family members. They will have questions and concerns, and deserve to have them addressed.

Family members often feel guilty over some issue with their loved one and need to have that clarified. Families need not feel guilty unless evidence of elder abuse is found.

Find a quiet place to speak to the family. It should be a place where they can sit comfortably and be together as a group. The nurses' station is never an appropriate place for meaningful communication other than the simple sharing of facts.

As nurse manager, the LPN needs to facilitate the sharing of information with the family. This could mean arranging an appointment with the social worker or assisting a family member to reach the physician.

The client's family is as important as the client. Generally strong personal relationships that are interdependent exist. Always treat the family members with the high level of respect and concern that you use with the client.

Interdisciplinary Team Communication

It is unrealistic to give quality care to elderly clients without the support of an interdisciplinary team (IDT). Generally, the care given to elders in all settings is based on the IDT approach. It is critical that the nurse manager be an active and contributing part of this team. Generally the nurse is with the patients 24 hours a day, or, if the elderly person is a home patient, the nurse generally sees the individual more frequently than other members of the team. This constant attendance of the nurse to the client provides a vast amount of personal and pertinent information. Therefore, it is essential that the nurse manager be active in contributing to the knowledge base and planning of the IDT (Fig. 3.1).

Figure 3.1 The interdisciplinary team conference is a place where the licensed practical nurse needs to assume the role of client advocate as well as to teach and explain nursing concepts to the other team members.

Again, concern arises over how to share the information the nurse has gathered about the patient. It needs to be shared with skill so that the message is received. This process is different in a group setting than it is with an individual client or family members. The group consists of professionals who have specialized knowledge regarding the elderly person. Unfortunately, rarely is there sufficient time to discuss the patients in a thorough and relaxed manner. Often a time crunch exists in IDT planning that establishes a unique atmosphere for communication. The following are strategies for communicating with an IDT:

Come prepared! There is no time to waste in these meetings, whether in groups or one-on-one.

Plan ahead and have priority concerns in your mind or on a piece of paper.

Remember that this is not a team of nurses, and they may not understand a nursing concept that is very familiar to you. Because nursing is its own specialty, you may be asked to justify your requests or concerns or to teach the team about a nursing concept.

In most situations, the nurse has the role of patient/resident advocate. This occurs naturally because of the amount of time nursing personnel spend with clients compared with that spent by other disciplines. This time allows for personal information and concerns to be communicated. It is critical that the patient advocacy role be accepted by the nurse, so that the patient is protected from the system and its depersonalizing effects.

ADDITIONAL COMMUNICATION SKILLS

Very specific skills are necessary for successful communication, and each of these skills can be used appropriately in all settings. Such skills are often necessary to clarify communication errors, or potential errors, and are commonly necessary in difficult situations. They are important for every LPN to add to the communication skills checklist, and their importance can be compared with that of being expert at cardiopulmonary resuscitation (CPR). You may not use the skills very often, but when they are necessary, you need to know how to use them.

Assertive Communication Skills

The normal physiological reaction to being attacked physically or verbally is "fight or flight." This occurs without thinking about it; it is normal physiology. When a situation occurs in which you are being attacked verbally or feel threatened by what is being said or done, the normal response is to fight back (an argument) or to take flight (avoidance). In the framework of assertive communication, these two normal responses are more formally identified as: *aggressive*—fight or *passive*—flight. The third concept that belongs on a continuum between these two is *assertive*—dealing with the problem.

Assertive behavior occurs when someone has violated the rights of an individual either verbally or physically. Assertive behavior is the most effective response to that violation. The major rule regarding the concept of assertive communication is simply that the assertive response *does not* violate the rights of the person who just infringed on your rights. What does that look like? An argument is the best example. Someone comes to the nurses' station and criticizes you in an angry, loud manner. Of course, there are residents, visitors, and coworkers in the area listening to this *aggressive* communication. It is embarrassing and humiliating to be the victim of a communication delivered in such an inappropriate way. The normal physiological response is to either run away, perhaps crying (*passive*), or to scream back (*aggressive*). Screaming back or starting an argument is a violation of the other person's rights. It does not matter if "He deserves it!" It is still wrong. The *passive* behavior or running away does not violate the other person's rights, but it does prevent a resolution of the problem.

Assertive communication requires that the person being violated *not* respond in a normal physiological fashion to the situation. Instead, it is necessary to resist the normal response and use the skills of communication to promote problem solving. Assertive communication often follows this response format:

"*I feel*"—Tell the other person how the aggressive attack made you feel. Perhaps you feel frustrated, devalued, angry, or frightened. Many other options are available for you to describe how you feel about what has been said.

"*When you*"—Describe for the person the behavior that has caused you to feel the way you do. It could be when you raise your voice at me, talk about private concerns in public, demand things from me that I cannot do, or criticize me in front of others. Again, many other statements could be used here. The statements used here must not be personal statements that attack the other person. Assertive communication is effective only if you describe objective behaviors rather than make a personal attack.

"*Could we*"—This is where you negotiate a solution to the problem. You could say, "Could we go into the office (clean holding area, utility room, day room) to discuss this?" Simply responding with something rational rather than fighting back or running away often defuses the other person's anger so that real communication can take place. The purpose is to negotiate a method of correcting the problem so that it does not happen again.

Assertive communication is a learned behavior. It is something that does not come naturally: As a nurse manager, it is critical for you to have this skill to promote the effective workings of your professional environment.

Active Listening

Another communication skill that complements assertive behavior is that of *active listening*. Most people respond to aggressive and negative remarks with defensive communication. While the aggressor is making comments, the person being attacked generally is mentally preparing the defense to the aggressor's attack. These are the defensive comments that often provoke an argument. They follow the script of "It is not my fault, now let me tell you why!"

Active listening requires that the person being verbally attacked listen to what is being said. Because of the natural inclination to "prepare a defense," this is a challenging thing to do. Just listen and, while listening, try to determine the cause of the problem beyond the apparent anger.

The person who is out of control must be removed to a private setting, such as an office or the clean holding area. This prevents that individual from self-embarrassment in front of others, and it places you in an environment with fewer distractions.

After the angry person has finished saying all the aggressive things there are to say, he or she will take a deep breath and stop talking. This is where the person uneducated in communication skills presents "the defense." But you, the nurse manager, need skills beyond the ordinary person. Active listening is one of those skills. The deep breath is the signal to use the information you learned while listening to clarify the problem and negotiate a solution.

Comments like "You seem so frustrated with . . ." or "It is unlike you to be so upset. How can I help?" are effective ones to use. They are not what the aggressive person expects to hear and generally prevent the person from losing control again. They are helpful comments that show caring and problem-solving skills. These are hallmark behaviors for nurse managers. The next move is for the two people involved to sit down and rationally look at the problem and work on a solution. The whole process begins with the nurse being able to stop self-defending and focus on listening.

The format for active listening is:

Remove the conversation to a private setting.
Listen.
Do *not* prepare a defense.

Listen for the deep breath that means the person has finished speaking.
Show support for the other person's feelings.
Negotiate how to resolve the problem.

Some LPNs reading this text may feel concern over being responsible for assertive communication and active listening skills. They are two of many possible communication skills that could have been discussed in this book. They are listed for a very specific purpose. LPNs in management roles have very challenging positions, which may place them in very serious situations that must be managed rather than ignored. Some people will say, "But I am just an LPN!" and feel that their role does not involve managing and solving problems of this nature. However, it is important to recognize that if you are a nurse manager, you have an obligation to develop the skills necessary for managing these acute and potentially destructive problems.

THE PLANNING HOOP

Every day, decisions must be made regarding the workload of the LPN and others that affect the scope of the LPN's practice. These are decisions that should be made with careful thought and planning rather than casually and without attention to detail. The decision that may be required of you could be as simple as who will get first bath as you give morning care; but even this decision may have serious implications for the patients or residents who are receiving your care. Other decisions that will be required of the LPN nurse manager could be counseling an employee whose behavior is unacceptable, making client care assignments, confronting a doctor or therapist with an alternate plan of care for a resident, or managing daily staffing. None of these tasks and the many others that are required of a nurse manager are easy or simple. They require the highest level of skill and attention to manage the process of making such decisions effectively.

To set priorities and make excellent decisions, the LPN nurse manager must understand the importance of planning, which is an intelligent process of thinking based on facts and information, rather than on emotion and wishes. An example is the holiday schedule. Staff members want Christmas Day off to be with their families. You, the manager, want everyone on your staff to be happy, but you have a clear picture as to what would happen if you granted everyone's wishes for Christmas Day! Instead, you need to intelligently make a rotation plan for the holidays, or perhaps draw names out of a hat, assign requests according to seniority, or determine some other way for the Christmas Day shift to be adequately staffed.

Planning is a process that never ends. It can be thought of as a hoop with notches where you stop and enter another phase of the planning process; then you continue going around the hoop over and over again. It is unrealistic to develop a plan and think that it will never change. It may be perfect for the moment, a week, or even an entire year; but the complexity of health care and the individuality of clients and staff require that your excellent plan be continuously reevaluated. The planning (Fig. 3.2) hoop begins with an assessment.

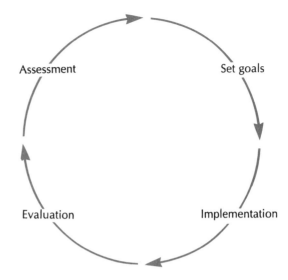

Figure 3.2   The planning hoop. The effective nurse manager must learn that planning is critical to getting the total workload done effectively.

Assessment

What is the problem or potential problem that concerns you? You know how to do a client physical assessment. This is a similar process. Look at the problem "from head to toe" and assess what really is wrong. If it is a staffing problem in a nursing home, look at the mix of licensed and unlicensed personnel. Is it right for the needs of the residents?

Is the problem a lack of knowledge? If it is, you need to assess where the lack is, who needs to know the information, and how to most effectively teach it. Do not be distracted by other issues as you do your assessment. Keep focused on the problem you are trying to resolve and learn all you can about it. This would be similar to trying to assess two residents at the same time. One does not get a clear picture of the problem unless a very focused effort is made. The next step in the planning hoop is to set goals.

Goal Setting

Now that you have a complete set of data regarding the problem, you have enough information to set goals. This, again, is very similar to the nursing process. Instead of writing a care plan, you are preparing a plan to resolve a management problem. Make the goals reasonable and achievable. As we saw, not everyone can have Christmas Day off. If the problem is an unbalanced mix of licensed and unlicensed personnel, your goal could be to correct the mix through attrition and selective hiring within the next 6 months. If the problem is knowledge, your goal would be to have 100% of your staff attend a class on the information needed by a specific date. The goals should be meaningful and demonstrate your most careful and organized thinking.

Implementation

This is the test of good planning. Was your assessment done accurately and are your goals realistic? Perhaps the actual implementation requires you to not hire an RN or LPN when they apply because your staff has too great a proportion of licensed personnel. Or implementation may mean you need to find the budget money to pay the staff to attend the education program you determined they needed. In addition, you need a plan for getting everyone to attend. This could involve bonus money or other rewards, and, in all likelihood, it would mean presenting the education program several times. Implementation is the actual "doing" of your plan.

Evaluation

Did your plan work? Was Christmas Day successfully staffed and did the staff feel that the staffing decisions were made with fairness? Within 6 months, was your staff mix at the level at which you needed it to be? How effective was your education program? Did it bring about the change you wanted? Such questions initiate the process of evaluation. A nurse manager cannot just "do something" and consider the problem solved. Instead, a careful evaluation must be performed so that the cycle of the planning hoop can begin again. That is right, once you have evaluated your plan, you need to do another assessment and begin the circle again!

Many people do not spend a great deal of time planning their workload solutions to the unit's problems, or to client-care problems. The profession of nursing is filled with "doing" types of people. One of the critical skills of being a manager is to learn to quit "just doing" and begin "planning to do." It is a challenge to take the time necessary to plan because planning does not enter into the conventional description of a "good nurse."

When a person is planning, that person is sitting somewhere quietly and thinking. The profession of nursing generally does not see that as productive because beds need to be made, and there are baths and treatments to be done. With those unfinished care issues, how can a *real* nurse take the time to just sit and think? A *real* nurse manager soon learns that doing the thinking or planning is critical to getting the total workload done effectively. So, fight the urge to be "busy" when planning is needed. Teach your staff that the time you spend planning is critical to the overall picture of care for clients and job satisfaction for them. Be courageous enough to use the planning hoop to resolve problems and prevent new ones. Because if you do not, you will become a victim of *crisis management*!

Crisis Management

A crisis manager is a person who does not take the time to plan. This manager waits until the week before Christmas to resolve the problem of the staffing crisis. A great deal of hysteria, excess energy, and distress are involved in solving problems when they occur rather than in foreseeing them and taking the time to plan a solution for the problem. The phrase "All I do is run around and put out fires!" is indicative of the crisis manager. It is not effective management and can be prevented by the implementation of the planning hoop into your management style. Look to the future and anticipate problems. Then, devise a plan for solving them before a crisis happens.

Some situations will still become a crisis for even the best manager. Accept that, solve the problem, design a plan so it will not be a crisis the next time, and move on to the next situation.

PRIORITY SETTING

Every LPN has learned how to prioritize the work of giving patient or resident care. Traditionally, the sickest patient is to receive the nurse's attention first and the least seriously ill person waits until last. This concept assumes that each patient is assessed and observed frequently, rather than being ignored until her or his turn comes to receive care.

Priority setting in management situations has a similar format. The priority of each management problem is determined after the assessment of the situation has been completed. The method for determining priority problems generally is based on determining what is essential for the organization or the person at the time. Staffing for Christmas Day is essential, as is giving pain medications in a timely manner.

The nurse manager needs to think of the entire organization when determining priorities. They often are divided into two categories: (1) concerns that relate to patient or resident care, and (2) concerns that relate to the process of running the business of the institution.

Each category should be considered separately, although a great deal of overlap of concerns occurs in implementing problem solutions. Each concern needs to be listed as a *need* or a *want*. Obviously, needs should be met before wants. It is helpful to use this method for categorizing your management concerns before prioritizing them.

MANAGING PERSONNEL

As a nurse manager, you will be involved in, if not responsible for, the hiring and evaluating of employees. This is a critical aspect of your job and one that requires the highest level of professional skill and performance. This work cannot be done by intuition or "best guess." All personnel decisions directly affect the lives of the employees of the institution. These people deserve as much care and attention as your patients.

The hiring process is where the employee begins a career with your organization or, if not employed, will leave with an impression that will be taken out to the community. It should be your desire to have that impression be a good one. Many legal issues are involved in the hiring process. Be sure to clarify those with your personnel manager or administrator. Laws exist that involve the advertisement of a job and how the interview is conducted, and federal rules identify questions that cannot be asked in an interview because of concern over discrimination. Be alert to these rules and follow them.

The philosophy of interviewing someone for employment is to find someone who "fits" with the philosophy and image of your institution. The applicant needs the licensure or certification that the job description demands and the experience to perform the job at a satisfactory level. The interview also allows the nurse manager to determine the shift availability and whether the potential employee is available for part-time or full-time work. Moreover, an effort should be made to learn the specific interests of the applicant so plans can be made to use any special skills and knowledge the person possesses. The screening process of the personnel department presumably will eliminate anyone unqualified for the job. It should not be necessary for such people to be interviewed.

Interview

The purpose of the interview is to exchange information. Be prepared to give positive information about your facility to all applicants whether they are to be employed or not. Remember, you want applicants to say favorable things about your organization even if they are not selected for the job. During the interview, the nurse manager is expected to determine the applicant's:

Dependability
Skill level
Willingness to assume the responsibilities of the job
Willingness and ability to work with others
Interest in the job
Adaptability
Consistency of goals with available opportunities
Conformity of manner and appearance to job requirements

The interview has definite purposes and should be carried out in a professional manner. It is not the place for social chit-chat; however, some warm and friendly comments at the beginning of the interview should put the applicant at ease so the interview can be emotionally comfortable.

The greatest predictor of the applicant's future success is past performance. Is this someone who has worked with the elderly previously and enjoyed it? Has the applicant sought additional educational experiences that will enhance work in your type of setting? Was this person a desirable employee at the last place of employment or, if a new graduate, a good student at school? These critical pieces of information should be noted on the application and verified in the interview.

It is your responsibility as the nurse manager to set the tone for honesty in the interview. Be specific and direct in your comments. It is helpful to have an interview guide available to use for every interview. This guide is a written document that contains questions, directions, and pertinent information to be shared with the applicant. The presence of an interview guide ensures you, the applicant, and the institution that the same process is being used in every interview. It avoids gathering of prejudicial information and provides consistency in the interview process.

Questions on the interview guide should cover subjects such as which shifts the applicant is willing to work, whether part-time or full-time work is desired, and feelings about working with the elderly. It also could contain a brief case study or scenario about a gerontologically focused situation that requires a response from the applicant. The presence of two or three such questions gives you additional information about the potential employee. All applicants must be asked the same questions to avoid discrimination or the appearance of discrimination in choosing future employees. You also need to carefully review the Title VII Civil Rights Act prior to doing any interviewing. This federal law prohibits discrimination in any personnel decision on the basis of race, color, sex, age, religion, or national origin. A comfortable format for an interview is presented below:

> Use an opening to establish rapport and put the applicant at ease.
> Share the interview procedure with the applicant.
> Discuss the applicant's interests in being employed at your facility.
> Obtain an educational history.
> Discuss future plans of the applicant, for example, upward mobility, future education.
> Share case studies and situations and discuss them.
> Inform the applicant about the organization.
> Allow time for the applicant to ask questions and get answers.
> Close by clarifying how to reach the applicant after the interview, informing the person when the decision will be made, and thanking the applicant for considering your organization for employment.

Employee Evaluation

After the nurse manager has made a decision to hire an applicant, a very focused effort must be made to give that person a thorough and extensive orientation to the job, its standards, and its expectations. The quality of personnel hired and retained in the organization determines the success of the organization and the quality of the orientation directly determines the overall success for both the organization and the employee.

After the employee has had the opportunity to work with other qualified employees and to establish an effective working routine, this new employee can be allowed to work independently. A resource person should always be available in some way to the new employee for the first 3 months of employment to indicate a sincere effort is being made to ensure success for both the organization and the new employee.

Each organization has an established process for evaluating employees. The first evaluation may come at 3 months, 6 months, or 12 months. Earlier and more frequent evaluations take more of the manager's time but also provide regular feedback for the employee. Overall, it is generally time well spent. Your organization should also have an established written form for evaluating employees. Again, this process should be consistent for all employees to avoid discrimination.

For all employing organizations, a performance appraisal may be based on the five basic realistic assumptions outlined below:

1. The appraisal will help an employee improve the management of the workload.
2. Employee appraisal is a difficult process, but a skill that can be mastered with hard work.

3. Few people like the current form (a perfect one simply does not exist!).
4. The appraisal will be made by the employee's supervisor.
5. Information must be gathered on a day-to-day basis.

The challenge to the nurse manager is that the performance appraisal *must* accurately reflect the person's actual job performance. It cannot contain prejudicial information, hearsay, or undocumented information. It is designed to be helpful to the employee and, by assisting the employee to improve, it will be helpful to the organization.

Traditionally, potential evaluation problems can contribute to a less than accurate evaluation. The first one is *leniency error*. This occurs when a supervisor wants everyone to "be buddies" or "be the manager's best friend." It results when the manager "looks the other way" or gives an employee "the benefit of the doubt" rather than finding out what really happened.

A competent nurse manager cannot afford to be "best friends" with employees. The manager needs to be the manager. It is critical to success for the manager to be an honest and fair person who does not lose the ability to be objective. The leniency error does not help an employee improve and it does not contribute to the overall functioning of the organization.

The *recency error* is an indication of a manager who has forgotten the basic assumptions of evaluation and who has not kept records of employee performance over the year. Because of the lack of written record, the manager than evaluates only on what is remembered "most recently." All employees know when their annual review is scheduled and often find it easy to "look good" during the time just prior to their evaluation. Again, this type of evaluation process enhances neither the performance of the employee nor that of the organization.

The *halo error* is allowing one trait to influence the entire evaluation. It could be either a strongly positive trait or a strongly negative one. Either way, it clouds the objective evaluation of an employee if only the halo behavior is remembered. Evaluations need to be fair and comprehensive regarding the employee's behavior and skills.

The evaluation process is critical to the growth and stability of the organization. Evaluation standards cannot be ambiguous to be successful. The process of rewarding a strong employee and counseling a poor employee must be valid. This happens only if the manager maintains a professional and consistent attitude toward the evaluation process.

Negative or probationary evaluations are very difficult for all managers to give. Use the same process you would use for a positive evaluation. Make it fair and comprehensive, and share the information you have in a professional manner. For all terminations, the process of counseling the employee must be carefully documented over time. This is an act of fairness toward the employee and a protection against litigation for the institution.

Making Client Care Assignments

One of the day-to-day management skills used by LPNs is that of making client-care assignments (Fig. 3.3). The skill of making effective assignments is critical to any

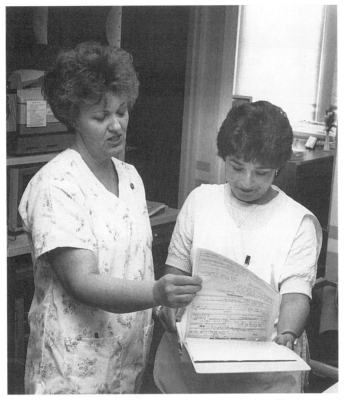

Figure 3.3 The licensed practical nurse is often responsible for making the care assignments to nursing assistants.

clinical area. The goal of making client-care assignments is to match the worker with the client in a manner that allows for the best nursing care to be administered and received, and that affords the highest level of employee satisfaction. This requires sensitivity, awareness of the skills and attitudes of others, and the ability to form a plan and to follow through on it. Several aspects of making client-care assignments should be examined.

Consider the personal skills of each nursing assistant. Is one better at doing colostomy care and another skilled at feeding a resident with a cerebrovascular accident (CVA)? Praise employees for their special skills and *allow them to use them.* Assist employees in developing skills related to their interests and abilities and recognize them for that specific skill development. Then, assign them clients who will benefit from the skill and knowledge of the employee. This enhances both client care and employee self-esteem. The entire organization benefits from this enhancement concept.

Make assignments according to skill level. A new nursing assistant should not be given the most difficult client on the floor just because the other employees are tired of caring for the individual. Instead, assign the new employee a mentor—a skilled nursing assistant—to guide the new person through the multiple, intricate dimensions of giving excellent client care.

Give all employees assignments they can be successful in doing, which provides excellent care for the client and bolsters the self-esteem of the employee.

When working with the elderly, it is generally more effective to assign the same employee to a client for several days in succession. This allows the caregiver to learn the personal needs and nuances of the client and address them successfully. When a "new" person is assigned to a client each day, it puts a demand on the client to need to explain again that he cannot hear out of his right ear, or that he wants two cups of coffee on his breakfast tray, or that it is his right knee that does not work very well. Generally, a comfortable camaraderie or sense of teamwork develops between the caregiver and the care receiver that enhances the work of healing when they are allowed to work together over time.

Sometimes a difficult or demanding client requires more energy and patience than most employees can provide day after day. When this occurs, the nurse manager should rotate the assignment or make a double assignment of nursing assistants to the client in a direct effort to avoid burn-out of the employees.

Another consideration for making assignments is that of physical demands. Often when caring for the elderly or chronically ill, a heavy physical demand is made in turning, positioning, and assisting the client to ambulate. When the nurse manager makes the assignment, the physical, muscular work of the care should be considered to not overwork a particular employee. Another consideration is that of placement of the rooms assigned geographically. It is unnecessary to make assignments that require an employee to have clients on both ends of the hall or in other diverse patterns. Make a strong effort to group the room numbers assigned to avoid unnecessary walking by personnel. Most work days are tiring enough.

At times, it is appropriate to ask an employee for a preferred care assignment for that day or week. Some special behavior or something else of interest may have attracted an employee to a client. It is a positive thing to address these interests when possible.

MANAGING THE QUALITY OF CARE

The process of managing and evaluating the quality of health care is not new. Florence Nightingale (1859) urged that all nursing care be carefully evaluated. Because of her innovative nursing care practices *and* her ability to measure and evaluate nursing care, she was able to measure changes in the health of patients. At one hospital during the Crimean War, she measured a decrease in patient mortality of 50% down to 20% after her nursing-care ideas were instituted. Different outside organizations measure the quality of care given in hospitals and nursing homes. The Joint Commission on Accreditation of Hospitals (JCAH) was founded in 1952 to evaluate health-care services. Two nursing organizations followed this trend in the late 1950s. The American Nurses Association developed and published standards of care for the various nursing specialities and the National League of Nursing published standards that the public could expect from nursing. Quality health care is the right of persons who enter the health-care system. The organizations just listed provide outside evaluation of the organization. Other methods for making self-evaluation that involve the LPN exist, however.

Total Quality Management

Total quality management (TQM) is a management philosophy that emphasizes a commitment of excellence throughout the entire health-care organization. The principles are widely used throughout many business organizations in addition to health care. The overall purpose of TQM is to improve quality of service and ensure customer satisfaction.

The four major characteristics of TQM are: (1) customer/client focus, (2) total organizational involvement, (3) use of quality tools and statistics for measurement, and (4) identification of key processes for improvement. The LPN is involved in all four aspects of the TQM process.

Most nurses naturally believe that their focus is the customer or client. This is the overall theme of TQM and calls for all personnel in each department to focus on the needs of the client. An example would be a smoother admission process, given that process is often an area that provokes customer complaints. Another example is the housekeeper responding to the patient. This could be simply friendly visiting or putting aside the housekeeper's usual work to go get a nurse for a patient.

The customer focus of TQM is most effective when all employees in a hospital or nursing home respond to the challenge to focus on the needs of the client. This philosophy eliminates the idea of "That is not my job!" Instead, everyone works toward the overall goal of satisfied customers. This may make it necessary for a nurse to assist the housekeeper in making beds because of the large number of admissions and discharges done in one shift. Or a physician may need to transport a patient from the emergency room to the unit; respiratory therapists may assist patients to the toilet; the unit secretary may need to transport patients who are being discharged to their car. The point is that everyone is committed to the idea of customer satisfaction and is willing to fulfill whatever role might be necessary to meet that commitment.

The use of high-quality tools and statistics to measure the level of care that is being given is an important consideration. An organization cannot determine whether the quality of care is being improved unless accurate measurement takes place. This generally is not the responsibility of the LPN, but an upper management or administrative assignment. The LPN may need to complete forms or make reports that contribute to overall measurement of the work being done, but such an assignment will be made by someone else in the system to you, as the LPN.

The fourth component of TQM is identification of key processes for improvement. All activities in an organization can be described in terms of people working together. The term identification of key processes refers to the efficiency or effectiveness of the work people or teams do together. One example is the *PDCA* cycle. This is the *P*lan, *D*o, *C*heck and *A*ct cycle. It very simply defines the process a group or team should be following as they do their work.

Continuous Quality Improvement

Continuous Quality Improvement (CQI) designates the process used to improve quality and performance of organizations and the people in them, whereas TQM designates the overall philosophy behind it. The terms "TQM" and "CQI" are often used interchangeably, which is not, however, an accurate description of these concepts.

CQI is used to systematically investigate ways to improve patient-resident care. It is a never-ending process that examines at what level standards of care are met and ways to make improvement. It always involves multiple persons from different departments. You, as the LPN, will be often asked to serve on a CQI team to evaluate and improve an aspect of health-care service. The most significant role you will have within this system is to provide excellent, individualized care to your "customer," the human being who depends on you for nursing care.

SUMMARY

Many skills are needed by the nurse manager, but this is just a chapter, not a management textbook. The basic information shared here is the most important for the LPN to master for the management position. The textbooks listed at the end of this chapter cover the subject more extensively, and the case study and test questions at the end of the chapter will give you practice in considering management issues. Finally, it is important for you to find a mentor to assist you with the real world of management.

CASE STUDY

It is 7:35 A.M. and you are the nurse in charge of a 25-bed skilled nursing facility (SNF) unit at the nursing home where you work. The night nurse went home early because she was ill, and you have just discovered that only half of the 6:00 A.M. medications have been distributed. You have a new LPN orienting with you, but she is a recent graduate, and you are not yet sure of her skill level.

You have an 8:00 A.M. meeting with the social worker and a family that is struggling with the decision of whether to allow their mother to die or to place her on stronger life-support mechanisms. The final concern you have is making up the payroll. It is your responsibility to have the paperwork completed on the payroll by 9:00 A.M. If the payroll forms are not in the personnel office, a 3-day delay will occur in paying the employees on your unit. It is the week before Christmas.

As you are struggling to set priorities for the morning, Dr. N. comes onto the unit in a rage and begins talking to you in a raised voice and with an angry non-verbal appearance. This is a physician who is known as a bully with both nurses and families, yet you have learned by working with him that he really does care for his residents. You stop everything you are doing to listen to him degrade you with his unprofessional manner. The halls are full of residents and employees who are watching this situation. As the charge nurse, you are responsible for all activities on the unit.

Please make a priority list with an explanation for the ranking of each item. Then, in narrative form, describe how you would implement the priority list you have made. Good luck!

CASE STUDY
DISCUSSION

PRIORITY LIST

1.
Explanation:

2.
Explanation:

3.
Explanation:

4.
Explanation:

Narrative Explaining My Decisions

CASE STUDY
SOLUTION

1. The medications must be distributed.
   Explanation: The medications already are an hour and a half late. This could have very serious physiological consequences for the frail elderly residents on the unit. This is a critical need.

2. The physician must be managed.
   Explanation: He is preventing me from resolving the other problems on the unit and some of them are critical. In addition, he is very disruptive to the people (including residents) on the unit.

3. The meeting with the social worker and the resident's family.
   Explanation: This is a very emotional situation for this family and it is unethical and unkind to ask them to wait or come back at a more convenient time. An issue of this importance cannot be delayed once people are ready to deal with it. It is listed third because the meeting could go ahead without me since the social worker will be there.

4. The payroll forms need to be completed.
   Explanation: It is unfair not to have the employees paid in a timely manner. Yet people are always more important than paperwork. This could wait since paperwork does not bleed, die, or have feelings.

NARRATIVE EXPLANATION OF THIS LIST

I would ignore the physician and his screaming; in the meantime I would call an experienced nurse on another unit. I would quickly explain to her the medication errors and the availability of only my newly hired LPN for assistance. My request would be for her to come to my floor and work with the new LPN to pass the medications that were missed. I am asking her for 30 minutes of her time in an emergency situation. I would not turn this assignment over to the new LPN because I am unsure of her skill level. This is a critical situation that demands immediate correction by someone with a very high skill level.

Because I know the physician really cares about his residents, I would resist the desire to humor him; instead, I would let him know that I had a resident emergency and could see him about his problem after 10:30 A.M. This is not a good example of problem solving with him, but it is an excellent example of setting priorities. He might still be angry with me, but I would be keeping my residents in the best health possible with my decisive action. My hope would be that his natural caring for residents would prevail and he would cooperate in this situation.

I would notify the social worker that I would be at the meeting, but that I might be late. And finally, I would call the personnel office and explain to them that a crisis involving the residents occurred and that the paperwork would be delivered to them by noon. If that did not allow for the employees on the unit to be paid in a timely manner, I would request that an employee from their office come to the floor and do the necessary paperwork.

I would not make lengthy explanations to any of these people. Instead I would count on my professional reputation to underlie the urgency of the situation. After the day was under control and all of the problems resolved, I would very carefully go to each person involved and thank him or her for the cooperation and give the explanation the person deserves. I would call the night nurse and let him or her know of the situation and ask the nurse to come in within 24 hours to complete the medication error forms. I already would have made the necessary phone calls to the physicians informing them of the medication errors.

Study Questions

Circle the correct choice(s) to complete each statement.

1. Every LPN must practice within the definition of the State Nurse Practice Act. The best way for an LPN to determine whether the current job description is within the current Nurse Practice Act is to:
   a. Ask the supervisor.
   b. Discuss it with the personnel office during the hiring interview.
   c. Read the Nurse Practice Act.
   d. Ask another LPN.

2. The authoritarian style of leadership is the most effective to use in gerontological settings because:
   a. The work gets done in a timely manner.
   b. Geriatric settings have many emergencies to manage.
   c. Authoritarian leaders are very person focused.
   d. Authoritarian leadership is not strongly compatible with elder-care settings.

3. The most honest form of communication is:
   a. Nonverbal communication
   b. Verbal communications with facial movements
   c. Sitting quietly and listening
   d. The written word

4. Assertive communication is:
   a. Inappropriate for an LPN to use
   b. A meaningful way to share angry feelings
   c. A learned behavior that allows for effective communication
   d. A normal physiological response to stressful communication

5. The purpose of an employee interview is to:
   a. Learn the prejudices of the applicant prior to employment
   b. Exchange information
   c. Fill the employment quota of minorities
   d. Make new friends

Reference

Nightingale, F. (1946). *Notes on nursing, replica edition: What it is, and what it is not.* Philadelphia: Lippincott-Raven Publishers.

Bibliography

Anderson, M. A. (1996). *Leadership, management and role transition of the LPN / LVN.* Philadelphia: F. A. Davis.
   This textbook is written specifically for the leadership / management role of the licensed practical nurse. It is written with a strong clinical application and is specific to the role of the LPN.
Sullivan E. J., & Decker, P. J. (1997). *Effective leadership and management in nursing.* Menlo Park, CA: Addison-Wesley Longman.
   This textbook provides general information on the basic concepts of nursing management. It covers all major issues concerned with management skill development.

Chapter

KATHLEEN R. CULLITON

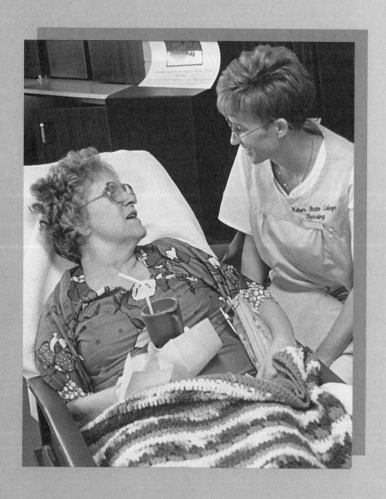

4

The Use of the Nursing Process and Nursing Diagnosis in the Care of Older Adults

Learning Objectives

After completing this chapter, the student will be able to:

1. Describe the nursing process as a problem-solving technique in the context of the older adult's assessment, plan of care, nursing interventions, and nursing documentation.
2. Identify the use of the nursing process, Minimum Data Set (MDS), and Resident Assessment Protocols (RAPs) in developing nursing care plans for residents in nursing facilities.
3. Use the nursing process to develop a care plan for the presented case study.

INTRODUCTION

Licensed practical nurses (LPNs) work in a variety of care settings. Each setting may require the practical nurse to function in a different capacity, yet each practice area expects the practical nurse be involved with the assessment, planning, implementation, and evaluation of older patients and the care they receive.

ENVIRONMENTS OF CARE

Home Care

A relatively new practice area for LPNs is working in home care. Practical nurses in home care work under the direction of a registered nurse. They provide nursing care such as changing dressings, monitoring blood glucose levels, administering medications, and assessing the status of chronic disease processes in the older adult's home.

Hospital Care

Licensed practical nurses work in a variety of capacities with the acutely ill older person who is hospitalized. Often they are paired with a registered nurse to form a care team in providing nursing care. Other care delivery models may require the LPN to have a specific task on the unit, such as treatments or passing medications for all of the hospitalized patients.

Long-Term Care Facilities

The LPN may be employed in many types of long-term care facilities. Skilled nursing facilities and nursing facilities were previously thought of as nursing homes. They generally provide a high level of nursing intervention. Assisted living facilities provide care to older persons who may need assistance with activities of daily living (ADLs), but who do not require complex, skilled intervention. Continuing care retirement communities have several levels of care including those offered in a skilled nursing facility, assisted living, and independent living apartments. Wellness clinics are frequently provided for independent apartment living residents. LPNs could be employed in any one of these long-term care settings.

In the long-term care environment, the practical nurse collects admission data, provides input to the plan of care, carries out the nursing interventions that are outlined in the plan of care, and evaluates the effectiveness of these interventions in meeting the goals of the older adult's care plan. Often the LPN confers with other members of the health-care team (dieticians, physical therapists, occupational therapists, recreational therapists, social workers, and nursing assistants) to share observations and clarify the plan of care. Very often, the LPN in these settings is responsible for working with nursing assistants to be sure the plan of care is carried out. Practical nurses even call physicians to clarify orders and to report changes in the resident's health status. The practice of LPNs in nursing facilities is the reference practice model for this chapter.

THE NURSING PROCESS

An LPN walks into a resident's room and finds the person with a supper tray in place. The resident is unable to talk and is turning blue. The nurse thinks that the resident is choking. Quickly, the nurse moves the meal tray out of the way and uses a two-handed thrust under the resident's diaphragm to attempt to dislodge the food that is obstructing the airway. After the nurse does the abdominal thrusts, the resident is assessed for respiratory movements. If the person is breathing again, the nurse takes a deep breath, cuts the resident's meat into smaller pieces, and observes the resident eating the rest of the meal. If the resident is not breathing, the nurse may attempt another abdominal thrust or reposition the resident so another abdominal thrust can be done from behind.

This short scenario is an example of the nursing process (Fig. 4.1). When the practical nurse entered the room and saw the older person with hands clenched on throat and turning blue, the nurse was collecting data. In a split second, the nurse identified the resident's problem as choking. The nurse's next thought was to set a goal for this resident's care: "The resident will expel the food that is causing the choking." With the goal of expelling the lodged food, the nurse designs the plan from nursing knowledge and immediately implements abdominal thrusts. After the nursing intervention, the nurse evaluates the situation to determine whether the resident has expelled the food. If the resident has not, the nurse must rethink and redesign the plan and immediately implement the revised nursing actions.

The nursing process is a problem-solving model that describes what nurses do. It identifies the way nurses approach patient care and recognizes the ongoing and changeable nature of the care that nurses provide, care which is based on the individual needs of the patient.

Nurses are faced with the many problems of the older person every day. The nursing process provides a structure for nurses to plan and give high-quality, individualized care.

Figure 4.1 Nursing process model. The circular nature of this model demonstrates that the process is ongoing.

Assessment

The first step in the nursing process is to collect all the information the nurse will need to clearly identify the older person's strengths, and current and potential problems. Usually, the assessment starts with the call or written summary from the agency or department that is transferring the older person to your nursing care area. The information that it is important to receive before the actual transfer of the older person includes:

> Name, age, insurance identification numbers
> Medical diagnoses, advanced directives, disease prognosis
> Family support
> Need for equipment (Does the client need special equipment, such as a special bed, oxygen, intravenous [IV] setup, or feeding pump?)
> Functional ability (How does the client transfer, ambulate, move in bed, bathe, toilet, and eat?)
> Medications (Which prescription and over-the-counter medication does the client take?)
> Cognitive ability (Is the client oriented? How is the client's memory?)
> Special needs (Is the client depressed, at risk for skin breakdown or other health risks?)

This information is very important for the preparation of the older person's bed and room and makes the transfer to your care as smooth as possible.

Once the older person is transferred, the nurse makes a focused assessment that culminates in a comprehensive assessment. The admission assessment includes observations, physical examination, review of laboratory values, interview of the older person and the family, and a nursing history.

In 1987, the federal government enacted legislation that set minimum standards for the assessment and care planning processes in nursing facilities certified for Medicare reimbursement. This legislation is known as the Omnibus Budget Reconciliation Act of 1987 (OBRA 1987). This was followed by OBRA 1990, which clarified some of the questioned areas of OBRA 1987. The MDS and RAPs were a part of the legislation that had been implemented across the country in nursing facilities that accept Medicare and Medicaid funding as reimbursement for the care they provide. The MDS and the RAPs are two components of the mandated assessment process entitled the Resident Assessment Instrument (RAI).

The MDS provides an outline of the most necessary information that must be collected about every resident admitted to a nursing facility. Nursing observations, physical assessment, health history, and interview of the older adult and the family, and completion of the RAPs added to the MDS, make a comprehensive assessment. (An example of a comprehensive assessment is included in the case study at the end of this chapter and in the Appendix at the end of the book.)

What does a nurse do with all the information that has been collected during assessment? The MDS refers care providers to a list of problem areas that must be addressed in the plan of care. Each of these problem areas also has a RAP that lists areas that require further assessment and consideration before designing the plan of care (Box 4.1).

BOX 4.1   EIGHTEEN PROBLEM AREAS IDENTIFIED FROM THE MINIMUM DATA SET

Delirium
Cognitive loss/dementia
Visual function
Communication
Activities of daily living: function/rehabilitation potential
Urinary incontinence and indwelling catheter
Psychosocial well-being
Mood state
Behavior problem
Activities
Falls
Nutritional status
Feeding tubes
Dehydration/fluid maintenance
Dental care
Pressure ulcers
Psychotropic drug use
Physical restraints

Frequently, the RAPs are not actually incorporated into the assessment process. These protocols, however, extend the assessment from the minimum information of the MDS and offer a more thorough review of the problem area identified by the MDS.

The Nursing Diagnosis

Developing the nursing diagnosis is a primary responsibility of the registered nurse. It involves the use of diagnostic reasoning to reflect the older person's strengths, problems, and potential problems. The registered nurse considers the assessment data and organizes them to decide whether they meet criteria for a specific nursing diagnosis. The North American Nursing Diagnosis Association (NANDA) has identified diagnoses that are widely accepted and understood by multiple disciplines and are viewed as the national standards for nursing diagnoses. The NANDA diagnoses are not specific to older people, but they are useful in providing consistent expression of nursing diagnoses for all disciplines and in all settings. An example of a NANDA diagnosis is: *Comfort altered, Pain, related to: degenerative joint disease.*

In the long-term care setting, nurses often prefer to use nursing diagnoses that incorporate the MDS language and format. An example of an MDS-related nursing diagnosis is: Potential for joint pain due to degenerative joint disease. Common nursing diagnoses for older adults include:

Self Care Deficit
Physical Mobility, impaired
Nutrition, altered: less than body requirements

Injury, high risk for
Urinary Elimination, altered
Constipation
Thought Process, altered
Skin Integrity, impaired: high risk for

It is the responsibility of the registered nurse to ensure that nursing diagnoses address the comprehensive assessment. The nursing diagnosis is an important part of the nursing process and addresses the potential and actual problems of the older adult.

Nursing Diagnosis and Medical Diagnosis

There are two basic ways to communicate the nature of an older client's health problems. One way is by medical diagnoses and another is by nursing diagnoses. Medical diagnoses are made by a physician and describe a disease or a disease process. Diseases are diagnosed by identifying a specific group of signs and symptoms. For example, diabetes mellitus is diagnosed when a client has elevated fasting blood sugar levels, weight loss, thirst, and a large urine output. A client who has an area of dead brain tissue on magnetic resonance imaging (MRI) and computerized tomography (CT) scan along with speech and swallowing difficulty and left-sided paralysis would be diagnosed with a cerebrovascular accident (CVA). Both of these medical diagnoses are common for older persons and communicate information to the nurse about what physical or psychological process is happening to the client.

The major problem with planning care based only on medical diagnoses is that they do not describe the individual problems of the older adult or the impact the disease has on the patient's day-to-day life. Nursing diagnoses, on the other hand, are specific to the individual older person's nursing care needs and frequently relate to the areas in which the older person has difficulty functioning.

For example, an obese client who is newly diagnosed with diabetes mellitus may have the following nursing diagnoses:

Nutrition, altered: more than body requirements and *Knowledge Deficit related to poor dietary practices.*

A long-term diabetes patient may be experiencing problems with a heel ulcer that will not heal. In this case, the nursing diagnosis will be:

Skin Integrity, altered

Both of these clients have the same medical diagnoses but different health-care needs, as shown in their nursing diagnoses.

Planning

After organizing the assessment data and noting the nursing diagnoses identified by the registered nurse, the practical nurse working with the older adult, the family, and the health-care team, begins the planning part of the nursing process. The planning portion of the nursing process includes setting priorities, identifying goals and outcomes of care, and designing and documenting interventions.

Setting Priorities

The nurse reviews the nursing diagnoses and places them in priority order. Remember the example at the beginning of this section? Removing the lodged food so the resident could breathe would be a higher priority than putting on residents' shoes!

One of the most popular models used to assist the nurse in setting priorities is Abraham Maslow's hierarchy of needs. This framework gives life-sustaining needs the highest priority. These needs are followed by safety and security needs, love and belonging needs, self-esteem needs, and self-actualization needs. Using this framework, the following nursing diagnoses would be placed in this order:

1. *Nutrition, altered: less than body requirements*
   Resident refuses to eat and drink.
2. *Injury, high risk for*
   Resident is unsteady ambulating to the bathroom; resident has fallen twice in the past week.
3. *Thought Process, altered*
   Resident constantly asks staff where he is; resident is unable to remember dates.

Because the nursing process is focused on the older person as an individual, it is also necessary to consider the priorities of the resident. Often a resident will state that the highest priority is to go home. The resident may refuse treatments, medications, and activities that will maintain personal health because no one will be assisting in the patient's discharge. Although discharge may not be realistic (at this time), the practical nurse will probably be more successful in providing nursing care if the plan of care addresses discharge to home as a high priority.

1. *Nutrition, altered: less than body requirements*
   Resident refuses to eat and drink.
   Discuss with the resident what is usually eaten at home and how it is prepared.
   Review how the person's current health status would affect the ability to buy food, prepare it, and eat at home.
   Discuss strategies and plans for ensuring that the resident is able to eat after returning home.
   Include the resident's food preferences in meals.

The nature of the work setting and other factors can affect priority setting. This includes considerations of expense, time, personnel resources, and schedule. The resident might be able to be discharged if the person received nursing care at home 24 hours a day. However, most people cannot financially afford that level of care, and generally insurance plans do not cover the cost. Therefore, discharge cannot be a high priority at this time.

Goal Setting or Identifying Outcomes

After identifying the priorities for the resident's care, the nurse identifies goals or outcomes for each of the nursing diagnoses. Setting goals is something that most of us do all of the time. Sometimes our personal goal may be to "clock out on time" or to "survive a busy day." The goals that are part of the planning process, however, describe the specific resident outcomes and identify the goals that direct nursing care. To direct care and describe outcomes, goals must be:

Measurable—measurable outcomes need to be identified. "Eating 100% of a meal" can be measured, whereas it is difficult to measure "appetite will improve."

Realistic—the goal must fit in with the resident's abilities. "The resident will recall the correct data and time" is probably an unrealistic goal for a resident with Alzheimer's disease.

Specific—the goal should identify certain behaviors or conditions to aid in their attainment and evaluation. "The resident will feel better" is not specific. It could be better worded as, "The resident will state that he has less nausea."

Timely—a time frame needs to be established for the attainment of each goal. "The resident will walk 100 feet" does not specify a time frame for achievement of this goal. Adding "by the end of December" provides a time frame.

Attainable—the goal should be written in such a way as to communicate a motivating factor to the resident and the nursing care staff. For an older adult with left hemiplegia, a goal such as "The resident will be independent in self-care by the end of the year" may be a strong motivator to work harder at the occupational and physical therapy sessions.

In nursing facilities, the documentation regulations under OBRA 1987 and OBRA 1990 require that the status of goal attainment be systematically addressed. These documentation requirements are the monthly summaries (a comprehensive review of outcomes every 30 days) and the quarterly reviews (comprehensive interdisciplinary review of the resident's plan of care every 90 days) (Box 4.2). With new admissions or specific insurance carriers, the nurse may be required to do monthly comprehensive assessments of the outcome of care. This provides a 30- or 90-day time framework in which goals can be designed. It also helps the nurse to think about what is realistic in that specific time frame. For a resident who is rehabilitating after

---

BOX 4.2 ASSESSMENTS NEEDED FOR EACH NURSING HOME RESIDENT

COMPREHENSIVE ADMISSION ASSESSMENT including
  RESIDENT ASSESSMENT INSTRUMENT (RAI)
   1. Minimum data set (MDS)
   2. Resident assessment protocols
   3. Ongoing nursing assessment
ANNUAL REASSESSMENT including RAI
SIGNIFICANT CHANGE IN STATUS ASSESSMENT including RAI
QUARTERLY ASSESSMENT including part of MDS

having a hip replacement, "Ambulate independently" may be a realistic goal in 6 months. "Stand and walk ten steps with a walker" may be a more realistic goal for 30 days. The following are examples of goals:

> The resident will eat more than 75% of each meal for the next 30 days.
> The resident will toilet independently when reminded to go to the bathroom in the next 90 days.
> The resident will attend one activity daily for the next 90 days.
> The resident will have no signs and symptoms of a urinary tract infection for the next 90 days.
> The resident's supplemental oxygen needs will be decreased to 1 L in the next 30 days.

Look back at these goals. What do you notice about them? Each goal identifies something that the resident will or will not do, or will or will not experience. The resident's behavior is the major focus of goals as outcomes. Nursing care is not part of the goal. "Bathe the resident" is a nursing intervention, not an outcome or a goal. Nursing standards also are not part of the goal statements. "Administer all medications within 30 minutes of their ordered time" is a nursing standard, not a resident goal.

This important distinction can be illustrated in two simple exercises. Identify the correctly stated resident-based outcomes or goals in the following list. Where the outcomes or goals are not properly expressed, explain what is wrong. The correct answers and rationales follow.

1. The resident will walk more in the next 90 days.
2. The nurse will toilet the resident every 2 hours for the next 30 days.
3. The resident will have no areas of skin breakdown in the next 90 days.
4. The resident's nutrition will improve.
5. The resident will drink 1500 mL a day for the next 90 days.

Answers and rationales:

1. This goal is not measurable. It would be better stated as follows: the resident will walk 100 ft in the next 90 days.
2. This is a nursing intervention rather than a goal. It would be better stated as follows: the resident will void when toileted by the nursing staff every 2 hours for the next 90 days.
3. This is a realistic, specific, and attainable goal. The outcome of care can be measured.
4. This is a noble goal, but it is not specific or measurable. It would be better stated as follows: the resident will gain 2 lbs in the next 30 days.
5. This is a realistic, specific, and attainable goal. The outcome of care can be measured.

Designing and Documenting the Plan of Care

Once the goals or outcomes of care are identified, the practical nurse, along with the other members of the interdisciplinary team, begins planning the activities that will help the older person reach the goals. The planning phase involves discussion and pen-and-paper activity. Discussing and documenting the plan of care allows input from all members of the team and provides one way for the plan to be communicated to all staff members who are providing care for that resident. Standards of nursing practice and federal regulations require that each resident have a written, comprehensive, and interdisciplinary plan of care. The plan of care includes the problem or potential problem to be identified, the actions or interventions to be taken to address the problem, the person or discipline responsible for each action, and the goals to be achieved. An example of interventions in an interdisciplinary plan of care follows:

> Document percentage of food eaten at each meal—nursing
> Feed resident and assess swallowing ability—speech
> Review dietary preferences—dietary services
> Promote feeding of self—restorative nursing

The focus of this chapter is on developing interdisciplinary plans of care using the nursing process. As you can see, all disciplines caring for the resident need to be represented in an actual plan of care. This is an important criterion for planning interventions: planned interventions must complement the interventions of other therapies. For example, it would be confusing for the resident to be ambulated with a walker by physical therapy and encouraged to walk with two canes by the nursing staff.

It is critical that members of all disciplines discuss and develop the components of the interdisciplinary plan of care so that confusion among the staff does not occur. Residents who are asked to perform one way in physical therapy and another way on the nursing unit can become confused as to how they should perform. A coordinated approach between physical therapy and nursing helps residents improve more quickly and maintain function longer. A coordinated approach among all disciplines enhances the effectiveness of the care given to the resident and minimizes duplication of efforts.

Nursing interventions must also consider the safety of the resident. "Administering a diuretic and a sleeping pill at bedtime" is an unsafe nursing action. The resident may fall while going to the bathroom at night if still groggy from the sleeping pill. Transferring a resident who is able to stand only with the assistance of a staff member may place that resident at risk of falling.

Selected nursing interventions should help to attain the identified goal. If a resident's goal is to "lose 1 lb a week," giving "dietary supplements between meals and at bedtime" would not assist in achieving this weight loss. When the resident's goal is "will ambulate 100 ft by the end of the month," a nursing intervention must state that the nursing staff will "assist the resident to ambulate."

Nursing interventions also must be realistic for the resident, staff, resources, and equipment. A reality in the workplace is that there often is not extra time for staff to talk to the residents. Therefore, providing "30 minutes of one-on-one time discussing pain every shift" is an unrealistic intervention. Stating that "each staff member will ask the resident about hip pain whenever they interact with the resident" is a more realistic intervention.

To be successful and effective, nursing interventions must be developed with input from the certified nursing assistants (CNAs). CNAs are important members of the interdisciplinary team. Nursing assistants spend more time with clients in nursing facilities, assisted living facilities, retirement communities, and sometimes in the client's home, than any other member of the interdisciplinary team. They can offer important specific information for the assessment of the client. Because CNAs are so familiar with the daily routine and functioning of the clients, they can offer pertinent, realistic suggestions for individualized interventions to deal with specific problems. They are also frequently the first people to notice subtle changes in residents' conditions that may indicate onset of a new problem or success or failure of an intervention. A care plan meeting including representatives of all disciplines is generally held to discuss assessment information and develop the interdisciplinary plan of care. The CNA who works with the resident to be discussed must be invited to this meeting and arrangements made to facilitate the CNA's attendance. The time away from the unit for the CNA is minimal compared with the value of the CNA's input into the care planning process.

Successful nursing interventions require the resident's input and should be important to the resident. A resident may not want to "lift weights to strengthen and increase flexibility of his arms" but may be very willing to "comb his hair and wash his face." "Encourage the resident to drink 1000 mL of water" may not work as well as "encourage the resident to drink 1000 mL of fruit juice and water."

Nursing interventions also must include continuing assessment and monitoring of disease processes and effects of medications and treatments. If a resident has an IV, the IV site must be "assessed every shift for signs of infiltration, irritation, and infection." If a resident is receiving therapy with digoxin (Lanoxin), the "apical pulse must be taken and recorded before each dose." Residents with congestive heart failure (CHF) should be "assessed for edema and dyspnea."

Remember that the plan of care is part of the resident's permanent record. It needs to be routinely reviewed and updated as the resident's health status improves or declines. The monthly and quarterly review times provide an excellent opportunity to revise the care plan to ensure that the resident is receiving appropriate nursing care.

Implementation

Implementation is the part of the nursing process that nurses do best. Being at the "bedside" of the resident providing care is one of the most rewarding aspects of being a nurse. Implementation means actually putting the plan of care into action. Along with providing the nursing care that has been outlined in the resident's nursing care plan, the LPN continues to collect data that can be used to update and revise the plan of care.

Many interventions from the plan of care will be assigned to CNAs. This is another strong reason for having CNAs attend the care plan development meeting. If the CNAs have an opportunity to provide input into the plan of care and they are present when it is discussed and developed, they will be more likely to carry out the interventions than if they are merely told what to do or handed a care plan to read.

Because nursing assistants on all shifts cannot attend the care plan meeting, a major challenge for the practical nurse is communicating the plan of care to all

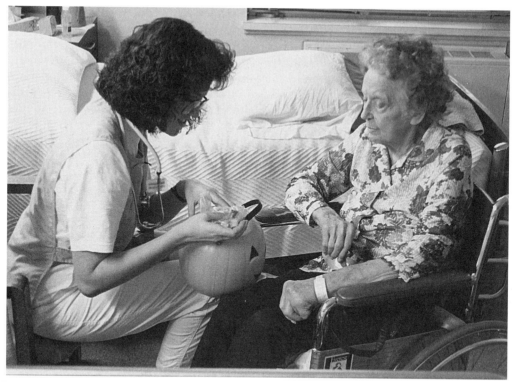

Every visit with the resident is an opportunity to reassess your nursing diagnoses and their implementation.

CNAs. A variety of communication techniques can be used. Some facilities provide nursing assistants with written assignments that list all of the interventions for each resident assignment made. Many facilities place the plan of care in a book and make it available to the staff. Very often, however, the book is rarely consulted. Meeting regularly with nursing assistants to discuss the plan of care, giving each CNA written assignments with information on the plan of care, and using primary CNAs who care for the same residents each day, will ensure the implementation of the plan of care and make it a working document rather than a useless piece of paper completed only to comply with regulations.

Another difficult part of implementation is that it also must be documented. Charting is an important part of implementing the plan of care. Documentation of interventions requires not only recording that the intervention was done but also the resident's responses to the intervention. An entry such as the following provides no information about the resident's response to the treatment:

12/16/93 1420 Wet to dry saline packing to coccyx ulcer

A better picture is given in the following chart:

12/16/93 1420 Wet to dry saline packing to coccyx pressure ulcer. Small amount of yellow serous drainage on old packing. Resident complained of pain when old packing removed and new packing inserted. Ulcer is 3×2 cm and 1.5 cm deep. Ulcer margins are pink and there is granulation tissue evident in the base of the ulcer. Two small (6 mm) scabs on left buttocks from tape irritation. No redness or drainage noted.

In addition to the required information, this chart provides new data that should be addressed in the plan of care: "Two small (6 mm) scabs on left buttocks from tape irritation." A simple model that can be used to document the nursing process with nursing interventions and resident responses is presented below:

Assessment
What the nurse observed and assessed
Objective measurements (blood pressure, laboratory values)
What the resident did (response to nursing intervention)
What the resident said

Action
What the nurse did (nursing interventions): treatments, turning the resident, giving a medication, increasing the oxygen flow rate, hanging a tube feeding, inserting a catheter

Plan
What the nurse plans to do: call the doctor, call the family, reassess with the next treatment, refer resident to social service

The assessment-action-plan charting format is simple, yet it sets up a framework for documenting the nursing process in a narrative format.

CNAs may also be involved in documentation and may provide information for the practical nurse's documentation. Flow sheets that include interventions from the plan of care and activities from the resident's day can be completed by nursing assistants. Flow sheets can be used to document such interventions as ADLs, walking programs, bowel and bladder training programs, and dietary intake and feeding programs. Results and trends from the flow sheets can be incorporated into the LPN's regular progress charting.

Evaluation

Evaluation is the final step in the nursing process. The main purpose of evaluation is to decide whether the resident has met the identified goals and to assess the outcomes of the nursing care provided. Remember how, in the discussion of implementation, the importance of assessing the resident and documenting the resident's responses to care was emphasized? The chart and resident assessments are reviewed as part of evaluation (Box 4.3).

When goals have been stated in measurable terms, the LPN should be able to review all of the data and decide whether the goal has been met, has been partially met, or remains unmet. This is a straightforward look at the resident's response to the nursing interventions. The evaluation of goal achievement needs to be documented in a monthly summary, quarterly review, or the nursing notes.

Evaluation also requires that the nurse review the nursing process. This helps to keep the plan of care up to date and reflects changes in the resident's health status. It also is an opportunity to decide which nursing interventions were ineffective

---

BOX 4.3 SIGNIFICANT CHANGE IN RESIDENT'S STATUS

Decrease in level of functioning in two or more activities of daily living
Decrease or increase in the ability to walk or the use of hands to grasp small
objects
Decline in health status that is not responsive to treatment
Changes in behavior or mood that cause daily problems

---

in assisting the resident to achieve goals and which goals may be unrealistic for the resident.

The reassessment of the resident and the plan of care in evaluation really address the dynamic strength of the nursing process. Although it follows specific, organized steps, no step excludes collecting more data. This is done by assessing the resident, updating goals and interventions, and conducting an ongoing evaluation of the outcome of the care that is provided. Nurses seem to use the nursing process even when they do not identify it as such. Here are some examples.

Mary Jones always was incontinent during the 1:00 A.M. rounds. The nursing staff decided to toilet her at 12:30 A.M.

In this example, the nursing staff assessed incontinence as a problem. Their unstated goal was, "the resident will not be incontinent at 1:00 A.M. rounds." Their intervention was to toilet the resident 30 minutes before she was usually incontinent. After toileting the resident at 12:30 A.M., the resident would be checked for urinary incontinence at 1:00 A.M. If she was not incontinent, the goal would be achieved and the staff would continue to toilet the resident at 12:30 A.M. to maintain that outcome. If the resident was toileted at 12:30 A.M. and she still was incontinent at 1:00 A.M., the staff may decide to toilet the resident at midnight. The care plan and charting examples provided in Figure 4.2 demonstrate the use of evaluation.

As this example shows, evaluation is ongoing and takes place daily, not just at the mandatory reassessment intervals. Thus, evaluation does not take place only when the quarterly assessment is due. Would you continue to carry out an intervention that was not working for 3 months until the quarterly review was due? Many people help you evaluate the plan of care each day. Residents give you information by their behavior and by telling you if an intervention is helping or not. Families tell you about changes they notice. Nursing assistants frequently note subtle changes in residents and may alter interventions to accommodate the change in the residents.

Making daily changes in the actual care given is common. Translating these changes into the written plan of care is less common. For the sake of communication and consistency among all staff, it is very important to be sure that the written plan of care is updated to reflect the actual care you want to be given.

COMPUTERS AND THE NURSING PROCESS

More and more nursing facilities throughout the country are installing computers to help nursing staff complete the MDS assessment and care plans. The practical nurse

Nursing Diagnosis Problems Addressed	Goals Outcomes of Care	Nursing Interventions	Evaluation
Physical Mobility, impaired related to musculoskeletal impairment as manifested by inability to transfer and ambulate without assistance	Resident will increase ambulation with walker in PT to independent use with minimal supervision in 90 days	▪ Assess and document: Orthostatic BPs (lying/sitting/standing ROM and strength of legs and arms Walking ability with walker and amount of assistance needed ▪ Have walker in resident's reach at all times and use for all transfers and walking in room ▪ Physical therapy for quad-strengthening exercises and ambulation with walker ▪ Put on jogging pants for daily physical therapy	

DOCUMENTATION

October 11, 1994, 1:45 p.m.: Resident is transferred from bed to wheelchair with assistance of one. Uses walker to steady himself when standing. Ambulates with hold-on assistance from physical therapist using a walker. Ambulated two steps withou hold-on assistance before becoming unsteady. Orthostatic BPs lying—138/82, sitting—110/80, standing—106/76, complained of being light-headed when he sat up. Dizziness passed in 5 minutes. Instructed to move slowly from lying-sitting-standing positions and not to move to another position until any dizziness or light-headedness passes. Will review medications and fluid intake for possible causes of orthostatic hypotension.

Figure 4.2　Sample care plan.

may be asked to enter MDS data directly on the computer or to complete the written form while another nurse enters the assessment data on the computer for all residents. Many different kinds of software are available that can be used by nurses to complete the MDS, RAPs, and care plans. Each software program is somewhat different, and generally no one program will do everything that you want it to do.

If you have never worked on a computer before, you may be fearful of using it for your assessment and care plans. Completing the MDS and the care plan on the computer, however, has many benefits that warrant overcoming your fears. One of the most time-consuming portions of the MDS is computing the triggers, that is, identifying the potential problem areas that need to be further assessed through the RAPs (Fig. 4.3). Most MDS software packages compute the triggers in a matter of seconds. Completing the interdisciplinary care plan on the computer saves the nurse from a great deal of handwriting and lends itself to regular updating without further lengthy handwriting. Some software packages will print out nursing assistant forms that include all the interventions from the plan of care assigned to the nursing assistant. These forms can be used as assignment sheets that communicate the plan of care to the CNA.

CASE STUDY

RESIDENT ADMISSION

December 1, 1997, 1:00 P.M.: Mr. B., 82-year-old white widowed male, is admitted to Room 112 of Quality Care Health Facility from Mercy Hospital via ambulance accompanied by daughter-in-law. Admitted with diagnosis of fractured left wrist, multiple hematomas and abrasions, Alzheimer's disease, diabetes mellitus, and a history of CHF. Dr. Ben Johnston notified of admission and verified orders. Dietary notified of 2 g sodium/no concentrated sweets diet. Medication orders faxed to the pharmacy:

furosemide (Lasix) 40 mg q.d. for CHF and COPD
digoxin (Lanoxin) 0.125 mg q.d. for CHF
potassium chloride (K-tabs) 2 tabs q.d. for CHF
glipizide (Glucotrol) 5 mg q. A.M. for diabetes
oxazepam (Serax) 20 mg q.h.s. for insomnia
haloperidol (Haldol) 1 mg b.i.d. for agitation
ducosate (Dulcolax) sodium suppository q.d. prn constipation
acetaminophen (Tylenol) gr 10 q.4h. p.r.n. pain
duoderm to open area on coccyx change q.o.d.
mupirocin (Bactroban) to abrasions b.i.d.
nystatin (Mycostatin) ointment to perineal rash b.i.d. $\times$ 10 days
ace wrap and splint to left wrist at all times
return to clinic in 2 weeks

Son has durable power of attorney for both financial and health-care decisions and has signed the advanced directives form for do not resuscitate. Resident has a living will and his wishes are known to his family.

Daughter-in-law reports that he has no known allergies, wears bifocals and reads large-print *Reader's Digest* occasionally, has upper and lower dentures, does not use a hearing aid, and has minimal difficulty hearing unless in a noisy room. Uses a cane to ambulate. Height—5'9"; weight—124 lb.

Mr. B. is alert and oriented to self and daughter-in-law but states that it is 1936, that the season is winter, the month is September, and that he is in Denver. Since his wife died 6 months ago, he has been living with his son and his family. His daughter-in-law has been his principal caregiver. Caring for Mr. B. has been quite stressful at times. He does not strike out but repeatedly asks the same questions over and over, even when the question has been answered. His daughter-in-law took a leave of absence from her job because Mr. B. could no longer stay in the house alone without becoming very anxious. He would call

---

CHF = congestive heart failure; COPD = chronic obstructive coronary disease, b.i.d. = twice daily; p.r.n. = as needed; q. A.M. = every morning; q.o.d. = every other day; q.4h. = every 4 hours; q.h.s. = before bedtime, every hour of sleep.

friends on the phone repeatedly and ask for his deceased wife. He would often go for walks and get lost.

Mr. B. was admitted to Mercy Hospital after he had fallen on an uneven sidewalk four blocks from home and suffered a concussion, multiple facial hematomas, abrasions on his right arm and shoulder, a fractured left wrist, and a large hematoma on his left hip. His daughter-in-law had been in the basement folding laundry when Mr. B. left the house. The family is expressing much guilt over the decision to place Mr. B. in a long-term care facility, but they admit that he would be safer there.

Mr. B is able to walk with his cane but favors the left hip when he stands and is very unsteady. He forgets where he is and cries out for help. He is able to dress himself but must have supervision to remind him of what he is doing. Mr. B. is able to feed himself but has not been eating and has lost a significant amount of weight in the past 3 months. Mr. B. has been generally continent of his bladder and bowel except while in the hospital, where he was incontinent of both.

Mr. B. had been an accountant before he retired, and he would often spend hours with a paper and pencil "doing the books." He has always enjoyed classical music and was quite an accomplished pianist. He had season tickets to the ballet and the opera and would go quite often before his wife died 6 months ago.

PHYSICAL ASSESSMENT

General Appearance	Thin white male
Head and Neck	White hair. Scalp dry with multiple areas of white dry flaking. Face symmetrical, two 5-cm hematomas on left cheek and jaw. Two-cm hematoma on left forehead, skin is also dry. Eyes are clear with no drainage, conjunctivae pink, pupils are equal at 5 mm and react briskly to light, consensual, and accommodative. No drainage from nose; patient is able to breathe through both nostrils. No drainage from ears. Did not appropriately respond when asked in a whisper to raise his arm. Oral mucous membranes are pink and dry. No denture irritation noted. No saliva pooling noted between gum and cheek. Tongue pink with no coating; remains at midline when extended from mouth. Throat dry with no pharyngeal drainage or redness noted: no cervical lymph nodes palpable: no thyroid nodules or enlargement palpated.
Chest	Symmetrical chest movements. Breath sounds clear throughout except for expiratory crackle in base of left lower lobe that cleared with cough. Apical pulse—78 and regular. No extra heart sounds

	noted. Back has multiple waxy, light brown to medium brown, 2×3 cm flat raised lesions. Moderate kyphosis of spine.
Abdomen and Buttocks	Large (8×12 cm) hematoma over left hip and left lower abdominal area. Hard stool in rectum. Active bowel sounds in all quadrants. Abdomen soft. No masses palpable. 2×1.5 cm stage 2 pressure ulcer over coccyx that is oozing serous drainage. Three small fluid-filled vesicles in gluteal fold of right buttocks.
Genitourinary	Normal male genitalia. Urinary meatus reddened. Urine dark amber and foul smelling. Fiery red rash noted on inner aspects of both upper thighs and scrotum.
Extremities	Full range of motion (ROM) of shoulders, elbows, right wrist, and fingers. Left wrist is splinted with a rigid plastic splint and wrapped with an ace bandage that he is constantly unwrapping. Radial and brachial pulses strong and equal bilaterally. Healing abrasions noted over lateral aspect of left upper arm and left shoulder. Limited ROM of both hips with complaints of pain with movement of left hip. Full ROM of both knees and ankles. Femoral and popliteal pulses strong and equal bilaterally. Left pedal pulse weak and 1+ pitting edema noted in left ankle. Right pedal pulse strong and right ankle edematous with no pitting noted. Homans' sign negative bilaterally and no complaints of calf tenderness to palpation. 1-cm eschar noted along medial nail of the left great toe. No drainage noted but there is slight redness around the eschar.

December 6, 1997, 2:00 P.M.: Mr. B. was found in another resident's room pulling clothes out of the closet. This is a daily occurrence. Mr. B. cannot explain why he is in the other resident's room and does not know the way back to his room. He yells at his roommate to get out and yells randomly at other residents in the facility. When he is in his room, he cries for help but does not have any requests or needs when the staff members answer. He went 3 days without having a bowel movement and was incontinent of stool in the hallway 30 minutes after being given a suppository. Mr. B. attends activities when asked to go, but he often leaves the activity early. He naps for about 1–2 hours in the afternoon and is awake frequently at night, when he has to be reminded to stay in bed. He was found one night stuck between the side rails and incontinent of urine.

The MDS for Mr. B. is shown in Figure 4.3.

Numeric Identifier _784393_

MINIMUM DATA SET (MDS) — *VERSION 2.0*
FOR NURSING HOME RESIDENT ASSESSMENT AND CARE SCREENING
BASIC ASSESSMENT TRACKING FORM

SECTION AA. IDENTIFICATION INFORMATION		GENERAL INSTRUCTIONS
1.	**RESIDENT NAME** ⊛	*George T. Blair* a. (First) b. (Middle Initial) c. (Last) d. (Jr./Sr.)	*Complete this information for submission with all full and quarterly assessments (Admission, Annual, Significant Change, State or Medicare required assessments, or Quarterly Reviews, etc.).*

2.	**GENDER** ⊛	1. Male 2. Female 【 **1** 】
3.	**BIRTHDATE** ⊛	【 1 0 】 – 【 1 5 】 – 【 1 9 1 5 】 Month Day Year
4.	**RACE/** ⊛ **ETHNICITY**	1. American Indian/Alaskan Native 4. Hispanic 2. Asian/Pacific Islander 5. White, not of 3. Black, not of Hispanic origin Hispanic origin 【 **5** 】
5.	**SOCIAL** ⊛ **SECURITY AND** ⊛ **MEDICARE NUMBERS** [C in 1st box if non Med. no.]	a. Social Security Number 【 0 0 5 】 – 【 0 6 】 – 【 7 8 0 0 】 b. Medicare number (or comparable railroad insurance number) 【 0 0 5 0 6 7 8 0 0 A 】
6.	**FACILITY PROVIDER NO.** ⊛	a. State No. 【 (shaded) 】 b. Federal No. 【 5 4 0 9 】
7.	**MEDICAID NO.** ["+" if pending, "N" if not a Medicaid ⊛ recipient]	【 N 】
8.	**REASONS FOR ASSESSMENT**	[Note—Other codes do not apply to this form] a. Primary reason for assessment 1. Admission assessment (required by day 14) 2. Annual assessment 3. Significant change in status assessment 4. Significant correction of prior assessment 5. Quarterly review assessment 0. *NONE OF ABOVE* 【 **1** 】 b. *Special codes for use with supplemental assessment types in Case Mix demonstration states or other states where required* 1. *5 day assessment* 2. *30 day assessment* 3. *60 day assessment* 4. *Quarterly assessment using full MDS form* 5. *Readmission/return assessment* 6. *Other state required assessment*
9.	**SIGNATURES OF PERSONS COMPLETING THESE ITEMS:**	
a.	Signatures *A. Jones, R.N.* Title Date *12/2/97*	
b.	Date	

⊛ = Key items for computerized resident tracking

▨ = When box blank, must enter number or letter

| a. | = When letter in box, check if condition applies

Code "NA" if information unavailable or unknown.

TRIGGER LEGEND

1	- Delirium	10A	- Activities (Revise)
2	- Cognitive Loss/Dementia	10B	- Activities (Review)
3	- Visual Function	11	- Falls
4	- Communication	12	- Nutritional Status
5A	- ADL-Rehabilitation	13	- Feeding Tubes
5B	- ADL-Maintenance	14	- Dehydration/Fluid Maintenance
6	- Urinary Incontinence and Indwelling Catheter	15	- Dental Care
7	- Psychosocial Well-Being	16	- Pressure Ulcers
8	- Mood State	17	- Psychotropic Drug Use
9	- Behavioral Symptoms	17*	- For this to trigger, O4a, b, or c must = 1-7
		18	- Physical Restraints

Form 1728HH R196   © 1995 Briggs Corporation, Des Moines, IA 50306   (800) 247-2343   PRINTED IN U.S.A.
 Copyright limited to addition of trigger system.

1 of 8

Figure 4.3 Sample minimum data set.

Resident _____ George Blair _____   Numeric Identifier _____ 784393 _____

MINIMUM DATA SET (MDS) — *VERSION 2.0*
FOR NURSING HOME RESIDENT ASSESSMENT AND CARE SCREENING
BACKGROUND (FACE SHEET) INFORMATION AT ADMISSION

SECTION AB. DEMOGRAPHIC INFORMATION		
1.	DATE OF ENTRY	*Date the stay began. Note — Does not include readmission if record was closed at time of temporary discharge to hospital, etc. In such cases, use prior admission date.* `1 2` – `0 1` – `1 9 9 7` Month Day Year
2.	ADMITTED FROM (AT ENTRY)	1. Private home/apt. with no home health services 2. Private home/apt. with home health services 3. Board and care/assisted living/group home 4. Nursing home 5. Acute care hospital 6. Psychiatric hospital, MR/DD facility 7. Rehabilitation hospital 8. Other `1`
3.	LIVED ALONE (PRIOR TO ENTRY)	0. No 1. Yes 2. In other facility `0`
4.	ZIP CODE OF PRIOR PRIMARY RESIDENCE	`8 4 4 0 3`
5.	RESIDEN-TIAL HISTORY 5 YEARS PRIOR TO ENTRY	*(Check all settings resident lived in during 5 years prior to date of entry given in item AB1 above.)* Prior stay at this nursing home — a. Stay in other nursing home — b. Other residential facility — board and care home, assisted living, group home — c. MH/psychiatric setting — d. MR/DD setting — e. NONE OF ABOVE — f. ✓
6.	LIFETIME OCCUPA-TION(S) (Put "/" between two occupations)	`a c c o u n t a n t`
7.	EDUCATION (Highest level completed)	1. No schooling 5. Technical or trade school 2. 8th grade/less 6. Some college 3. 9-11 grades 7. Bachelor's degree 4. High school 8. Graduate degree `7`
8.	LANGUAGE	*(Code for correct response)* a. Primary Language 0. English 1. Spanish 2. French 3. Other `0` b. If other, specify
9.	MENTAL HEALTH HISTORY	Does resident's RECORD indicate any history of mental retardation, mental illness, or developmental disability problem? 0. No 1. Yes `0`
10.	CONDITIONS RELATED TO MR/DD STATUS	*(Check all conditions that are related to MR/DD status that were manifested before age 22, and are likely to continue indefinitely)* Not applicable — no MR/DD (Skip to AB11) — a. MR/DD with organic condition Down's syndrome — b. Autism — c. Epilepsy — d. Other organic condition related to MR/DD — e. MR/DD with no organic condition — f.
11.	DATE BACK-GROUND INFORMA-TION COMPLETED	`1 2` – `0 2` – `1 9 9 7` Month Day Year

`▓` = When box blank, must enter number or letter
`a.` = When letter in box, check if condition applies
Code "NA" if information unavailable or unknown.

SECTION AC. CUSTOMARY ROUTINE		
1.	CUSTOMARY ROUTINE *(In year prior to DATE OF ENTRY to this nursing home, or year last in community if now being admitted from another nursing home)*	*(Check all that apply. If all information UNKNOWN, check last box only)*
		CYCLE OF DAILY EVENTS
		Stays up late at night (e.g., after 9 pm) — a.
		Naps regularly during day (at least 1 hour) — b.
		Goes out 1+ days a week — c.
		Stays busy with hobbies, reading, or fixed daily routine — d.
		Spends most of time alone or watching TV — e.
		Moves independently indoors (with appliances, if used) — f. ✓
		Use of tobacco products at least daily — g.
		NONE OF ABOVE — h.
		EATING PATTERNS
		Distinct food preferences — i.
		Eats between meals all or most days — j.
		Use of alcoholic beverage(s) at least weekly — k.
		NONE OF ABOVE — l. ✓
		ADL PATTERNS
		In bedclothes much of day — m.
		Wakens to toilet all or most nights — n. ✓
		Has irregular bowel movement pattern — o.
		Showers for bathing — p.
		Bathing in PM — q.
		NONE OF ABOVE — r.
		INVOLVEMENT PATTERNS
		Daily contact with relatives/close friends — s. ✓
		Usually attends church, temple, synagogue (etc.) — t.
		Finds strength in faith — u.
		Daily animal companion/presence — v.
		Involved in group activities — w.
		NONE OF ABOVE — x.
		UNKNOWN — Resident/family unable to provide information — y.
		END

SECTION AD. FACE SHEET SIGNATURES			
SIGNATURES OF PERSONS COMPLETING FACE SHEET:			
a. Signature of RN Assessment Coordinator *A. Jones, R.N.*			Date 12/2/97
b. Signatures	Title	Sections	Date
c.			Date
d.			Date
e.			Date
f.			Date
g.			Date

NOTE: Normally, the MDS Face Sheet is completed once, when an individual first enters the facility. However, the face sheet is also required if the person is reentering this facility after a discharge where return had not previously been expected. It is **not** completed following temporary discharges to hospitals or after therapeutic leaves/home visits.

Form 1728HH   © 1995 Briggs Corporation, Des Moines, IA 50306 (800) 247-2343 PRINTED IN U.S.A.
Copyright limited to addition of trigger system.

2 of 8   MDS 2.0 10/18/94N

Resident _George Blair_   Numeric Identifier _784393_

MINIMUM DATA SET (MDS) — *VERSION 2.0*
FOR NURSING HOME RESIDENT ASSESSMENT AND CARE SCREENING
FULL ASSESSMENT FORM
(Status in last 7 days, unless other time frame indicated)

SECTION A. IDENTIFICATION AND BACKGROUND INFORMATION

1. RESIDENT NAME

George T. Blair

a. (First)   b. (Middle Initial)   c. (Last)   d. (Jr./Sr.)

2. ROOM NUMBER `1` `1` `2`

3. ASSESSMENT REFERENCE DATE

a. *Last day of MDS observation period*

`1` `2` – `1` `4` – `1` `9` `9` `7`
Month   Day   Year

b. Original (0) or corrected copy of form (enter number of correction)   `0`

4a. DATE OF REENTRY Date of reentry from most recent temporary discharge to a hospital in last 90 days (or since last assessment or admission if less than 90 days)

☐ ☐ – ☐ ☐ – ☐ ☐ ☐ ☐
Month   Day   Year

5. MARITAL STATUS
1. Never married   3. Widowed   5. Divorced
2. Married   4. Separated   `3`

6. MEDICAL RECORD NO. `7` `8` `4` `3` `9` `3`

7. CURRENT PAYMENT SOURCES FOR N.H. STAY
(Billing Office to indicate; check all that apply in last 30 days)
Medicaid per diem	a.	VA per diem	f.
Medicare per diem	b. ✔	Self or family pays for full per diem	g.
Medicare ancillary part A	c.	Medicaid resident liability or Medicare co-payment	h.
Medicare ancillary part B	d.	Private insurance per diem (including co-payment)	i.
CHAMPUS per diem	e.	Other per diem	j.

8. REASONS FOR ASSESSMENT

[Note—If this is a discharge or reentry assessment, only a limited subset of MDS items need be completed]

a. Primary reason for assessment
1. Admission assessment (required by day 14)
2. Annual assessment
3. Significant change in status assessment
4. Significant correction of prior assessment
5. Quarterly review assessment
6. Discharged—return not anticipated
7. Discharged—return anticipated
8. Discharged prior to completing initial assessment
9. Reentry
0. NONE OF ABOVE   `1`

b. Special codes for use with supplemental assessment types in Case Mix demonstration states or other states where required
1. 5 day assessment
2. 30 day assessment
3. 60 day assessment
4. Quarterly assessment using full MDS form
5. Readmission/return assessment
6. Other state required assessment

9. RESPONSIBILITY/ LEGAL GUARDIAN
(Check all that apply)
Legal guardian	a.	Durable power of attorney/financial	d. ✔
Other legal oversight	b.	Family member responsible	e.
Durable power of attorney/health care	c.	Patient responsible for self	f.
		NONE OF ABOVE	g.

10. ADVANCED DIRECTIVES
(For those items with supporting documentation in the medical record, check all that apply)
Living will	a. ✔	Feeding restrictions	f.
Do not resuscitate	b. ✔	Medication restrictions	g.
Do not hospitalize	c.	Other treatment restrictions	h.
Organ donation	d.	NONE OF ABOVE	i.
Autopsy request	e.		

SECTION B. COGNITIVE PATTERNS

1. COMATOSE (Persistent vegetative state/no discernible consciousness)
0. No   1. Yes *(If yes, skip to Section G)*   `0`

2. MEMORY (Recall of what was learned or known)
a. Short-term memory OK—seems/appears to recall after 5 minutes
0. Memory OK   1. Memory problem 2   `1`

b. Long-term memory OK—seems/appears to recall long past
0. Memory OK   1. Memory problem 2   `1`

☐ = When box blank, must enter number or letter.

a. = When letter in box, check if condition applies

Code "NA" if information unavailable or unknown.

Form 1728HH   © 1995 Briggs Corporation, Des Moines, IA 50306 (800) 247-2343 PRINTED IN U.S.A.
Copyright limited to addition of trigger system.

---

3. MEMORY/ RECALL ABILITY
(Check all that resident was normally able to recall during last 7 days)
Current season	a.	That he/she is in a nursing home	d.
Location of own room	b.	NONE OF ABOVE are recalled	e. ✔
Staff names/faces	c.		

4. COGNITIVE SKILLS FOR DAILY DECISION-MAKING
(Made decisions regarding tasks of daily life)
0. INDEPENDENT—decisions consistent/reasonable
1. MODIFIED INDEPENDENCE—some difficulty in new situations only 2
2. MODERATELY IMPAIRED—decisions poor; cues/ supervision required 2
3. SEVERELY IMPAIRED—never/rarely made decisions 2, 5B   `3`

5. INDICATORS OF DELIRIUM— PERIODIC DISORDERED THINKING/ AWARENESS
(Code for behavior in the last 7 days.) [Note: Accurate assessment requires conversations with staff and family who have direct knowledge of resident's behavior over this time.]
0. Behavior not present
1. Behavior present, not of recent onset
2. Behavior present, over last 7 days appears different from resident's usual functioning (e.g., new onset or worsening)

a. EASILY DISTRACTED—(e.g., difficulty paying attention; gets sidetracked) 2 – 1, 17*   `1`

b. PERIODS OF ALTERED PERCEPTION OR AWARENESS OF SURROUNDINGS—(e.g., moves lips or talks to someone not present; believes he/she is somewhere else; confuses night and day) 2 – 1, 17*   `1`

c. EPISODES OF DISORGANIZED SPEECH—(e.g., speech is incoherent, nonsensical, irrelevant, or rambling from subject to subject; loses train of thought) 2 – 1, 17*   `0`

d. PERIODS OF RESTLESSNESS—(e.g., fidgeting or picking at skin, clothing, napkins, etc.; frequent position changes; repetitive physical movements or calling out) 2 – 1, 17*   `0`

e. PERIODS OF LETHARGY—(e.g., sluggishness; staring into space; difficult to arouse; little body movement) 2 – 1, 17*   `0`

f. MENTAL FUNCTION VARIES OVER THE COURSE OF THE DAY—(e.g., sometimes better, sometimes worse; behaviors sometimes present, sometimes not) 2 – 1, 17*   `0`

6. CHANGE IN COGNITIVE STATUS
Resident's cognitive status, skills, or abilities have changed as compared to status of **90 days ago** (or since assessment if less than 90 days)
0. No change   1. Improved   2. Deteriorated 1, 17*   `0`

SECTION C. COMMUNICATION/HEARING PATTERNS

1. HEARING (With hearing appliance, if used)
0. HEARS ADEQUATELY—normal talk, TV, phone
1. MINIMAL DIFFICULTY when not in quiet setting 4
2. HEARS IN SPECIAL SITUATIONS ONLY—speaker has to adjust tonal quality and speak distinctly 4
3. HIGHLY IMPAIRED/absence of useful hearing 4   `1`

2. COMMUNICATION DEVICES/ TECHNIQUES
(Check all that apply during last 7 days)
Hearing aid, present and used	a. ✔
Hearing aid, present and not used regularly	b.
Other receptive comm. techniques used (e.g., lip reading)	c.
NONE OF ABOVE	d.

3. MODES OF EXPRESSION
(Check all used by resident to make needs known)
Speech	a.	Signs/gestures/sounds	d. ✔
Writing messages to express or clarify needs	b.	Communication board	e.
American sign language or Braille	c.	Other	f.
		NONE OF ABOVE	g.

4. MAKING SELF UNDERSTOOD
(Expressing information content—however able)
0. UNDERSTOOD
1. USUALLY UNDERSTOOD—difficulty finding words or finishing thoughts 4
2. SOMETIMES UNDERSTOOD—ability is limited to making concrete requests 4
3. RARELY/NEVER UNDERSTOOD 4   `1`

5. SPEECH CLARITY
(Code for speech in the last 7 days)
0. CLEAR SPEECH—distinct, intelligible words
1. UNCLEAR SPEECH—slurred, mumbled words
2. NO SPEECH—absence of spoken words   `0`

6. ABILITY TO UNDERSTAND OTHERS
(Understanding verbal information content—however able)
0. UNDERSTANDS
1. USUALLY UNDERSTANDS—may miss some part/intent of message 2, 4
2. SOMETIMES UNDERSTANDS—responds adequately to simple, direct communication 2, 4
3. RARELY/NEVER UNDERSTANDS 2, 4   `2`

7. CHANGE IN COMMUNICATION/ HEARING
Resident's ability to express, understand, or hear information has changed as compared to status of **90 days ago** (or since last assessment if less than 90 days)
0. No change   1. Improved   2. Deteriorated 17*   `0`

3 of 8   MDS 2.0   10/18/94N

Resident __George Blair__   Numeric Identifier __784393__

SECTION D. VISION PATTERNS

1.	VISION	*(Ability to see in adequate light and with glasses if used)* 0. *ADEQUATE*—sees fine detail, including regular print in newspapers/books 1. *IMPAIRED*—sees large print, but not regular print in news-papers/books 3 2. *MODERATELY IMPAIRED*—limited vision; not able to see newspaper headlines, but can identify objects 3 3. *HIGHLY IMPAIRED*—object identification in question, but eyes appear to follow objects 3 4. *SEVERELY IMPAIRED*—no vision or sees only light, colors, or shapes; eyes do not appear to follow objects	1
2.	VISUAL LIMITATIONS/ DIFFICULTIES	Side vision problems—decreased peripheral vision (e.g., leaves food on one side of tray, difficulty traveling, bumps into people and objects, misjudges placement of chair when seating self) 3 a. Experiences any of following: sees halos or rings around lights; sees flashes of light; sees "curtains" over eyes b. *NONE OF ABOVE* c. ✓	
3.	VISUAL APPLIANCES	Glasses; contact lenses; magnifying glass 0. No 1. Yes	1

SECTION E. MOOD AND BEHAVIOR PATTERNS

1. INDICATORS OF DEPRES-SION, ANXIETY, SAD MOOD

(Code for indicators observed in last 30 days, irrespective of the assumed cause)
0. Indicator not exhibited in last 30 days
1. Indicator of this type exhibited up to five days a week
2. Indicator of this type exhibited daily or almost daily (6, 7 days a week)

VERBAL EXPRESSIONS OF DISTRESS			
a. Resident made negative statements—e.g., "Nothing matters; Would rather be dead; What's the use; Regrets having lived so long; Let me die" 1 or 2 = 8	0	h. Repetitive health complaints—e.g., persistently seeks medical attention, obsessive concern with body functions 1 or 2 = 8	0
b. Repetitive questions—e.g. "Where do I go; What do I do?" 1 or 2 = 8	2	i. Repetitive anxious complaints/concerns (non-health related) e.g., persistently seeks attention/reassurance regarding schedules, meals, laundry/clothing, relationship issues 1 or 2 = 8	0
c. Repetitive verbal-izations— e.g., calling out for help ("God help me") 1 or 2 = 8	0	SLEEP-CYCLE ISSUES	
d. Persistent anger with self or others—e.g., easily annoyed, anger at placement in nursing home; anger at care received 1 or 2 = 8	1	j. Unpleasant mood in morning 1 or 2 = 8	0
		k. Insomnia/change in usual sleep pattern 1 or 2 = 8	0
e. Self deprecation—e.g., "I am nothing; I am of no use to anyone" 1 or 2 = 8	0	SAD, APATHETIC, ANXIOUS APPEARANCE	
		l. Sad, pained, worried facial expressions—e.g., furrowed brows 1 or 2 = 8	0
f. Expressions of what appear to be unreal-istic fears—e.g., fear of being abandoned, left alone, being with others 1 or 2 = 8	0	m. Crying, tearfulness 1 or 2 = 8	0
		n. Repetitive physical movements—e.g., pacing, hand wringing, restless-ness, fidgeting, picking 1 or 2 = 8, 17*	0
g. Recurrent statements that something terrible is about to happen—e.g., believes he or she is about to die, have a heart attack 1 or 2 = 8	0	LOSS OF INTEREST	
		o. Withdrawal from activities of interest—e.g., no interest in longstanding activities or being with family/ friends 1 or 2 = 8	0
		p. Reduced social inter-action 1 or 2 = 8	0

2.	MOOD PERSIS-TENCE	One or more indicators of depressed, sad or anxious mood were not easily altered by attempts to "cheer up", console, or reassure the resident over last 7 days 0. No mood indicators 1. Indicators present, easily altered 8 2. Indicators present, not easily altered 8	2
3.	CHANGE IN MOOD	Resident's mood status has changed as compared to status of 90 days ago (or since last assessment if less than 90 days) 0. No change 1. Improved 2. Deteriorated 1, 17*	2
4.	BEHAVIORAL SYMPTOMS	*(A) Behavioral symptom frequency in last 7 days* 0. Behavior not exhibited in last 7 days 1. Behavior of this type occurred 1 to 3 days in last 7 days 2. Behavior of this type occurred 4 to 6 days, but less than daily 3. Behavior of this type occurred daily *(B) Behavioral symptom alterability in last 7 days* 0. Behavior not present OR behavior was easily altered 1. Behavior was not easily altered	

		(A)	(B)
a. WANDERING (moved with no rational purpose, seemingly oblivious to needs or safety) A = 1, 2, or 3 = 9, 11		3	2
b. VERBALLY ABUSIVE BEHAVIORAL SYMPTOMS (others were threatened, screamed at, cursed at) A = 1, 2, or 3 = 9		3	2
c. PHYSICALLY ABUSIVE BEHAVIORAL SYMPTOMS (others were hit, shoved, scratched, sexually abused) A = 1, 2, or 3 = 9		0	0
d. SOCIALLY INAPPROPRIATE/DISRUPTIVE BEHA-VIORAL SYMPTOMS (made disruptive sounds, noisiness, screaming, self-abusive acts, sexual behavior or disrobing in public, smeared/threw food/feces, hoarding, rummaged through others' belongings) A = 1, 2, or 3 = 9		3	2
e. RESISTS CARE (resisted taking medications/injections, ADL assistance, or eating) A = 1, 2, or 3 = 9		0	0

5.	CHANGE IN BEHAVIORAL SYMPTOMS	Resident's behavior status has changed as compared to **status** of 90 days ago (or since last assessment if less than 90 days) 0. No change 1. Improved 9 2. Deteriorated 1, 17*	2

SECTION F. PSYCHOSOCIAL WELL-BEING

1.	SENSE OF INITIATIVE/ INVOLVE-MENT	At ease interacting with others a. At ease doing planned or structured activities b. At ease doing self-initiated activities c. Establishes own goals 7 d. Pursues involvement in life of facility (e.g., makes/keeps friends; involved in group activities; responds positively to new activities; assists at religious services) e. Accepts invitations into most group activities f. ✓ *NONE OF ABOVE* g.	
2.	UNSETTLED RELATION-SHIPS	Covert/open conflict with or repeated criticism of staff 7 a. Unhappy with roommate 7 b. ✓ Unhappy with residents other than roommate 7 c. ✓ Openly expresses conflict/anger with family/friends 7 d. Absence of personal contact with family/friends e. Recent loss of close family member/friend f. ✓ Does not adjust easily to change in routines g. *NONE OF ABOVE* h.	
3.	PAST ROLES	Strong identification with past roles and life status 7 a. ✓ Expresses sadness/anger/empty feeling over lost roles/status 7 b. Resident perceives that daily routine (customary routine, activities) is very different from prior pattern in the community 7 c. *NONE OF ABOVE* d.	

SECTION G. PHYSICAL FUNCTIONING AND STRUCTURAL PROBLEMS

1. (A) ADL SELF-PERFORMANCE—*(Code for resident's PERFORMANCE OVER ALL SHIFTS during last 7 days—Not including setup)*

0. *INDEPENDENT*—No help or oversight—OR—Help/oversight provided only 1 or 2 times during last 7 days
1. *SUPERVISION*—Oversight, encouragement or cueing provided 3 or more times during last 7 days—OR—Supervision (3 or more times) plus physical assistance provided only 1 or 2 times during last 7 days
2. *LIMITED ASSISTANCE*—Resident highly involved in activity; received physical help in guided maneuvering of limbs or other nonweight bearing assistance 3 or more times—OR—More help provided only 1 or 2 times during last 7 days
3. *EXTENSIVE ASSISTANCE*—While resident performed part of activity, over last 7-day period, help of following type(s) provided 3 or more times:
   —Weight-bearing support
   —Full staff performance during part (but not all) of last 7 days
4. *TOTAL DEPENDENCE*—Full staff performance of activity during entire 7 days
8. *ACTIVITY DID NOT OCCUR* during entire 7 days

(B) ADL SUPPORT PROVIDED—*(Code for MOST SUPPORT PROVIDED OVER ALL SHIFTS during last 7 days; code regardless of resident's self-performance classification)*

0. No setup or physical help from staff
1. Setup help only
2. One person physical assist
3. Two+ persons physical assist
8. ADL activity itself did not occur during entire 7 days

			(A) SELF-PERF	(B) SUPPORT
a.	BED MOBILITY	How resident moves to and from lying position, turns side to side, and positions body while in bed A = 1 = 5A, A = 2, 3, or 4 = 5A, 16 : A = 8 = 16	0	0
b.	TRANSFER	How resident moves between surfaces—to/from: bed, chair, wheelchair, standing position (EXCLUDE to/from bath/toilet) A = 1, 2, 3, or 4 = 5A	0	0
c.	WALK IN ROOM	How resident walks between locations in his/her room A = 1, 2, 3, or 4 = 5A	2	2
d.	WALK IN CORRIDOR	How resident walks in corridor on unit A = 1, 2, 3, or 4 = 5A	2	2
e.	LOCOMO-TION ON UNIT	How resident moves between locations in his/her room and adjacent corridor on same floor. If in wheelchair, self-sufficiency once in chair A = 1, 2, 3, or 4 = 5A	2	2
f.	LOCOMO-TION OFF UNIT	How resident moves to and returns from off unit locations (e.g., areas set aside for dining, activities, or treatments). If facility has only one floor, how resident moves to and from distant areas on the floor. If in wheelchair, self-sufficiency once in chair A = 1, 2, 3, or 4 = 5A	2	2
g.	DRESSING	How resident puts on, fastens, and takes off all items of **street** clothing, including donning/removing prosthesis A = 1, 2, 3, or 4 = 5A	3	2
h.	EATING	How resident eats and drinks (regardless of skill). Includes intake of nourishment by other means (e.g., tube feeding, total parenteral nutrition) A = 1, 2, 3, or 4 = 5A	1	1
i.	TOILET USE	How resident uses the toilet room (or commode, bedpan, urinal); transfers on/off toilet, cleanses, changes pad, manages ostomy or catheter, adjusts clothes A = 1, 2, 3, or 4 = 5A	2	1
j.	PERSONAL HYGIENE	How resident maintains personal hygiene, including combing hair, brushing teeth, shaving, applying makeup, washing/ drying face, hands, and perineum (EXCLUDE baths and showers) A = 1, 2, 3, or 4 = 5A	2	2

Form 1728HH   © 1995 Briggs Corporation, Des Moines, IA 50306 (800) 247-2343 PRINTED IN U.S.A.
Copyright limited to addition of trigger system.

4 of 8

MDS 2.0 10/18/94N

Resident **George Blair**   Numeric Identifier **784393**

2.	BATHING	How resident takes full-body bath/shower, sponge bath, and transfers in/out of tub/shower (EXCLUDE washing of back and hair). **Code for most dependent** in self-performance and support. A = 1, 2, 3 or 4 -**5A** (A) BATHING SELF-PERFORMANCE codes appear below. 0. Independent—No help provided (A) (B) 1. Supervision—Oversight help only 2. Physical help limited to transfer only 3. Physical help in part of bathing activity 4. Total dependence 8. Activity itself did not occur during entire 7 days (Bathing support codes are as defined in Item 1, code B above)		(A) 3 (B) 2

3.	TEST FOR BALANCE (See training manual)	(Code for ability during test in the last 7 days) 0. Maintained position as required in test 1. Unsteady, but able to rebalance self without physical support 2. Partial physical support during test; or stands (sits) but does not follow directions for test 3. Not able to attempt test without physical help		
		a. Balance while standing		2
		b. Balance while sitting—position, trunk control 1, 2, or 3 = **17***		1

4.	FUNCTIONAL LIMITATION IN RANGE OF MOTION (see training manual)	(Code for limitations during last 7 days that interfered with daily functions or placed resident at risk of injury) (A) RANGE OF MOTION (B) VOLUNTARY MOVEMENT 0. No limitation 0. No loss 1. Limitation on one side 1. Partial loss 2. Limitation on both sides 2. Full loss (A) (B)		
		a. Neck	0	0
		b. Arm—Including shoulder or elbow	0	0
		c. Hand—Including wrist or fingers	1	2
		d. Leg—Including hip or knee	2	1
		e. Foot—Including ankle or toes	0	0
		f. Other limitation or loss	0	0

5.	MODES OF LOCOMOTION	(Check all that apply during last 7 days)		
		Cane/walker/crutch a. ✔	Wheelchair primary mode of locomotion d.	
		Wheeled self b.		
		Other person wheeled c.	NONE OF ABOVE e.	

6.	MODES OF TRANSFER	(Check all that apply during last 7 days)		
		Bedfast all or most of time **16** a.	Lifted mechanically d.	
		Bed rails used for bed mobility or transfer b. ✔	Transfer aid (e.g., slide board, trapeze, cane, walker, brace) e.	
		Lifted manually c.	NONE OF ABOVE f.	

7.	TASK SEGMENTATION	Some or all of ADL activities were broken into subtasks during **last 7 days** so that resident could perform them 0. No 1. Yes	1

8.	ADL FUNCTIONAL REHABILITATION POTENTIAL	Resident believes he/she is capable of increased independence in at least some ADLs **5A**	a.
		Direct care staff believe resident is capable of increased independence in at least some ADLs **5A**	b. ✔
		Resident able to perform tasks/activity but is very slow	c.
		Difference in ADL Self-Performance or ADL Support, comparing mornings to evenings	d.
		NONE OF ABOVE	e.

9.	CHANGE IN ADL FUNCTION	Resident's ADL self-performance status has changed as compared to status of **90 days ago** (or since last assessment if less than 90 days) 0. No change 1. Improved 2. Deteriorated	0

SECTION H. CONTINENCE IN LAST 14 DAYS

1.	CONTINENCE SELF-CONTROL CATEGORIES (Code for resident's PERFORMANCE OVER ALL SHIFTS) 0. CONTINENT—Complete control (includes use of indwelling urinary catheter or ostomy device that does not leak urine or stool) 1. USUALLY CONTINENT—BLADDER, incontinent episodes once a week or less; BOWEL, less than weekly 2. OCCASIONALLY INCONTINENT—BLADDER, 2 or more times a week but not daily; BOWEL, once a week 3. FREQUENTLY INCONTINENT—BLADDER, tended to be incontinent daily, but some control present (e.g., on day shift); BOWEL, 2-3 times a week 4. INCONTINENT—Had inadequate control. BLADDER, multiple daily episodes; BOWEL, all (or almost all) of the time		
a.	BOWEL CONTINENCE	Control of bowel movement, with appliance or bowel continence programs, if employed 1, 2, 3 or 4 = **16**	3
b.	BLADDER CONTINENCE	Control of urinary bladder function (if dribbles, volume insufficient to soak through underpants), with appliances (e.g., foley) or continence programs, if employed 2, 3 or 4 = **6**	3
2.	BOWEL ELIMINATION PATTERN	Bowel elimination pattern regular—at least one movement every three days a.	Diarrhea c.
			Fecal impaction 17* d.
		Constipation 17* b. ✔	NONE OF ABOVE e.

3.	APPLIANCES AND PROGRAMS	Any scheduled toileting plan a. ✔	Did not use toilet room/commode/urinal f.
		Bladder retraining program b.	Pads/briefs used **6** g.
		External (condom) catheter **6** c.	Enemas/irrigation h.
		Indwelling catheter **6** d.	Ostomy present i.
		Intermittent catheter **6** e.	NONE OF ABOVE j.

4.	CHANGE IN URINARY CONTINENCE	Resident's urinary continence has changed as compared to status of **90 days ago** (or since last assessment if less than 90 days) 0. No change 1. Improved 2. Deteriorated	2

SECTION I. DISEASE DIAGNOSES

Check only **those diseases that have a relationship** to current ADL status, cognitive status, mood and behavior status, medical treatments, nursing monitoring, or risk of death. (Do not list inactive diagnoses)

1.	DISEASES	(If none apply, CHECK the NONE OF ABOVE box)		
		ENDOCRINE/METABOLIC/NUTRITIONAL	Hemiplegia/Hemiparesis	v.
		Diabetes mellitus a. ✔	Multiple sclerosis	w.
		Hyperthyroidism b.	Paraplegia	x.
		Hypothyroidism c.	Parkinson's disease	y.
		HEART/CIRCULATION	Quadriplegia	z.
		Arteriosclerotic heart disease (ASHD) d.	Seizure disorder	aa.
		Cardiac dysrhythmias e.	Transient ischemic attack (TIA)	bb.
		Congestive heart failure f. ✔	Traumatic brain injury	cc.
		Deep vein thrombosis g.	**PSYCHIATRIC/MOOD**	
		Hypertension h.	Anxiety disorder	dd.
		Hypotension 17* i.	Depression 17*	ee.
		Peripheral vascular disease **16** j.	Manic depression (bipolar disease)	ff.
		Other cardiovascular disease k.	Schizophrenia	gg.
		MUSCULOSKELETAL	**PULMONARY**	
		Arthritis l.	Asthma	hh.
		Hip fracture m.	Emphysema/COPD	ii.
		Missing limb (e.g., amputation) n.	**SENSORY**	
		Osteoporosis o.	Cataracts **3**	jj.
		Pathological bone fracture p.	Diabetic retinopathy	kk.
		NEUROLOGICAL	Glaucoma **3**	ll.
		Alzheimer's disease q.	Macular degeneration	mm.
		Aphasia r.	**OTHER**	
		Cerebral palsy s.	Allergies	nn.
		Cerebrovascular accident (stroke) t.	Anemia	oo.
		Dementia other than Alzheimer's disease u.	Cancer	pp.
			Renal failure	qq.
			NONE OF ABOVE	rr.

2.	INFECTIONS	(If none apply, CHECK the NONE OF ABOVE box)		
		Antibiotic resistant infection (e.g., Methicillin resistant staph) a.	Septicemia	g.
			Sexually transmitted diseases	h.
		Clostridium difficile (c. diff.) b.	Tuberculosis	i.
		Conjunctivitis c.	Urinary tract infection in last 30 days **14**	j.
		HIV infection d.	Viral hepatitis	k.
		Pneumonia e.	Wound infection	l.
		Respiratory infection f.	NONE OF ABOVE	m. ✔

3.	OTHER CURRENT OR MORE DETAILED DIAGNOSES AND ICD-9 CODES	Dehydration 276.5 = **14**		
		a. Fx L wrist	814.00
		b. Hematomas	924.8
		c. Abrasions	919.0
		d.	.
		e.	.

SECTION J. HEALTH CONDITIONS

1.	PROBLEM CONDITIONS	(Check all problems present in last 7 days unless other time frame is indicated)		
		INDICATORS OF FLUID STATUS	Dizziness/Vertigo 11, 17*	f.
		Weight gain or loss of 3 or more pounds within a 7 day period **14** a.	Edema	g. ✔
			Fever **14**	h.
		Inability to lie flat due to shortness of breath b.	Hallucinations 17*	i.
			Internal bleeding **14**	j.
		Dehydrated; output exceeds input **14** c.	Recurrent lung aspirations in last 90 days 17*	k.
		Insufficient fluid; did NOT consume all/almost all liquids provided during last 3 days **14** d. ✔	Shortness of breath	l.
			Syncope (fainting) 17*	m.
			Unsteady gait 17*	n. ✔
		OTHER	Vomiting	o.
		Delusions e.	NONE OF ABOVE	p.

Resident __George Blair__   Numeric Identifier __784393__

2.	**PAIN SYMPTOMS**	(Code the **highest level of pain** present **in the last 7 days**) **a. FREQUENCY** with which resident complains or shows evidence of pain — 0. No pain (**skip to J4**) 1. Pain less than daily 2. Pain daily **b. INTENSITY** of pain 1. Mild pain 2. Moderate pain 3. Times when pain is horrible or excruciating	a. **2** b. **2**
3.	**PAIN SITE**	(If pain present, **check all sites** that apply in last 7 days) Back pain a. / Bone pain b. / Chest pain while doing usual activities c. / Headache d. / Hip pain e. ✔ / Incisional pain f. / Joint pain (other than hip) g. / Soft tissue pain (e.g., lesion, muscle) h. / Stomach pain i. / Other j.	
4.	**ACCIDENTS**	(Check all that apply) Fell in **past 30 days** 11, 17* a. / Fell in **past 31-180 days** 11, 17* b. / Hip fracture in last **180 days** 17* c. / Other fracture in **last 180 days** d. ✔ / **NONE OF ABOVE** e.	
5.	**STABILITY OF CONDITIONS**	Conditions/diseases make resident's cognitive, ADL, mood or behavior patterns unstable—(fluctuating, precarious, or deteriorating) a. / Resident experiencing an acute episode or a flare-up of a recurrent or chronic problem b. / End-stage disease, 6 or fewer months to live c. / **NONE OF ABOVE** d. ✔	

SECTION K. ORAL/NUTRITIONAL STATUS

1.	**ORAL PROBLEMS**	Chewing problem a. / Swallowing problem 17* b. / Mouth pain 15 c. / NONE OF ABOVE d. ✔	
2.	**HEIGHT AND WEIGHT**	Record (a.) height in inches and (b.) weight in pounds. Base weight on most recent measure in **last 30 days**; measure weight consistently in accord with standard facility practice— e.g., in a.m. after voiding, before meal, with shoes off, and in nightclothes.	a. HT (in.) **6 9** b. WT (lb.) **1 2 4**
3.	**WEIGHT CHANGE**	a. Weight loss—5% or more in last 30 days; or 10% or more in **last 180 days** 0. No 1. Yes 12	**1**
		b. Weight gain—5% or more in last 30 days; or 10% or more in **last 180 days** 0. No 1. Yes	**0**
4.	**NUTRITIONAL PROBLEMS**	Complains about the taste of many foods 12 a. / Regular or repetitive complaints of hunger b. / Leaves 25% or more of food uneaten at most meals 12 c. ✔ / NONE OF ABOVE d.	
5.	**NUTRITIONAL APPROACHES**	(Check all that apply in last 7 days) Parenteral/IV 12, 14 a. / Feeding tube 13, 14 b. / Mechanically altered diet 12 c. / Syringe (oral feeding) 12 d. / Therapeutic diet 12 e. ✔ / Dietary supplement between meals f. / Plate guard, stabilized built-up utensil, etc. g. / On a planned weight change program h. / NONE OF ABOVE i.	
6.	**PARENTERAL OR ENTERAL INTAKE**	(**Skip to Section L if neither 5a nor 5b is checked**) a. Code the proportion of **total calories** the resident received through parenteral or tube feedings in the **last 7 days** 0. None 1. 1% to 25% 2. 26% to 50% 3. 51% to 75% 4. 76% to 100%	**0**
		b. Code the average fluid intake per day by IV or tube in last 7 days 0. None 1. 1 to 500 cc/day 2. 501 to 1000 cc/day 3. 1001 to 1500 cc/day 4. 1501 to 2000 cc/day 5. 2001 or more cc/day	**0**

SECTION L. ORAL/DENTAL STATUS

1.	**ORAL STATUS AND DISEASE PREVENTION**	Debris (soft, easily movable substances) present in mouth prior to going to bed at night 15 a. / Has dentures or removable bridge b. / Some/all natural teeth lost—does not have or does not use dentures (or partial plates) 15 c. / Broken, loose, or carious teeth 15 d. / Inflamed gums (gingiva); swollen or bleeding gums; oral abscesses; ulcers or rashes 15 e. / Daily cleaning of teeth/dentures or daily mouth care—by resident or staff Not ✓ = 15 f. ✔ / NONE OF ABOVE g.	

SECTION M. SKIN CONDITION

1.	**ULCERS** (Due to any cause)	(Record the number of ulcers at each ulcer stage— regardless of cause. If none present at a stage, record "0" (zero). Code all that apply during **last 7 days**. Code 9 = 9 or more.) [**Requires full body exam.**]	**Number at Stage**
		a. **Stage 1.** A persistent area of skin redness (without a break in the skin) that does not disappear when pressure is relieved.	**0**
		b. **Stage 2.** A partial thickness loss of skin layers that presents clinically as an abrasion, blister, or shallow crater.	**1**
		c. **Stage 3.** A full thickness of skin is lost, exposing the subcutaneous tissues—presents as a deep crater with or without undermining adjacent tissue.	**0**
		d. **Stage 4.** A full thickness of skin and subcutaneous tissue is lost, exposing muscle or bone.	**0**
2.	**TYPE OF ULCER**	(For each type of ulcer, **code for the highest stage in the last 7 days** using scale in item M1—i.e., 0=none; stages 1, 2, 3, 4)	
		a. Pressure ulcer—any lesion caused by pressure resulting in damage of underlying tissue 1 = 16; 2, 3, or 4 = 12, 16	**2**
		b. Stasis ulcer—open lesion caused by poor circulation in the lower extremities	**0**
3.	**HISTORY OF RESOLVED ULCERS**	Resident had an ulcer that was resolved or cured in **LAST 90 DAYS** 0. No 1. Yes 16	
4.	**OTHER SKIN PROBLEMS OR LESIONS PRESENT**	(Check all that apply during last 7 days) Abrasions, bruises a. ✔ / Burns (second or third degree) b. / Open lesions other than ulcers, rashes, cuts (e.g., cancer lesions) c. / Rashes—e.g., intertrigo, eczema, drug rash, heat rash, herpes zoster d. / Skin desensitized to pain or pressure 16 e. / Skin tears or cuts (other than surgery) f. / Surgical wounds g. / NONE OF ABOVE h.	
5.	**SKIN TREATMENTS**	(Check all that apply during last 7 days) Pressure relieving device(s) for chair a. / Pressure relieving device(s) for bed b. / Turning/repositioning program c. / Nutrition or hydration intervention to manage skin problems d. / Ulcer care e. ✔ / Surgical wound care f. / Application of dressings (with or without topical medications) other than to feet g. ✔ / Application of ointments/medications (other than to feet) h. ✔ / Other preventative or protective skin care (other than to feet) i. / NONE OF ABOVE j.	
6.	**FOOT PROBLEMS AND CARE**	(Check all that apply during last 7 days) Resident has one or more foot problems—e.g., corns, calluses, bunions, hammer toes, overlapping toes, pain, structural problems a. / Infection of the foot—e.g., cellulitis, purulent drainage b. / Open lesions on the foot c. / Nails/calluses trimmed during last 90 days d. / Received preventative or protective foot care (e.g., used special shoes, inserts, pads, toe separators) e. / Application of dressings (with or without topical medications) f. / NONE OF ABOVE g. ✔	

SECTION N. ACTIVITY PURSUIT PATTERNS

1.	**TIME AWAKE** 10B only if BOTH N1a = ✓ and N2 = 0	(**Check appropriate time periods over last 7 days**) Resident awake all or most of time (i.e., naps no more than one hour per time period) in: Morning 10B a. ✔ / Afternoon b. / Evening c. / NONE OF ABOVE d.	

(IF RESIDENT IS COMATOSE, SKIP TO SECTION O)

2.	**AVERAGE TIME INVOLVED IN ACTIVITIES**	(When awake and not receiving treatments or ADL care) 0. Most—more than 2/3 of time 10B 1. Some—from 1/3 to 2/3 of time 2. Little—less than 1/3 of time 10A 3. None 10A	**1**
3.	**PREFERRED ACTIVITY SETTINGS**	(Check all settings in which activities are preferred) Own room a. / Day/activity room b. ✔ / Inside NH/off unit c. / Outside facility d. / NONE OF ABOVE e.	
4.	**GENERAL ACTIVITY PREFERENCES** (Adapted to resident's current abilities)	(Check all PREFERENCES whether or not activity is currently available to resident) Cards/other games a. / Crafts/arts b. / Exercise/sports c. / Music d. ✔ / Reading/writing e. / Spiritual/religious activities f. / Trips/shopping g. / Walking/wheeling outdoors h. / Watching TV i. / Gardening or plants j. / Talking or conversing k. / Helping others l. / NONE OF ABOVE m.	

Resident __George Blair__   Numeric Identifier __784393__

5.	**PREFERS CHANGE IN DAILY ROUTINE**	Code for resident preferences in daily routines 0. No change 1. Slight change 2. Major change		
		a. Type of activities in which resident is currently involved *1 or 2 = 10A*		0
		b. Extent of resident involvement in activity *1 or 2 = 10A*		0

SECTION O. MEDICATIONS

1.	**NUMBER OF MEDICATIONS**	*(Record the number of different medications used in the last 7 days; enter "0" if none used)*	10
2.	**NEW MEDICA-TIONS**	*(Resident currently receiving medications that were initiated during the last 90 days)* 0. No 1. Yes	1
3.	**INJECTIONS**	*(Record the number of DAYS injections of any type received during the last 7 days; enter "0" if none used)*	0
4.	**DAYS RECEIVED THE FOLLOWING MEDICATION**	*(Record the number of DAYS during last 7 days; enter "0" if not used. Note—enter "1" for long acting meds used less than weekly)* (NOTE: For **17** to actually be triggered, O4a, b, or c MUST = 1-7 AND at least one additional item marked **17*** must be indicated. See sections B, C, E, G, H, I, J, and K.)	
		a. Antipsychotic *1-7 = 17* d. Hypnotic	7
		b. Antianxiety *1-7 = 11, 17* e. Diuretic *1-7 = 14*	8 7
		c. Antidepressant *1-7 = 11, 17*	8

SECTION P. SPECIAL TREATMENTS AND PROCEDURES

1. **SPECIAL TREAT-MENTS, PROCE-DURES, AND PROGRAMS**	**a. SPECIAL CARE**—Check treatments or programs received during the **last 14 days**

TREATMENTS			PROGRAMS	
		Ventilator or respirator		l.
Chemotherapy	a.			
Dialysis	b.	Alcohol/drug treatment program		m.
IV medication	c.	Alzheimer's/dementia special care unit		n.
Intake/output	d.			
Monitoring acute medical condition	e.	Hospice care		o.
Ostomy care	f.	Pediatric unit		p.
Oxygen therapy	g.	Respite care		q.
Radiation	h.	Training in skills required to return to the community (e.g., taking medications, house work, shopping, transportation, ADLs)		r.
Suctioning	i.			
Tracheostomy care	j.			
Transfusions	k.	NONE OF ABOVE	✓	s.

b. THERAPIES—Record the number of days and total minutes each of the following therapies was administered (for at least 15 minutes a day) in the **last 7 calendar days** (Enter 0 if none or less than 15 min. daily) [Note—count only post admission therapies]

(A) = # of days administered for 15 **minutes or more**

(B) = total # of **minutes** provided in last 7 days

	DAYS (A)	MINUTES (B)
a. Speech-language pathology and audiology services	0	
b. Occupational therapy	0	
c. Physical therapy	0	
d. Respiratory therapy	0	
e. Psychological therapy (by any licensed mental health professional)	0	

2.	**INTERVEN-TION PROGRAMS FOR MOOD, BEHAVIOR, COGNITIVE LOSS**	(Check all interventions or strategies used in last 7 days—no matter where received)	
		Special behavior symptom evaluation program	a.
		Evaluation by a licensed mental health specialist in last 90 days	b.
		Group therapy	c.
		Resident-specific deliberate changes in the environment to address mood/behavior patterns—e.g., providing bureau in which to rummage	d.
		Reorientation—e.g., cueing	e.
		NONE OF ABOVE	f. ✓

3.	**NURSING REHABILI-TATION/ RESTOR-ATIVE CARE**	Record the NUMBER OF DAYS each of the following rehabilitation or restorative techniques or practices was **provided to the resident for more than or equal to 15 minutes** per day in the last 7 days (Enter 0 if none or less than 15 min. daily).	

a. Range of motion (passive)	0	f. Walking		
b. Range of motion (active)	0	g. Dressing or grooming		0
c. Splint or brace assistance	0	h. Eating or swallowing		0
TRAINING AND SKILL PRACTICE IN:		i. Amputation/ prosthesis care		0
		j. Communication		0
d. Bed mobility	0	k. Other		0
e. Transfer				

4.	**DEVICES AND RESTRAINTS**	(Use the following codes for **last 7 days**:) 0. Not used 1. Used less than daily 2. Used daily	
		Bed rails	
		a. —Full bed rails on all open sides of bed	2
		b. —Other types of side rails used (e.g., half rail, one side)	0
		c. Trunk restraint *1 = 11, 18. 2 = 11, 16, 18*	0
		d. Limb restraint *1 or 2 = 18*	0
		e. Chair prevents rising *1 or 2 = 18*	0
5.	**HOSPITAL STAY(S)**	Record number of times resident was admitted to hospital with an overnight stay in last 90 days (or since last assessment if less than 90 days). (Enter 0 if no hospital admissions)	1
6.	**EMERGENCY ROOM (ER) VISIT(S)**	Record number of times resident visited ER without an overnight stay in last 90 days (or since last assessment if less than 90 days). (Enter 0 if no ER visits)	0
7.	**PHYSICIAN VISITS**	In the LAST 14 DAYS (or since admission if less than 14 days in facility) how many days has the physician (or authorized assistant or practitioner) examined the resident? (Enter 0 if none)	0
8.	**PHYSICIAN ORDERS**	In the LAST 14 DAYS (or since admission if less than 14 days in facility) how many days has the physician (or authorized assistant or practitioner) changed the resident's orders? Do not include order renewals without change. (Enter 0 if none)	0
9.	**ABNORMAL LAB VALUES**	Has the resident had any abnormal lab values during the **last** 90 days (or since admission)? 0. No 1. Yes	1

SECTION Q. DISCHARGE POTENTIAL AND OVERALL STATUS

1.	**DISCHARGE POTENTIAL**	a. Resident expresses/indicates preference to return to the community 0. No 1. Yes	0
		b. Resident has a support person who is positive toward discharge 0. No 1. Yes	0
		c. Stay projected to be of a short duration—discharge projected **within 90 days** (do not include expected discharge due to death) 0. No 2. Within 31-90 days 1. Within 30 days 3. Discharge status uncertain	0
2.	**OVERALL CHANGE IN CARE NEEDS**	Resident's overall self sufficiency has changed significantly as compared to status of **90 days ago** (or since last assessment if less than 90 days) 0. No change 1. Improved—receives fewer supports, needs less restrictive level of care 2. Deteriorated—receives more support	2

SECTION R. ASSESSMENT INFORMATION

1.	**PARTICI-PATION IN ASSESSMENT**	a. Resident: 0. No 1. Yes	0
		b. Family: 0. No 1. Yes 2. No family	1
		c. Significant other: 0. No 1. Yes 2. None	0

2. SIGNATURES OF PERSONS COMPLETING THE ASSESSMENT:

a. _A. Jones, R.N. (O, P, Q, R)_
   Signature of RN Assessment Coordinator (sign on above line)

b. Date RN Assessment Coordinator signed as complete

Month	Day	Year
1 2	1 4	1 9 9 7

	Signature	Title	Sections	Date
c. Other Signatures	J. Spencer, LPN		(A, B, C, D, J, K, L)	12/12/97
d.	M. Moeller, LPN		(G, H, I, M)	12/14/97
e.	S. Miller, TRT		(N)	12/14/97
	a. Schmidt MSW		(E, F)	12/10/97
f.				Date
g.				Date
h.				Date

TRIGGER LEGEND

1 - Delirium	5B - ADL-Maintenance	10A - Activities (Revise)	14 - Dehydration/Fluid Maintenance
2 - Cognitive Loss/Dementia	6B - Urinary Incontinence and Indwelling Catheter	10B - Activities (Review)	15 - Dental Care
3 - Visual Function	7 - Psychosocial Well-Being	11 - Falls	16 - Pressure Ulcers
4 - Communication	8 - Mood State	12 - Nutritional Status	17 - Psychotropic Drug Use
5A - ADL-Rehabilitation	9 - Behavioral Symptoms	13 - Feeding Tubes	17* - For this to trigger, O4a, b, or c must = 1-7
			18 - Physical Restraints

Form 1728HH © 1995 Briggs Corporation, Des Moines, IA 50306 (800) 247-2343 PRINTED IN U.S.A.
Copyright limited to addition of trigger system.

MDS 2.0 10/18/94N

SECTION V. RESIDENT ASSESSMENT PROTOCOL SUMMARY   Numeric Identifier __784393__

Resident's Name: George T. Blair	Medical Record No.: 784393

1. Check if RAP is triggered.
2. For each triggered RAP, use the RAP guidelines to identify areas needing further assessment. Document relevant assessment information regarding the resident's status.
   - Describe:
     - Nature of the condition (may include presence or lack of objective data and subjective complaints).
     - Complications and risk factors that affect your decision to proceed to care planning.
     - Factors that must be considered in developing individualized care plan interventions.
     - Need for referrals/further evaluation by appropriate health professionals.
   - Documentation should support your decision-making regarding whether to proceed with a care plan for a triggered RAP and the type(s) of care plan interventions that are appropriate for a particular resident.
   - Documentation may appear anywhere in the clinical record (e.g., progress notes, consults, flowsheets, etc.).
3. Indicate under the Location of RAP Assessment Documentation column where information related to the RAP assessment can be found.
4. For each triggered RAP, indicate whether a new care plan, care plan revision, or continuation of current care plan is necessary to address the problem(s) identified in your assessment. The Care Planning Decision column must be completed within 7 days of completing the RAI (MDS and RAPs).

A. RAP Problem Area	(a) Check if Triggered	Location and Date of RAP Assessment Documentation	(b) Care Planning Decision—check if addressed in care plan
1. DELIRIUM	✔	Mood + behavior problems \ Admit notes Nsg notes	✔
2. COGNITIVE LOSS	✔	Poor STM & LTM \ Nsg. notes	✔
3. VISUAL FUNCTION	✔	Wears glasses \ Admit note	✔
4. COMMUNICATION	✔	Difficulty making needs known + following instruc \ Nsg. notes	✔
5. ADL FUNCTIONAL/ REHABILITATION POTENTIAL	✔	Assist c̄ ADL's \ Nsg. notes	✔
6. URINARY INCONTINENCE AND INDWELLING CATHETER	✔	Incont. of urine \ Admit note Nsg. note	✔
7. PSYCHOSOCIAL WELL-BEING	✔	Verbally abusive \ Nsg. note	✔
8. MOOD STATE	✔	Expressions of distress \ Nsg. note	✔
9. BEHAVIORAL SYMPTOMS	✔	Wandering + inapprop behavior \ Nsg. notes	✔
10. ACTIVITIES			
11. FALLS	✔	Fell in last 2 wks \ Admit note	✔
12. NUTRITIONAL STATUS	✔	Wgt. loss, spec. diet \ Admit note Nsg note	✔
13. FEEDING TUBES			
14. DEHYDRATION/FLUID MAINTENANCE	✔	Constipation \ Nsg. note	✔
15. ORAL/DENTAL CARE			
16. PRESSURE ULCERS	✔	Coccyx pressure ulcer \ Admit note	✔
17. PSYCHOTROPIC DRUG USE	✔	Haldol bid + Oxazepam HS \ Admit note Nsg note	✔
18. PHYSICAL RESTRAINTS			

B. A. Jones, R.N.
1. Signature of RN Coordinator for RAP Assessment Process

2. | 1 | 2 | – | 1 | 4 | – | 1 | 9 | 9 | 7 |
   Month   Day   Year

A. Jones, R.N.
3. Signature of Person Completing Care Planning Decision

4. | 1 | 2 | – | 1 | 4 | – | 1 | 9 | 9 | 7 |
   Month   Day   Year

Form 1728HH © 1995 Briggs Corporation, Des Moines, IA 50306 (800) 247-2343 PRINTED IN U.S.A.
Copyright limited to addition of trigger system.
8 of 8

MDS 2.0 10/18/94N

RESIDENT ASSESSMENT PROTOCOL TRIGGER LEGEND FOR REVISED RAPS (FOR MDS VERSION 2.0)

Resident _____ Numeric Identifier _____

Key:
- ● = One item required to trigger
- ② = Two items required to trigger
- ✻ = One of these three items (O4a, O4b, O4c), plus at least one other item (●✻) required to trigger
- ●✻ = Psychotropic Drug Use triggered only when at least one of the three items (O4a, O4b, O4c) identified by ✻ also apply
- (a) = When both ADL triggers present, maintenance takes precedence

Proceed to RAP Review once triggered

Column legend:
1. Delirium
2. Cognitive Loss/Dementia
3. Visual Function
4. Communication
5A. ADL-Rehabilitation Trigger A (a)
5B. ADL-Maintenance Trigger B (a)
6. Urinary Incontinence and Indwelling Catheter
7. Psychosocial Well-Being
8. Mood State
9. Behavioral Symptoms
10A. Activities Trigger A (Revise)
10B. Activities Trigger B (Review)
11. Falls
12. Nutritional Status
13. Feeding Tubes
14. Dehydration/Fluid Maintenance
15. Dental Care
16. Pressure Ulcers
17. Psychotropic Drug Use
18. Physical Restraints

MDS 2.0 ITEM	DESCRIPTION	CODE	1	2	3	4	5A	5B	6	7	8	9	10A	10B	11	12	13	14	15	16	17	18	ITEM
B2a	Short term memory	1		●																			B2a
B2b	Long term memory	1		●																			B2b
B4	Decision making	1,2		●																			B4
B4	Decision making	3		●				●															B4
B5a-B5f	Indicators of delirium	2	●																		●✻		B5a-B5f
B6	Change in cognitive status	2	●																		●✻		B6
C1	Hearing	1,2,3				●																	C1
C4	Understood by others	1,2,3				●																	C4
C6	Understand others	1,2,3		●		●																	C6
C7	Change in communication	2																			●✻		C7
D1	Vision	1,2,3			●																		D1
D2a	Side vision problem	✓			●																		D2a
E1a-E1p	Indicators of depression, anxiety, sad mood	1,2									●												E1a-E1p
E1n	Repetitive movement	1,2																			●✻		E1n
E1o	Withdrawal from activities	1,2											●										E1o
E2	Mood persistence	1,2									●												E2
E3	Change in mood	2		●																	●✻		E3
E4aA	Wandering	1,2,3										●			●								E4aA
E4bA-E4eA	Behavioral symptoms	1,2,3										●											E4bA-E4eA
E5	Change in behavioral symptoms	1										●											E5
E5	Change in behavioral symptoms	2																			●✻		E5
F1d	Establishes own goals	✓								●													F1d
F2a-F2d	Unsettled relationships	✓								●													F2a-F2d
F3a	Strong id, past roles	✓								●													F3a
F3b	Lost roles	✓								●													F3b
F3c	Daily routine different	✓								●													F3c
G1aA	Bed mobility	1					●																G1aA
G1aA	Bed mobility	2,3,4					●													●			G1aA
G1aA	Bed mobility	8																		●			G1aA
G1bA-G1jA	ADL self-performance	1,2,3,4					●																G1bA-G1jA
G2A	Bathing	1,2,3,4					●																G2A
G3b	Balance while sitting	1,2,3																			●✻		G3b
G6a	Bedfast	✓																		●			G6a
G8a,b	Resident, staff believe capable	✓					●																G8a,b
H1a	Bowel incontinence	1,2,3,4																		●			H1a
H1b	Bladder incontinence	2,3,4							●														H1b
H2b	Constipation	✓																			●✻		H2b
H2d	Fecal impaction	✓																			●✻		H2d
H3c,d,e	Catheter use	✓							●														H3c,d,e
H3g	Use of pads/briefs	✓							●														H3g
I1i	Hypotension	✓																			●✻		I1i
I1j	Peripheral vascular disease	✓																		●			I1j
I1ee	Depression	✓																			●✻		I1ee
I1jj	Cataracts	✓			●																		I1jj
I1ll	Glaucoma	✓			●																		I1ll
I2j	UTI	✓																●					I2j
MDS 2.0 ITEM AND DESCRIPTION		CODE	1	2	3	4	5A	5B	6	7	8	9	10A	10B	11	12	13	14	15	16	17	18	ITEM

Form 1729HH BRIGGS, Des Moines, IA 50306 (800) 247-2343 PRINTED IN U.S.A.
R396

MDS 2.0 RAP TRIGGER LEGEND
MDS 2.0 10/18/94N

RESIDENT ASSESSMENT PROTOCOL TRIGGER LEGEND FOR REVISED RAPS (FOR MDS VERSION 2.0)

Key:
- ● = One item required to trigger
- ② = Two items required to trigger
- ★ = One of these three items (O4a, O4b, O4c), plus at least one other item (●*) required to trigger
- ●* = Psychotropic Drug Use triggered only when at least one of the three items (O4a, O4b, O4c) identified by ★ also apply
- (a) = When both ADL triggers present, maintenance takes precedence

Proceed to RAP Review once triggered

Column legend (numbered headers):
1 Delirium · 2 Cognitive Loss/Dementia · 3 Visual Function · 4 Communication · 5A ADL-Rehabilitation Trigger A (a) · 5B ADL-Maintenance Trigger B (a) · 6 Urinary Incontinence and Indwelling Catheter · 7 Psychosocial Well Being · 8 Mood State · 9 Behavioral Symptoms · 10A Activities Trigger A (Revise) · 10B Activities Trigger B (Review) · 11 Falls · 12 Nutritional Status · 13 Feeding Tubes · 14 Dehydration/Fluid Maintenance · 15 Dental Care · 16 Pressure Ulcers · 17 Psychotropic Drug Use · 18 Physical Restraints

MDS 2.0 ITEM	DESCRIPTION	CODE	1	2	3	4	5A	5B	6	7	8	9	10A	10B	11	12	13	14	15	16	17	18	ITEM
I3	Dehydration diagnosis	276.5																(●)					I3
J1a	Weight fluctuation	✓																(●)					J1a
J1c	Dehydrated	✓																(●)					J1c
J1d	Insufficient fluid	✓																●					J1d
J1f	Dizziness	✓													●						●*		J1f
J1h	Fever	✓																●					J1h
J1i	Hallucinations	✓																			●*		J1i
J1j	Internal bleeding	✓																●					J1j
J1k	Lung aspirations	✓																			●*		J1k
J1m	Syncope	✓																			●*		J1m
J1n	Unsteady gait	✓																			(●*)		J1n
J4a,b	Fell	✓													(●)						●*		J4a,b
J4c	Hip fracture	✓																			●*		J4c
K1b	Swallowing problem	✓																			●*		K1b
K1c	Mouth pain	✓																	●				K1c
K3a	Weight loss	1														(●)							K3a
K4a	Taste alteration	✓														●							K4a
K4c	Leave 25% food	✓														(●)							K4c
K5a	Parenteral/IV feeding	✓														●	●						K5a
K5b	Feeding tube	✓															●	●					K5b
K5c	Mechanically altered	✓														●							K5c
K5d	Syringe feeding	✓														●							K5d
K5e	Therapeutic diet	✓														(●)							K5e
L1a,c,d,e	Dental	✓																	(●)				L1a,c,d,e
L1f	Daily cleaning teeth	Not ✓																	●				L1f
M2a	Pressure ulcer	2,3,4													(●)					(●)			M2a
M2a	Pressure ulcer	1																		●			M2a
M3	Previous pressure ulcer	1																		●			M3
M4e	Impaired tactile sense	✓																		●			M4e
N1a	Awake morning	✓												(②)									N1a
N2	Involved in activities	0												②									N2
N2	Involved in activities	2,3											●										N2
N5a,b	Prefer change in daily routine	1,2											●										N5a,b
O4a	Antipsychotics	1-7																			(★)		O4a
O4b	Antianxiety	1-7													●						★		O4b
O4c	Antidepressants	1-7													●						★		O4c
O4e	Diuretic	1-7																(●)					O4e
P4c	Trunk restraint	1													●							●	P4c
P4c	Trunk restraint	2													●					●		●	P4c
P4d	Limb restraint	1,2																				●	P4d
P4e	Chair prevents rising	1,2																				●	P4e

MDS 2.0 10/18/94N

CASE STUDY
DISCUSSION

Use the following nursing diagnoses to organize your assessment data and develop a nursing care plan for Mr. B.

1. Nursing Diagnosis: *Self Care Deficit* related to confusion manifested by inability to perform ADLs independently secondary to Alzheimer's disease and fractured wrist.

ADL FUNCTION/REHABILITATION POTENTIAL
VISUAL FUNCTION

2. Nursing Diagnosis: *Injury, high risk for* related to altered mobility as manifested by unsteadiness and wandering, secondary to hip injury and Alzheimer's disease.

FALLS
BEHAVIOR PROBLEMS

3. Nursing Diagnosis: *Nutrition, altered: less than body requirements* related to lack of appetite as manifested by significant weight loss in last 30 days secondary to Alzheimer's disease.

NUTRITIONAL STATUS
DEHYDRATION/FLUID MAINTENANCE

4. Nursing Diagnosis: *Urinary Elimination, altered* and *Incontinence* related to confusion mobility as manifested by not going to the bathroom to void secondary to Alzheimer's disease.

URINARY INCONTINENCE AND INDWELLING CATHETER

5. Nursing Diagnosis: *Thought Processes, altered* related to inaccurate interpretation of environment as manifested by inability to state season, date, remember names of staff members, inability to follow commands secondary to Alzheimer's disease, and possible use of antipsychotic and sedative medication.

DELIRIUM
COGNITIVE LOSS/DEMENTIA
COMMUNICATION
MOOD STATE
BEHAVIOR PROBLEM
PSYCHOTROPIC DRUG USE
PSYCHOSOCIAL WELL-BEING

6. Nursing Diagnosis: *Skin Integrity, impaired* related to a fall and being restrained in bed during hospitalization manifested by hematomas, abrasions, blisters, and stage 2 coccyx pressure ulcer.

PRESSURE ULCER

7. Nursing Diagnosis: *Constipation* related to decreased fluid intake as manifested by bowel movements hard and difficult to pass and use of suppository secondary to Alzheimer's disease, altered nutrition intake, and dehydration.

DEHYDRATION/FLUID MAINTENANCE
NUTRITIONAL STATUS

Study Questions

Select the one best answer to each question.

1. The nursing process is:
   a. A type of standardized care plan
   b. A framework for providing nursing care
   c. A procedure that registered nurses use to make care assignments
   d. An instinctive method of providing care

2. The steps in the nursing process are:
   a. Admission, inpatient care, and discharge
   b. Assessment, intervention, and documentation
   c. Assessment, nursing diagnosis, planning, intervention, and evaluation
   d. Admission, physical examination, interview, nursing history, and planning

3. Nursing diagnoses differ from medical diagnoses because they:
   a. Address the problems of the older person
   b. Are written in language that nurses understand
   c. Are standardized for any person who is receiving nursing care
   d. Are designed to address the medical treatment plan

4. When setting priorities during the planning stage of the nursing process, it is important to consider:
   a. The needs of the physician
   b. The needs of the family
   c. The needs of the nursing staff
   d. The needs of the client

5. Evaluation of the nursing care plan is documented by means of:
   a. The nurse's notes
   b. The resident care plan
   c. The doctor's orders
   d. Revising the admission note

Bibliography

Ackley, B. J., & Ladwig, G. B. (Eds.). (1997). *Nursing diagnosis handbook: A guide to planning care* (3rd ed.). St. Louis: Mosby-Year Book.
   This is a complete and comprehensive reference guide for making nursing diagnoses and writing care plans. It provides plans of care for every NANDA-approved nursing diagnosis.
Atkinson, L. D., & Murray, M. E. (1986). *Understanding the nursing process* (3rd ed.). New York: Macmillan.
   This text is a classic. When I first taught nursing fundamentals and care planning in 1981, this is the text that I found to explain the whole nursing process. Some of my lecture notes and "classic" care planning and nursing process lectures still have their basis in the content and humor of this text.
Burggraf, V., & Stanley, M. (Eds.). (1989). *Nursing the elderly: A careplan approach*. Philadelphia: J. B. Lippincott.
   This text uses nursing care plans to comprehensively cover the nursing process (nursing diagnoses, goals, and nursing interventions). Each chapter is based on a body system or on a problem of older people. The chapter begins with discussion of assessment criteria and ends with care plans based on aspects of that specific body system assessment.

Doenges, M. E., Moorhouse, M. F., & Geissler, A. C. (1993). *Nursing care plans: Guidelines for planning and documenting patient care* (3rd ed.). Philadelphia: F. A. Davis.
   An excellent text on writing meaningful care plans.
Eliopoulos, C. (Ed.). (1990). *Caring for the elderly in diverse care settings.* Philadelphia: J. B. Lippincott.
   Easy-to-read overview of the issues and problems of older people. Discusses nursing practice in acute, home, and long-term care. I especially enjoyed chapters that discussed the diversity of practice that gerontological nurses are undertaking.
Fischbach, F. T. (1991). *Documenting care: Communication, the nursing process and documentation standards.* Philadelphia: F. A. Davis.
   This text is the best that I have found in terms of covering most of the aspects of documentation in a comprehensive and easy-to-read format.
Krechting, J. L., & Koper, V. E. (1995). *Interdisciplinary care plans for long-term care.* Rockville, MD: Aspen Publishers.
   This book is specifically oriented to the long-term care resident and approaches care planning from an interdisciplinary perspective.
March, C. S. (1997). *The complete care plan manual for long-term care.* Chicago: American Hospital Publishers.
   This is a complete manual that addresses all aspects of writing care plans in the nursing facility.
Needham, J. F. (1996). *Gerontological nursing (plans of care for specialty practice).* Albany, NY: Delmar Publishers.
   This reference provides plans of care for specific problems of the older adult. The plans can be applied in a variety of settings.
Wilkinson, J. M. (1992). *Nursing process in action: A critical thinking approach.* Redwood City, CA: Addison-Wesley.
   A high-energy and enthusiastic text for understanding and using the nursing process. Uses questions in the form of "think breaks" and other very creative learning activities. This is a complete and convenient reference to help nurses.

Chapter

MARY ANN ANDERSON

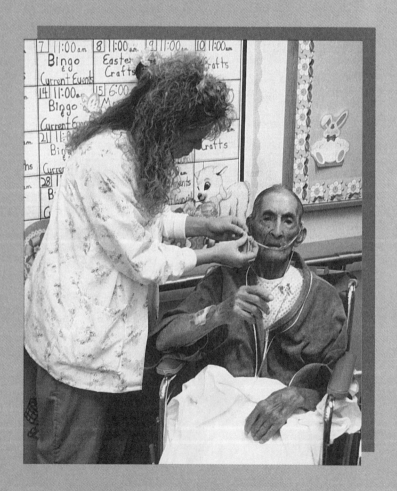

Legal and Ethical Considerations Regarding the Elderly

Learning Objectives

After completing this chapter, the student will be able to:

1. Compare and contrast the terms *legal* and *ethical*.
2. Define the guiding principles of a restraint-free environment.
3. Outline the role of the licensed practical nurse (LPN) in using advanced directives and informed consent.
4. Describe the legal definition of elder abuse and the LPN's role in reporting it.
5. Express an understanding of the ethical responsibility of working with elderly clients in meeting client's sexual needs.

INTRODUCTION

Health-care decisions that are made daily across the nation are based on the legal and ethical definitions of health care. Advances in technology, increased resources, newer drug therapies, and other modalities of treatment continue to bring with them both ethical and legal problems and solutions to the health-care system that are unprecedented. While the legislators and ethics committees of this country debate the merits of treatment approaches, health-care providers deliberate every day as to their role and often wonder if it is one of help or hindrance.

ETHICS

Ethics is the study of moral actions and values. It is based on the principles of conduct that govern both individuals and groups. Many people envision ethics as dealing with principles and moral concepts that determine what is good or bad behavior. The problem with this concept is determining who decides what is good and what is bad. Is this decision one for the elderly patient, the nurses, the family, or an outside group?

A broader definition of ethics considers the value system of a person and the relationship of those values in determining what is good for an individual or group. It is important for LPNs to understand their own value systems and the ethical framework underlying the work performance that springs from it. The personal values of all the persons involved in making health-care decisions for elderly persons form the most important aspect of the nurse's delivery of ethical health care.

Patient's Bill of Rights

The Patient's Bill of Rights is a document published by the American Hospital Association in 1975 (Box 5.1). It outlines the ethical behavior that is seen as appropriate and proper for care of those who are patients in a hospital. The nursing home organization has a Resident's Bill of Rights for those people who are in nursing homes. Other organizations such as the American Nurses' Association, American Dental Association, and National Respiratory Therapy Association have ethical codes that are based on the principles in the patient's and resident's bills of rights.

The bill of rights for any client is based on that persons's individual right to make decisions regarding health-care treatment. It is designed to serve as a model that defines acceptable behavior toward those in your care. All work done with clients of every age and condition should be based on the principles in the Patient's Bill of Rights. Please read and review the Bill of Rights in Box 5.1. It should be the foundation for the work you do with clients, and it has a very special significance when dealing with the elderly.

THE LAW

The legal system is based on rules and regulations that guide society in a formal and binding manner. These are man-made rules capable of being changed by the legisla-

Box 5.1   A Patient's Bill of Rights*

1. The patient has the right to considerate and respectful care.
2. The patient has the right to and is encouraged to obtain from physicians and other direct caregivers relevant, current, and understandable information concerning diagnosis, treatment, and prognosis.

Except in emergencies when the patient lacks decision-making capacity and the need for treatment is urgent, the patient is entitled to the opportunity to discuss and request information related to the specific procedures and/or treatments, the risks involved, the possible length of recuperation, and the medically reasonable alternatives and their accompanying risks and benefits.

Patients have the right to know the identity of physicians, nurses, and others involved in their care, as well as when those involved are students, residents, or other trainees. The patient also has the right to know the immediate and long-term financial implications of treatment choices, insofar as they are known.

3. The patient has the right to make decisions about the plan of care prior to and during the course of treatment and to refuse a recommended treatment or plan of care to the extent permitted by law and hospital policy and to be informed of the medical consequences of this action. In case of such refusal, the patient is entitled to other appropriate care and services that the hospital provides or transfer to another hospital. The hospital should notify patients of any policy that might affect patient choice within the institution.
4. The patient has the right to have an advance directive (such as a living will, health care proxy, or durable power of attorney for health care) concerning treatment or designating a surrogate decision maker with the expectation that the hospital will honor the intent of that directive to the extent permitted by law and hospital policy.

Health-care institutions must advise patients of their rights under state law and hospital policy to make informed medical choices, ask if the patient has an advance directive, and include that information in patient records. The patient has the right to timely information about hospital policy that may limit its ability to implement fully a legally valid advance directive.

5. The patient has the right to every consideration of privacy. Case discussion, consultation, examination, and treatment should be conducted so as to protect each patient's privacy.
6. The patient has the right to expect that all communications and records pertaining to his/her care will be treated as confidential by the hospital, except in cases such as suspected abuse and public health hazards when reporting is permitted or required by law. The patient has the right to expect that the hospital will emphasize the confidentiality of this information when it releases it to any other parties entitled to review information in these records.
7. The patient has the right to review the records pertaining to his/her medical care and to have the information explained or interpreted as necessary, except when restricted by law.

*These rights can be exercised on the patient's behalf by a designated surrogate or proxy decision maker if the patient lacks decision-making capacity, is legally incompetent or is a minor.

BOX 5.1   A PATIENT'S BILL OF RIGHTS (*Continued*)

8. The patient has the right to expect that, within its capacity and policies, a hospital will make reasonable response to the request of a patient for appropriate and medically indicated care services. The hospital must provide evaluation, service, and/or referral as indicated by the urgency of the case. When medically appropriate and legally permissible, or when a patient has so requested, a patient may be transferred to another facility. The institution to which the patient is to be transferred must first have accepted the patient for transfer. The patient must also have the benefit of complete information and explanation concerning the need for, risks, benefits, and alternatives to such a transfer.

9. The patient has the right to ask and be informed of the existence of business relationships among the hospital, educational institutions, other health care providers, or payers that may influence the patient's treatment and care.

10. The patient has the right to consent to or decline to participate in proposed research studies or human experimentation affecting care and treatment or requiring direct patient involvement, and to have those studies fully explained prior to consent. A patient who declines to participate in research or experimentation is entitled to the most effective care that the hospital can otherwise provide.

11. The patient has the right to expect reasonable continuity of care when appropriate and to be informed by physicians and other caregivers of available and realistic patient care options when hospital care is no longer appropriate.

12. The patient has the right to be informed of hospital policies and practices that relate to patient care, treatment, and responsibilities. The patient has the right to be informed of available resources for resolving disputes, grievances, and conflicts, such as ethics committees, patient representatives, or other mechanisms available in the institution. The patient has the right to be informed of the hospital's charges for services and available payment methods.

A Patient's Bill of Rights was first adopted by the American Hospital Association (AHA) in 1973. This revision was approved by the AHA Board of Trustees on October 21, 1992.

© 1992 by the American Hospital Association. Reprinted with permission of the American Hospital Association, Copyright 1992.

tive and judiciary systems of this country. The law gives you, the health-care provider, a general foundation for guiding your work; it may or may not complement your personal value system.

Ideally, the care you give is both ethical and legal. However, it is possible for a legal approach to care to seem unethical to you because it conflicts with your value system. This is when ethical-legal dilemmas occur. For example, the law recognizes the right of a competent patient to refuse therapy. The patient has that right regardless of the health-care system's agreement or disagreement with the decision. For example, a client has the right to refuse to have a pacemaker replaced. Such replacement is essentially a benign procedure with minimal risk, and not to have it done amounts to a death sentence. However, it is the client's right to accept or refuse this therapy. Your values do not change the principles of the law.

Another example is shared by Dr. Jean Watson, nurse theorist. Dr. Watson's theory is the Science of Human Caring and is explained in detail in her book *Nursing: Human Science and Human Caring—A Theory of Nursing.* In it she emphasizes the importance of valuing clients as individuals and avoiding objectifying them. She explains that a nurse gives legal care when going into a patient's room to perform a complicated dressing change and assesses the wound site, removes the old dressing, and replaces it with a new dressing. The law does not indicate that the nurse needs to talk to the patient or to explain the procedure or the healing process. However, for that care to be ethical, the nurse must take the time to talk to the patient and treat the person as a human being rather than an object with a wound to dress. Another very simple example is that of bathing persons with dementia. Federal law requires that persons in nursing homes be kept clean. However, it is possible for a nursing assistant to give a resident a bath that was abusive; that is, allowing no protection of modesty, not waiting for the water to warm, being verbally abusive. This could be described as a legal, but unethical, bath. In the midst of the time pressures of healthcare's complex world, one must be careful to determine the difference between legal and ethical care.

As an LPN, you are required to function under the mandates of the nurse practice act in your state. You are not allowed to practice nursing outside of the law as it is outlined in the practice act. An important consideration or "rule of thumb" to keep in mind as you administer care is to always consider "What is reasonable under the circumstances?" If you have the knowledge to answer that question whenever you have doubts, you should be able to make a legal and ethical decision. If you do not have the knowledge to answer that question, you need to go to someone with more knowledge or education than you have to assist in making the right decision. If you were ever on trial for a decision you made in your practice as a nurse, the question "What is reasonable under the circumstances?" would be the main question the judge would want answered. The judge would possibly interview expert witnesses to determine what other LPNs would do in the same situation. The assumption is that most LPNs act in a reasonable manner, and if your behavior agrees with that exhibited by other LPNs in similar situations, you are being reasonable in your care administration.

Acts of Negligence and Omission

There are two very specific legal concepts that you should be familiar with as a licensed nurse: negligence and omission. Lawsuits frequently are based on these two principles.

Negligence is failure to exercise adequate care. The determination of negligence is based on the level of performance that is expected of an LPN as determined by the state nurse practice act, the policies and procedures for the facility where the LPN works, and what is considered safe and prudent care by other LPNs. For example, if you start an intravenous (IV) procedure even in an emergency situation, and you are not IV-certified, you have broken the law, as outlined in the nurse practice act, and you are liable for your behavior even if there is a good outcome from your actions. Why? Because you broke the law. Even if the outcome is good, you could be sued because you have broken the law.

The second example refers to following the policies and procedures in your workplace. Imagine that you are working the night shift and have a nursing assistant call in sick. You are responsible for the care that is given regardless of the number of people who report to work. After a great deal of effort, you are still unable to replace the sick assistant, and the entire shift is minus one person. On the unit, you have a resident who is notorious for wandering at night. Without the additional nursing assistant, you do not have adequate staff to watch the resident and keep him from falling, so you restrain him. The night goes well, and you feel that you have successfully used good judgment. However, the restraint is still on the resident when his daughter comes to assist him with breakfast. She approaches you with an angry look and states that her father has been unlawfully restrained. She leaves the unit to contact other family members and eventually an attorney. The policies and proce-

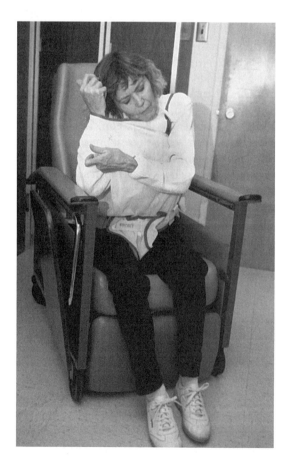

The use of restraints on elderly people is the result of ageist thinking and old nursing traditions.

dures for your nursing home will determine if the family will win this case or not. If your unit has a policy of a restraint-free environment that requires resident or family permission to restrain (as required by the Omnibus Budget Reconciliation Act [OBRA]), or has a policy of calling the administrator whenever there is not adequate staff, you will lose the case. The policies and procedures in your work environment are "the law" of the facility and must be obeyed carefully to protect clients as well as your licensure.

Safe and prudent care is what most LPNs would give in the same situation. If you were being sued for putting the restraint on the nursing home resident described above, your attorney might ask three or four qualified LPNs to testify about what they would do. This is the same principle as that used with the question "What is reasonable under the circumstances?" This legal concept should force every nurse to think in terms of safe and prudent care with each activity performed. The question is, "Would another LPN do the same thing under the same circumstances?"

The concept of omission is very straightforward. It occurs when you omit something that is either ordered or expected as a normal part of treatment for a client. Classic examples of omission involve treatment or medication. Omission could also involve failure to notify a supervisor or physician of a situation with a client. Many lawsuits are based on omissions of care.

There are many issues within the realm of nursing that are profoundly affected by both ethical and legal concepts. The purpose of this chapter is to discuss issues closely associated with nursing care of the elderly, such as the use of restraints, advanced directives, informed consent, and elder abuse.

USE OF RESTRAINTS

The long-practiced tradition of using restraints has been an accepted aspect of nursing care of the elderly until recently. According to the National Center of Health Statistics (1990), at any point in time approximately 41% of the people in nursing homes in this country were subject to physical restraints. According to the Nursing Home Coalition of New York State (Rudder, 1990), 60% of nursing home residents in that state were in restraints in 1990. In addition, 93% of those who are placed in restraints remain in them for the rest of their stay. A U.S. Food and Drug Administration (FDA) survey indicated that a national average of 22% of nursing home residents were kept in physical restraint and 27% were chemically restrained. It is important to note that the use of restraints in this country is significantly higher than in European countries. Only 4% of nursing home residents are restrained in Scotland and England, and the numbers are fewer in Sweden and Denmark (Powell, 1993). Fortunately the numbers have changed regarding restraint use in nursing homes during the past few years. Current literature now shares research and information on how to work with elderly persons in an effort to avoid restraint use. This is a positive sign. Even so, health-care statistics still indicate that 500,000 persons a day are restrained for some reason while in the care of health-care providers.

Thoughts about the ageism that exist in our society have been shared in Chapter 1 of this book. One of the premises of this author is that restraints are allowed as a "care" modality with elderly clients because of ageism. The fact that society allows the use of restraints for frail elderly people and refers to that intervention as nursing care should be appalling to anyone who reads this book. The feeling of being appalled over something is a feeling based on ethical thinking, structured after the value system of you, the person with the feeling.

The implementation of OBRA in 1987 had a positive impact on decreasing restraint use in nursing homes. The OBRA regulation states that the resident has the right to be free from any physical restraint imposed or psychoactive drug administered for the purposes of discipline or convenience and not required to treat the resident's medical symptoms. Federal statistics state that the use of restraints has declined by 50% since 1987 because of the implementation of OBRA.

The OBRA Interpretative Guidelines define physical restraints as: any manual method or physical or mechanical device, material, or equipment attached or adjacent to the resident's body that the individual cannot remove easily which restricts free movement or normal access to one's body. Physical restraints include leg restraints, arm restraints, hand mitts, soft ties or vasts, and wheel chair safety bars (Health Care Financing Administration, 1992). Chemical restraints are defined as ". . . a pharmacological drug used for discipline or convenience and not required to treat medical symptoms" (Health Care Financing Administration, 1992).

The nursing home industry is successfully striving to reduce the use of restraints and to make restraint alternatives the standard of care. Current federal laws clearly create a strong reason not to use chemical or physical restraints. The law places on the nursing home that uses restraints the burden of justifying their use as the least restrictive alternative available. Many LPNs work in nursing homes and have to deal with the ethical and legal concerns surrounding the use of restraints on a daily basis.

What are the laws that govern the use of restraints in hospitals? These laws are written by the individual state legislatures and are not managed under the umbrella of a federal law. They also are controlled by current hospital policy. This makes the use of restraints in hospitals not only a legal issue but an ethical issue of great importance. It is often true that where there are less restrictive laws written, there is a need for a higher ethical awareness and concern. Generally, the laws regarding the use of restraints on elderly people in hospitals are less defined and the decision to apply restraints is the decision of the nurse who is responsible for the elderly person. How does a nurse make the decision to apply restrictive devices on a person, generally without that person's permission? And what theory of nursing or nursing principle allows that to happen without being questioned by other health-care providers?

Why Are Restraints Used?

The main reason restraints are used on elderly people is to prevent injury from a fall or a wandering episode. This is a laudable reason; however, in the current environment of resident/patient rights, the use of restraints should be re-examined. Other than the desire to prevent injury, the decision to use restraints comes from two recognizable sources. The first is nursing tradition. Prior to the 1960s and the invention of the antipsychotic drugs, severely mentally ill people were placed in state mental hospitals and often were securely restrained to avoid their hurting themselves or others. Once drugs were invented that managed their psychotic behavior, most of these clients were released from restraints and actively participated in psychotherapy. Those who did not respond or did not respond sufficiently to the drugs continued to be retrained.

How did this nursing tradition of protecting psychotic people from themselves and each other become translated to a standard of care for the elderly? As the citizens of this nation have aged, there are more and more "old, old" people who demonstrate the normal losses of aging. The percentages of old people with dementia has increased simply because more people are living to be older. Somehow in this scenario, nurses and other health-care providers have decided that a treatment modality for psychotic individuals is acceptable for frail elderly persons. It is important to question the ethics of that decision. Does it demonstrate the art of nursing, the science of nursing, the value system of nurses in general, or does it represent a misplaced, outdated nursing tradition?

The second reason many nurses use restraints is the fear of litigation. Often when given a viable option for care that does not require a restraint (e.g., validation therapy, as described in Chapter 11), nurses still use a restraint to avoid being sued. They want to avoid a lawsuit that results from the fall of an unrestrained elderly person. The most frequently cited reason for using restraints is to prevent the elderly person from falling. Yet few nurses recognize that 200 deaths of institutionalized elderly clients per year are attributed to the use of restraints. Choking on a vast restraint is the most common form of death while restrained (Weick, 1992). Numerous studies (Evans and Strumpf, 1990; Johnson, 1990; Kapp, 1992) have been reviewed in search for injury outcomes, including serious falls, which were related to the prolonged use of restraints. The results showed that elderly people are injured, sometimes fatally, while becoming agitated and trying to escape from their restraints. Examples from these studies include climbing over the siderails, strangling and suffocating with a restraint that has slipped or been improperly applied, and the failure of staff to monitor and adjust restraints at regular, timely intervals. The use of chemical restraints often results in confusion and/or personality alteration.

Many nurse managers feel that apprehension over liability, or at least being caught as an involuntary party in litigation, is frequently the reason for using restraints. However, it is time for nurses to examine themselves professionally and consider whether the behavior is based more on a paternalistic bias toward the elderly, is done for staff convenience, or derives from a desire to control client behavior. The motivation for this practice needs to be strongly examined both in terms of legal and ethical principles.

I feel that if restraints were removed from the standard repertoire of the LPN, creative and effective nursing-care strategies would surface. Care would be based on the individual needs of each elderly person, and each person would be treated as an individual of value. The objective of care could and should be a restraint-free environment. Once restraint-free environments are in place for a period of time, a new and improved nursing tradition will have been created.

A Restraint-Free Environment

One of the important concepts for you, the licensed nurse, to understand is that there is no scientific basis to support the use of restraints to protect elderly people from injury. The exact opposite is true. Careful scientific research has shown that restraints can reduce a person's functional capacity and create problems with most body systems. With that in mind, the development of a restraint-free environment should be a priority for health-care providers who sincerely care about the physical and emotional condition of their clients. How is that type of environment established?

Use of Least Restrictive Devices

You, the caregiver, should always be thinking in terms of the least restrictive device possible for each client. The truth is that you do *not* want a resident to fall and sustain an injury, or to wander out of the building and become lost, or worse. The least restrictive approach would include the use of pillows, wedge cushions, pads, and lap trays. The criterion for each of these items is that they can be removed by the elderly person. The devices should serve as a reminder rather than a restraint. The concern over wandering can be dealt with in numerous ways. There are many commercial alarms available that will warn the employees when a resident walks through the doorway. Placing a rope or Velcro strip across doorways that should not be used by confused residents will work as a reminder in some situations. Having well-educated and caring volunteers available at peak activity times enhances both the safety and enjoyment of most residents. The use of validation therapy (See Chapter 11) will often reduce the anxiety and, therefore, pacing behavior of some people.

When establishing a restraint-free environment, it is important to see each resident as an individual with rights and a history. Do some people pace or wander at a specific time each day because of a lifelong habit? A recurring concern? An unresolved life event? It is important to determine whether the resident's history is the cause of the wandering behavior.

Other Considerations

The staff in either a hospital on nursing home should have some common strategies for managing confused older people. There may need to be a policy of placing mattresses on the floor or of lowering the bed near the floor to keep a night wanderer from falling out of bed. There should be a means of communicating very clearly and deliberately to the staff those people who are at risk for falls and have a program of monitoring them that is effective. If wandering occurs more frequently at night or in the late afternoon, then these are the times the staff should be increased so residents can be closely monitored. Currently in most facilities, evening and night shifts are times of minimal staffing.

Implementing a restraint-free environment requires the education of everyone on staff, including ancillary people, to the principles of working in a restraint-free environment. Along with the education program, it is important to assist staff to focus on their personal values regarding care for the elderly. This should help in establishing desirable approaches to care. A restraint-free environment is an innovative care strategy that also requires thought by bright and creative people who feel a commitment to the rights of all people, especially the elderly.

ADVANCED DIRECTIVES

One of the most difficult situations that health-care professionals face when caring for the elderly is how to assist patients and families trying to make decisions about whether to start, continue, or stop life-sustaining treatments. Elderly people as a group comprise 73% of deaths each year, making end-of-life treatment decisions far more prevalent among them. Documents that assist the health-care team in making such complex decisions are advanced directives. There are two types of advanced directives documents available: the durable power of attorney for health care (also called health-care proxy) and living wills.

The *health-care proxy* has the authority to make health-care decisions if the individual loses the ability to make decisions or communicate personal wishes. The proxy can make decisions as the need arises and is not restricted to a decision that was make previously without knowledge of the current situation. The other type of advanced directive is known as a *living will* (Fig. 5.1). This is a legal document that allows individuals to share their opinions and wishes regarding their death. The legal statutes that govern the use of advanced directives vary from state to state. You, as a licensed nurse, must clearly understand the advanced directive laws where you work.

Advanced directives came into use when legal cases such as those involving Karen Ann Quinlan and Nancy Cruzan surfaced in the judicial system. Both were situations in which a young woman was kept alive, on life-support equipment but had no quality of life at the time and no possibility of improvement in the future. In both cases, the family members decided to remove the life-support equipment and allow their daughters to die. In both cases, the health-care facility refused to remove the equipment and the parents sued.

In 1989, the U.S. Supreme Court ruled that not even the family should make decisions for an incompetent patient without "clear and convincing evidence" that indicated the person's desire was to die if incompetent. In a five-to-four decision by the U.S. Supreme Court, the following rights were listed for states (*Cruzan v. Director,* 1990):

* The state has a right to assert an unqualified interest in the preservation of human life.
* A choice between life and death is a very personal matter.
* Abuse can occur when incompetent patients do not have loved ones available to serve as surrogate decision makers.

After this court ruling, the majority of state legal systems began requiring an advanced directive on admission to health-care facilities to predetermine the actions that should be taken if a patient became incompetent. As an LPN, you need to deter-

INSTRUCTIONS

CHOICE IN DYING
LIVING WILL

PRINT YOUR
NAME

I, _____,
being of sound mind, make this statement as a directive to be followed if I become permanently unable to participate in decisions regarding my medical care. These instructions reflect my firm and settled commitment to decline medical treatment under the circumstances indicated below:

I direct my attending physician to withhold or withdraw treatment if I should be in an **incurable or irreversible mental or physical condition with no reasonable expectation of recovery.**

These instructions apply if I am a) **in a terminal condition;** b) **permanently unconscious;** or c) **if I am minimally conscious but have irreversible brain damage and will never regain the ability to make decisions and express my wishes.**

I direct that treatment be limited to measures to keep me comfortable and to relieve pain, including any pain that might occur by withholding or withdrawing treatment.

While I understand that I am not legally required to be specific about future treatments, **if I am in the condition(s) described above I feel especially strongly about the following forms of treatment:**

CROSS OUT ANY
STATEMENTS
THAT DO NOT
REFLECT YOUR
WISHES

    I do not want cardiac resuscitation (CPR).
    I do not want mechanical respiration.
    I do not want tube feeding.
    I do not want antibiotics.

    However, I **do want** maximum pain relief, even if it may hasten my death.

ADD PERSONAL
INSTRUCTIONS
(IF ANY)

Other directions (insert personal instructions):

Figure 5.1   Living Will. For instructions on completing this document see Appendix B. To obtain a copy of a legally valid living will for a specific state, contact Choice in Dying at 1-800-989-WILL. (Reproduced with permission from Choice in Dying, Inc.)

These directions express my legal right to refuse treatment, under federal and state law. I intend my instructions to be carried out, unless I have rescinded them in a new writing or by clearly indicating that I have changed my mind.

SIGN AND DATE THE DOCUMENT AND PRINT YOUR ADDRESS

Signed: _____ Date: _____

Address: _____

_____

WITNESSING PROCEDURE

I declare that the person who signed this document is personally known to me and appears to be of sound mind and acting of his or her own free will. He or she signed (or asked another to sign for him or her) this document in my presence.

Witness: _____

Address: _____

_____

TWO WITNESSES MUST SIGN AND PRINT THEIR ADDRESSES

Witness: _____

Address: _____

_____

PAGE 2

mine what the law is in your state regarding advanced directives. If they are required on admission, you need to know where they are and what they say regarding your clients. It is the role of the nurse to be an advocate for the people to whom care is given. Knowledge about the advanced directive and the state laws that govern its use is very important to you.

When one is working with advanced directives there is more involved than just knowing the law. The law represents legal responsibilities. These are serious responsibilities and should not be ignored; however, as in every issue, there is also an ethical component. It is the ethical responsibility of every nurse to be sure that the person signing the advanced directive is not coerced and has full understanding of what is being signed. In most states the nurse is *not* allowed to witness this document. It is important that outsiders who would not wield undue influence act as witnesses.

Whenever you are giving care to a patient who is in a terminal condition, it is important that you listen to them as they talk and give them honest answers to their questions. If someone feels concern over what was written in the advanced directive, you should bring that to the attention of the nurse manager. In all situations, it is necessary to keep in mind the primary objective of the advanced directive: to follow the wishes of the person who wrote it.

INFORMED CONSENT

Another very similar legal and ethical concern is the concept of *informed consent*. The Patient's Bill of Rights clearly outlines a person's right to information before giving consent to treatment. The law says there needs to be a signature on the consent form. The ethical aspect of this situation is that the client has the right to all the information available on the treatment or procedure for which consent is being given. Again, the nurse assumes the role of patient advocate. Would you stop a patient from going to surgery if, as you were assisting him or her onto the cart, the patient asked, "Tell me again, what it is the doc is going to do?" Legal and ethical knowledge says you should.

Obviously, there are better ways to manage this type of situation than to postpone the scheduled surgery. One is to simply be sure ahead of time that the patient has the information needed to make decisions about the health and treatment plan. This can become challenging when the patient is a frail elderly person who is experiencing behavior that ranges from forgetfulness to dementia. Is it enough just to get the signature when you know the client will not remember the instructions? The answer to that question must come from your value system, that ethical aspect of yourself. Do you value the patient and the patient's rights as outlined in the Patient Bill of Rights? Do you value the principle behind the informed consent rule? Hopefully, you do. If that is so, you have a great deal of work to do to protect the rights of all clients. That work may involve reporting the forgetfulness or dementia to the nursing manager. In a nursing home environment, it would be important to share that information at the interdisciplinary team (IDT) meeting; this is a weekly meeting where the interdisciplinary professionals meet to discuss and resolve resident problems. Talking to the family may be something you do or that is delegated to the social worker. The priority is to ensure that the elderly person has full information when asked to make a decision regarding health care.

ELDER ABUSE

Occurrences of elder abuse are on the increase in this country. It is estimated that 5% of elderly people are abused each year, most often by a close family member. Abuse exists in family homes, nursing homes, and hospitals. It is done by family members, paid caregivers, and strangers. It seems to be a consequence of life in Western society, which moves faster and faster, with more and more demands. Into this scenario comes an increasing number of older people who, as a natural consequence of aging, move more slowly and experience mental changes that require patience from caregivers. This country has never had so many older citizens, and society does not seem adequately prepared to adapt to them and their needs.

Because of this lack of emphasis on understanding and meeting the needs of the elderly, caregivers tend to experience burnout. Accompanying this phenomenon is the tendency to abuse the elder for causing the feelings of burnout and frustration. I believe that elder abuse is the most extreme and destructive form of ageism that can be demonstrated. Elder abuse also is against the law.

Every state in this country has laws against elder abuse. Again, it is your responsibility, as a licensed nurse, to determine what the law is in your state, as well as the policies and procedures for handling abuse in the organization where you work. Whatever the particulars of the law are, it will state that you are responsible, under the law, to report all suspected cases of elder abuse.

Elder abuse can occur in many forms. Some of them are:

- Inflicting pain or injury
- Withholding food, money, medication, or care
- Confinement; physical or chemical restraint
- Theft or intentional mismanagement of assets
- Sexual abuse
- Threatening to do any of the above

The composite picture of the person most likely to be abused is a female client, 75 years old, who lives with a relative. She is physically, financially, or socially dependent on others. For LPNs who work in home health care or in day-care centers, this description should be one to keep in mind. Do any of your clients have unexplained bruises or other markings? Do they seem unusually hungry or frightened? Are they unwilling to talk about their family member or do they act fearful when you mention the family member who is responsible for their care? Any of these behaviors could be indications of abuse and deserve your attention.

If you are an LPN in a nursing home or hospital, it is critical to be alert for staff members who treat clients in negative and degrading ways. If a confused client is even more confused or is screaming and crying after receiving "care" from a particular staff member, be on the alert. Another cue is when residents have more bruises after a particular staff member has worked than at other times. Residents who are

The social worker is an excellent resource when dealing with suspicions of elder abuse.

complaining of things being lost may actually be victims of theft. An older person should not have a fearful countenance when a family or staff member comes near; be on the lookout for such behavior.

It is critical that all cases of suspected abuse be reported to the proper authorities. In all settings it is proper for you, the LPN, to report suspected abuse to your supervisor. If nothing is done to prevent the behaviors that seemed suspicious to you, it is both an ethical and legal mandate that you find the proper avenue for reporting your information to a legal authority. You will determine the proper protocol for reporting abuse by reviewing the abuse laws in your state and the policies and procedures in your work setting that govern this situation.

In most situations that elderly person will be moved to a safer environment, or the employee who was performing the acts of abuse will be put on probation, terminated, or arrested. If the abuse is occurring in the home, the situation becomes very complex. The family that allows elder abuse is obviously dysfunctional. Perhaps the abuse is occurring because of parental abuse of the child when the child, now turned caregiver, was younger. Perhaps it is simply a response to the distress of caring for an aging parent. Sometimes, the abused elder does not want to be moved out of the situation because of concern over being moved into a nursing home or other facility. This is a choice the elder person is allowed to make. However, in most situations the family members will be required to receive counseling in an effort to alter abusive behavior.

SEXUAL NEEDS

Another ageist concept in our society is that old people are asexual. Biologically this is simply not true. Sexual needs are as basic as eating and socializing. The aging process does not remove that need from the physiological schema of your clients. The question is how do you provide for the fulfillment or manage the needs of older people for whom you are responsible?

Older people need love, too. I recall attending a conference many years ago where the presenter, a music therapist, made the statement that every person needs 14 hugs a day. I do not believe that she had any scientific data to validate her point, but when she said it, I believed her! She continued to say that most of society finds old people very unlovable and, therefore, unhuggable. I immediately began a lifelong quest to provide as many hugs to older people as I could give in a lifetime. Old people in our society are touch starved; people do not like to touch or hug them. Does this flash of unscientific insight bring to your awareness that *you* can do something positive about meeting this need for your elderly clients? It would be very exciting to see a care plan that said: 14 hugs a day evenly distributed over 24 hours. This approach to the elderly would be positive in assisting them to meet their normal, physical needs identified as sexual.

A myth that needs to be dispelled is that "dirty old men are always reaching and grabbing inappropriate parts of my body!" When this accusation is made, it generally is directed at an older, confused man. Instead of restraining or isolating that individual, you should assess him on a professional level. Sitting with him and asking, "You miss your wife, don't you?" to provoke a discussion of his sexual feelings would be very appropriate. After your discussion with this client, you may learn strategies that will help him manage his sexual feelings in a more appropriate manner. Perhaps he needs a picture of his deceased wife that he can keep with him at all times, for instance, in the dining room, or when he is in the hallway in his wheelchair. It may take something as simple as teaching the nursing assistants to point to the picture of his wife and ask him to tell them about her to ward off his confused attempts at meeting his sexual needs. Perhaps the solution is more complex, and the nursing assistants need to be taught how to stop his inappropriate behavior in a respectful manner that recognizes sexual needs as normal and confusion as a reality. It is your responsibility, in an ethical framework, to determine the approaches and strategies that will provide for effective management of the sexual needs of your clients.

Another problem that occurs at times is that of masturbation. Masturbation is a normal sexual outlet for people who are experiencing sexual frustration. Teenagers generally masturbate as part of their sexual experimentation. Adults often masturbate as part of their sexual relationships with other persons. It is not abnormal for older people to masturbate. It is something they have either done intermittently or have worked hard at suppressing throughout their lives. It is not wrong for an older adult to masturbate; however, because of different levels of cognitive ability, a client may be participating in this activity in an inappropriate place. Masturbating in the day room or in any environment in front of others is not appropriate behavior. If this should occur, it is your responsibility to gently and kindly stop the activity and take the client to his or her room. It is appropriate to leave the person alone there to do as the person wishes. This approach is an effective one to use if the client is acting out for attention or is forgetful or confused. If you walk into a client's room and the person is masturbating, just excuse yourself and close the door.

Often in nursing home settings, there is controversy about allowing married couples to room together or to have time for conjugal visits. Sometimes it is not wise to have couples room together because one may need more care than the other, and the stronger person becomes worn out trying to administer to every need of the ill or degenerating spouse. Abusive behavior brought on because of dementia could be another reason. But only reasons that would jeopardize the health of one or both of the people involved are valid for keeping a married couple separated. It is normal for married people to live together. It is normal for married people to have sex together. The facility that recognizes that normalcy and individual right is to be commended.

Another situation that can occur is that of unmarried, consenting adults having intimate moments. You have the ethical and legal responsibility of protecting demented or mentally ill clients from the sexual advances of others. If that person does not have the ability to make day-to-day decisions, neither does the person have the ability to make the normal, everyday decision to have an intimate relationship. As a licensed nurse, you are responsible for protecting such a person from what could be defined as sexual abuse.

What of those who are not cognitively impaired? Counselors do not go around the halls of high schools or universities to keep teenagers and young adults from holding hands or kissing. Why does society think it is necessary to do that for older adults?

Sexual feelings and expressions are a normal part of living even if one is old, handicapped, or confused. Every dependent human being has the right to expect protection from sexual abuse; but by the same token, every human being has the right to express sexual feelings within the framework of society's norms.

SUMMARY

This chapter covers several diverse topics that have legal and ethical ramifications in giving care to elderly clients. Every topic is one of importance and needs to be addressed by you as a gerontological nurse. Older people have rights and when these people come into the health-care system, you, the licensed nurse, are the unofficial advocate for them. Their legal and ethical rights are your responsibility. The concepts explained in this chapter should help to provide you with a strong foundation for fulfilling that role.

CASE STUDY

As the 11–7 charge nurse on a 20-bed unit at Cherry Dale Nursing Home, you have had concerns over the staffing on your shift. Often you have found the nursing assistants restraining residents "for their own good" without telling you. You have discussed the problem with the nursing assistants and have taught them the rules for restraint application at Cherry Dale, but there still is one "old time" nursing assistant who does not follow the facility's rules and regulations and clearly ignores your instructions.

This is your first charge nurse position as an LPN. You recognize that the nursing assistants see you as an inexperienced nurse. This is especially true of the older nursing assistant. During your first 6 weeks on the job, you feel you have made progress in earning the trust you need from the nursing assistants. However, one or two are still restraining residents at night without telling you or without trying other alternatives.

You discussed this problem with your nurse manager and she simply told you that you were a charge nurse now and it was your responsibility to follow the policies of the facility. The policy indicates that restraints are not used for the convenience of the staff and are not applied without a written order from the physician and permission from the resident or the resident's guardian.

What are the ethical and legal ramifications regarding your current dilemma?

CASE STUDY
DISCUSSION

Because you are the licensed nurse responsible for what occurs on your shift, you are both legally and ethically accountable for the behavior of the nursing assistants who work with you. Because they are violating facility policy, it is as if you were actually performing the act.

It is both unethical and illegal to restrain people without their permission. When this occurs and it also breaks the rules and regulations of the facility, your legal accountability is compounded. It is important you realize that the law is being broken every time the residents are restrained. It does not matter if you know about it or not. The point is that, as the charge nurse, you are supposed to know about it! Reporting the situation to your supervisor does not release you from responsibility either. She gave you clear instructions as to what to do; you are to follow the facility's policy regarding restraints. The ethical problems of restraining residents are as serious as the legal ones.

CASE STUDY
SOLUTION

There is more than one approach that could resolve this problem. The truth is that you may have to use them all before you find an appropriate solution.

- Make it perfectly clear to all the nursing assistants that the law is being broken and the act of restraining residents on your shift is a criminal offense. Then . . .
- Use the experience and wisdom of the nursing assistants to process different solutions to the problem of residents wandering or potentially falling at night. The nursing assistants will appreciate being asked to assist in solving the problem rather than being told what to do. Try all ideas that do not go against the policy of the institution, the law, or your ethical standards.
- Share your creative solutions with the nurse manager. Let her know how "prudent and safe" the care is on your shift. (Remember that prudent and safe care is the care that most LPNs would give in the same situation.) You also should build a case for additional staffing on your shift, if that is the problem.
- Document the unique approaches of care you use on your shift and share them with the other shifts by means of verbal report and the nursing care plan.

Study Questions

Please select the one best answer.

1. Ethics is the study of moral actions and values. One of the dilemmas within ethical thinking is concern over:
   a. Who decides what is right and what is wrong.
   b. Whoever pays the bill deciding what is ethical.
   c. Ethical and legal behavior being the same.
   d. The rules of ethical behavior changing daily.

2. Although you were not IV-certified, if you were to find a client bleeding and in need of immediate fluids to save his life, one of the following defines your legal role. Mark the correct answer.
   a. Under the Good Samaritan Act, you are required to do all you can to save the person's life, so you would start IV fluids and call the doctor.
   b. Call the RN and have her handle it. After all, she has the advanced license.
   c. Call an ambulance for immediate transport.
   d. Administer first aid, leave a nursing assistant with the resident, and call the physician or the RN.

3. The legal concept of omissions in care applies when:
   a. The physician has missed a diagnosis and, therefore, you have omitted treatment for it because nothing was ordered.
   b. You have intentionally or unintentionally missed an antibiotic dose.
   c. Residents are given baths only every other day.
   d. The RN does not work the weekend.

4. A restraint-free environment consists of an environment where:
   a. Many of the residents fall or wander, but they do not sue the facility because they want to be without restraint.
   b. Mattresses are placed on the floor so residents will not fall out of bed.
   c. The least restrictive device is used on each resident.
   d. Restrictive devices are not used for any reason.

5. Elder abuse is a growing concern in modern society. Which of the following statements is correct?
   a. It is against the law to threaten abuse as well as perform abusive acts.
   b. Elder abuse includes inflicting pain or injury, but not confining an older person.
   c. Elder abuse is likely to happen to a male client, over age 85, who lives with a relative.
   d. It is the legal responsibility of the RN to report all suspected cases of elder abuse; this is not the responsibility of the LPN.

REFERENCES

American Hospital Association. (1992). *A patient's bill of rights.* New York: American Hospital Association.

Cruzan v. Director, Missouri Department of Health, 110 U.S. 2841 (1990).

Evans, L. K., & Strumpf, N. E. (1990). Myths about elder restraints. *Image: Journal of Nursing Scholarship, 22,* 124–125.

Health Care Financing Administration. (1992). *Interpretative guidelines to OBRA.* (No. 263-H). Washington, DC: U.S. Government Printing Office.

Johnson, S. (1990). The fear of liability and use of restraints in nursing homes. *Law, Medicine & Health Care.* 263–264.

Kapp, J. D. (1992). Nursing home restraints and legal liability. *The Journal of Legal Medicine, 13,* 1–32.

National Center for Health Statistics. (1990). *Characteristics of nursing home residents' health status and care received: National nursing home survey.* (No. PHS 81-1721). Washington, DC: U.S. Government Printing Office.

Powell, S. (1993). Restraint reduction: Customizing approaches to care. *Provider, 1* (2), 76–77.

Rudder, C. (1990). *Restraint reduction: A consumer perspective.* New York: Nursing Home Community Coalition.

Watson, J. (1985). *The science of human caring.* New York: National League for Nursing.

Weick, M. D. (1992). Physical restraints? An FDA update. *American Journal of Nursing, 11* (8), 102–103.

BIBLIOGRAPHY

Braun, J. V., & Lipson, S. (1993). *Toward a restraint free environment.* Baltimore: Health Professions Press.
   This book is well written and comprehensive in dealing with the issue of restraints on elderly people. It covers current legal and ethical implications and includes OBRA regulations.

Edge, R. S., & Grover, J. R. (1994). *The ethics of health care.* Albany, NY: Delmar Publishers.
   This is an excellent clinical guide to ethical behavior in health care.

Mazey, M., Bottrell, M. M., Ramsey, G., & the NICHE Faculty. (1996). Advance directives protocol: Nurses helping to protect patient's rights. *Geriatric Nursing, 18* (5), 204–210.
   This article thoroughly discusses the definitions, use and ramifications of advanced directives.

Chapter

MARY McCARTHY SLATER AND KATHLEEN R. CULLITON

6

Environments of Care

Learning Objectives

After completing this chapter, the student will be able to:

1. Discuss the role of the licensed practice nurse (LPN) as environmental manager.
2. Describe at least two components of the physical environment that nurses need to consider.
3. Discuss the aspects included in a climate of caring.
4. Identify at least four settings in which nursing care for older adults is provided.
5. Describe how nurses in various care settings meet the needs of older adults.
6. Discuss relocation trauma and ways in which a nurse can help an older person adjust to a new environment.

INTRODUCTION

One of the most important tasks for a nurse is to manage the patient-care environment. Florence Nightingale saved the lives of hundreds of soldiers during the Crimean War simply by cleaning the wards, opening the windows, and providing the soldiers with daily hygiene. Miss Nightingale and her nurses also provided direct, caring, 'hands-on" nursing to the soldiers under her care. Prior to Miss Nightingale's interventions, there were more soldiers dying in the hospitals because of the lack of hygenic conditions than there were dying in the actual battles. Improved health for the men dying during the Crimean War required both environmental management and quality nursing care.

The role of a nurse is not that of a housekeeper but that of an environmental manager. To be effective care givers, nurses must be aware of the influence of environment on the health and functioning of the patient. Nurses are responsible for the manipulation of environmental conditions to improve patient care. In Miss Nightingale's era, environmental management included such tasks as opening windows to clear the patient's room of stale, potentially illness-producing air; managing raw sewage because plumbing was not available; and controlling the population of mice and rats in the hospital. Modern nurses also must understand the effect that the environment can have in enhancing or impeding the progress and functioning of older adults.

ENVIRONMENTAL MANAGEMENT

Providing care to older adults must include environmental management. Assessment of the environment is the first step. The nurse needs to examine the total environment starting with where the older person is living. Good questions to ask include: What is the neighborhood like? Is it a safe neighborhood for an older person? Is there a security system in the home or building? Are there locks to secure the doors and windows? Is there more than one entrance or exit into their living area? Does the home or building have a posted and recognized fire evacuation plan? How far does the older person have to travel to get groceries and medical care? Are there support services in the neighborhood? How can the older person get to the grocery store and doctor's office? If the person drives a car, is the car in safe running order? If the person walks, are the sidewalks and streets free of clutter and debris? Is the sidewalk even or is it raised or buckled in spots? Is the home or apartment in good repair? Is it well maintained and structurally sound? Does the elderly person have electricity, running water, sewage treatment, and garbage services? Do they have to climb stairs to get to their living area? Are the stairs in good repair, and do they have railings?

The assessment of the environment continues to the older adult's living area. This includes the kitchen, living room, bathroom, and bedroom. It is important to evaluate the other areas of the home as well, especially basement areas. Be careful not to assume that the person you are assessing simply stays in the bedroom all day because the individual may be climbing stairs to do laundry, to get food out of the pantry, or even to use the bathroom.

Does the older adult have a working telephone in the home? Does the person have an emergency plan for contacting someone if there is illness or injury? Is there an emergency alert button? Is the living area free of clutter and debris? Can the older adult carry out daily routine activities on one level of his or her home, or does the person have to climb stairs? Do the stairs in the home have handrails and is the stair covering intact without loose carpet or treads? Are there throw rugs in the living areas of the home? Is the furniture in good repair and safe for its intended function? Is the temperature of the living area warm enough or cool enough for the older person? Are electrical appliances in safe working order, and are the cords and electrical outlets safe (no frayed cords and only two cords plugged into any outlet at one time)? Is the older adult using alternative heat sources like electric heaters, kerosene heaters, fireplaces, kitchen stoves and ovens, and heating pads? Are the cords hot or warm to touch if an electric heat source is being used? Is the home properly vented for gas- and wood-burning heating units? Are there smoke and carbon dioxide detectors in the home? Is there a proper three-prong outlet for medical equipment in the home? Is the older person's living area free of noxious and unpleasant odors? How are cats, dogs, and other pets cared for? Is there a litter box? Who empties the litter box? Is food safely stored in the kitchen? Does the older adult have food in the cupboards and refrigerator? Can the person use the refrigerator and the stove? Does the person know how to operate the microwave? Is the older adult able to move about the kitchen well enough to prepare meals and clean up afterwards? Is the older adult able to get to and from the bathroom safely? How difficult is it to get off of the toilet and into and out of the bathtub? Does the bathroom have approved grab rails, or is the older adult using towel bars and other bathroom structures instead of grab bars? Is there a chair in the tub and the shower to avoid overexertion and falling during bathing? Is the living area of the home on the first level and the bathroom on the second level? Are bathroom cleaning supplies in a secure area? Are medications and other drugs in a secure place? Is there enough room in the bathroom to perform procedures such as colostomy irrigation if necessary? If access to the bathroom is limited and the older adult is using a commode, how is the commode being emptied? How is the garbage being emptied? If the person is using products for incontinence, is it convenient to rinse and wash nondisposable diapers and properly dispose of disposable briefs? Are the bed and the bedroom safe? Does the older adult know how to operate the bed and other equipment in the bedroom?

Assessment of the physical environment includes all aspects of the older adult's living situation that can be seen, heard, touched, or smelled. Each of the physical items in the environment can either contribute to or detract from the optimal functioning of the older person. A room that is too hot may make the older person tired, lethargic, and unwilling to participate in personal care activities. A room that is too cold may likewise result in lack of activity because the older person is unwilling to get out of bed or to come out from under the cover of an afghan.

A critical question to ask throughout the assessment of the physical environment is how well the older person functions in the living areas. Is the environment as barrier free as possible? Can the older person walk unencumbered or wheel a wheelchair through the entire setting? Are there features in the environment to promote physical function? These may include grab bars in the bathroom by the commode, shower, or bathtub seat, and handrails by stairs. When assessing the older person carrying out activities of daily living, be aware of possible alterations that may improve function. Lowering a mirror or moving a storage area below shoulder level may improve both safety and convenience. The risk of falling can be decreased with adequate room lighting and the use of night lights. The room where the older person reads should have high-intensity illumination.

Another important part of the environmental assessment is assessing the climate of caring. The climate of caring involves the people in the environment and the environmental tone and atmosphere. The people in an older person's living environment may include family members, neighbors, friends, and paid caregivers.

The people in an environment are extremely important to the older person's potential for improvement and optimal function. Families, staff, and visitors can be encouraging and uplifting or depressing and demotivating. A climate of caring includes persons who present a positive but realistic outlook. The older adult's personal space is respected in a caring climate. Such an atmosphere also affords opportunities for privacy, encourages activity and involvement, and facilitates independence.

Safety

In any setting, safety for the older person is a primary concern. Are there any environmental hazards, such as frayed extension cords, malfunctioning equipment, or broken furniture? Falls among the elderly are common, and not all of them can be avoided, but is the environment free of fall risks? Such risks include clutter, throw rugs, wheelchair leg rests, and poorly fitting shoes or slippers. Many items in the kitchen, such as gas stoves, can be safety hazards if the older person does not have the cognitive abilities for good judgment.

Stimulation and Personalization

Opinions vary on whether environments for older persons with cognitive impairment should be very stark and nonstimulating or should contain eye-catching and stimulating components. More important, however, is a personalized environment for the older person. Personalized items help the older person relate to the environment and maintain a sense of identity. A special picture can be displayed in the hospital room as well as in the nursing home. In some settings, such as nursing homes and retirement communities, the entire bedroom or apartment can be personalized with cherished furniture and decorations.

A climate of caring facilitates optimal independence and autonomy for each older person living in the setting. There are times when the routines and regulations necessary to operate a large health-care facility, such as a hospital or nursing home, cannot accommodate the individual needs or desires of the older person. The nurse must assess, however, which rules and routines are absolutely necessary and which are the result of a controlling institution or individual staff member. While a nursing home may need to serve meals at particular times because of regulations and staffing, the rule that all elderly residents must be dressed for breakfast may be unnecessary. This rule does not allow for each resident to take the time to personally do as much of the dressing as possible. Such a rule forces the resident to be dependent on staff for dressing. A climate of caring provides multiple opportunities for individual choice in the environment and encourages the older person to function as independently as possible.

Personal Space and Territoriality

Personal space and territory are important to every human being. Personal space is the area around a person. Some individuals define their personal space very close to their bodies, whereas others define it as a broader area. It is viewed as an intrusion for someone to invade our personal space. In providing nursing care, nurses must frequently invade the personal space of the patient. Nurses must be conscious, however, that they do not do so unnecessarily.

Territory is the space used by a person and seen as owned by the person. When enrolled in a course, students will tend to sit in the same seats during each class session. Technically, the student does not own the seat, but the tendency exists to define a territory and return to it habitually. The seating arrangement in a dining room in a nursing home or retirement community is frequently consistent for each meal. This

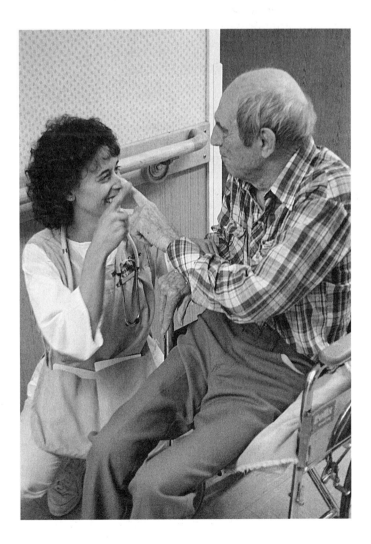

A climate of caring includes people who present a positive, realistic outlook.

tends to occur whether or not seats are assigned. Individuals will defend their territory if an unwanted person intrudes. An older person who has a favorite chair at home or in the nursing home may fiercely defend it from others to the point of physical aggression. The nurse needs to understand and respect the personal space and the territoriality of the older person.

Privacy

All human beings need time to be alone. People need to have opportunities for privacy as well as for human contact. At times, it is difficult for the older person living in a health-care setting to find opportunities for privacy. Many hospitals and nursing homes have multiple-occupancy rooms, so that the patient may never have a chance to be truly alone. As a nurse working with older persons in a congregate setting, you must be aware of the older person's needs for privacy. You should respect that right to privacy by knocking on the door before entering, pulling cubicle curtains during care, and arranging private time for the older person.

Activity and Involvement

As a person ages, the number of social roles fulfilled tends to diminish. An older woman who was once a daughter, a mother, a wife, a neighbor, an accountant, a scout leader, and a bridge player may hold none of these social roles at 90 years of age. Due to aging, death, and disability, these roles may no longer be possible. Involvement with others, however, is still a need. A climate of caring affords each individual multiple and diverse opportunities for activity and involvement with others.

As a nurse working with older people in multiple health-care settings, you can help to provide important opportunities for active involvement. It is important to find out the older person's prior social roles, particularly the ones most enjoyed. Activities that include tasks associated with these roles should be encouraged. It also is important to create opportunities for social interaction. By introducing the older client to others in the setting who may share like interests, and by arranging seating for natural conversation rather than against walls, the nurse can be instrumental in encouraging social exchanges.

RELOCATION TRAUMA

Moving from one environment to another is stressful. Anyone who has ever moved from one house to another, or from one city to another can appreciate the stress of relocation. It takes time to adjust to and become familiar with a new setting. During times of crisis or illness one has less energy available to deal constructively with stress. Older persons are particularly susceptible to being overcome with the stress of relocation.

Older people use a considerable amount of energy coping with chronic illness and disabilities. The onset of an acute illness or some other major crisis requires additional coping. If the crisis or illness results in the need to move to another living situation, the older person's coping abilities may be exhausted. A crisis, superimposed on the day-to-day stresses of living with disability and dysfunction frequently leaves the older person with little coping reserve to deal with the stress of relocation. When the stress is overwhelming and the older person is unable to cope with the situation, there will be signs of decompensation. These may include disorientation, agitation, acting out, and hallucinations. It is not uncommon for an older person newly admitted to any of the health-care settings described in this chapter to exhibit some of these signs. Thus, the movement from one environment to another can be extremely disruptive to the older adult; this disruption has been termed *relocation trauma*.

In addition to identifying and understanding relocation trauma, the nurse can help to relieve relocation stress. It is important to understand that relocation trauma is temporary, and the behavioral signs of decompensation should diminish as the older person becomes familiar with the new environment. You can, however, accelerate this process of adjustment.

Limit stimulation and the introduction of new activities and people on the older person's first day in the setting. Orient the older person to the environment slowly so that the person can incorporate new areas and routines gradually. On the first day, introduce only people and places that are absolutely necessary. Placing an older person in the dining room of a nursing home with 20 other residents shortly after admission may be overwhelming.

Look for ways to provide links between the old environment and the new one. The more familiar the new environment is to the older person, the easier the transition will be. Bringing favorite furniture and objects to the new setting will increase its familiarity to the older person. Including the older person in planning for the move is ideal. This is not always possible, however, if the move occurs because of an acute illness. If it can be arranged, involve the older person in selecting the items to take to the new location.

Scenario

Mrs. G. was moving from her home of 40 years to a retirement community. She had some short-term memory problems and walked with a slow gait. To expedite the move, Mrs. G's son packed for her and sorted through all of her belongings to identify what items to take and what to give away. Because many of her things were very old and worn, her son decided to purchase all new furniture and decorations for her new apartment. The new apartment looked beautiful. After moving, Mrs. G. became extremely disoriented and paranoid and accused everyone of stealing her belongings. As the nurse in the retirement community, what would you have taught Mrs. G's son about preparing his mother for relocation?

Including Mrs. G. in planning for the move to the retirement community would have facilitated her adjustment considerably, although it may have slowed down the process. Allowing her to take time to sort through all of her belongings and make her own choices on what to keep and what to discard either before or after the move would also have been helpful. Even if her own items may not have been the most beautiful, taking them with her would have helped the transition and brought familiarity to the new setting.

ENVIRONMENTS OF CARE

There are a variety of settings where older persons may receive health care and services. This chapter does not discuss all such settings or services but reviews some of the most commonly used environments of care.

Day Care

A number of communities now have adult day-care centers available to provide supervised activities for older adults. Day treatment centers for older people with psychiatric problems and day hospitals for older persons with considerable physical disability are available in many localities. Day treatment centers and day hospitals focus on a particular type of older person and provide specific services to meet their physical and psychiatric needs. Many day-care centers provide transportation to bring older persons to and from the center. Fees for day care may be charged on a sliding scale, according to the ability of the older adult to pay. Few insurance policies, including Medicare and Medicaid, cover the cost of day care, however. Generally, the older person or the family must pay for these services personally.

A typical day in this care setting includes planned activities, such as group discussion, current events, exercise, snacks, and lunch. Volunteers often visit a center to speak on community affairs, health-promotion topics, or to present entertainment programs that encourage group participation. Many centers have activity directors who plan and schedule events that are appealing, offer a variety of choices for the older adult, and promote group interaction.

Nurses working in a day-care setting provide a number of services, according to the needs of the individual. Assessment of the older person's physical, psychological, and emotional functioning is a critical component of the nurse's role in the day-care center. Health teaching to older persons and their families and ways to administer medication may also be included in the nurse's role.

Some older people may need assistance with mobility, toileting, or eating. Other older people may need help in taking medications, whereas still others simply need encouragement to participate in center activities. Nurses in day-care centers need a solid foundation in gerontological nursing to help them in their daily interactions with older people. Such a foundation assures that subtle physical or emotional changes are not disregarded or blamed simply on "old age."

Acute illnesses in older adults can present themselves in atypical fashion. The nurse who knows and appreciates normal aging is better prepared to assess subtle changes in older persons and to be alert to the possible implications of these changes. Because so many older adults have chronic illnesses, medication administration often becomes a major responsibility for the nurse in a day-care center. The nurse needs to be skillful at administering medications, knowing their expected effects and the possible side effects. The nurse also can use knowledge of medications to teach the older person and family members the importance of safe and accurate medication use. Do the older person and the family know which medications are being taken and why they were prescribed? Are the older person and the family aware of possible side effects, potential drug interactions, and the necessary steps to take if problems are suspected? The nurse as teacher has an important role in this setting.

Ongoing assessments of the day-care participants are especially important. Frequent contact with the older person allows nurses to see subtle changes in function that may signal serious underlying physiological problems. The nurse's powers of observation and knowledge of the aging process are critically important in detecting actual or impending illness. Is an older person experiencing mobility changes? Are you seeing decreased participation in formerly active participants? Has a older person had changes in weight or affect? If you are making these types of observations, the next questions becomes, "Why are you seeing these changes?" Good communication skills may uncover a change in family living conditions, changes in medication, or exacerbation of the effects of a chronic illness.

Day-care centers provide opportunities for socializing and staying involved in the world. Many families use day care to give respite to the main caregiver for the older adult. The stresses of caregiving can have a strong effect on the older person, caregiver, and family. Respite allows caregivers some time to see to their own needs. Grocery shopping, housekeeping, socializing with friends, and participating in enjoyable activities for the caregivers can often mean the difference between continued home care versus institutionalization for an older adult. Nurses in day-care centers are able to use their assessment skills to identify the older persons strengths and weaknesses, help elders to continue to participate in daily living activities, and provide information for older persons and their families about community resources.

Although day-care nurses may perform few technical nursing procedures, they use a variety of different nursing skills. Day-care nurses must have particularly strong physical and psychological assessment skills. They also must be adept in communication and teaching. A major responsibility of the day-care nurse is health teaching for older persons and families. Teaching may involve such areas as medication administration, diet restrictions, and safety issues in the home. The day-care nurse also must have a thorough knowledge of community resources and be able to refer the older person and family to appropriate services in the area.

With the increasing awareness and concern about care for people with dementia, there are some programs now available to provide day care specifically for older persons with cognitive impairments. These day programs are designed to give care that takes into account the abilities and safety needs of individuals with Alzheimer's disease or other dementias.

Scenario

You are the licensed nurse at the Golden Ages Adult Day Care Center. Mrs. Y. attends the center every Monday, Tuesday, and Wednesday until after lunch when her husband picks her up. This Tuesday you notice, for the second day in a row, that Mrs. Y. has been unsteady when she walks. She stops to rest frequently when moving around the center and has been falling asleep during group activities. These behaviors are unusual because Mrs. Y. normally ambulates well, participates enthusiastically in center activities, and often encourages others to "join the fun." What further assessment do you now want to make?

Certainly, vital signs will provide some basic information. It also would help to ask Mrs. Y. if she has noticed any changes in the way she feels or functions. When you speak with Mr. Y., you should ask about changes in Mrs. Y.'s routine and medications. He tells you, "She was so upset and restless last weekend, I had to give her one of my sleeping pills to help her calm down and get some rest Sunday night." By using your powers of observation and problem solving, you are able to uncover the need for medication administration teaching for Mr. Y.

Home Care

Home health-care agencies provide a number of services for older adults in the home. Such agencies provide nursing services, given by licensed nurses and nursing assistants, and therapy services, such as physical, occupational, and speech therapy. Many agencies also provide medical supplies and equipment. Most agencies are licensed and, therefore, eligible for state or federal reimbursement for services. Medicare, Medicaid, and community funding may pay for limited home health-care services if the older person qualifies for these types of reimbursement.

Home care may be provided on a daily basis or intermittently, according to the needs of the patient. Nursing care provided in the home has become more complex in the past two decades. It is not unusual for people who need help during their recovery to be discharged from the hospital "quicker and sicker." Chronically ill elders may be receiving home care to avoid frequent hospitalizations.

The LPN in home care works under the instructions of the registered nurse case manager. In the home-health role, the LPN will be assigned basic nursing care, medications administration and teaching, dressings and wound care, and may be asked to spend 4–24 hours in the home to provide respite care to the primary caregivers. The LPN is often asked to work with the certified nurse assistant (CNA) in coordinating care for the patient.

A certain amount of creativity is needed in home-care nursing due to limitations in the type of equipment and supplies that may be available. As in other settings, it is helpful for the nurse to be aware of resources available to the older adult and of ways to gain use of those resources. Nurses who choose home-nursing care can expect a variety of older persons and conditions. Caring for older adults in the home can be very rewarding and challenging. Because the home-health nurse generally visits the older person on a less than daily basis, patient and family teaching is very important. Teaching may be needed to help the family ensure a safe environment for the older adult. Educating older persons and families about fall prevention, medication safety, positioning, and transferring techniques may be needed. A family also may need to learn more complex procedures, such as how to change dressings or give injected medications.

The amount of time spent with older persons is often limited by the nurse's workload and the reimbursement for care given. The nurse is responsible for assessing and documenting care needs and providing prescribed treatments. Good communication skills are important to ensure that all members of the health-care team are aware of the older person's needs and progress.

Scenario

As an LPN for a visiting nurse group, you are assigned Mrs. E. Mrs. E. is 75 years old and lives with her husband in their home. Mrs. E. was just discharged from the hospital following surgery to pin her broken right hip. She is not capable of weight bearing, and the physical therapist is scheduled to visit her at home twice a week. Mrs. E. has mild dementia and frequently forgets that she is not permitted to walk. Her husband, Mr. E., wants to keep her in bed to remind her not to walk. What care do you need to teach Mr. E.?

It would be appropriate to talk with Mr. and Mrs. E. about the hazards of immobility and the need for Mrs. E. to be out of bed. Together with the physical therapist, you teach Mr. E. how to safely transfer his wife in and out of bed and on and off the toilet. With Mr. E., you work out a system to remind Mrs. E. that she cannot walk alone. This may include posted notes and frequent verbal reminders. You also suggest that Mr. E. try to keep his wife in the same room with him as much as possible. Finally, you teach Mr. E. how to do skin checks and observe his wife's bony prominences for signs of redness or breakdown.

Community-Based Care

Nursing opportunities are available in a variety of settings not linked to formal institutions such as hospitals or nursing homes. LPNs may provide care for older adults in a community clinic, dialysis center, or physician's office. In these noninstitutional settings, the nurse may practice under the direct supervision of a physician rather than a registered nurse. Practice in these settings often includes assisting with physical examination and treatments, and nurses in these settings are frequently an important source of information and clarification for patients. The nurse uses assessment skills and provides information on resources available in the community to meet the older person's needs. Contact with older adults in these settings may be more infrequent and briefer than in other care settings.

Scenario

You are the office nurse for Dr. A., a geriatrician. Mr. M., a patient of Dr. A.'s, is 74 years old and recently retired. On this day, Mr. M has an appointment with Dr. A. for a complaint of stomach upset. You notice that Mr. M. is quieter and more withdrawn than usual. What additional assessment would you make?

While you are waiting for Dr. A., you ask Mr. M. if he has had any changes in routinely lately. In reviewing his sleeping, eating, and activity patterns, you note that he said he is getting up early in the morning and not eating well. In the course of the conversation, Mr. M. tells you that he is tired all of the time and does not feel like living. You suspect depression and share your observations with Dr. A. before he examines the patient. Dr. A. assesses Mr. M. further and identifies a clinical depression with suicidal thoughts and prescribes an antidepressant. When he is leaving, you ask Mr. M. if he would mind if you call him in a few days to see how he is feeling.

Licensed practical nurses
working in community-based
care perform a role that does
not exist in other
environments.

Hospice

Hospice care is designed to provide care for the dying patient and the family. A team approach is central to the hospice concept. Team members include physicians, nurses, social workers, and nursing assistants, as well as other ancillary workers. The goal of the hospice is to help dying older persons remain at home, if possible, with all the support needed to ensure a "good death." In this case, "good" means that the older person is kept comfortable and able to receive the support of family and loved ones in a familiar setting.

Hospice work allows nurses to give direct patent care and develop a close relationship with the patient and family. As in the care settings previously discussed, the nurse's role as a teacher is especially helpful. Most families are not prepared to meet the needs of a dying family member. The hospice nurse can teach family members how to provide for the comfort of their loved ones. The nurse also can identify hospice resources available to help families and older persons cope during this extremely stressful time. Nurses who have not worked in a hospice setting may be reluctant to try this type of nursing because all the clients are terminally ill. Talking with nurses who work in a hospice, however, often shows that the team support and the closeness to patients and families provide a high degree of job satisfaction.

Scenario

You are the staff nurse on a medical unit at Hoover Medical Center. One of your patients is Mrs. O., a 69-year-old, married woman with chronic lung disease. Mrs. O. has been on your unit many times. This time, she and her husband realize that her lungs cannot last much longer, and she has expressed that she does not want to be put on a respirator. Mrs. O. wishes to die at home and tells you that she does not believe she will return to the hospital. She seems to have accepted the idea of death but tells you that she is worried about how her husband will deal with her passing. What suggestions can you offer Mrs. O.?

Hospice services are available to individuals with terminal illnesses. They are not exclusively for cancer patients. You talk with Mrs. O. about the services available through the hospice, including grief counseling for her husband before and after she dies. She is very receptive to the idea and you initiate the appropriate referrals.

Retirement Communities

As people age, there is a tendency to simplify lifestyles and living space. The size of the home needed to provide adequate living space for a family can become more of a burden than an asset to older adults. Retirement communities are an increasingly popular way for the elderly to have a home without homeowner responsibilities. Not having yard work and other maintenance tasks associated with a large home relieves a number of burdens. The communities offer a variety of living spaces and services. Apartments, duplexes, or individual homes may be located within the boundaries of a retirement complex. The goal for these retirement communities is to appeal to a broad range of older adults by offering security and a variety of conveniences and services. While communities for retirees have been popular for quite a while, retirement complexes that also provide services for older adults with physical care needs are now increasingly common.

The goal of assisted living units in retirement communities is to provide older persons with help in performing activities of daily living. Frail older persons who do not require continuous care are able to have help in such activities as meal preparation, grooming and bathing, laundry, and housekeeping. Most assisted living programs require that the older person be ambulatory and fairly independent. Much of the care provided is done by nursing assistants rather than LPNs. The practical nurse in an assisted living program often provides supervision for nursing assistants, medication administration, basic documentation of care given, and assessment of the older persons ability to function.

The assisted living nurse also must use creative talents to ensure that the environment is as homelike as possible. This means the nurse must be flexible in tailoring care to the individual needs of each older person. The nursing assistant in assisted living may be called a resident assistant and perform many functions that do not relate directly to activities of daily living. Assisted living nurses and nursing assistants are often very involved in activities and social planning for residents.

Continuing-care retirement communities are designed to meet the needs of older adults along a continuum from complete independence to total dependence. The centers offer not only apartments or cottages for independent older persons and assisted living services but also nursing home care.

For many older adults, the appeal of a continuing-care retirement center lies in the fact that clients are able to stay in a familiar environment regardless of their health status. Nursing in a continuing-care retirement center offers many opportunities. Home visits, health promotion or screening activities (such as blood pressure monitoring clinics), health teaching, or direct bedside care to nursing home patients are a few of the opportunities available to nurses in continuing-care communities. As in assisted living situations, supervisory ability is a valuable asset for the licensed nurse. Retirement community nursing allows nurses to work with older adults who have a variety of needs and abilities. The ability to apply your knowledge of the aging process in this setting helps you to enhance the quality of life for older persons in the setting.

Scenario

As a center staff nurse, you have been invited to the Evergreen Retirement Center's Monday Morning Coffee Club. The center's activity director has asked you to talk with club members about home safety. Make a list of at least four safety concerns for older adults. What suggestions would you give regarding these concerns in speaking to the Coffee Club Group?

Your talk might focus on the following areas:

Problem	Solution
Unable to read dials and gauges on thermostats	Bright, nonglare lighting to enhance visual ability
Potential for falls when walking into the home, while using the toilet, and getting in and out of the shower	Handrails and hand guards
Potential for falls through tripping over items or slipping on unsecured scatter rugs	Uncluttered environment
Hazard of living alone and falling or losing consciousness	Daily networking with family or friends

Nursing Homes

The nursing home is an area of practice that has been available to practical nurses for a number of years. With the growing number of frail elders and the old-old (85 and older), the need for nursing home care remains high. Some nursing home residents need a full range of nursing care; others may be independent physically but have cognitive changes that require a high degree of supervision to maintain their personal safety. In discussing nursing home care, there are two categories of care defined by federal regulation. The first category is the skilled nursing facility (SNF) and the second is the nursing facility (NF). The nursing facility level was previously referred to as intermediate care.

All nursing homes must be licensed by the state in which they operate. If they wish to receive reimbursement from Medicare or Medicaid for the services provided to residents, they also must meet additional federal requirements and be certified by the federal government. A nursing home may choose not to accept Medicare and Medicaid funding and admit only private-pay residents. Medicare, the federal health insurance program for older and disabled individuals, has two parts that can pay for some services in the nursing home. Most persons over 65 years of age have Medicare Part A. This will pay for up to 100 days of care in an SNF if the older person is being discharged from the hospital after a stay of at least 3 days and requires skilled nursing or therapy services. The requirements for skilled services are very specific and should be consulted before assuming Medicare will pay for nursing home care after a hospital stay. Medicare Part B is a voluntary insurance program that many older persons purchase. It will pay for some physician and therapy services and some medical equipment, but it does not pay the daily fee for the nursing home.

Medicaid is a welfare program that pays for over 50% of the nursing home care in this country. Older people must have a very low income to qualify for Medicaid. Many older persons pay for nursing home care privately at the start until they have spent all of their savings. They can then apply for Medicaid. The Medicaid program pays for all medical services in the nursing home.

In an SNF, care is provided by licensed nurses around the clock, and a registered nurse is present at least 8 hours a day, 7 days a week. A SNF unit also offers the services of allied health professionals, such as speech, physical, or occupational therapists, at least 5 days a week. An NF generally does not have the same level of staffing by registered nurses or therapists as an SNF.

Regardless of category, long-term care facilities offer a team approach to meeting the older person's needs over time. Facilities that receive federal funds are required to offer the services of a social worker as well as an activity director and dietetic consultant. Licensed nurses can gain input from a variety of sources in planning and delivering care.

The practical nurse in long-term care has traditionally been responsible for supervising the nursing assistants who give hands-on care to residents. In many facilities, practical nurses mainly give medications or do treatments. With the current emphasis on improving care in nursing homes, nurses can now be part of the team approach in planning and giving care.

The nurse interested in long-term care has the opportunity to get to know residents well over a longer period of time. Due to the changing needs and physical condition of residents, the long-term care nurse needs very good assessment skills. Skills such as monitoring resident responses to treatments, observing for signs of decreasing function, and assessing subtle changes in condition are used by long-term care nurses on a daily basis. Accurate documentation, skillful use of the nursing process, and good interpersonal skills in working with residents, staff, and family members are valuable tools in long-term care.

Care in a nursing home differs from hospital care in many ways. The skills required of the nursing home nurse are no less challenging and the tasks no less difficult than those of the hospital nurse. The goal for the hospital patient is to cure illness in a brief period of time. For the nursing home resident with multiple chronic conditions, cure is not possible. In the nursing home, care rather than cure is the primary focus.

Scenario

Mrs. H., an 85-year-old widow, was recently admitted to Sunny Acres Nursing Home after falling in her apartment and breaking a hip. She had surgery for a hip replacement and can walk short distances, but she is unsteady and tires easily. She is underweight, eats poorly, and does not want to be in the nursing home. Her family lives out of town and is not sure she can live on her own any longer. You are the nurse in charge at Sunny Acres. What are some of the most important areas you would want to assess for Mrs. H.?

Because Mrs. H. was functioning independently prior to her fall, and she does not want to be in the nursing home, the first area you assess is her potential for discharge. What is the prognosis for improvement in function? With what does she need help? Could she return to her own apartment with additional services in the home? Will she fit appropriately into an assisted living program? In addition to discharge planning, your assessment includes mobility function, eating patterns and ability, and evaluation for signs and symptoms of depression.

Acute Care

The final clinical site for working with older adults presented in this chapter is the acute care setting. Most admissions to hospitals comprise people aged 65 years and over. In fact, depending on the source used, it is estimated that 40%–65% of hospital admissions include older adults. Nursing practice in a hospital setting presents a number of opportunities and challenges. Usually, practical nurses are given responsibility for a set number of patients and depending on policy, they may perform a variety of procedures. Most patients are hospitalized only briefly. The emphasis on cost containment and federal mandates means that reimbursement for care is often limited to a set period of time. The concept of diagnostic related groups (DRGs) has allowed reimbursement for hospital treatment to be based on a specific number of hospital days for specific conditions. Hospital-based practice requires all the basic skills the practical nurse possesses. Acute care also generally involves brief contact with a large number of patients.

There are a number of challenges in giving nursing care to older adults in the hospital setting. They include establishing a trusting relationship over a short period of time, dealing with problems secondary to relocation or medications, and resisting the tendency to stereotype patients because of their age. In addition, a major challenge for the nurse working with older people in the hospital setting is to create a

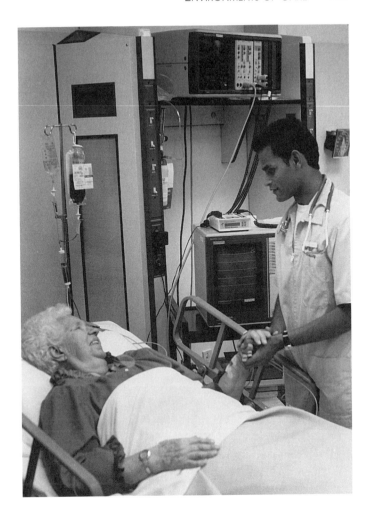

40%–65% of all admissions to acute care hospitals are people 65 years of age and older.

safe and caring environment that facilitates independence. This must be done while the tasks required for the cure and treatment of the patient are accomplished. Environmental management, as discussed earlier in this chapter, is the most difficult task to accomplish in the hospital setting. The short time frame and the urgency for treatment in many situations cannot accommodate the slowed responses and abilities of older persons.

Scenario

Mr. W. is a 90-year-old resident of a nursing home who was admitted to your floor at Hoover Medical Center for treatment of congestive heart failure. He has a significant dementia, is incontinent of bowel and bladder, and is very unsteady on his feet. As his primary nurse, what can you do to make his hospital environment more like home?

You call the nursing home nurse and talk with her about Mr. W.'s habits at the nursing home. You also ask her to send to the hospital any familiar items Mr. W. may appreciate having in the hospital. The nurse tells you that Mr. W. likes to stay up late and is accustomed to remaining in bed until after breakfast. You write this routine into the care plan and pass the information on to the night shift.

SUMMARY

This chapter has provided a brief overview of the nurse's role in environmental management and the various settings where older adults in our society receive health care. Of special significance for the older adult is the opportunity to receive care from a nurse who is familiar with the aging process and uses that knowledge when giving nursing care in any setting.

CASE STUDY

Your neighbor, Mrs. J., asks your advice about finding good care for her 80-year-old grandmother. The grandmother, Mrs. G., lives at home alone in an isolated section outside the city limits. She was recently discharged from the hospital after injuring her right arm in a home fall. The arm is in a cast, which makes it difficult for Mrs. G. to cook and perform other self-care activities. Your neighbor is unable to visit her grandmother daily because of work and child-care commitments and is worried about her grandmother's ability to remain at home. She wants her grandmother to move in with her for at least a month. However, Mrs. G. insists on staying in her own home. Mrs. J. asks for your advice. She ends the conversation with the statement, "I just don't know what else we can do to make sure Grandma is safe and taken care of in her home."

CASE STUDY
DISCUSSION

Based on the above situation and your readings from this chapter, what advice would you offer Mrs. J.?

CASE STUDY
SOLUTION

Considering Mrs. G.'s location and her desire for independence, Mrs. J. could look into home-care services. The assistance with bathing, grooming, and food preparation could be addressed by the home-health agency team and a plan for home care could be developed. There are no indications that Mrs. G. needs the type of care offered by the other agencies or facilities mentioned in the chapter.

Study Questions

Please select the one best answer.

1. Mr. D., 75 years old, is discharged from the hospital after a right-sided cerebrovascular accident. He requires at least 6 weeks further nursing care and physical therapy. The facility most likely to meet these needs is:
   a. A continuing-care retirement center
   b. Hospice care
   c. An intermediate care facility
   d. A skilled nursing facility

2. Hospice care provides a multidisciplinary approach to caring for people with:
   a. A chronic illness
   b. An acute exacerbation of a chronic illness
   c. A terminal illness
   d. A contagious illness

3. The major benefit of living in a continuing-care retirement community is:
   a. Low household maintenance requirements
   b. Services available for a continuum of health-care needs.
   c. A safe environment for elders
   d. The presence of a hospital in the complex

4. Mr. J., 83 years old, has Alzheimer's disease and has wandered from home on several occasions. Mrs. J. is concerned for her husband's safety and desires some respite services. You recommend that she investigate:
   a. A local nursing home
   b. The local senior center
   c. A home health-care agency
   d. Adult day care

5. In the home health-care setting, the licensed nurse can expect:
   a. A limited amount of equipment and supplies to be available
   b. Intermittent contact with patients
   c. To care for clients discharged from the hospital with a number of physical care needs
   d. All of the above.

Bibliography

Burnside, J. (1988). *Nursing and the aged: A self-care approach* (3rd ed.). St. Louis: McGraw-Hill.
   This insightful text shares with the reader concepts of self-care that allow the elderly person to live in diverse settings.
Eliopoulos, C. (1990). *Caring for the elderly in diverse care settings.* Philadelphia: J. B. Lippincott.
   This book provides in-depth information regarding the different care settings available to elderly people.
Hagship, B., & Leon, J. (1992). *Hospice care.* Newbury Park, CA: Sage Publications.
   A complete description of current approaches to hospice care.
Hamm, E. M. (1991). A community responds to respite need. *Geriatric Nursing, 12,* 188–190.
   This article shares ideas for keeping elderly people in their homes through the use of creative respite approaches.
Jacobson, R. B. (1983). Scenes from a nursing home. *Journal of Practical Nursing, 33,* 18–19.
   This is a classic article that gives a view of care in the nursing home environment.
Messner, R. L., & Darby, L. B. (1985). Hospice: A new horizon for nurses. *Journal of Practical Nursing, 35,* 30–31.
   This article provides a clear picture of the LPN's role in hospice care.

Audiovisual Resources

Home Care

Bosch, J. V. (Director). (1984). *My mother, my father* [Videotape]. Chicago: Terra Nova Films.

Bosch, J. V. (Director). (1991). *My mother, my father: Seven years later* [Videotape]. Chicago: Terra Nova Films.
> *These two videos tell the story of Alzheimer's disease from a very personal perspective. It is a portrayal of the beginning of the disease through the first 7 years. It is a touching and insightful set of videos.*

Films for the Humanities and Sciences (Producer). (1990). *Home care* [Videotape]. Princeton, NJ: Films for the Humanities and Sciences.
> *A meaningful description of home care skills for the LPN.*

Hospice

Kaiser Permanente (Producer). (1993). *Quality of time: An introduction to hospice* [Videotape]. Irvine, CA: Concept Media.
> *Excellent video productions on the hospice concept.*

Opportunities for Learning (Producer). (1992). *Death and dying, closing the circle* [Videocassette]. Mansfield, OH: Opportunities for Learning, Inc.

Community-Based Care

Age View, Inc. (Producer). (1990). *All about aging* [Videotape]. Lubbock, TX: Age View.

Centre Production (Producers). (1984). *Softfire* [Videotape]. Boulder, CO: Centre Productions.
> *These videos emphasize the importance of maintaining the elderly person in the home with home care support.*

Acute Care

Video Press (Producer). (1991). *Understanding your elderly patient* [Videotape]. Baltimore, MD: University of Maryland at Baltimore, School of Medicine.

Video Press (Producer). (1992). *Transitions* [Videotape]. Baltimore, MD: University of Maryland at Baltimore, School of Medicine.
> *These videos reinforce the importance of understanding the uniqueness of elderly clients when they are hospitalized.*

Long-Term Care

Bosch, J. V. (Director). (1989). *Seven days a week* [Videotape]. Chicago: Terra Nova Films.
> *Excellent videos that describe the nursing home environment and its uniqueness.*

Cohen, S. (Producer). (1991). *One seat* [Videotape]. Baltimore, MD: University of Maryland at Baltimore, School of Medicine.

Cohen, S. (Producer). (1991). *Working with families in long-term care* [Videotape]. Baltimore, MD: University of Maryland at Baltimore, School of Medicine.

CLINICAL PRACTICE

Chapter

MARY ANN JOHNSON

Common Medical Diagnoses

Learning Objectives

After completing this chapter, the student will be able to:

1. Identify differences between acute and chronic stages of common medical problems of older adults.
2. Describe at least two common physiological changes in each body system found with older adults that are thought to be "normal" as the person ages.
3. Describe nursing care appropriate for chronic care of an older adult who has one or more of the common pathologies discussed in this chapter.

INTRODUCTION

Older adults develop multiple health-care and medical problems that often complicate the nursing and medical treatment plans. Elderly clients often have at least three chronic diseases or health-care problems by the time they reach 65 years of age. In contrast, younger people frequently see a physician or enter a hospital with a single health problem.

This chapter has been developed to provide information in three areas. They are:

- The differences between the acute and chronic states of a problem or medical diagnosis. More emphasis is placed on problems related to chronic rather than acute situations because of the frequency of chronic problems in older adults.
- The differences between nursing care for acute and chronic medical conditions. For more detail regarding the acute phase of illness, the student is referred to the many texts that are available to explain signs and symptoms of the acute phase of medically diagnosed illnesses.
- The effect of the normal changes of aging on medical symptoms. These are discussed in terms of the specific effect that aging has on a health problem.

Five body systems have been selected for discussion. The changes in these systems are commonly found with older adults in any setting. Frequently seen medical conditions are included as examples of the disorders that affect each system. Often these conditions do not occur alone. For example, two or more cardiac problems may be present at the same time, and arthritis often occurs with other chronic conditions. The medical conditions to be discussed include the following:

CARDIOVASCULAR SYSTEM
Coronary heart disease (CHD)
Congestive heart failure (CHF)
Hypertension (HTN)
Peripheral vascular disease
NEUROLOGICAL SYSTEM
Cerebrovascular accident (CVA)
Parkinson's disease
Sensory changes
Vision
Hearing
PULMONARY SYSTEM
Chronic obstructive pulmonary disease (COPD)
MUSCULOSKELETAL SYSTEM
Osteoarthritis
Osteoporosis
ENDOCRINE SYSTEM
Diabetes mellitus
Hypothyroidism

ACUTE VERSUS CHRONIC CONDITIONS

Acute medical problems are those that develop rapidly. The person experiencing an acute problem notices symptoms for minutes to less than a month. These acute symptoms may be caused by some previous chronic condition, such as CHF, or the pathology may be caused by a change in body function that is related to aging. For example, changes in kidney function could induce acute renal failure. Conversely, an acute problem may be due to an infection.

Traditionally, chronic conditions exist for at least 6 months and create some disruption in biological, sociological, and psychological function. Examples include both physical and emotional conditions that are not limited to the older population. However, chronic health problems are common with older people. Approximately 80% of older people who live in the community have at least three chronic conditions. Arthritis, heart conditions (including hypertension), and sensory changes occur most frequently.

There are a number of ways to distinguish between acute and chronic medical conditions. Acute conditions may be thought of as requiring more immediate and often more sophisticated or technical levels of treatment. The goal in an acute condition is to cure the problem.

Chronic conditions develop over time and often are not noticed by the client until major deficits become manifest. These conditions tend to require more help from the informal system of caregiving, specifically from the family or home-health nurse. Often the client develops a partnership with members of the informal system to gain more control over the chronic disease. Cure is not the goal with chronic conditions. From a nursing standpoint, the goal is to provide care that is helpful in managing the chronic condition. This should be focused on assisting the client to function at the highest possible level in the physical, social, psychological, and spiritual arenas of life. Achievement of this goal should provide a higher quality of life for the individual and decreased morbidity (disability). An alternative goal is to work with the client to enable the person to die with dignity, a realistic goal that needs to be acknowledged when working with people who have chronic, debilitating diseases.

Nursing care requires observation of the patent's physical functioning, which makes this one of the responsibilities of the nurse. In the acute phase of illness, it is essential that the nurse note responses to medical treatments such as medications or surgery. New signs and symptoms may arise because of such treatments. All changes must be reported, because the new symptoms may be critical in determining whether to continue treatment, or they may indicate complications.

Nursing care for people with chronic diseases also requires the nurse to observe the person's physical functioning. In addition, it is important to have the observations of informal caregivers. The most critical information comes from the chronically ill person's observation of personal symptoms and overall condition. For treatment to be most effective, the person must be "tuned in" to the body's responses to treatment or to changes in total body function.

Various stressors may exacerbate a chronic but stable disease both in the short and in the long term. Such stressors can include uncertainty about the future, starting a new treatment, or the development of an acute condition. For example, a patient with emphysema may develop pneumonia, and although penicillin may cure the acute condition, the pneumonia may cause a flare-up of the previously controlled chronic emphysema.

Many nurses and other health-care workers have difficulty working with people with chronic conditions. There is a tendency to look for time lines, to place limits on how long the condition may last, or when it might get worse. It is critical for you, the licensed practical nurse (LPN), to recognize that each chronic condition has its own pattern. Some conditions, like cancer, may get progressively worse. On the other hand, for the person with a CVA, the recovery and return of ability depend on the part of the body affected. There is no accurate prediction or measure of recovery because of variabilities from person to person. Other conditions may not change over months or years. This can be seen with multiple sclerosis, in which a person goes through a period of remission or absence of symptoms that lasts for a prolonged period.

Patients with a chronic health problem, such as hypertension, may have to learn to cope with a disease in which there are no visible signs of pathology. Some patients may not realize the disease is even present. Medications for hypertension often have side effects that cause patients to stop taking the drugs. Other patients stop taking their medication for hypertension when they "feel good" or believe the condition has been "cured." This can occur with both physical and emotional conditions and is something that the knowledgeable nurse frequently assesses and works to deter.

Working with people with chronic conditions is a challenge for the nurse. It is not uncommon for people with chronic diseases to become discouraged. This type of nursing care calls on the creativity of the nurse in assisting the older person to conserve time and energy to participate in activities that have meaning for the individual. Fatigue should be prevented and ways have to be found to help the chronically ill person learn to cope with loss and change. Use of a self-care model in providing nursing care can help patients maintain their remaining abilities. The nurse, patient, and family form the team that is needed to encourage self-care. A crucial part of the team's function is maintaining good communication. This begins with an understanding of the past history of the older person. One part of that past history comes from a review of systems.

REVIEW OF SYSTEMS

To determine pathology and functional ability, a review of systems is used as part of the history and physical examination. This review covers all the body systems in an orderly fashion. One purpose of the review is to uncover symptoms that may be associated with the current health problem.

Another goal is to identify chronic conditions that may have persisted for years and to learn how the person has managed those conditions over time. The review also is a method of gathering data that can help in deciding on the appropriate type of treatment. For example, some medications may not be appropriate if the person has problems with falling.

The review is especially useful for an older adult because:

1. Older people frequently have nonspecific, atypical symptoms. The review helps to identify possible causes for present problems. It is a method of defining the usual and unusual for the individual.
2. Changes of aging may affect two or more body systems simultaneously. The review can help to demonstrate how an interaction between systems occurs.
3. Older people often have a complex history. Here, the review can help to tie the past into the present problem.

For the system review, each system and the usual questions asked are listed. Any positive response to a question is followed by other questions to determine the extent or duration of the problem and treatment, if any. It is desirable to have information about treatment used in the past and the effectiveness of those treatments. Treatments include medications bought "over the counter" (OTC), as well as those prescribed by a physician.

Pulmonary System

- History of frequent colds or upper respiratory infections?
- Cough? Productive or nonproductive of sputum?
- Appearance of sputum (not saliva)?
- Dyspnea whether on exertion, positional (orthopnea), or during the night (paroxysmal nocturnal dyspnea)?
- Immunization history (Pneumovax and influenza)?
- Exposure to anyone with tuberculosis and knowledge about a skin test (PPD) for tuberculosis?

Cardiovascular System

- History of hypertension?
- History of murmurs, irregular heart beat, or palpitations?
- Fainting or falls, especially when changing position?
- Chest pain (at rest or after exercising) or presence of edema?
- Easy bruising? Varicose veins? Anemia? Blood clots (if so, where)?

Gastrointestinal System

- Food and fluid intake (a typical 24-hour food intake, number and size of glasses of water and other fluids)? Who prepares the meals? Any food intolerances? Likes and dislikes? Vitamins taken? Use of alcohol or tobacco?
- Stomach or abdominal discomfort before or after meals?
- Problems with bowels and frequency of use of laxatives (what types)? Presence of hemorrhoids (any bleeding, pain, itching)?
- Nausea or vomiting (under what conditions)?

Musculoskeletal System

- Pain, stiffness, or discomfort in joints (when or under what situations)?
- Pain or cramping in muscles (when and under what situations)?
- Weakness of arms or legs? Swelling in joints? History of broken bones or other injuries to muscles or bones?
- Ability to walk? Distance traveled before stopping (reason for stopping)?
- Use of assistive devices such as cane or walker (if so, under what circumstances)?
- Type of daily exercise or activity?

Genitourinary System

- Difficulty holding urine and under what conditions?
- Burning, pain, or bleeding on urination?
- Sense of fullness in bladder even after urinating?

Women

- Number of pregnancies? Any problems?
- Symptoms associated with menopause?
- Vaginal drainage? Itching? Burning?
- If sexually active, any pain or discomfort?

Men

- Nocturia? Dribbling after urinating or difficulty starting to urinate?
- If sexually active, any problems?

Neurological System

- Falls or fainting with or without dizziness? Steady or unsteady gait?
- Periods of amnesia or forgetfulness?
- Inability to hold on to objects?
- History of stroke?
- Difficulty with vision or hearing? (If present, ask to describe).
- Loss of feeling or numbness in legs or arms?
- Headaches?

Endocrine System

- History of increased thirst, urination, or hunger?
- Dry skin, loss of hair, or thinning of hair?
- Intolerance to either heat or cold?

This review of systems provides only a baseline of information. As a physical examination is performed, the client frequently remembers other symptoms or events to be added to the history. Often the first contact with any client does not provide all the information that may contribute to an understanding of the person's health problems. The person may believe that symptoms were not important at the time, or the symptoms may simply have been forgotten, so that the review remains incomplete. Consequently the systems review is always left open for additional information that may help with both the planning and continuity of care.

CHRONIC ILLNESSES COMMONLY FOUND IN OLDER ADULTS

This section provides some background information about chronic conditions frequently found with older adults. The primary focus is on continuation of care rather than on immediate treatment and nursing care.

Cardiovascular Conditions

Coronary Heart Disease (CHD)

The term *coronary heart disease* indicates that the heart muscle is not receiving a blood supply adequate to meet its needs. Included under this category are angina pectoris, myocardial ischemia and infarction, arrhythmias, congestive heart failure, valvular diseases, and hypertension. Three of these are discussed to show how some of the changes of aging may compound a person's ability to manage the condition. The first example includes angina and myocardial infarction (MI).

A heart attack (MI) may be the first indication of CHD for an older person. This condition is found in both men and women over 65 years of age. The morality rate for those over 70 years of age is about twice the rate for younger individuals. Cardiovascular disease is the leading cause of death and disability in older adults. The symptoms of an MI for the older person are often atypical. Instead of chest pain, there may be delirium or a change in behavior, fainting, stroke, dyspnea, or gastrointestinal symptoms such as nausea and vomiting. Chest pain occurs even less often in the person over 85 years of age.

Because of the atypical symptoms, the diagnosis of myocardial ischemia or infarction may be difficult in older people. For example, the electrocardiogram (ECG) may not be as specific in diagnosing an MI as for younger people because of age-related changes such as ventricular hypertrophy. The cardiac enzymes, especially creatine kinase (CK; also known as creatine phosphokinase, CPK) may not be elevated as much as in a younger person because of decreased muscle mass. Therefore, nurses who work with older people need to be alert to the possibility of an MI even when the usual signs do not appear.

Medical management for the older person is essentially the same as that for a younger person. Coronary artery bypass surgery, for example, has been demonstrated to be effective in older adults. Decreasing risk factors such as obesity, smoking, and hypertension also help decrease the probability of a heart attack. One goal of medical care is to avoid complications. Congestive heart failure, arrhythmias, thrombi/emboli, and extension of the infarction are common complications. These may be prevented by close monitoring during the acute phase after MI.

Some people will restrict their activity following MI and become less capable of self-care. Decreased activity can lead to a situation called *deconditioning*. This may compound aging changes in the musculoskeletal system, such as decreased muscle mass and decreased muscle strength. The ability to balance activity and rest to avoid incapacity requires a strong cooperative effort among family, patient, and health-care personnel. Referral to cardiac rehabilitation may help the person to identify individual abilities and limitations and avoid deconditioning. Older people are capable of recovery and may return to their usual lifestyles. At other times, however, alterations in lifestyle may be necessary.

Congestive Heart Failure (CHF)

The majority of people with CHF are over 60 years of age. This condition is defined as one of congestion in the circulatory system, due to cardiac malfunction. The common causes of CHF in the elderly include hypertension, heart valve calcification, myocardial ischemia/infarction, cardiac hypertrophy, arrhythmias, thyroid disease, and anemia. An acute episode of CHF can be brought on by treatment for other conditions. For example, overaggressive intravenous fluid replacement (too much, too fast), or medications such as beta-blockers (e.g., propranolol [Inderal]) are common causes for some people. The symptoms of dyspnea and frequent nighttime wakening often lead to fatigue and decreased activity.

The goal of medical treatment is to reduce the workload on the heart and help the heart pump better. Older people are able to maintain a normal cardiac output unless they are under physical or emotional stress. The presence of CHF is a pathology that can decrease cardiac output. Use of drugs such as digoxin is still a primary treatment. Digoxin is most frequently used when atrial fibrillation occurs with the CHF. Some older people have taken digoxin for many years. Periodic blood level evaluation of this drug is necessary to prevent toxicity and ensure that the drug is still needed. If the dose is too high (even 0.25 mg may be too high), side effects, such as confusion, may result. Other drugs include diuretics and those that increase dilatation of the blood vessels. A side effect with these drugs is falling, which results from a drop in blood pressure with change in position (orthopnea).

Nursing responsibility in chronic CHF includes monitoring the older person for:

* Presence of edema in feet, legs, sacral area, lungs, abdomen, and around the eyes. Look for increased fluid in any "dependent" parts and weight gain, especially when appetite is decreased. Often people gain weight because of fluid retention but lose actual body weight. This type of weight gain and loss can lead to decreased endurance and increased workload on the heart. A weight record is helpful to monitor fluctuations daily to weekly, depending on severity or level of control of the CHF.
* Blood pressure changes with change in position (postural hypotension). Blood pressure and pulse should be checked after 5–10 minutes of rest in a flat position, again within 1 minute of sitting, and again 1 minute after standing. Also ask the person whether dizziness occurs with these changes. A drop of 20 mm

Hg in pressure on changing position is significant. Patients need to be taught how to control balance before walking and how to use support equipment, such as a cane. The medication may need to be changed, or the patient may not be drinking sufficient fluid. Postural hypotension may result from a physiological change of aging in which the body does not respond to pressure changes due to changes in pressure receptors in blood vessels. The cause of postural hypotension may be any or all three of the preceding possibilities.

- Maintaining a balance between rest and activity is critical to prevent fatigue and accompanying inability in self-care. Most patients find that they benefit from a daily routine that allows for short periods of activity followed by rest. During the acute phase, activity should usually be minimal: possibly sitting in a chair for 30 minutes three times a day. As cardiac function improves, increased activity is possible. The activity level should be determined by the physician and closely monitored by the nurse.
- Maintaining adequate diet to prevent loss of lean body mass. The person's appetite may be decreased, or fatigue may be so great that five instead of three meals a day are needed. A reduced-salt diet (2–3 g/d) may be prescribed, although many people do well on a diet with no added salt and no foods that are high in salt. Decreased sodium intake may make food unappetizing and can cause anorexia. Use of spices instead of salt (e.g., cinnamon, thyme, lemon) and commercial salt substitutes may improve the taste of some food.

Hypertension (HTN)

A blood pressure over 160/90 is regarded as HTN for any age group. This condition is still the leading cause of death and morbidity in the United States. The prevalence of HTN increases with age, and about 40% of those over age 65 are affected. Men, African-Americans, and obese people tend to be at greater risk. Most research now supports the need to treat a systolic HTN above 160 mm Hg and diastolic HTN over 90 mm Hg. Several factors associated with aging may predispose the older person to HTN. For example, stiffening of the aorta, increased cardiac afterload (the force needed to pump blood from the ventricle), and increased peripheral vascular resistance may be present. Changes in the baroreceptor reflexes may be indicated by fluctuation blood pressures during physical activity or emotional experiences. Other causes for HTN may include changes in the kidney and endocrine system due to aging.

Blood pressure measurement is one of the most important items of physical examination. The following are some guidelines for obtaining an accurate blood pressure reading in older adults:

- Allow the person to sit quietly for 3–5 minutes before taking a blood pressure reading. Older adults, especially when physically deconditioned, require more time to adjust to a baseline function even after a "minor" stress, such as walking into an examination area.
- Select the size of cuff appropriate to the person: the regular adult cuff may be too large or too small. Use of a pediatric cuff for small arms and a large adult

or leg cuff for obese people is essential for accuracy. The cuff should be about 20% larger than the diameter of the arm.

- An auscultatory gap is often found with older adults. To avoid an inaccurate systolic reading, palpate the brachial artery and inflate the cuff in increments of 10 mm Hg while palpating. When the pulse disappears, inflate the cuff another 20–30 mm Hg, then listen for the sounds as you deflate the cuff. The first sound may be followed by a "gap" of 20–30 mm Hg before the sounds are again heard.

- If this is the first contact with the older adult, take readings on both arms to determine whether there are differences of more than 10 mm Hg. If there is an arteriosclerotic plaque in the right subclavian artery, the blood pressure is lower in the right arm. The correct reading is then obtained from the left arm.

- Determination of orthostatic hypotension is needed especially when monitoring the effect of antihypertensive drugs. (See previous note under Congestive Heart Failure regarding technique.)

- If you have difficulty hearing the last sound for diastolic pressure, take the reading of a muffled sound as diastolic pressure. Make a note of this in your recording. One technique that can facilitate the diastolic reading is to elevate the arm above heart level.

Another nursing care technique for someone with HTN is the monitoring of medications to ensure the maintenance of regular doses and the person's willingness to continue taking the drugs. The usual reason for a person to discontinue the drug or alter the dosage schedule is the experience of unpleasant side effects. The specific side effect varies with the class of drug (e.g., angiotensin-converting enzyme inhibitor, calcium-channel blocker, diuretic). Examples of side effects that may cause the person to stop taking the drug include constipation, drowsiness, depression, cough, dizziness related to orthostatic hypotension, anorexia, and, in men, impotence. In addition, some patients stop taking diuretic medications if frequent trips to the bathroom interfere with their sleep or their daily activities.

When a person has had consistent systolic pressure reading of 150 mm Hg or above and then has a normal reading (120/80), further checking may be required. The drop may be due to side effects of medication, or the person may have altered lifestyle preferences. It could also be an indication of a heart attack. The usual symptoms of an MI may not be present, but the person will be more fatigued and have less strength or energy to do things.

Teaching good health habits related to diet and exercise is also a nursing function. Some people may be placed on dietary restrictions, such as no added salt, reduced cholesterol, or reduced calories. Severe restrictions are usually not needed, but basic teaching is needed to alert the client and family to factors that can help control blood pressure. If these measures are successful, medications may not be needed.

Efforts to reduce blood lipid levels in people over 75 years of age are still considered questionable by some practitioners. Measurements of fasting cholesterol and high-density lipoprotein (HDL) are minimal laboratory tests to determine lipid levels. The older person may have more difficulty than a younger person in changing a lifetime pattern of eating. Use of a food diary may help with this change. Periodic contacts with nursing staff should check not only adherence to the diet but also the person's reaction to the changes that have occurred. Emotional support provided in this way increases compliance with difficult dietary changes.

The use of regular exercise in controlling blood pressure is just as important for older people as it is for younger people. The physician may prescribe aerobic exercise, especially walking, as an adjunct to control blood pressure and weight. Regular exercise may be just as beneficial as medication for some people. When people do not exercise regularly, they tend to start too fast. Instructions should be given for a minimum of 5 minutes of warm-up and stretching, and a gradual increase in the amount of time spent in aerobic walking. Usually the older adult can start with 10 minutes of aerobic walking 2–3 times a week. The time and frequency of aerobic activity can gradually be increased by 5–10 minutes each week. The person should be taught how to take a pulse to ensure that the pulse does not go beyond that person's maximum limit during the peak workout time. The maximum is based on resting heart rate and age. A cool-down period of at least 5 minutes is also needed following exercise.

Peripheral Vascular Disease

The maintenance of good vascular supply to the extremities is critical for older people. When blood vessels are affected by both arteriosclerosis and aging changes, the nutrition of tissues is impaired. Both arteries and veins may be involved at the same time. This results in a depleted oxygen supply and retention of waste products in the body.

Evidence of decreased vascular function is indicated by skin ulcers resulting from venous statis. Venous stasis is marked by changes in the skin, such as thinning and dryness or overgrowth of epidermis. A permanent brown discoloration may appear because of small hemorrhages (petechiae). Any slight trauma to the area can break the skin and begin an ulceration. Prompt treatment is needed to avoid infection. Even when an ulcer is healed, the area is always at risk for further breakdown. Concern about the condition may cause the person to limit activity. Functional problems, e.g., limited ability to ambulate, may result.

Prevention of further trauma and interference with blood supply is the guide for nursing intervention. Patients can be taught to:

- Keep the legs elevated when sitting, unless arterial insufficiency is also present.
- Avoid constricting clothing, such as hose with elastic bands.
- Avoid extremes of temperature (hot or cold).
- Keep the legs uncrossed when sitting.
- Use cotton socks or stockings and properly fitted shoes.
- Report any break in the skin as soon as possible.
- Avoid applying tape or any irritants (salves) to the area.

Neurological Conditions

Cerebrovascular Accident (CVA)

The third leading cause of death for older adults continues to be a CVA or stroke. This is true despite increasing emphasis on prevention. One risk factor for stroke is advanced age. Other risk factors include hypertension, diabetes mellitus, transient ischemic attacks (TIAs), and heart disease (such as a myocardial infarction or CHF). The mortality rate has declined over the past decade, yet about 40% of those who experience a stroke die within 1 month. About 60% of those who do survive must cope with some disability and physical impairment. Such coping may involve sensory or motor abilities, memory, or language and other communication skills.

There are several ways to classify strokes. They are:

- By type: thrombosis (large vessel or small vessel, also called lacunar), embolism, or hemorrhage.
- Location of the ischemia or the infarction: the posterior or anterior circulation such as the brainstem, pons, cerebellum, or medulla; or the cortex.
- Rate of development of the stroke: slow (sometimes called *stroke in progress*) or sudden and massive.
- Brain hemisphere: right or left hemisphere, or dominant or nondominant hemisphere. This last classification is used herein for the discussion of treatment and continuity of care.

Once the patient has been stabilized, usually in the hospital, planning for discharge and follow-up care is needed. Rehabilitation should begin as soon as possible, preferably in the hospital. Such an early beginning helps prevent the development of some of the physical complications of a CVA. Two common complications are contractures and skin breakdown. Continued care aids in regaining prestroke abilities, providing emotional support, and maintaining physiological defense mechanisms, such as resistance to infections.

Classification of stroke on the basis of the involved hemisphere is important because it points to the type of nursing care required. The goals for care and the way the nurse interacts with the patient are particularly affected. Frequently, the patient with a right hemisphere stroke:

- Has problems accurately determining level of abilities
- Has problems in learning due to a shortened attention span
- Is easily distracted from tasks
- Is unable to transfer learning from one situation to another
- May show poor judgment about the lack of ability that occurred because of the CVA, and take risks leading to injury
- Is unable to determine distance or rate of movement of people or objects because of poor spatial perception
- Retains language abilities and can convince others of abilities that do not exist, such as stating, "I can walk" when in reality, the person cannot safely do so.
- May have visible deficits such as weakness or paralysis on the left, or nondominant, side of the body

These patients are a challenge for you, the nurse. The nurse has to help the patient and family cope with many frustrations, including conflict between the patient and caregivers, which may result from the patient's denial of disability or from impulsive behavior (acting without thinking). The patient may be totally unaware of the effect of this behavior, and the family must be constantly alert to the potential for injury to self or others. This type of behavior may persist throughout the remainder of the person's life.

In contrast, the person with a left hemisphere stroke will tend to have more visible disabilities. These include:

* Problems with language and physical function.
* A need for adaptation of all activities of daily living if the dominant hand is affected.
* A tendency to be more cautious than those who sustained a right hemisphere stroke in their behavior. The tendency is to take few risks and deny the extent of their abilities (rather than extent of disability).
* A tendency to engage in repetitive behavior such as washing the same body part over and over again.
* May have weakness or paralysis on the right, or dominant, side of the body.

The goal of care for the person with a left hemisphere CVA is to improve physical ability. Physical, occupational, and speech therapies should be included as part of the interdisciplinary team. Fatigue may require scheduled rest times, but limit should be placed on the length of time allowed for rest.

Other losses also occur that are independent of the hemisphere involved. Neglect of one side of the body may first demonstrate itself in failure to eat food placed on one side of the tray or by failure to turn toward a visitor. Homonymous hemianopsia (loss of vision in the left or right visual field; Fig. 7.1) or bitemporal hemianopsia (loss of the peripheral and/or temporal area of vision) may cause each of these symptoms. Therapy to teach the person to consciously look at a "total picture" of self and surroundings is needed.

Prevention of complications is a major component of poststroke care. After a stroke, the person is frequently at risk for infections (respiratory and urinary), falls, malnutrition, repeated strokes, and deconditioning due to lack of activity. Prevention of complications includes all of the following:

* At a minimum, immunizations for Pneumovax, influenza, and tetanus
* Keeping a routine for urination
* Monitoring fluid and food intake

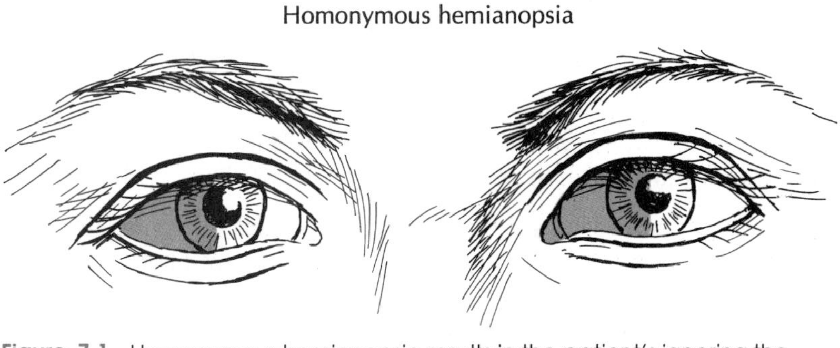

Homonymous hemianopsia

Figure 7.1 Homonymous hemianopsia results in the patient's ignoring the entire side of the body that he or she cannot see.

- Monitoring medications
- Maintaining mobility and independence at optimum levels

Older people tend to drink inadequate amounts of fluid. Teaching both the patient and family ways to ensure consumption of 1500–2000 mL of water per day is useful. Some people fill a quart bottle with water every morning and drink from that throughout the day, periodically refilling it. When encouraging fluids, however, be sure the client does not have difficulty swallowing. People with swallowing difficulties after a stroke frequently have more difficulty with fluids than they do while swallowing solids.

The client's appetite may be affected by an inability to use a knife and fork. Occupational therapy should help with instruction on new ways for self-feeding. Meal plans may need to be altered to help the patient lose weight or control sodium or cholesterol levels. Medications are often used to control HTN, cardiac arrhythmias, and blood clotting. When a person begins to feel better, it is common to believe some medications are no longer needed. It is critical that compliance with medications is frequently assessed. Accurate determination of blood pressure in the home or physician's office is essential. Listening to the apical heart beat instead of relying on radial pulse is advisable. Laboratory work to follow prothrombin time and international normalized ratio (PT/INR) is critical (see Chapter 14). Following a set schedule to maintain a balance between rest and activity helps to minimize fatigue and to promote activity. Many older people who live at home may need continued follow-up after discharge from the hospital or nursing home. Home-health care is important for the client to maintain optimum health.

Parkinson's Disease (PD)

Parkinson's disease is found more often in men than women. The condition can begin as early as the mid-40s but usually appears between 60 and 80 years of age. This is chronic, progressive disease that is marked by slow movement, rigidity, unstable posture, and tremors at rest. There are some known causes for Parkinson-like symptoms but no known cause for PD.

The primary treatment for PD is medication; most commonly carbidopa or levodopa (e.g., Sinemet). Selegiline hydrocloride (Eldepyrl) has proved beneficial for younger people but not for older adults.

This condition also requires active involvement of the person affected by the disease as well as the family. Education of the patient and family should be a primary objective for every nurse. Important information to be imparted includes:

- Defining the disease and its problems
- Side effects and individual reactions to medications
- Methods to promote independence and activity while providing for safety

Some people with PD become very depressed and withdraw from social contacts. The person with PD can help to prevent depression by identifying times when fatigue occurs. The beneficial effect of medication may "wear off" close to the time for the next dose. Activity planned around these times of fatigue and decreased drug effect will help to maintain physical and social function.

As the disease progresses, the person is at risk for several complications. Infections, gastrointestinal problems, and injury from falls are most common. Respiratory infections occur when swallowing is affected. Aspiration of food and fluids can lead to pneumonia and malnutrition. Urinary tract infections may result from urinary retention and from inadequate fluid intake. Eye infections may result from seborrhea (a dandruff-like skin problem).

Constipation is a common gastrointestinal problem due to a lack of bulk-type foods and fluids. Problems swallowing can lead to anorexia. Nausea and anorexia are common side effects of the medications. Consumption of semisolid foods or those with the consistency of pudding, and foods with a high water content, such as fruits, may help.

There is a tendency for the person with PD to be physically unstable. Many falls can be prevented by the use of a cane or walker. Safety devices should be installed in the home, such as handholds in the bathroom and banisters in the stairway. Floor coverings and furniture should provide a barrier-free route for walking. Shoes that fit well, are lightweight, support the foot, and do not cause either slipping or too much friction are needed.

The goal is to maintain the person's function for as long as possible. A secondary goal is to support the family as they help to manage the daily activities of the elderly person. Coping with the changes that usually occur is difficult for most families. Referral to support groups and helping with problem solving are two important nursing functions.

Sensory Losses

Many adults find that visual and hearing losses begin around 50 years of age. The eyeball changes shape for most people so they become farsighted and require glasses for near vision, for example, when reading. This aging change is referred to as *presbyopia*. Changes in the shape of the lens and a yellow discoloration may alter the person's ability to focus and to distinguish colors.

Three common pathological conditions experienced by older people include cataracts, glaucoma, and macular degeneration. Clouding of the lens resulting in cataracts is the most common pathology found with the eyes. Blurred vision and difficulty with nighttime driving may be the first clues of cataract formation. Current techniques for 1-day surgery have relieved the problem for most people who experience cataracts. Other eye conditions, however, require more adjustment.

Glaucoma is still a major cause of blindness and results from increased pressure in the eye that destroys the optic nerve. Central vision is usually retained, but peripheral vision is lost. People speak of having "tunnel vision." This condition is generally controlled with medications instilled in the eye daily. All people over 40 years of age should have a yearly examination for increased intraocular pressure (above 22 mm Hg).

Macular degeneration destroys the point of maximum sight—the macula. Blindness does not result, but the person losses central vision. Peripheral vision is retained around that central blind spot. Increased magnification helps many people. Some people learn to adjust head positions in order to use peripheral vision. Use of zinc and vitamin B supplements has been effective for some people in decreasing the extent of this degeneration.

Hearing loss increases with aging and is noted more among men then women. This may be due to an aging change called presbycusis that occurs without previous injury or other known cause. Hearing difficulties carry both social and emotional consequences because communication with others suffers. Many people tend to talk more loudly to those who are hard of hearing. Speaking loudly results in sounds' becoming more muddled, so that comprehension is worse. Some people are helped by the use of hearing aids, whereas others cannot be helped in this way because the type or extent of hearing loss. Adjustment to a hearing aid may be difficult because of lack of finger dexterity. The inability to tune out distracting noises may discourage individuals from using the aid.

The person with either visual or hearing loss should be informed about available services. Centers for the visually impaired in large cities can provide teaching and materials to assist people to use their remaining vision. Often people can be taught ways to compensate for the loss. Audio amplifiers are available for the hearing impaired. These can provide greater amplification and are especially useful in open-room areas.

Some general guidelines for nurses working with visually or hearing-impaired older adults are listed below:

- Face the person before beginning to speak. Avoid sitting in front of a window or light so there will not be any glare. Glare reduces the ability of a person to read lips.
- Speak clearly and slowly so that words are distinct.
- Try not to exaggerate your speaking voice.
- If possible use low pitch in speaking.
- Touch the person to indicate where you are.
- Identify yourself by name and explain why you are there.
- Keep the patient's glasses and hearing aid clean.
- Refer to local, state, or national resources for assistance (e.g., centers for the visually impaired, audiologists, Lion's Club for help with glasses).

Pulmonary System

Chronic Obstructive Pulmonary Disease (COPD)

Chronic obstructive pulmonary disease is a pathological condition resulting from exposure to irritants (especially tobacco smoke) and is not limited to older people. Chronic bronchitis, asthma, and emphysema are included in this very broad category. Chronic obstructive pulmonary disease is the fourth leading cause of death for those over 65 years of age. The primary signs and symptoms are cough and shortness of breath. The lungs become hyperinflated and the diaphragm flattens. The person must use abdominal and intercostal muscles (accessory muscles) to breathe. Use of these muscles requires more energy than use of the diaphragm.

Some older adults who develop a barrel chest appear to have developed COPD. Their appearances may be due to increased residual volume of air because of destruction of the alveolar walls. In this condition, there is less lung surface for diffusion of gases. Alternately, the person may have a severe kyphosis of the thorax. This condition should not be confused with COPD.

Different forms of COPD have distinct symptomatology; however, the end result for all forms is chronic lung disease with a strong negative effect on physiological and emotional function. Often there is one event, usually an infection, that causes the person to recognize the chronic nature of the condition. There is no "typical" pattern to the disease process, except that COPD is progressive and serious complications do occur, especially repeated infections. Hypoxemia may result with any form of COPD.

Deconditioning occurs when a person is inactive. Deconditioning is defined as loss of muscle strength and endurance. The person becomes less able to care for self or to engage in social and physical activity. A vicious cycle may result: inactivity leads to loss of muscle strength, which in turns leads to more deconditioning.

The adjustments a person with COPD has to make in lifestyle, habits, and work can be overwhelming. Prevention of complications is the primary goal of chronic care. Each person (and family member/significant other, when available) needs knowledge about the disease process and how to aid in self-care. Teaching self-care includes:

- Ways to prevent infections with balanced diet, balanced rest and activity, avoidance of situations in which spread of infection may occur, and use of influenza and pneumococcal immunizations.
- How to recognize signs and symptoms of infection, such as increased cough, change in sputum, and decreased tolerance for activity.
- Instruction in self-medication, including the use of oxygen, the purpose of each medication, and side effects to be expected.
- How to keep track of the medication schedule and medications to avoid, such as cough suppressants.
- Explaining the need for adequate hydration (2000 mL/d unless other conditions such as heart disease rule this out).
- How to distinguish between anxiety and airway obstruction on the one hand, and measures to control both, on the other.
- How to develop a support group or how to locate one.

Musculoskeletal System

Osteoarthritis/Degenerative Joint Disease (DJD)

Osteoarthritis is the major chronic condition reported by older adults. The incidence of arthritis increases with increasing age. Destruction of the joint cartilage occurs, often followed by overproduction of tissue at the joint margins. The result is a visible enlargement of the joint, especially in the knees and fingers. The most common form, degenerative joint disease (DJD) or primary osteoarthritis, develops from an unknown cause. Inflammation of the joint usually does not occur. Primary arthritis is permanent and progressive. However, it can also fluctuate or vary in intensity. Secondary osteoarthritis develops from a combination of physical stress on joints and a medical problem such as diabetes or inflammation. Gout and rheumatoid arthritis are examples of this form.

The person with DJD usually reports joint stiffness in the morning with limitation of motion and muscle aches, cramps, or spasms. The extent of these symptoms varies from person to person. Some people have very little joint pain or stiffness. Others may experience joint pain most of the day. There is no specific treatment; however, the goals for treatment include:

- Control of pain with nonsteroidal medications, such as ibuprofen
- Weight loss if the person is overweight

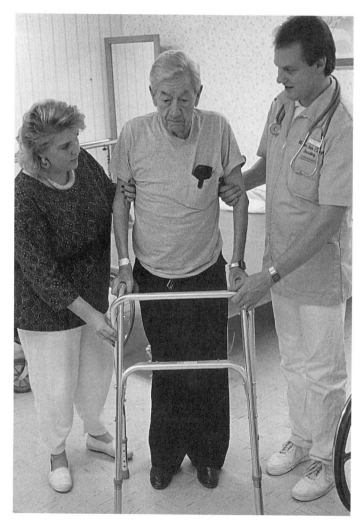

Use of a walker and other devices can decrease the pain and stress on joints while exercising.

- Maintaining activity
- Coping with physical and lifestyle changes

To reach these goals, it is usually helpful for the person to understand the nature of the condition to avoid the use of unhelpful ("quack") treatments. It also is important to learn to identify events or activities that increase and decrease pain in order to promote self-care.

Another critical aspect of care is to teach the client to use medications to prevent pain, rather than to control pain after it has started, for example, before activity or on a routine basis. Meal planning is another challenge. The meals should meet but not exceed caloric needs. (This can be a problem for those with low income, with minimal sources of emotional support, or lack of energy to change eating habits). The nurse should teach the client to plan activities around the time of day when the person feels best and there is less pain.

Learning the proper use of moist heat, physical therapy exercises, and equipment (e.g., a walker) to decrease pain or stress on joints can be done with a physical therapist. Keep in mind that the walker or other equipment may need to be examined to ensure that it is appropriate for the person's needs. The nurse should focus on teaching the client self-expression to maintain self-esteem, decrease depression, and promote social interaction. Referral to an arthritis support group and use of their teaching materials may be helpful to the person and family.

Osteoporosis

The term "brittle bones" has been used to describe this condition. Actually the bone is not brittle, but bone mass is decreased because bone is reabsorbed faster than it is formed. This results in greater risk for fractures. There are two forms of osteoporosis: type I and type II. Type I is found primarily with women after menopause and is thought to be related to lack of estrogen. White women with fair complexions and women (white and Asian) with small body build are especially at risk. Type II can occur among both sexes with increasing age. (See Box 7.1 for other risk factors.)

Type I affects the spongy (trabecular) portion of bone such as the one in the ends of long bones. Type II affects both compact bone found in the middle portion (diaph-

---

Box 7.1   RISK FACTORS FOR OSTEOPOROSIS

Positive family history for osteoporosis
Inactivity or immobility
Low calcium intake (below 800 mg/d)
Gastric or small bowel resection
Smoking
High intake of alcohol
High intake of caffeine
Long-term use of glucosteroids or anticonvulsant drugs
Hyperparathyroidism
Low body weight

ysis) of long bones and trabecular bone. Regardless of type, the person may not be aware of having osteoporosis until minimal trauma results in a fracture of a rib or wrist.

A major goal when working with someone with osteoporosis is to maintain safety. Injury due to a fall, especially a hip fracture, is one of the most frequent consequences. The resulting loss of mobility and restriction of activity creates emotional problems and places the person at risk for other physical problems such as skin breakdown and constipation. In addition, treatment is long and costly.

A major nursing responsibility is to teach the person and family to identify hazards in the home and community. Some "simple" techniques that can be used to help maintain safety are the use of grab bars by the toilet in the tub or shower and the use of a sliding board or tub chair for bathing. The house should be carefully examined for safety hazards such as "trippers" (e.g., scatter rugs, electric cords, uneven pavement, and pets). The client should be taught to maintain postural balance by rising slowly and avoiding sudden movement or hyperextension of joints such as neck and hip. Another area in which teaching is beneficial is the identification of risk factors, for example, limiting use of caffeine sources to one a day. Limiting the use of tobacco and alcohol may help decrease the progress of osteoporosis. Increasing the consumption of sources of calcium, such as fortified low-fat milk, yogurt, and cottage cheese will also increase the intake of vitamin D.

Metabolic and Endocrine Diseases

Noninsulin-Dependent Diabetes Mellitus (NIDDM)

This form of diabetes mellitus is more common with older adults than the insulin dependent form. Although the pancreas continues to produce insulin, the amount is not sufficient for carbohydrate metabolism. The reason for this pathology is not clear. Some people believe that a virus is responsible for triggering the destruction of the beta cells that produce insulin in the pancreas. This view is consistent with the state of immunodeficiency that is present with aging. Others believe that the body becomes resistant to insulin as the percentage of body fat increases and lean body mass (muscle) decreases with aging. The latter belief has been supported by the effect of weight loss on control of hyperglycemia.

The way in which an older person may demonstrate symptoms of NIDDM is different from that of younger people. Older people tend to have anorexia, dehydration, confusion/delirium, incontinence, and decreased vision. In addition, it is not unusual for the older person to have high triglyceride and cholesterol levels along with high glucose level. The main complication of NIDDM is hyperglycemic, hyperosmolar, nonketotic coma. In this case, the serum glucose level is elevated, but ketosis is not present as it is with insulin-dependent diabetes mellitus.

There is no cure for NIDDM, but usually it can be controlled with diet alone. When the person is overweight, a reduced caloric intake coupled with regular exercise is recommended. Oral hypoglycemic drugs may be used if control is not achieved with diet and exercise. Some older adults may need insulin when control is not achieved. In most instances, medications should be avoided because they may cause hypoglycemia.

The usual precautions against diabetes are needed for people with NIDDM. The types of complications found in diabetes mellitus, such as skin lesions and renal and neurological problems, may also be typical of aging. Therefore, teaching about skin care, protection of the feet, periodic eye examination, dental care, and recognition of infections is just as important for people with NIDDM as for those who are insulin dependent. The nurse also needs to teach the client how to follow a regular schedule involving medication, diet, exercise, and blood glucose monitoring.

Hypothyroidism

This condition has been found to be common, especially among older women. The presence of a low thyroid level is often overlooked, because of the similarity between the symptoms of hypothyroidism and characteristics of aging. Symptoms of hypothyroidism thought to be typical among older adults are fatigue, memory loss, slowing of thought processes, slowed speech, intolerance to cold, loss of equilibrium, constipation, and sleep apnea.

The current belief is that older people benefit from treatment with thyroxine even if they have subclinical hypothyroidism. Caregivers often attribute behavioral changes in an older person only to aging. Even small deficits of thyroxine or small increases in thyroid-stimulating hormone can result in slowed reactions. A follow-up of

Hypothyroidism is common among older women. The symptoms are often ignored because they are confused with characteristics of aging.

blood levels of the thyroid replacement is needed within 4–5 weeks after beginning therapy or within the same period after a dosage is changed. People must be taught how to recognize signs and symptoms of over- or undermedication. It is especially important to monitor respiratory and cardiac function. People usually begin to notice improved function within a few days of starting treatment.

SUMMARY

Although all these conditions have been discussed separately, you have probably noted that there are similarities in approaches that can be used. Involvement of the patient has been stressed throughout. The need for exercise, high-quality meals with lowered caloric intake, and prevention of complications are three common themes. The following case study serves as an example of thinking out a unified approach to the care of people with chronic conditions.

Case Study

Mrs. O. is an 82-year-old widow who has lived alone since the death of her husband last year. She was able to care for herself with all activities of daily living and had help with light housekeeping, shopping, and banking. During the past 6 months, her energy and endurance have lessened and she has gained 10 pounds. Her appetite has not changed, and her food intake is reported as "the same as before." Her social activities include church and contact with her three children and grandchildren at least once a week. Mrs. O. has been told she has "beginning" cataracts in both eyes, which need to be checked every 2 months. The only symptoms she has noted are blurring of vision and increased glare, especially at night. She has been treated for several medical problems including osteoarthritis, hypertension, and congestive heart failure. Current medications include:

Ibuprofen	650 mg q.6 h. to control arthritic pain
Hydrochlorothiazide	12.5 mg q.d. for hypertension
Digoxin (Lanoxin) and Lisinopril (Zestril)	0.125 mg and 20 mg q.d. respectively for congestive heart failure
Current weight	175 lb
Height	5′4″

Her mental status has been intact and she takes pride in her good memory.

An appointment with her physician resulted in hospitalization for 4 days. The following were reported on admission: BP 187/98; P = 90 (apical) irregular beat; R = 24 with some dyspnea on exertion. The physician heard inspiratory crackling in both lower lung bases (posterior) up to the midscapular area. He made a tentative diagnosis of acute CHF with atrial fibrillation. After 4 days in the hospital, she was sent home. Lanoxin was increased to 0.25 mg q.d., and Mrs. O. was given a no-added-sodium diet and was told to decrease the amount of fat in her diet.

Case Study
Discussion

1. What nursing approaches, especially monitoring through home care or physician office visits, can you suggest that may have helped to prevent this acute attack and hospitalization?
2. What chronic health-care problems might interfere with total self-care? What activities needing increased assistance might you anticipate?
3. What positive characteristics of Mrs. O. could be used to help her monitor her own health condition?
4. What referral sources can you think of that could be of help to Mrs. O.?

CASE STUDY
SOLUTION

1. You should consider the desired effect of the medications, the possible side effects of each, as well as whether there are any interactions among the medications. In addition, consider how frequently blood pressure needs to be checked (probably every 1–2 weeks after a medication is started; consider the use of a home-health nurse to monitor this, or use of a senior center if there is one where blood pressure monitoring can be done). Check for edema, especially in the lower extremities, sacral area, and lungs. The area of edema depends on whether heart failure is right- or left-sided: right-sided failure results in edema in the lower extremities, sacral area, and abdomen; left-sided failure results in fluid in the lungs. In each case, the location of edema is related to where the backup of pressure occurs. Monitoring should also include a review of food actually eaten: 24-hour diet recall, keeping a diary of food eaten, or looking at salt content as well as quantity of food and fluids. Even after a patient has been on medications for some time, reviews of diet, activity, ability to take medications as prescribed, even ability to pay for the medications (to avoid skipping doses) are needed. One critical factor to monitor is weight. People with CHF may increase in weight because of fluid retention and not of increase in lean body mass. They may "look" healthy, because of that weight, but fluid accumulation decreases their ability to function by putting more stress on the heart; both cardiac output available for daily activities and endurance are, thereby, decreased.

2. You should discuss the effect of gradual loss of vision with possible development of cataracts: what does this do to the person's ability to take medications as ordered, to shop, to obtain transportation, to use the telephone, and to feel safe, especially at night? When that person is also hampered by osteoarthritis, a vicious cycle may develop. Chronic pain may limit activity, which in turn creates more stiffness and decreased range of motion; as a result, the person needs to exert more energy to do even simple housekeeping and leads a more sedentary lifestyle; so the cycle continues. When these limitations are superimposed on the chronic conditions of HTN and CHF, the person may gradually lose not only the ability but also the desire for self-care. These psychosocial losses are then added to the physiological losses, and the need for assistance with activities of daily living (bathing, transfers, toileting) is increased. You might also want to discuss the differences between acute and chronic pain and the effect of chronic on daily activities, perception of self-care abilities, involvement in social activities, and the effect that complaints about this type of pain have on social interaction.

3. One could make some assumptions that would need to be checked out about involvement with family. The case history indicates that Mrs. O. has been able to be self-sufficient and that she has some support from family members. Family tends to be the first line of defense for older people and only if family help is not available, will they rely on community support or formal and gov-

ernmental agencies. The history of the individual is usually a good indication of what that person will do as an older adult provided that there is some support when problems occur. Apparently Mrs. O. has good cognitive ability and is capable of learning. Therefore, teaching and helping her to establish a program of monitoring herself (such as weight, food intake, type of food, shopping for inexpensive food) and teaching her ways to simplify housekeeping, conserve energy, and develop a daily schedule to do energy-requiring activities when she has the most energy could be very effective. Involvement of the patient in developing this program of care is essential: avoid "doing for" when the patient is able to be part of the decision-making process.

4. Look at community resources in her area. Investigate the county agencies on aging, home-health agencies, nutrition programs, transportation resources, availability of neighbors or friends as well as family. What help is available to assist with visual problems? Control of arthritic pain, such as water aerobics? Physical therapy? Talk about or visit some of these resources to determine if they will help Mrs. O.

Study Questions

Please select the one best answer.

1. Chronic health conditions differ from acute conditions in which of the following ways?
   a. Chronic conditions being at an earlier age.
   b. Acute conditions tend to take time developing.
   c. Chronic conditions require active work by patient or family.
   d. Acute conditions occur only once and then disappear.

2. A "review of systems" helps the nurse identify which of the following?
   a. Possible interaction among health-care problems
   b. Whether the person has been taking care of his or her health properly
   c. How much the patient can remember about past health history
   d. Whom the patient should be referred to based on a "system" need

3. When a person has a right-sided neglect due to a stroke, one way to ensure the patient's continued attention to both sides of the body is to do which of the following?
   a. Observe for equal length of both arms.
   b. Observe the condition of the skin and mucous membranes on the affected side.
   c. Continue to teach the patient to strength the unaffected side to avoid overuse of the affected extremities.
   d. Continue to approach the patient from the unaffected side to encourage communication.

4. One of the major concerns with older adults who have chronic conditions such as osteoarthritis is lack of activity. Which of the following is an unwanted result of decreased activity?
   a. Diarrhea
   b. Poor hygiene
   c. Loss of sense of touch
   d. Deconditioning

5. An older person with a chronic condition such as HTN may not take prescribed medications routinely. The *main* reason for this is which of the following?
   a. Inability to remember a medication schedule
   b. Lack of symptoms that indicate blood pressure is high
   c. Fear of becoming dependent on the medication
   d. Conflicting information about the purpose of the medication

Bibliography

Baines, E. M. (Ed.). (1993). *Perspectives on gerontological nursing.* Newbury Park, CA: Sage Publications.
   This edited publication provides the student with a holistic view of aging and the nurse's role in the care of older people. One of the major sections provides information about chronic physiological and psychological conditions as well as the concept of chronicity. Rehabilitation and ethical and legal issues also are included.

Ebersole, P., & Hess, P. (1994). *Toward healthy aging: Human needs and nursing response* (4th ed.). St. Louis: Mosby.
   This edition continues to provide a view of aging from the perspective of theories of aging and Maslow's need theory. Rather than focus on specific disease conditions, the authors divide the chapters according to the hierarchy of needs. They provide a view of aging that encompasses care in any setting and the nurse's responses in those settings. Although this is not a text intended for practical nursing students, it does provide excellent information.

Hogstel, M. O. (Ed.). (1992). *Clinical manual of gerontological nursing.* St. Louis: Mosby-Year Book.
   The editor describes this publication as a clinical guide to the care of older adults. As such the student, faculty, and practicing nurse are provided with clear guidelines in the form of charts designed to assist with assessment and nursing interventions. The topics of this spiral-bound volume are presented in a body-systems format to allow for easy reference on the basis of diagnosis and planning of nursing care.

Journal of Geriatric Nursing
   This bimonthly journal produced by the Mosby Year Book Company provides short, concise articles of clinical importance. Efforts are made to include topics that pertain to any care setting and to focus on practical information that could be applied by students as well as practicing nurses.

Chapter

KAY MARTIN GROTT and KATHLEEN R. CULLITON

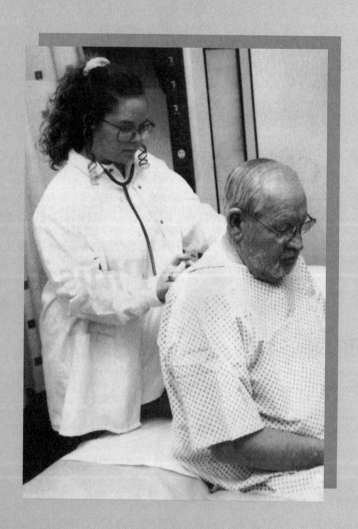

Physiological Assessment

Learning Objectives

After completing this chapter, the student will be able to:

1. Describe two unique aspects of physiological assessment for the older adult population.
2. Describe at least three normal aging changes for each body system.
3. List two tools that are commonly used to evaluate functional status.
4. Discuss the importance of nutrition to the physiological well-being of the older adult.
5. Describe at least two important components to include in a home assessment.

INTRODUCTION

This chapter outlines the parts of a physical, functional, discharge, and wellness assessment. The interrelationship of physical health, psychological well-being, and safety (Fig. 8.1) is highlighted. The licensed practical nurse (LPN) should be prepared to make a complete and thorough health assessment of the older adult to assist the person in being as independent as possible. This chapter outlines the essential elements in completing such an evaluation.

PHYSICAL ASSESSMENT

Each of the major areas included in a physical examination is reviewed with a focus on identifying normal assessment findings, distinguishing normal variations, and recognizing abnormal assessment findings. Included are questions used to collect subjective health history information. Questions related to the aging process are highlighted. Physical assessment steps (inspection, palpation, percussion, auscultation) are followed for each body area. The techniques for physical examination included in this chapter are not all-inclusive of the techniques used to conduct a total examination. However, this assessment outline assists you in completing a head-to-toe physical examination of an older adult. It is important to remember to report any abnormal findings to the registered nurse or the physician.

Head, Neck, and Face

History

Evaluate the older adult's past medical history for head injury, increased level of stress, thyroid dysfunction, neck injury, or infection.

Physical Examination

The assessment of the head and neck is the same for older adults as for younger people.

Inspection

Observe the older individual's head position. Note the size, shape, symmetry, and proportion of the head. If it appears abnormally large or small, measure the circumference or distance around the head. Evaluate hair distribution, pattern of baldness, and dryness of the scalp. Note if lice are found in the hair. The presence of lice demands immediate intervention. Assess the face for color, symmetry, and distribution of facial hair. Evaluate facial muscles by having the older adult demonstrate different facial expressions: raise eyebrows, close eyes, puff out cheeks, smile, show teeth, and frown. Note any wrinkles or dryness of the skin. Note the size of the neck. The trachea should be aligned with the midline of the suprasternal notch. Observe for symmetry of the neck muscles. Are they equal in size? Note venous distention, invol-

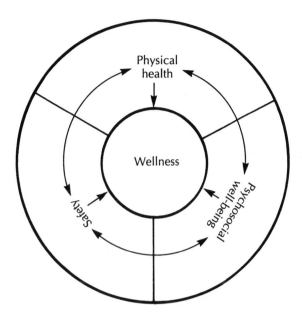

Figure 8.1 The interrelationship of physical health, psychosocial well-being and safety.

untary muscle tension, or swelling in the neck. Assess the active range of motion (ROM) of the neck by having the older adult tilt the head backward, forward, from side to side, and in a circular motion. Range of motion of the neck should be completed without limitation or pain.

Palpation

Palpate the alignment of the trachea. Palpate the cervical muscles and note any tenderness. Palpate the carotid pulses one at a time. What does the pulse feel like? Is it bounding? Weak? Or does it have a vibration-type movement? As the older adult moves the neck, palpate over the spinal area for crepitus. Crepitus is a slight grating sensation and is not normal.

Abnormal findings include edema of the face (especially around eyes), involuntary facial movements (tic, tremor, droop), lack of symmetry, unusual size and contour, and tenderness.

Nose and Sinuses

History

Epistaxis (nosebleed) can be severe and difficult to treat. Older people commonly have bleeding from the posterior portion of the nose. Causes of epistaxis include trauma, septal perforation, hypertension, tumors, blood diseases, allergies, frequent respiratory infections, and frequent use of nasal sprays.

Physical Examination

INSPECTION

Observe the size, shape, and color of the nose. Note any flaring of the nostrils during breathing and any nasal drainage. Examine the nasal cavity for swelling, drainage, polyps, and bleeding. The nasal mucosa should be moist and dark pink. Frequently, men have an increased amount of nasal hair. Assess the movement of air through each nostril by occluding the nostril not being examined and asking the older adult to inhale and exhale through the nose. Assess the older adult's ability to smell by asking the person to identify different common smells (almond, vanilla, cinnamon, coffee). It is abnormal for the smell perceived to be different in each nostril.

PALPATION

Palpate the nose for tenderness or masses. Abnormal findings include swelling of mucosa, bleeding, discharge, perforation, polyps, deviation of nasal septum. It is common to find nasal blockage, infection, crusting, and dryness.

Eyes

History

The nurse needs to discuss the following: vision changes, pain, excessive tearing or discharge, diplopia, infection, and cataracts. Ask whether the patient wears glasses. When are the glasses worn? When was the last ophthalmic examination?

Physical Examination

INSPECTION

Assess both the external eye and visual acuity. Examine the eyes for position and alignment. Note the symmetry of the eyebrows, eyelashes, pupils, and irises. Changes in the appearance of the eyelids can be due to systemic diseases such as hyperthyroidism, myasthenia gravis, or nerve palsy. The eyes should be evaluated for redness, swelling, and discharge. Pupils should be equal in size unless they have been unequal throughout life or have become unequal as a result of surgery or trauma. They may react slightly more slowly to light than they did in the patient's youth. Normally the pupils are black, equal in size, round, and smooth. If the older adult has cataracts, the pupils may appear cloudy. Before testing visual acuity, the nurse needs to make sure that adequate light is available. If the older adult wears glasses, the lenses should be checked for cleanliness and alignment. These two factors can affect visual acuity. The line of the bifocals may cause double vision if the glasses are misaligned. Evaluate distant vision with a Snellen's eye chart. Test each eye separately, with and without glasses. After testing separately, test the eyes together with and without glasses. Any patient with 20/40 vision or less should be referred to a physician or nurse practitioner. To test near vision, use a newspaper or other conventional reading material for the older adult; measure the distance from the face to the reading material.

Ears

History

The nurse needs to help determine the effect of hearing loss on the older person's life. Does the older adult use any corrective devices, such as amplifiers or hearing aids? Consider any risk factors, such as environmental hazards, chemical exposure, and uncontrolled, loud noises.

The following are some questions that can be used to elicit a history: Have you experienced pain from your ears? Have you had dizziness? In what situations? How long did it last? What relieved the dizziness? Have you had any discharge from your ears? What color? What consistency? Did it have an odor? Have you experienced a sudden or rapid change in your hearing? What were you doing when it occurred? Does it come and go?

Physical Examination

INSPECTION

Observe the older individual in conversation. Does the person lean forward or cup a hand to the ear to hear? Is a loud speaking voice used? Does the person request repetition of what has been said? If hearing loss is identified, speak to the person in a normal tone of voice and speak toward the better ear. Assess the ear for size, shape, symmetry, redness, inflammation, swelling, discharge, and lesions.

PALPATION

The surface of the skin of the ear should have a smooth texture. Palpate around the ear and ask the older adult whether any pain or tenderness is present.

Mouth and Throat

History

The first aspect of history taking related to the mouth is to establish whether the patient has any dental complaints. The following questions can be used to elicit a history:

Do you have any pain or discomfort? Are any of your teeth especially sensitive to hot or cold temperatures? Have you noticed any swelling in your mouth or throat? Do you have any difficulty chewing or swallowing? How does food taste? Is your mouth dry?

Do your dentures fit properly? Do you have any sore or lesions in your mouth or throat? How often do you brush your teeth, dentures, or tongue? Do you use dental floss? If so, how often? When was the last dental exam? What was the result? Do you clean your dentures at night in a cleaning solution?

What are your eating habits? Food consistency? Twenty-four–hour diet recall? Do you smoke? What type of tobacco? Cigarettes? Cigar? Smokeless tobacco? Do you dip snuff or tobacco? How often? For how many years?

What medications are you taking? Prescriptions? Over-the-counter drugs?

Physical Examination

INSPECTION AND PALPATION

Inspection and palpation are used concurrently during the oral cavity examination. Use a gloved hand and a gauze pad to perform this part of the examination. If the older adult wears dentures, remove them before starting the examination. Evaluate both the fit of the dentures to the gums or alveolar surfaces and the dentures themselves. Dentures are considered to fit improperly if there is inflammation and ulceration of the palate, mucosa, and alveolar ridges. Examine the dentures for cracks, missing pieces, and rough edges. Dentures should be stable and remain securely fixed during chewing. Underlying tissues should be pink and adhere tightly to the bone. There should not be food, debris, or excessive denture adhesive on the inside of the denture. If the older adult does not have dentures, examine the teeth. Note the number and position of teeth. Are they in good repair or can you see cavities and broken teeth? The gums should be pink, moist, and smooth. Inspect for signs of inflammation and lesions. The hard palate should be pale. The soft palate should be pink. Inspect for inflammation, lesions, pallor, and any purulent drainage or a white coating on the tongue. The uvula should be midline and red. It should move up as the older adult says, "Ah." Tonsils, if present, should be small, pink, and symmetrical. Check the gag reflex. Both the top and bottom of the tongue should be examined. A smooth, painful tongue may indicate vitamin B_{12} deficiency. The tongue and mucous membranes should be pink, moist, and free of swelling and lesions. The tongue should relax on the floor of the mouth. Varicose veins on bottom surfaces of the tongue are common. To examine the tongue, ask the older adult to stick out the tongue. While you hold it out with a piece of gauze, inspect all sides of the tongue and the floor of the mouth. Report any white, scaly patches. The lips should be moist, smooth, and pink. Check the corners of the mouth for cracks (angular cheilitis). These cracks are a prime spot for *Candida* (yeast) infections.

Neurological System

History

Does the patient have any problems with headaches? In assessing the neurological system, the nurse should also ask if the older adult has experienced seizures. Is there an existing seizure disorder? What type of treatment has been received? What were the circumstances occurring before, during, and after the seizure?

Physical Examination

INSPECTION

Initially, examine the older adult's level of orientation. Is the person alert, lethargic, or nonresponsive? Oriented to place, time, and/or person? As the older adult answers questions, observe the face for symmetry of movement when smiling, talking, grimacing, or frowning. Evaluate the older adult's appearance throughout the examination. Is the person dressed appropriately? Is the person wearing multiple layers of clothing? If so, are they appropriate for the weather outdoors? Is there body odor? Does the person appear well groomed? Is the older adult's behavior appropriate? Evaluate the strength and symmetry of the older adult's upper and lower extremities. Ask the person to walk across the room and observe the gait for symmetry, balance, and coordination during ambulation. Note any weakness.

Peripheral Vascular System

History

Some key history questions related to peripheral vascular functioning are listed below:

Are you overweight? Do you smoke? Do you drink? What medications do you take? Prescription? Over-the-counter? Do you have diabetes? Do you wear garters or girdles? Do you wear ankle-, knee-, or thigh-high hosiery? When you take off your hosiery, is there an indentation in your leg that does not go away for several minutes? Do your shoes fit tightly? Do you have pain in your calves after walking? Do you ever experience pains, aches, numbness, or tingling in your calves, feet, buttocks, or legs? Are there any activities that you cannot do because of pains and aches in your extremities? What aggravates your pain? What relieves the pain? Does walking or climbing stairs cause pain? Do you ever notice change in the color of your extremities, that is, red, blue, or pale? Have you noticed any hair loss over any part of your legs? Does your family have a history of problems with the legs? Do you sit for long periods of time with your legs crossed? Do you experience swelling of your legs at the end of the day? Does swelling return to normal in the morning?

Physical Examination

The physical examination of the peripheral vascular system includes inspection, palpation, and auscultation. The nurse should always compare one side of the body with the other when using these assessment methods.

INSPECTION

Skin color should be evaluated with the older adult lying down. Inspect the upper and lower extremities. Venous insufficiency is indicated if the legs are cyanotic when they are dependent (hanging down), or when petechiae or broken pigmentation is present on the skin over the legs. Chronic venous insufficiency is common in the elderly. If the legs become pale when they are elevated and turn dark red when they dangle, arterial insufficiency is indicated. The signs of chronic venous insufficiency are as follows: distended *tortuous* veins, hair loss, hyperpigmentation, cool or normal skin temperature, pretibial edema/pedal edema (Fig. 8.2) that is worse during the

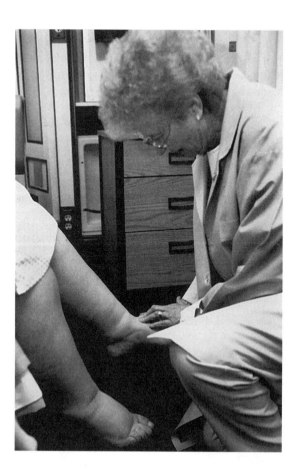

Figure 8.2 Pedal edema should improve during the night while the patient is asleep.

day but improves at night when the older adult lies down to sleep. The signs of chronic arterial insufficiency include thin, shiny, atrophic skin; hair loss over feet and toes; thick and rigid toenails; and cool skin. Edema of the legs and feet should be noted. The nurse may choose to record the width of the edematous area by using a measuring tape. When measuring the legs to assess edema, be sure to measure at the same place on each leg. If you wish to monitor changes in edema, lightly mark the location on the leg you are measuring with a felt-tipped marker and measure in the same place each day. Stasis ulcers are rare with varicose veins but commonly occur with deep vein insufficiency. Venous stasis ulcers are located on the sides of the ankles. Arterial ulcers may involve toes or places where the skin has been bumped or bruised.

PALPATION

Check the skin temperature of the older adults arms and legs by using the back of your hand. Increased temperature can be caused by a localized response to inflammation. Cool temperature denotes decreased blood flow. Peripheral pulses should be evaluated by using the pads of the index and middle fingers. The pulse is evaluated for rate, rhythm, amplitude, and symmetry. Normal vessels feel smooth and resilient. In most elders, increased resistance to compression may be palpated because of rigid and tortuous artery walls. The nurse should practice palpating the pulses of both a young person and an older person to be able to differentiate the changes associated with aging. Pulses should be evaluated one at a time (carotid, brachial, radial, femoral popliteal, dorsalis pedis, and posterior tibial). They should be regular, strong, and equal bilaterally. In the older adult, the dorsalis pedis and posterior tibial pulses are harder to find. Lack of symmetry between extremities indicates possible impaired circulation. If you have difficulty finding a pulse, feel throughout the area where it is expected to be and vary the pressure of your finger. Be sure you are not feeling your own pulse. The rate you feel should be different from your own heart rate. If you had difficulty finding a pulse, you can mark its location once it is found. Use a felt-tipped pen to mark the spot so that it will be easier to find the next time.

Cardiac System

History

Older adults should be asked questions for assessment of cardiac disease risk factors. It is a good idea to have older adults write down their diet for the past 3 days and assess it. Then, continue with health history questions. The following are some questions that can be used to elicit a history:

Have you lost or gained weight in the past 6 months? How do you deal with stress? Do you use tobacco? What kind (cigarettes, cigars, chewing tobacco)? How much do you use each day? How many drinks of alcohol and/or beer do you have each day? Which prescription and over-the-counter medications do you take? Do you use any vitamins, herbs, or nutritional supplements? Do you have a regular exercise regimen? How often and for how long do you exercise? Do you have any problems with dyspnea? Does your shortness of breath increase with activity (dyspnea on exertion)? Do you have chest pain? When does it occur? What are you doing when it occurs? Is the chest pain relieved by rest?

Physical Examination

INSPECTION

A cardiac physical examination procedure is the same for both older and younger persons. The older adult should be evaluated while lying down, sitting up, and standing. Observe the neck and chest to detect any visible pulsations, lifts, or heaves. The heartbeat is usually not visible, but it may be if the individual is emaciated. It is abnormal to observe the heart beating on the chest wall of an older adult who is obese or of normal weight. Note any cough, shortness of breath, venous or abdominal distention, or cyanosis of mucous membranes and nailbeds. The legs, ankles, and feet should be observed for edema.

PALPATION

Feel the front of the chest over the heart for any thrills, heaves, or lifts. A *thrill* is palpable vibration. A *lift* or *heave* is a pulsation that is more forceful than anticipated. There should be minimal changes in the pulse when the older adult changes positions between lying, sitting, and standing. Press on the nailbeds and observe for the return of a pink color. This should occur quickly and is called *capillary refill*. It is abnormal for a refill to take longer than 2 seconds. Skin temperature should be palpated for unusual coolness or heat. The blood pressure should be checked with the older adult lying, sitting, and standing. Five minutes should be allowed between each measurement. This will assist in determining whether the older adult has hypertension or orthostatic hypotension. Orthostatic hypotension is a common problem with older adults.

AUSCULTATION

The elderly have more rapid and less distinct heartbeats. Many older persons live normal, everyday lives with chronic atrial fibrillation. Any irregularity of the heartbeat noted while listening to the heart should be reported to the RN or physician. Infrequent extra beats (ectopic) are fairly common. Another common abnormal finding is a heart murmur. A heart murmur is caused by thickened and rigid heart valves and decreased strength of myocardial contractions. It sounds like a hum or click and results from turbulent or backward flow of blood through the heart. If detected, it should be reported.

Respiratory System

History

Questions that are used to assess an older adult's respiratory status include: Do you have any difficulty breathing? Do you get short of breath with exercise or exertion? Do you have a cough? Is your cough dry or productive? What color and consistency is the mucous that you cough up? Is there any blood in the mucus? Dyspnea or difficulty breathing is not a part of normal aging. It is often related to congestive heart failure (CHF), pneumonia, anemia, and other lung diseases. It is present in only one half of the elderly with pneumonia. The first signs of pneumonia often include a nonspecific deterioration in health, for instance, slight cough, altered mental status, and tachycardia.

Ask the older adult if there is any history of lung disease. If so, what effect does it have on activities of daily living? Is oxygen used? Ask questions to determine if the older adult is using oxygen safely in the home. Other questions that can be used to elicit history of lung disease follow:

Do you smoke? If so, for how many years? How many packs of cigarettes do you smoke per day? Do you live in a smoking environment? Do you chew tobacco? Dip snuff? Does you live in an area that has air pollution? Have you or any member of your family ever had tuberculosis? What is the date of your last chest x-ray? Have you had the pneumonia vaccine (Pneumovax)? If so, when did you receive the Pneumovax? Have you had an influenza shot this year? Have you received one within the last year? Have you had a tuberculosis skin test? When?

Physical Examination

INSPECTION

In the older adult population, barrel chest, slight use of intercostal muscles, and slightly prolonged respirations may occur normally. If these signs and symptoms occur suddenly, they should be considered abnormal. The respiratory rate for normal older adults is 12–24 respirations per minute. A rate of 24 or greater is considered *tachypnea*. Observe for the use of accessory muscles and nasal flaring. A rate of less than 12 respirations per minute is considered *bradypnea*. Overt signs of the lower oxygen levels resulting from bradypnea include decreased consciousness, confusion, and lethargy. The character of respirations also should be evaluated. A normal respiratory rate is even and unlabored. The older adult's skin, lips, and nail color should be inspected for cyanosis and pallor. Posture while sitting and standing should be noted. Posture affects the ability to breathe.

PALPATION

The anterior and posterior chest should be palpated for masses and tenderness of the ribs. The tracheal area should be palpated for any deviation.

AUSCULTATION

Remember that an older adult can become dizzy from hyperventilation if asked to take deep breaths for a long time. Allow the patient periods of normal breathing between deep breaths. Listen fully to inspiration and expiration. Softer vesicular sounds and diminished breath sounds in the bases of the lungs are normal. Listen for abnormal (adventitious) sounds. These sounds are superimposed on the normal breath sounds. Crackles are often heard when the older adult has CHF or pulmonary edema. Crackles result from air passing through moisture and sound like hair being rubbed between the fingers. Scattered crackles in dependent lung segments of some older adults should not be mistaken for bronchitis or CHF. If the crackles disappear after coughing, they are not pathological. If they are present after coughing, pathology may be present. Wheezes are a whistling noise caused by air passing through a narrowed airway. This happens with bronchospasm and swelling of the bronchioles. It is commonly heard in chronic obstructive pulmonary disease (COPD) and in older adults with asthma. Pleural friction rub is due to inflammation between the membranes lining the chest cavity. It sounds like leather being rubbing together.

Gastrointestinal System

History

In taking a gastrointestinal (GI) history, the nurse needs to focus on nutritional status, bowel habits, and medications. Ask the older adult or family member to give a 24-hour recall of the older person's diet. Evaluate the reported intake for nutritional balance. Is it full of fatty foods? Is it low fiber? Does it have a high starch content? Calculate the amount of fluids the older adult drinks in a 24-hour period. The older adult needs 2000–3000 mL of fluids per day. Continue with more health history questions:

How do you tolerate eating and drinking? Do you have problems with swallowing? Do you experience pain with swallowing? Do you have difficulty swallowing liquids? Solids? Do you have the sensation of food stuck in your throat? What is your bowel routine? Do you have abdominal pain? Do you use laxatives? Have you used laxatives in the past? How long did you use them? What kind of laxatives? How often were they used? Have you experienced any recent injury or infection?

Evaluate the medications the older adult is currently taking using the methods described previously.

Physical Examination

INSPECTION

Inspect the skin of the abdomen and note any lesions caused by rubbing of belts or corsets over the years. Check for fungal rashes in skin folds of those who are obese or incapacitated. Does the abdomen look rigid? If so, refer the individual to the RN or physician. Abdominal rigidity can indicate bowel obstruction.

AUSCULTATION

Listen to the abdomen with your stethoscope. Auscultate each quadrant continuously for 5 minutes if you are unable to hear bowel sounds. Bowel sounds are decreased in the older adult because of decreased gastric motility that accompanies normal aging. While the history was being taken, did the older adult complain of pain in the abdomen? Ask the older adult to point to the area of pain. Right lower quadrant pain may indicate appendicitis. Left lower quadrant pain may indicate diverticulitis. Tenderness at the base of the xiphoid process may indicate stomach pain, hiatal hernia, or referred pain from the aorta. Palpation will provide further information.

PALPATION

Relaxation of the abdominal muscles enhances palpation. If the older adult is obese, palpation may be difficult. If you palpate a mass in the abdomen, it could indicate diverticulitis, fecal impaction, mesenteric thrombosis, or cancer.

Integumentary System

History

History taking is the most important aspect of the skin assessment. The most common skin complaints are pain, pruritus, paresthesia, and dermatitis. The nurse needs to find out as much as possible about any skin problem mentioned. Questions to ask include:

Do you have any skin problems? What kind? How were they treated? Are there any other symptoms? What are they? Have they been treated? What was the treatment? Are you allergic to any drugs or environmental allergens? What are they? How long have you had the allergy? Have you been exposed to an infectious disease? What is your history of sun exposure? What is your skin care regimen? Evaluate all medications the older adult is taking. Anything that can cause an allergic reaction, no matter how long the product has been used, should be discussed. Common allergens are soaps and topical medications.

Physical Examination

INSPECTION

Look at the older person's skin in a well-lit room. Skin folds should be evaluated for dampness, irritation, and fissures. Common skin folds are under the breasts and inguinal areas. Observe the scalp, behind the ears, the fingernails and toenails, genitalia, buttocks, and face. How clean is the older adult's skin? Is there an odor present? Assess skin color for variations that are not uniform and have changed since the previous examination. Note any pallor, jaundice, cyanosis, erythemia, petechiae, and ecchymosis. Older adults with deeply pigmented skin tones should be evaluated for changes in color such as duskiness, graying, and blackish areas. Jaundice in a person of color should be evaluated on the hard palate and the soles of the hands and feet. Check pressure points over bony prominences, especially on individuals who are debilitated or immobilized. Pay particular attention to the areas over the scapulae, back of the head, ear lobes, hips, heels, coccyx, and elbows.

The Braden scale is one common assessment tool used to evaluate the risk of pressure ulcer formation. This is a helpful assessment to complete on every older individual who enters a health-care setting. It will provide baseline information on the older person's risk for pressure ulcer formation. Individuals at high risk should have preventive measures implemented from the start. The Braden scale (Fig. 8.3) also can be used for periodic assessment of the older person. If the older adult's risk for pressure ulcer development increases over time, new and more aggressive interventions for prevention should be implemented.

Evaluate the skin for lesions. Some lesions are normal. Table 8.1 describes normal and abnormal skin lesions. Note the consistency of the lesions. If there has been a change in color, consistency, edges or growth, the lesion may have changed from normal to abnormal.

PALPATION

Check the skin for turgor. Gently pinch the skin on the forehead or anterior chest to see how quickly it returns to place. Poor turgor may be a normal aging change. It also could indicate dehydration and/or malnutrition. Palpate skin texture and note the temperature. Notice if the skin has become rough, dry, or coarse. Normally the skin is smooth with some dryness. Check the skin temperature with the back of your hand. During this evaluation, note the symmetry of temperature and texture.

Braden Scale
FOR PREDICTING PRESSURE SORE RISK

Patient's Name _____   Evaluator's Name _____   Date of Assessment

SENSORY PERCEPTION Ability to respond meaningfully to pressure-related discomfort	**1. Completely Limited:** Unresponsive to painful stimuli (does not moan, flinch, or grasp), due to diminished level of consciousness or sedation. OR Limited ability to feel pain over most of body surface.	**2. Very Limited:** Responds only to painful stimuli. Cannot communicate discomfort except by moaning or restlessness. OR Has a sensory impairment which limits the ability to feel pain or discomfort over ½ of body.	**3. Slightly Limited:** Responds to verbal commands, but cannot always communicate discomfort or need to be turned. OR Has some sensory impairment that limits ability to feel pain or discomfort in 1 or 2 extremities.	**4. No Impairment:** Responds to verbal commands. Has no sensory deficit that would limit ability to feel or voice pain or discomfort.
MOISTURE Degree to which skin is exposed to moisture	**1. Constantly Moist:** Skin is kept moist almost constantly by perspiration, urine, and so on. Dampness is detected every time patient is moved or turned.	**2. Very Moist:** Skin is often but not always moist. Linen must be changed at least once a shift.	**3. Occasionally Moist:** Skin is occasionally moist, requiring an extra linen change approximately once a day.	**4. Rarely Moist:** Skin is usually dry, linen requires changing only at routine intervals.
ACTIVITY Degree of physical activity	**1. Bedfast:** Confined to bed	**2. Chairfast:** Ability to walk severely limited or nonexistent. Cannot bear own weight and/or must be assisted into chair or wheelchair.	**3. Walks Occasionally:** Walks occasionally during day, but for very short distances, with or without assistance. Spends majority of each shift in bed or chair.	**4. Walks Frequently:** Walks outside the room at least twice a day and inside room at least once every 2 hours during waking hours.

Figure 8.3 Braden scale for predicting pressure sore risk. (From Braden, B.J. & Bergstrom, N. (1992). Pressure reduction. In G. Bulechek & J. McCloskey (Eds.), *Nursing Interventions* (2nd ed., p. 63). Philadelphia: W.B. Saunders, with permission.

	1. Completely Immobile: Does not make even slight changes in body or extremity position without assistance.	2. Very Limited: Makes occasional slight changes in body or extremity position but unable to make frequent or significant changes independently.	3. Slightly Limited: Makes frequent though slight changes in body or extremity position independently.	4. No Limitations: Makes major and frequent changes in position without assistance.
MOBILITY Ability to change and control body position				
NUTRITION *Usual* food intake pattern	**1. Very Poor:** Never eats a complete meal. Rarely eats more than ⅓ of any food offered. Eats 2 servings or less of protein (meat or dairy products) per day. Takes fluids poorly. Does not take a liquid dietary supplement. OR is NPO and/or maintained on clear liquids or IVs for more than 5 days.	**2. Probably Inadequate:** Rarely eats a complete meal and generally eats only about ½ of any food offered. Protein intake includes only 3 servings of meat or dairy products per day. Occasionally will take a dietary supplement. OR receives less than optimum amount of liquid diet or tube feeding.	**3. Adequate:** Eats over ½ of most meals. Eats a total of 4 servings of protein (meat, dairy products) each day. Occasionally will refuse a meal, but will usually take a supplement if offered. OR is on tube feeding or TPN regimen, which probably meets most of nutritional needs.	**4. Excellent:** Eats most of every meal. Never refuses a meal. Usually eats a total of 4 or more servings of meat and dairy products. Occasionally eats between meals. Does not require supplementation.
FRICTION AND SHEAR	**1. Problem:** Requires moderate to maximum assistance in moving. Complete lifting without sliding against sheets is impossible. Frequently slides down in bed or chair, requiring frequent repositioning with maximum assistance. Spasticity, contractures, or agitation leads to almost constant friction.	**2. Potential Problem:** Moves feebly or requires minimum assistance. During a move, skin probably slides to some extent against sheets, chair, restraints, or other devices. Maintains relatively good position in chair or bed most of the time but occasionally slides down.	**3. No Apparent Problem:** Moves in bed and in chair independently and has sufficient muscle strength to lift up completely during move. Maintains good position in bed or chair at all times.	

Figure 8.3 (*Continued*)

TABLE 8.1 NORMAL AND ABNORMAL SKIN LESIONS	
Normal Skin Lesions	
Lesion	**Description**
Seborrheic keratosis	Raised; vary in size; tan to black in color; appear "warty" or greasy; frequently appear on trunk.
Senile purpura	Vivid purple patch; well demarcated; eventually fades.
Senile lentigines	Brown; irregularly shaped patches; "age" or "liver" spots; occur most frequently on back of hands, forearms, and face.
Cherry angioma	Bright; ruby red elevated area; frequently found on trunk; common; insignificant; increase in size and number with age.
Sebaceous hyperplasia	Yellowish, flat, solid elevations with central depression; looks like a small doughnut; common on face, forehead and nose; more common in men.
Abnormal Lesions	
Senile or actinic keratosis	Precancerous; superficial patch covered by a persistent scale; common on sun-exposed areas.
Squamous cell carcinoma	Firm, red-brown nodule; may arise from senile keratosis; common on sun-exposed areas and in fair-skinned clients.
Basal cell epithelioma	Starts as pearly colored solid elevation on face or ear; ulcerates leaving a crater with an elevated border and depressed center.
Malignant melanoma	Brown, black lesion; may have flecks of red, white, or blue irregular border, irregular surface; arise from moles or appear as new pigmented, irregular lesion.
Lentigo maligna melanoma	Less aggressive form of malignant melanoma specific to the elderly; arise from lentigens that enlarge laterally.

Source: McGovern, M., & Kuhn, J. K. (1992). Skin assessment of the elderly client, *Journal of Gerontological Nursing, 18* (8), 40–41, with permission.

Musculoskeletal System

History

The most common musculoskeletal complaints are related to the joints. Complaints include pain, stiffness, redness, limitation in movement, and joint deformity. If the older person complains of pain, determine where the pain originates and where it radiates. The most common soft-tissue problem is pain in and around the shoulder joint. If the older adult has a sudden onset of low back pain, report it to the RN or physician. This could mean a compression fracture of the spine.

Physical Examination

INSPECTION

If possible, observe the older adult while the person is participating in activities of daily living (ADLs) and instrumental activities of daily living (IADLs). (See Functional Assessment section in this chapter.) This allows the nurse to assess range of motion, muscles mass, and level of independence in self-care. Some decline in range of motion is expected. There is a general rigidity of the lower extremities.

Observe the older adult's ability to walk. Have the person ambulate a specified distance to determine endurance. It is normal for older men to have a slight anterior-flexion of the upper body while the arms and knees are slightly flexed. Note the kind of shoes worn by the older adult. Intervention is necessary if the person has an unstable gait yet wears high-heeled shoes. Have the older adult transfer in and out of the bed and chair, on and off the commode, and from the commode to the bathtub. Observe for symmetry of movement. Determine if the person needs assistance. Some older people may be independently mobile with the use of a wheelchair. Assess their ability to maneuver the wheelchair in the environment. Check the older adult's feet for lesions and deformity because these can interfere with gait and mobility. As with physical examination of all of the systems, report all abnormal findings of the musculoskeletal system to the RN or physician.

Reproductive System

History: the Female Patient

Although questions about sexual functioning and the reproductive organs may be uncomfortable for both the nurse and the older adult, it is important to ask them. Ask the older woman if she knows about breast self-examination (Fig. 8.4). If not, there is a need for education on the subject. Do not be surprised if she is familiar with breast self-examination and does it regularly. Many older adult women are more compliant than younger women in performing this examination. Inquire about symptoms of breast cancer. Does the patient have any pain, nipple discharge, lumps, skin discoloration, or change in breast shape? Is there any family history of breast cancer or other cancerous conditions? Determine if the older woman has used estrogen or other medications that affect the breasts, such as digitalis, thyroid drugs, and antihypertensives. Has the patient ever had an abnormal Papanicolaou (Pap) smear? If so, was the patient been treated? Did the patient receive any medications for menopausal symptoms? Was there any unusual bleeding since menopause? Some common physical complaints that older women experience with intercourse include vaginal dryness, pain, and limited mobility from arthritis. These complaints should be addressed and ways to deal with them should be suggested. Lubricants and using different positions during intercourse, such as the side-lying position, can help the older woman manage these concerns.

History: the Male Patient

The older man should be evaluated for symptoms of benign prostatic hyperplasia (BPH). Is there any change in the urinary stream? Any dribbling of urine? A sense that the bladder is not completely empty after urinating? Is there urinary frequency? Urgency? Burning on urination? Does the patient experience nocturia? How often? Review his medications and note whether he takes diuretics or an anticholinergic that might worsen BPH. Does he realize the importance of checking his breasts periodically? It is possible for males to develop breast cancer but not as often as women.

**3 Ways
Most Women Use
To Check Their
Breasts**

How To Check
Your Breasts
for Cancer

Find breast cancer early and save your life. You can do this. Just follow all 3 steps in this booklet.

1. Take A Shower
Or Bath

A good time to check your breasts for cancer is anytime you are taking a shower or a bath. Hands move easier over wet skin.

Move your flat hand over each breast. Do this slowly over every part of the breast. Use the right hand to check the left breast. Use the left hand for the right breast.

Feel for any lump, hard knot or thick mass.

2. Stand
in front
of a
Mirror

Hold your arms at your sides. Look at your breasts.

Next, raise your arms above your head. Hold them high.

Look for any of these signs:

Next, put hands on hips. Press down on your hips.
Do this so that your chest muscles stand out.

Left and right breasts do not match on most people. You need to know what is normal for you. Look for changes in the shape of your breasts from one month to the next.

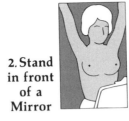

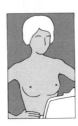

3. Lie down on
the bed

Get a pillow or folded towel. Put it under your right shoulder. Place right hand behind your head. Hold your left hand flat. Place left hand on your right breast.

* Feel all of your breast and that part of your body that goes from your breast to your shoulder. If your breast is small you should take at least 2 minutes to check it. If your breast is large, take more than 2 minutes. You do not want to miss any part of your breast.

* Now check your left breast the same way you checked your right breast.

* When you check each breast, find out where it is soft. Where is it firm? Are there any ridges? A ridge in the lower part of your breast is normal. Take your thumb and finger and squeeze the nipple a little bit. If your nipple bleeds, go see your doctor.

Figure 8.4 How to check your breasts for cancer. (From American Cancer Society. *How to check your breasts for cancer.* Used with permission of American Cancer Society, Tennessee Division, Inc.)

Physical Examination

INSPECTION

During the examination process you should inspect the external genitalia on both the male and female older adult. Assess for skin or mucous membrane lesions, rashes, discoloration, hair loss, inflammation, discharge, asymmetry, and circumcision.

Urinary System

History

In gathering information about the urinary tract, the nurse needs to find out the chief complaint and the nature and extent of the older adult's underlying problem. The most common complaints are urgency to void, leakage when changing position, pain on urination, frequency of urination, voiding small amounts, and incontinence caused by coughing, sneezing, and laughing. The subject of urinary incontinence frequently causes the older adult to feel embarrassed. Incontinence may cause the older person to withdraw from usual social contact for fear of having an accident. It is also a major risk factor for pressure ulcer formation and urinary tract infections. Thus, despite the difficulties and embarrassment that may be associated with discussing incontinence, it is a serious problem that can have multiple untoward effects. If the older adult reports any complaints related to the urinary tract, determine the person's normal urinary/bowel habits before the symptoms began. Assess the past medical history for childbirths, previous surgeries involving the lower abdomen and pelvic floor, renal disease, and bladder cancer. Evaluate the older adult's medications. Diuretics and antiparkinsonian drugs can affect the urinary system. Periods of prolonged rest or immobility can cause urinary stasis. Urine that is allowed to pool in the bladder creates a favorable environment for the development of infection. To fully empty the bladder, it is important for the older adult to be able to use the sitting-with-legs-dependent position. Full bladder emptying may not be possible on a bedpan. Decreased fluid intake results in low urine volume and infrequent urination. This can create pooling of the urine and increase the risk for infection. It also can lead to dehydration, elevated blood sugar levels, and electrolyte imbalance. These conditions may manifest themselves in the older adult through alterations in mental status.

Physical Examination

INSPECTION

Assess urine amount and color for the presence of any sediment.

PALPATION

Palpate the abdomen for distention of the bladder and signs of pelvic discomfort or masses.

FUNCTIONAL ASSESSMENT

For an older adult, a functional assessment is as important as a physical assessment. Very often, the older person demonstrates changes in function as the first or only sign indicating the onset of illness. Although the older person has many chronic illnesses, these typically are not problematic until function is affected.

Functional assessment includes a holistic approach to evaluating the older adult that includes physical, cognitive, and social function. Physical function is comprised of the individual's current health status in addition to how well the person performs ADLs and IADLs. Cognitive function includes the individual's memory, judgment, and thinking abilities. Cognitive function is discussed in Chapter 10 and is not included in this section on functional assessment. Social function involves a psychosocial approach to determine how the individual interacts with the environment and with others.

Functional assessment involves evaluating the older adult to determine what the person can do (strengths) and cannot do (deficits). What the health-care team members see as a deficit may not correlate with what the older adult views as a problem. Both the older adult's true abilities, as assessed by the nurse, and the older adult's perception of these abilities must be considered.

Functional assessment assists in setting realistic goals. Cure, as a goal, is not appropriate for an elderly individual with chronic, irreversible conditions. The goal, for this person, would be to maximize functional strengths and compensate for deficits to achieve and maintain optimal independence in function.

An interdisciplinary team (IDT) approach is necessary for the older person to reach maximum independence. No single discipline can thoroughly evaluate or provide all of the needed services for older persons. An interdisciplinary approach helps to uncover problems and their cause, define the older adult's strengths and resources, and prevent fragmentation of care. The focus is to plan, implement, and coordinate interventions to address both the older adult's deficits and strengths.

In almost any health-care setting, the nurse is the health-care professional who spends the most time with the older adult. This affords the nurse many opportunities to observe physical functioning. A decline in functional ability may represent a change in an underlying chronic disease or the onset of a new acute illness. Monitoring functional status helps track improvements and setbacks. It also indicates when additional services are needed. Use of a formal tool to evaluate functional status allows the nurse to validate, monitor, and clearly communicate clinical impressions to other members of the IDT.

Activities of Daily Living

The Katz ADL scale (Fig. 8.5) is widely used to assess ADLs. It is a well-rounded tool that is appropriate for use in most settings, including home, hospital, and nursing home. Activities of daily living are those performed in taking care of oneself. The following areas are considered ADLs: bathing, dressing, toileting, feeding, ambulating or transferring, and continence. Direct observation is the most valid indicator in assessing ADLs. Watch the older adult perform ADLs and check for abnormal body movements. Rate the older adult on each of the ADL items of the Katz scale. Using the scale supplies specific information on how the older adult performs in each of the ADL areas, and the composite score can give you and others on the IDT an overall view of the patient's level of ability. The score also gives an objective means to monitor progress over time. Goals in each of the ADL areas can be set on the basis of scores on the scale.

Activities of Daily Living (ADL) Scale
Evaluation Form

Name _____ Day of evaluation _____

For each area of functioning listed below, check description that applies. (The word "assistance" means supervision, direction, or personal assistance.)

Bathing—either sponge bath, tub bath, or shower

☐	☐	☐
Receives no assistance (gets in and out of tub by self, if tub is usual means of bathing)	Receives assistance in bathing only one part of the body (such as back or a leg)	Receives assistance in bathing more than one part of the body (or not bathed)

Dressing—gets clothes from closets and drawers, including underclothes, outer garments, and using fasteners (including braces, if worn)

☐	☐	☐
Gets clothes and gets completely dressed without assistance	Gets clothes and gets dressed without assistance, except for assistance in tying shoes	Receives assistance in getting clothes or in getting dressed, or stays partly or completely undressed

Toileting—going to the "toilet room" for bowel and urine elimination; cleaning self after elimination and arranging clothes

☐	☐	☐
Goes to "toilet room," cleans self, and arranges clothes without assistance (may use object for support such as cane, walker, or wheelchair and may manage night bedpan or commode, emptying same in morning)	Receives assistance in going to "toilet room" or in cleansing self or in arranging clothes after elimination or in use of night bedpan or commode	Doesn't go to room termed "toilet" for the elimination process

Transfer

☐	☐	☐
Moves in and out of bed as well as in and out of chair without assistance (may be using object for support, such as cane or walker)	Moves in and out of bed or chair with assistance	Doesn't get out of bed

Continence

☐	☐	☐
Controls urination and bowel movement completely by self	Has occasional "accidents"	Supervision helps keep urine or bowel control; catheter is used or person is incontinent

Feeding

☐	☐	☐
Feeds self without assistance	Feeds self except for getting assistance in cutting meat or buttering bread	Receives assistance in feeding or is fed partly or completely by using tubes or intravenous fluids

SOURCE: Courtesy of Sidney Katz, MD. Reprinted with permission.

For additional information on administration and scoring refer to the following references:
1. Katz S. Assessing self-maintenance: activities of daily living, mobility, and instrumental activities of daily living. *J Am Geriatr Soc.* 1983;31:721–727.
2. Katz S, Akpom CA. A measure of primary sociobiologic functions. *Int J Health Services.* 1976;6:493–508.
3. Katz S, Downs TD, Cash HR, et al. Progress in development of the index of ADL. *J Gerontol.* 1970;10(1):20–30.

Figure 8.5 The Katz Activities of Daily Living scale. (From Katz, S., Ford, A., & Moskowitz, R. (1963). The index of ADL: A standardized measure of biological and psychosocial function. *Journal of the American Medical Association 185*, 914. Copyright 1963, American Medical Association, with permission.)

Instrumental Activities of Daily Living

Instrumental activities of daily living include the ability to use the telephone, cook, shop, do laundry, manage finances, take medications, and prepare meals. These activities are needed to support independent living. Lawton's scale for IADLs is used widely (Fig. 8.6).

If possible, observe the older adult while the person is performing IADLs. Look for abnormal body movements such as tremors or twitching, for lack of balance, or for poor vision. In addition to checking the person's ability to complete the IADL, it is important to assess the older adult with regard to safety. The older person may be able to cook a meal, but if the burner is left on, a serious safety concern exists.

Many times in completing an IADL assessment, the nurse must rely on reports from the older adult or family members. Keep in mind that individuals tend to overrate their abilities and family members tend to underrate them.

Tools for assessing ADLs and IADLs are used to measure the elder's ability to do self-care and home-care tasks. They can be used to help identify needed services and to monitor the progress or deterioration of the older individual.

Social Function

Social function involves how the older adult interacts with self, the environment, and others. It is the degree to which a person functions as a member of the community. Cultural and socioeconomic background and the older adult's environment define and limit social activities and relationships. Self-concept affects the older adult's ability to perform self-care activities. Psychological interventions may be necessary to enhance the older person's self-esteem before achieving independent functioning.

Strategies to Enhance the Well-Being of the Older Adult

Reinforce positive health behaviors through acknowledgment and praise so that the moral-ethical component of self-concept is strengthened. Avoid emphasis on self-care deficits so that the tendency for heightened criticism and lowered physical self-concept is not accentuated. Ensure that the older adult possesses the knowledge and competence necessary to engage in health-promoting self-care activities, for example, information on diet, nutrition, exercise, sleep, medications, and other disease-management strategies. Encourage the older adult to engage in ADLs that contribute to achieving a reasonable level of independent function so that a sense of independence is maintained through self-care. Maintain professional behavior in interacting with the older adult so that respect and caring are communicated.

Instrumental Activities of Daily Living (IADL) Scale

Self-Rated Version Extracted from the Multilevel Assessment Instrument (MAI)

1. Can you use the telephone:
   without help, — 3
   with some help, or — 2
   are you completely unable to use the telephone? — 1

2. Can you get to places out of walking distance:
   without help, — 3
   with some help, or — 2
   are you completely unable to travel unless special arrangements are made? — 1

3. Can you go shopping for groceries:
   without help, — 3
   with some help, or — 2
   are you completely unable to do any shopping? — 1

4. Can you prepare your own meals:
   without help, — 3
   with some help, or — 2
   are you completely unable to prepare any meals? — 1

5. Can you do your own housework:
   without help, — 3
   with some help, or — 2
   are you completely unable to do any housework? — 1

6. Can you do your own handyman work:
   without help, — 3
   with some help, or — 2
   are you completely unable to do any handyman work? — 1

7. Can you do your own laundry:
   without help, — 3
   with some help, or — 2
   are you completely unable to do any laundry at all? — 1

8a. Do you take medicines or use any medications?
   (If yes, answer Question 8b) Yes — 1
   (If no, answer Question 8c) No — 2

8b. Do you take your own medicine
   without help (in the right doses at the right time), — 3
   with some help (take medicine if someone prepares it for you and/or reminds you to take it), or — 2
   (are you/would you be) completely unable to take your own medicine? — 1

8c. If you had to take medicine, can you do it
   without help (in the right doses at the right time), — 3
   with some help (take medicine if someone prepares it for you and/or reminds you to take it), or — 2
   (are you/would you be) completely unable to take your own medicine? — 1

9. Can you manage your own money:
   without help, — 3
   with some help, or — 2
   are you completely unable to handle money? — 1

SOURCE: Lawton MP, Brody EM. Assessment of older people: self-maintaining and instrumental activities of daily living. *Gerontologist*. 1969;9:179–185. Reprinted with permission.

For additional information on administration and scoring refer to the following references:
1. Lawton MP. Scales to measure competence in everyday activities. *Psychopharm Bull*. 1988;24(4):609–614.
2. Lawton MP, Moss M, Fulcomer M, et al. A research and service-oriented Multilevel Assessment Instrument. *J Gerontol*. 1982;37: 91–99.

Figure 8.6 Instrumental Activities of Daily Living scale. (From Lawton, M. P., & Brody, E. M. (1969). Assessment of older people: Self maintaining and instrumental activities of daily living. *Gerontologist*, 9, 179–185. Copyright © The Gerontological Society of America, with permission.)

DISCHARGE PLANNING AND ASSESSMENT

Discharge planning requires the application of many types of assessment. Such planning is essential for the older individual leaving any kind of health-care setting. Although it is most traditionally thought of in terms of discharge from the hospital, discharge planning is appropriate when the older person leaves the nursing home, the day-care center, or any type of formal health-care service.

The key to discharge planning is to start early. It should be initiated on the day of admission to the health-care setting or service and should involve the older adult, family members, and members of the health-care team. Initiating discharge plans early allows time for appropriate education for the older adult and the family. If necessary, outside resources, such as hospice and home-health agencies, should be contacted so that they can become familiar with the older adult and the care that will be required. Discharge planning should assume a holistic approach to the older individual to avoid overlooking important areas and ensure continuity of care.

It is best if an objective assessment tool is used during the initial assessment process to identify potential discharge needs. Blaylock developed a "nurse friendly" bedside tool for discharge planning. The Blaylock risk assessment screen (BRASS) assists in overcoming difficulties with discharge planning (Fig. 8.7). If it is used at the time of admission, older adults that are at risk for prolonged hospitalization can be identified and the need for discharge resources can be assessed (Blaylock & Cason, 1992). This tool was developed to reflect the needs of the older adult.

Home Visit

In many situations, it is more economically feasible for the older adult to remain in the home than to be institutionalized. It is also desirable for the older person to remain in a familiar home environment for as long as possible. Once the older person becomes significantly dependent in ADLs, however, home-care costs can surpass the cost of living in a nursing home. This presents a major dilemma for the family. Often the nurse assists by listening and being supportive or referring the family to a social worker.

A home visit is a valuable component of discharge planning from any health-care environment. The home visit is conducted prior to discharge and provides an opportunity for the older adult and the nurse to evaluate the home setting. During the home visit, the nurse should evaluate the person's ability to function in the home setting, opportunities for socialization, and safety of the environment.

Information from the home visit should be used to prepare both the older adult and the home for the person's return to the home setting. The nurse's role is to assist the older person and the caregivers in maintaining an environment conducive to the elder's optimal level of independence (Frisch, 1993). The nurse must be able to identify the older adult's problems, strengths, and resources to complete an effective home visit.

Blaylock Discharge Planning Risk Assessment Screen

Circle all that apply and total. Refer to the Risk Factor Index.*

Age
   0 = 55 Years or less
   1 = 56 to 64 years
   2 = 65 to 79 years
   3 = 80 + years

Living Situation/Social Support
   0 = Lives only with spouse
   1 = Lives with family
   2 = Lives alone with family support
   3 = Lives alone with friends' support
   4 = Lives alone with no support
   5 = Nursing home/residential care

Functional Status
   0 = Independent in activities of daily living
       and instrumental activities of daily living
   Dependent in:
   1 = Eating/feeding
   1 = Bathing/grooming
   1 = Toileting
   1 = Transferring
   1 = Incontinent of bowel function
   1 = Incontinent of bladder function
   1 = Meal preparation
   1 = Responsible for own medication
       administration
   1 = Handling own finances
   1 = Grocery shopping
   1 = Transportation

Cognition
   0 = Oriented
   1 = Disoriented to some spheres† some of the
       time
   2 = Disoriented to some spheres all of the
       time
   3 = Disoriented to all spheres some of the time
   4 = Disoriented to all spheres all of the time
   5 = Comatose

Behavior Pattern
   0 = Appropriate
   1 = Wandering
   1 = Agitated
   1 = Confused
   1 = Other

Mobility
   0 = Ambulatory
   1 = Ambulatory with mechanical assistance
   2 = Ambulatory with human assistance
   3 = Nonambulatory

Sensory Deficits
   0 = None
   1 = Visual or hearing deficits
   2 = Visual and hearing deficits

Number of Previous Admissions/
Emergency Room Visits
   0 = None in the last 3 months
   1 = One in the last 3 months
   2 = Two in the last 3 months
   3 = More than two in the last 3 months

Number of Active Medical Problems
   0 = Three medical problems
   1 = Three to five medical problems
   2 = More than five medical problems

Number of Drugs
   0 = Fewer than three drugs
   1 = Three to five drugs
   2 = More than five drugs

Total Score:

*Risk Factor Index: Score of 10 = at risk for home care resources; score of 11 to 19 = at risk for extended discharge planning; score greater than 20 = at risk for placement other than home. If the patient's score is 10 or greater, refer the patient to the discharge planning coordinator or discharge planning team.
†Spheres = person, place, time, and self.
Copyright 1991 Ann Blaylock

Figure 8.7 Blaylock Discharge Planning Risk Assessment Screen. (From Blaylock, A., & Cason, C. L. (1992). Discharge planning: Predicting patients' needs. *Journal of Gerontological Nursing 18*(7), 5–9, with permission.)

Some questions should be asked during a home visit. What do you feel are your main problems? What do you find is the most difficult for you to do at home? Is the treatment you are currently receiving helpful? Why? What do you want to result from your care? Use the information obtained from these questions in your discharge plan. Build on the information you collect. The older adult's goals of care should be based on the person's expectations and the health-care professional's input. If the elder's goals do not agree with yours, negotiation may be necessary to accommodate both.

As Figure 8.1 illustrates, physical health, psychosocial well-being, and safety interrelate to determine the holistic health-care needs of the older adult. All these areas must be reviewed during the home visit. An outline for completing a home visit that incorporates all of these elements appears below:

1. Before the visit, review the older adult's medical records, if available, for
   A. *Demographic information*
      Neighborhood. Is it known to be safe, or crime-ridden?
      Type of housing.
      With whom does the older adult reside?
      What is its proximity to health-care services?
   B. *Previous health history and physical examinations*
      Previous complaints
      Major diagnosis
      Functional ability
      Cognitive state
2. In the home
   A. Determine the elderly person's chief complaint.
   B. Complete portions of health history and physical examination pertinent to the older adult's chief complaints.
   C. Complete ADL/IADL evaluation by using the scales of Katz and Lawton.
   D. Complete cognitive evaluation (refer to Chapter 10).
      Minimental status exam
      Short portable mental status exam
   E. Complete the home safety checklist.
   F. Determine from findings if referrals are needed to other members of the health-care team for more extended evaluation. This may include the physical therapist, occupational therapist, respiratory therapist, social worker, and dietician.

During the course of the home visit, evaluate the older adult's communication skills. If the caregiver is available, how does that person interact with the older adult? Is the situation one of tension and anxiety, or of peace and tranquility? Watch facial expressions and body language. Frequently nonverbal communication tells more about the stability of relationships than verbal communication.

Remember, the point of the home visit is to identify anything that may compromise the older person's quality of life. The data from the home visit should be integrated into a specific plan of care. Success can then be measured by the social and functional independence that the older adult achieves.

Safety

The nurse has the responsibility of ensuring safety for the older adult in any environment, including the nursing home, the hospital, or the home. To do this, the nurse has to be knowledgeable about normal aging changes and how they affect the elder's optimal level of independence. In addition to physical safety in the environment, the nurse has a responsibility to assess the older adult's safety from neglect and mistreatment. Figure 8.8 is an example of an evaluation tool for the environment. This particular example is for an in-home assessment that can be completed together with the older adult. With some modifications, however, it can be used in the nursing home and the hospital. Aspects of the environment that are unsafe or promote dependency should be altered prior to the older adult's discharge. Realistic focused interventions can be developed to utilize knowledge of the elder's independence in ADLs and IADLs as they relate to the environmental assessment findings.

Safety assessment also involves evaluating the older adult for signs of neglect or mistreatment in the home setting. Mistreatment of older persons often goes undetected and/or is ignored and is a major problem with the aging population in our country. Nurses have the skills to detect signs and symptoms of abuse. According to Fulmer & Birkenhauer (1992), some common indicators of elderly mistreatment include abrasions, lacerations, contusions, burns, frostbite, depression, fractures, sprains, dislocations, pressure ulcers, dehydration, malnutrition, inappropriate clothing, poor hygiene, oversedation, overmedication or undermedication, untreated medical problems, and behavior that endangers others.

The nurse has the responsibility to report every suspicion of mistreatment to the state's department of aging (Fulmer & Birkenhauer, 1992). It is the responsibility of the state, along with adult protective services, to evaluate the older adult to determine if the elder has suffered mistreatment. The nurse's report needs to carefully document comments made by the older adult and family or staff members. Physical appearance, physical examination findings, and suspected cause of any injuries and measures initiated to ensure safety also must be thoroughly documented. The nurse should not include any editorial or subjective comments in the report. Only facts and findings are appropriate.

In whatever setting the elder resides, a mistreatment evaluation should be completed. Check with your state or local agency on aging for an evaluation tool. The nurse has a professional responsibility to include this assessment as part of the evaluation process. The most important aspect to keep in mind is the older adult's safety and well-being.

Wellness Assessment

Wellness involves health promotion and building on an individual's strengths. It encompasses not only physical health but mental, emotional, and spiritual health as well. The focus of wellness is on behavior and lifestyle. Wellness has become a major area of attention for the U.S. government. A health-care reform movement for our nation is being planned, using wellness as a major goal. As mentioned in an earlier chapter, *Healthy People 2000* is a government publication that includes a national

HOME SAFETY CHECKLIST

This checklist is used to identify fall hazards in the home. After identification, hazards should be eliminated or reduced. One point is allowed for every *NO* answer. A score of 1 to 7 is excellent, 8 to 14 is good, 15 or higher is hazardous.

	YES	NO
Housekeeping		
1. Do you clean up spills as soon as they occur?	___	___
2. Do you keep floors and stairways clean and free of clutter?	___	___
3. Do you put away books, magazines, sewing supplies, and other objects as soon as you're through with them and never leave them on floors or stairways?	___	___
4. Do you store frequently used items on shelves that are within easy reach?	___	___
Floors		
5. Do you keep everyone from walking on freshly washed floors before they're dry?	___	___
6. If you wax floors, do you apply 2 thin coats and buff each thoroughly or else use self-polishing, nonskid wax?	___	___
7. Do all small rugs have nonskid backings?	___	___
8. Have you eliminated small rugs at the tops and bottoms of stairways?	___	___
9. Are all carpet edges tacked down?	___	___
10. Are rugs and carpets free of curled edges, worn spots, and rips?	___	___
11. Have you chosen rugs and carpets with short, dense pile?	___	___
12. Are rugs and carpets installed over good-quality, medium-thick pads?	___	___
Bathroom		
13. Do you use a rubber mat or nonslip decals in the tub or shower?	___	___
14. Do you have a grab bar securely anchored over the tub or on the shower wall?	___	___
15. Do you have a nonskid rug on the bathroom floor?	___	___
16. Do you keep soap in an easy-to-reach receptacle?	___	___
Traffic Lanes		
17. Can you walk across every room in your home, and from one room to another, without detouring around furniture?	___	___
18. Is the traffic lane from your bedroom to the bathroom free of obstacles?	___	___
19. Are telephone and appliance cords kept away from areas where people walk?	___	___
Lighting		
20. Do you have light switches near every doorway?	___	___
21. Do you have enough good lighting to eliminate shadowy areas?	___	___
22. Do you have a lamp or light switch within easy reach from your bed?	___	___
23. Do you have night lights in your bathroom and in the hallway leading from your bedroom to the bathroom?	___	___
24. Are all stairways well lighted?	___	___
25. Do you have light switches at both the tops and bottoms of stairways?	___	___
Stairways		
26. Do securely fastened handrails extend the full length of the stairs on each side of stairways?	___	___
27. Do rails stand out from the walls so you can get a good grip?	___	___
28. Are rails distinctly shaped so you're alerted when you reach the end of a stairway?	___	___
29. Are all stairways in good condition, with no broken, sagging, or sloping steps?	___	___

Figure 8.8 Home safety checklist. (From National Safety Council in cooperation with the National Retired Teachers Association and the American Association of Retired Persons. (1992). Falling–The Unexpected Trip. A safety program for older adults. Program Leader's Guide, reprinted with permission from Family Safety & Health, Published by the National Safety Council, 1121 Spring Lake Dr., Itaska, IL 60143.)

health-promotion and disease-prevention program. This publication points out three major goals for our nation to achieve during the 1990s (U.S. Public Health Service, 1990). They are:

- Increase the span of healthy life for Americans
- Reduce health disparities among Americans
- Achieve access to preventive services for all Americans

Although our national goals are broad, they serve as the basis of health-promotion and disease-prevention programs. One of the goals of the nursing professional is to assist individuals to reach their optimal level of health and wellness. This level of wellness coincides with our national goals for health care. Consequently, nurses are in an ideal position to have a major impact on health care in the future.

Health promotion involves nutrition, exercise, and stress and weight management. Additional areas that commonly require attention in the geriatric population are medication management and substance abuse evaluation, that is, alcohol and tobacco. Any health-care promotion program for the elderly population should focus on building endurance and self-reliance to promote self-care and quality of life. The nurse assists the older adult with a wellness program by helping identify lifestyle changes that promote health and prevent disease. The older adult identifies reasons to participate in the program. Unless the older person values participation in the program, the likelihood of noncompliance is extremely high. Pascucci (1992) has developed a tool that can assist the nurse to understand the older adult's incentives for undertaking wellness behaviors. Clear communication is extremely important for the success of the program.

A major incentive for wellness behaviors is cost. This becomes particularly relevant if the older person has a limited income. It is more economical to prevent disease and disability than it is to treat them.

Understanding the older adult's motivation and goals is crucial for the nurse to help the older adult define the most beneficial behaviors. "Self-motivation does not change with age" (Rhoads, Dean, Cason, & Blaylock, 1992). Therefore, if the incentives are clear, the older adult will be self-motivated. Health promotion and prevention should take place in all health-care settings. It is as essential as treatment of disease and disability, and nurses must integrate it with equal emphasis into the educational system.

CASE STUDY

Miss S. is an 85-year-old woman who lives alone. You are to make a home visit to assess her ability to live safely in her home. When you enter her home you notice only one light is on in the living room. You check the bulb, and it is 40 watts. She has throw rugs scattered throughout her house. You notice roaches crawling on her appliances and on her food in the kitchen. The back door in her kitchen has the glass broken out. You notice she smells of dried urine. When you see her teeth you notice she is partially edentulous. The refrigerator has only a quart of milk, some cheese, and some eggs. You notice that Miss S. is feeding her cat the same food she is eating. Miss S. is able to function independently and is alert and oriented.

CASE STUDY
DISCUSSION

1. What environmental safety hazards did you assess?
2. What environmental hygiene problems are present?
3. What personal hygiene issues cause you concern?
4. What agencies would you contact to assist Miss S.?
5. Would you recommend that Miss S. be institutionalized? Why?

CASE STUDY
SOLUTIONS

1. Poor lighting (40-watt bulb); scattered rugs; glass in door broken out.
2. Roaches; lack of proper food for nourishment.
3. Partially edentulous state; smell of urine.
4. Meals on Wheels to have two hot meals delivered daily; area agency on aging to see what services are available to fix the glass door, remove roaches, provide light bulbs; health department for social worker referral.
5. No. I would use all possible community resources first and see how she adapts. If, after a specified time period, these interventions do not work, I would reassess and plan for potential institutionalization.

Study Questions

Please select the one best answer.

1. The following are normal aging changes except:
   a. Presbyopia, presbycusis
   b. Presbyopia, urinary incontinence
   c. Kyphosis, ptosis
   d. Osteoporosis, arteriosclerosis

2. Activities of daily living include:
   a. Shopping
   b. Managing finances
   c. Bathing
   d. None of the above

3. A common tool used for evaluating ADLs is:
   a. Lawton's scale
   b. The mini-mental status exam
   c. The Katz scale
   d. a and c

4. A common symptom of myocardial infarction with the older adult is:
   a. Chest pain
   b. Lethargy
   c. Confusion
   d. b and c

5. An important health problem the nurse should help the older adult prevent is:
   a. fecal impaction
   b. dehydration
   c. malnutrition
   d. all of the above

References

Blaylock, A., & Cason, C. L. (1992). Discharge planning: Predicting patients' needs. *Journal of Gerontological Nursing, 18*(7), 5–9.

Frisch, N. (1993). Home care nursing and psychosocial emotional needs of clients. *Home Health Care Nurse, 11*(2), 64–65, 70.

Fulmer, T., & Birkenhauer, D. (1992). Elder mistreatment assessment as a part of everyday practice. *Journal of Gerontological Nursing, 18*(3), 42–43.

Pascucci, M. A. (1992). Measuring incentives to health promotion in older adults: Understanding neglected health promotion in older adults. *Journal of Gerontological Nursing, 18*(3), 16–23.

Rhoads, C., Dean, T., Cason, C., & Blaylock, A. (1992). Comprehensive discharge planning. *Home Health Care Nurse, 10*(6), 13–18.

U.S. Public Health Service. (1990). Healthy People 2000: National health promotion and disease prevention objectives [excerpts]. *Journal of Allied Health, 19*(4), 297–311.

Bibliography

Videotapes

Concept Media (Producer) (1990).
   617 Series:
      Normal Physiologic Changes
      Physical Assessment I
      Physical Assessment II
      Functional Assessment
      Mental and Socioeconomic Assessment

Available from:
  Concept Media
  2493 Dubridge Avenue
  Irvine, CA 92714-5022
  714-660-0727
  1-800-233-7078
  FAX 714-660-0206

  These videotapes provide additional supportive detail for those who want to learn more about physical assessment. They include the important issues of normal physiological changes and functional assessment.

Medcom Inc.
  The Natural Process of Aging
  Medication Use by the Elderly
  OBRA Resident Assessment: Cognitive and Sensory Functioning
  OBRA Resident Assessment Physical Functioning

Available from:
  Medcom
  12601 Industry Street
  Garden Grove, CA 92641

  This set of videotapes adds supplemental information for the student working toward mastery of the world of the elderly client. It emphasizes the normal aging process and provides additional information about medication use and OBRA-focused assessments.

Organizations

Help for Incontinent People (HIP)
  HIP Inc.
  P. O. Box 544
  Union, SC 29379

  This organization provides both information and consultation regarding incontinence in the elderly.

National Gerontological Nursing Association (NGNA)
  7250 Parkway Drive
  Suite 510
  Hanover, MD 21076
  1-800-723-0560

  NGNA is a national organization that invites membership from all levels of nursing. The purpose of the organization is to promote gerontological nursing issues in the national arena. It provides scholarships for undergraduate and graduate nursing students, promotes research, and supports excellence in clinical practice.

Chapter

VIVIAN J. KOROKNAY

9

Common Clinical Problems: Physiological

Learning Objectives

After completing this chapter, the student will be able to:

1. Identify the age-related factors that place the older client at risk for impaired mobility.
2. Describe how the nurse can help the older client maintain mobility.
3. Delineate two categories of risk factors for falls in the older population and name three risk factors specific to each category.
4. Identify two categories of incontinence.
5. Explain how prompted voiding and habit training schedules can be utilized by the nurse for prevention or reversal of incontinence.
6. Identify the mechanical and physiological risk factors for pressure ulcers.
7. Discuss the problems pertaining to adequate food intake in the older population.
8. Describe two sleep disorders common to the older population.
9. State the common changes in sleep patterns in the older population.
10. Define iatrogenesis and list common iatrogenic problems experienced by the older patient.

INTRODUCTION

With aging, every body system undergoes some changes. These changes, although not necessarily resulting in illness or disease, cause health problems, which are more prevalent in the older age group. It is commonly stated that 80% of the aged population has at least one chronic illness. The combination of normal aging changes along with underlying chronic diseases means that the older person has less physical reserve than a younger counterpart; that is, the body has a decreased ability to respond when an increased demand, such as an illness, is placed on it. With diminished physical reserve, the older person is less capable of adapting to physical stressors and is, therefore, at increased risk for suffering such clinical problems as immobility, falls, incontinence, pressure ulcers, and alteration in nutrition and sleep. This chapter reviews the clinical problems that are common to older adults. In addition, effective management approaches, based on the nursing diagnoses, are discussed.

ALTERATION IN MOBILITY

The process of aging, combined with the presence of chronic illness, places the older person at risk for developing an alteration in mobility status. Immobility is a major medical disability for the aged, and one that is frequently overlooked by health-care providers. Immobility often leads to numerous complications for older people in long-term care facilities as well as in the hospital and the community. The ability to move is essential to the functioning of all body systems. The elderly population is particularly susceptible to the physiological and psychological complications of immobility. The body changes related to aging and those caused by immobility have many features in common. Taken together, the two often cause serious problems for older people. Nursing management is essential to maintaining and improving the older person's ability to be mobile.

The Musculoskeletal System

Normal aging changes that occur in the musculoskeletal system increase the risk of developing problems related to mobility. The bones of an older person are less dense and more brittle. This is due to changes in the formation of bone at the cellular level. As a result, the older population is likely to develop osteoporosis and to suffer the subsequent risk of bone fractures.

With a fracture, mobility is restricted still further. Mechanical stresses, such as walking and standing, tend to stimulate the process of bone formation. When the body is immobilized, there is bone dissolution. This process is called *disuse osteoporosis,* and it will make the bones of the older person still more brittle. Thus, the aging process, when combined with an underlying illness such as a fracture, exacerbates osteoporosis and increases the risk of immobility.

Generalized muscle weakness is also a normal aging process. There is a noticeable decrease in muscle strength with aging. The antigravity muscles are most affected by this change so that standing up can be a difficult movement. In time, if muscles are not used, walking, balancing, and turning become severely impaired. At complete rest, muscle strength can decline at a rate of 5% a day (Brummel-Smith,

1990). The loss of muscle mass is not just a symptom of generalized deterioration but also a factor in the risk of falling. As muscle strength decreases, there is a decrease in endurance. This makes it more difficult for the individual to be active and maintain mobility. Consequently, a cycle develops in which limited activity causes a decline in muscle strength and endurance; this, in turn, causes immobility, which further depletes muscle strength.

The mobility of the joints is affected by the length and composition of the muscle fibers. When there is immobility, the muscles that bridge the joint shorten. With decreased muscle length, as well as thickening of the joint cartilage (the connective tissue that surrounds the moveable surfaces of the joint), the joints become stiff. Stiffness affects the mobility of the joint. Such changes lead to fatigue and higher susceptibility to osteoarthritis.

Osteoarthritis, or degenerative joint disease, occurs in 83%–87% of people when they are between 55 and 64 years of age. It is marked by deterioration of the cartilage and formulation of new bone at the joint surfaces (Burrage, 1991). With aging, the cartilage is less elastic, thicker, and more easily stretched. As a result, the joint is stiff and there is decreased range of motion to the joint. Over time, the older person can lose the ability to mobilize efficiently as a result of stiffness in the joints. As joints are immobilized, contractures (a permanent contraction of the muscles that bridge the joint) can develop and further limit mobilization.

The Cardiovascular System

Many of the changes in the cardiovascular system that accompany aging are closely related to inactivity. Similarly, these aging changes can be exacerbated, or become more severe, when there are prolonged periods of immobility. One such aging change is that in oxygen consumption, which is referred to as $\dot{V}O_2$. $\dot{V}O_2$ measures the body's ability to transport oxygen from the atmosphere to the various tissues of the body. In aging, as well as during periods of immobilization, this ability decreases. $\dot{V}O_2$ is affected by cardiac output (the amount of blood pumped from the heart to the body), which is known to diminish in aging. Physical exercise causes the active tissue to utilize more oxygen and eliminate carbon dioxide, and this increases cardiac output; however, with prolonged immobility, cardiac output during exercise does not increase as efficiently as in an active ambulatory person.

Oxygen consumption and cardiac output also are known to decrease with aging. This change is evident from the fact that the pulse rate of an older person does not increase in response to exercise as efficiently as in younger people. After physical exertion, the pulse takes longer to return to a normal level. The inefficient cardiac response to activity causes activity intolerance. Elderly people are at greater risk for immobility because of diminished exercise tolerance. When an older person is immobilized, the cardiac response to activity is even less efficient, which impedes mobility still further.

The Respiratory System

As is true of the musculoskeletal system, aging changes to the respiratory system put the older person at risk for complications when immobility is present. Normal anatomical changes in the aging body compromise lung function. Increased rigidity of the rib cage, kyphosis, and osteoporosis reduce the compliance of the chest wall, making it more difficult to fully inflate the lungs. The reduced compliance of the chest wall makes it more difficult for the older person to maintain activity, and it also increases the potential for complications caused by immobility. The lungs of most older clients have diminished vital capacity (the amount of air that can be expelled from the lungs following inspiration). Other changes include less efficient gas exchange by the alveoli and less stretchability of the lung tissue. The result is impaired ventilation and decreased blood supply to the lungs. Such changes may not only hinder the older person's ability to mobilize, but more importantly, place the older patient at increased risk for developing atelectasis (collapsed lung) and pneumonia, when immobilized.

Response to Illness

Chronic health problems may cause older people to restrict their movement. For instance, poor eyesight may cause someone of any age to avoid activity because of fear of falling over an obstacle. Pain in the joints due to arthritis or pain in the lower extremities due to impaired circulation generally limit ambulation and cause older persons to become sedentary. Shortness of breath or angina secondary to chronic cardiopulmonary diseases may cause the individual to avoid activity. With the prevalence of chronic health problems in the older population, these situations are not uncommon.

Acute health problems may also lead to immobility. The onset of an acute illness, whether or not it requires hospitalization, may lead to confinement in bed. Often well-meaning family and health-care providers may actually encourage immobility. Bed rest often is ordered during hospitalization for an acute illness. Unfortunately, unlike a younger person, the older adult who is on bed rest deteriorates rapidly and may develop irreversible complications. Although rest can promote healing, immobility promotes deterioration. Prolonged immobility is detrimental to both the physical and mental health of a person of any age. When immobilized, the older person can develop complications such as contractures, pneumonia, pulmonary emboli, thrombophlebitis, pressure ulcers, incontinence, constipation, renal stones, dehydration, loss of appetite, and psychological problems related to sensory deprivation and depression.

Nursing Implications. Although immobility is a prevalent health problem, it is not often addressed in the care of the elderly. Identifying immobility as a patient-care problem and intervening to prevent it are central to nursing care of the older client. In addressing the mobility needs of an elderly patient the licensed practical nurse may prevent complications and shorten the length of time the resident is ill.

Nurses, as well as the older people to whom they give care, need to be aware that promoting physical activity not only prevents complications but also slows the rate of the aging process. In the hospital setting, the time for enforced bed rest needs to be limited as much as possible. As soon as it is medically safe to do so, the nurse needs to ensure that the patient is up and out of bed. If orders for bed rest are in effect, it is the nurse's responsibility to inquire whether such orders can be changed. Even transferring the patient from a supine to a sitting position has beneficial effects.

While on bed rest, elderly patients can be taught isometric and active range-of-motion exercises. If the patient is incapable of performing these exercises independently, then the nurse must assist the patient to meet this need. Passive range-of-motion exercises maintain joint flexibility and, to some extent, delay muscle wasting.

As soon as it is medically indicated, the patient should be ambulated with assistance. This intervention is as important to the patient's health as receiving the proper medication or a dressing change. If, after a prolonged period of illness, the patient is too weak to ambulate with assistance, then a physical therapy referral is indicated. In the older population, a referral for rehabilitative therapies may be overlooked. There may be a fear that the older person might fall or be harmed as a result of frailty; however, even patients well into their 80s have been shown to benefit from efforts at rehabilitation. Nursing staff should augment therapy services by ensuring that appropriate, sturdy footwear, eyeglasses, and any assistive devices such as canes or walkers are brought from home. Because of reimbursement issues, hospital stays are becoming shorter. Therefore, as soon as the patient is physiologically able, attempts to restore functional ability should begin.

As in the hospital setting, promoting functional mobility is central to the care of the older person at home or in a nursing home. The nursing home environment offers different possibilities for fostering mobility. Unlike the hospital setting, where the presence of an acute state may impede the nurse's attempts to restore function and where time is limited due to reimbursement constraints, the nursing home setting allows the nurse to monitor and promote mobility over an extended period of time. All residents should be considered for assisted walking unless the underlying chronic illness absolutely precludes such an activity. The older person who does not walk deteriorates even further and eventually loses all ability to walk. Therefore, persons who are unable to ambulate independently are in particular need of nursing interventions to promote mobility. Walking programs have been found to be helpful in ensuring that the mobility needs of all residents—even those who are unable to walk alone or cannot do so safely—are being met. Although staff are often reluctant to encourage ambulation with a resident whose gait is unsafe, many older people would rather risk falling than being placed in a wheelchair. The nurse, too, needs to consider the risk of falling versus the negative effects of prolonged immobility.

The effects of mobility on promoting health and function are well known. Any mobility goal, no matter how limited, assists the older person in obtaining the highest level of independence. This in turn improves the individual's quality of life. As the health-care provider who is central to maintaining and/or supporting a person's ability to move about, the nurse's role is essential to the promotion of activity and the prevention of immobility.

POTENTIAL FOR INJURY FROM FALLS

As with alteration in mobility, the potential for falls is closely related to many of the bodily changes that occur with aging. The aging of the musculoskeletal system, which may cause a deterioration in mobility, may also increase the older person's risk for falling. One third of adults over 65 years of age living in the community and one half of those over 80 years of age fall each year. In nursing homes, a fall rate of two per resident per year has been reported. Most falls do not result in serious injury;

however, 230,000 falls per year result in hip fractures (Sattin, 1992), and 9,500 persons 65 years of age or older die each year as the result of a fall or fall-related injury (Tinnetti, 1990). The presence of chronic illness accompanying the aging process places the nursing home resident, in particular, at increased risk for falls.

When an older person falls, the person often becomes fearful of falling again. This may cause the older individual to limit activities, to become more withdrawn and dependent on others, to become less mobile, and to become more at risk for future falls due to the harmful effects of immobility. Caregivers also may place restrictions on the older person's mobility to prevent another fall. At home, the family may admonish the older person to restrict activities so that a fall will not occur again. In the health-care setting, restraints may be used to prevent the risk of another fall. These options do not promote health for the patient.

Factors that predispose to falling are typically divided into two categories: intrinsic and extrinsic. Intrinsic factors include factors inherent to the individual, such as normal aging changes, deficiencies in health status, changes in mental status, immobility, and changes in functional ability. Extrinsic factors refer to environmental conditions, which may include poor lighting, slippery floors, inappropriate or poorly placed furnishings, and inadequate footwear. Falls among older adults often stem from the presence of intrinsic factors that hinder the older person's ability to manage the environment or from environmental conditions (extrinsic factors).

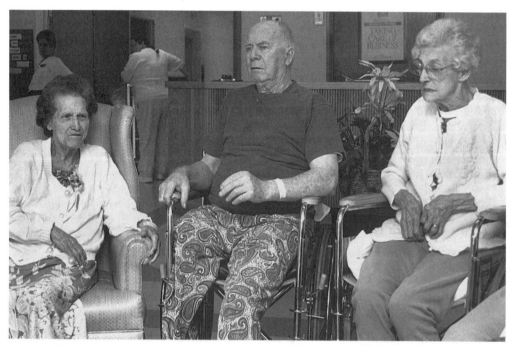

The potential for falls is closely related to many of the bodily changes that are associated with aging. Clients who need assistance to ambulate or require a wheelchair need monitoring to avoid falls.

Intrinsic Factors

Age-related changes in posture, balance, gait, and vision predispose the older person to falls. Postural changes are common in older people and are due to a decline in strength and flexibility. In older adults, the head tends to be carried forward, the shoulders may be rounded, and the upper back may have a slight curvature, or kyphosis. Changes in posture and spinal alignment can affect balance and increase the risk of falls.

Posture and Balance

The body's ability to maintain its coordination in a standing position and to react to prevent a fall is dependent on coordination among the musculoskeletal system, the neurosensory system, and the visual system. Postural sway occurs when one or more of these three systems is not functioning at an optimal level. Balance problems are associated with postural sway, which can cause falls. Prolonged bed rest, aging changes, medications, and the presence of some chronic diseases are contributors to postural sway.

Postural reflexes (reflexes that respond to balance disturbances when standing or walking) play a role in fall prevention by responding to disturbances in balance during standing or walking. With aging, these reflexes become slower; therefore, older people are less able to "catch" themselves when they trip or begin to fall. Inactivity may result in a slower response to disturbances in balance.

Gait

With aging, the gross motor movements necessary for maintaining posture and gait, or walking, are altered. The gait of older people is often marked by decreased speed and step height; small, hesitant steps; diminished arm swing; and stooped posture. These changes are almost universal in the population over 80 years of age. The alterations in speed of movement and maintenance of upright posture adversely affect balance and often lead to a higher incidence of falls by the older person.

Vision

All older people experience changes in vision as part of the normal aging process. With aging, there is a decline in visual acuity, peripheral vision, depth perception, night vision, and tolerance for glare (Stone & Chenitz, 1991). The loss of vision that accompanies aging is a risk factor for falls because there is a decreased ability to focus on objects at a distance and to judge distances correctly. The result is that an older person may miss a step or trip over a curb. The decline in peripheral vision may cause an individual to trip over objects at the edge of the visual field. Visual deficits can compound a gait disability because vision is necessary to maintain stability while walking.

These normal, age-related changes in posture, gait, and vision, when compounded by the presence of an underlying chronic or acute illness, make falls the leading cause of death from injury in the group over 65 years of age (Sattin, 1992). Because of the presence of these intrinsic factors, many older people are less capable of coping with the extrinsic factors that may be in the environment.

Extrinsic Factors

At least 50% of the falls affecting older adults result from environmental factors. Such factors may include clutter in the halls, inadequate lighting or glare, or unsafe furniture or equipment in the person's immediate area. Attempting to function in an area that is not designed to accommodate the aging person's needs can diminish the older person's confidence. The individual may begin to fear falling and may eventually become more sedentary. Such behavior eventually leads to a loss of function and an increased need to depend on others for activities of daily living.

Nursing Implications. As health-care providers, it is important for nurses to understand the role that both intrinsic and extrinsic factors play in falls. The individual's ability to maneuver safely in the immediate environment is best monitored by the nurse. In both the home and the institution, most falls occur in the bedroom and the bathroom. Therefore, it is important to assess the older person walking about the bedroom, getting into and out of bed, and getting on and off the toilet. Only by assessing the individual's ability to move in these daily activities and in the environment can the nurse begin to anticipate needs and take steps to prevent a fall before it occurs.

Having assessed the older client's safety, the nurse, along with other members of the health-care team, should plan care according to the observed need. For instance, the nurse may observe that the older person cannot safely get on and off the toilet independently and may advise the individual not to attempt this maneuver unassisted. If the person is not cognitively intact, the nurse may utilize a toileting schedule to discourage the individual from attempting self-toileting when the nurse is not present to assist. If the older person cannot safely ambulate alone, the health-care team may decide that physical therapy is indicated or that a program of daily assisted ambulation should be initiated. Older persons who cannot safely stand or walk unassisted, but who may still attempt these actions, should not be left alone for extended periods of time. One idea is to bring the person out of the room so staff members can observe the person and in that way keep the individual safe. When someone who is not safe is left alone, mobility alarms should help the staff know when the individual is getting up unassisted. Certainly, all members of the team need to remember to remove clutter and maintain clear walking paths for older people, to adjust lighting to provide an optimum environment, and to wipe up spills from the floor as soon as they occur or are noticed.

ALTERATION IN ELIMINATION

Urinary Incontinence

Urinary incontinence, an affliction that affects approximately 10 million Americans, is defined as an involuntary loss of urine that is sufficient to be a problem (Agency for Health Care Policy Research, 1992b). It is a problem most often seen in the elderly; 15%–30% of noninstitutionalized people over 60 years of age and half of the 1.5 million nursing home residents are affected. The cost of caring for individuals with urinary incontinence is approximately $7 billion annually for individuals dwelling in the community and approximately $3.3 billion for nursing home residents (Agency for Health Care Policy Research, 1992b).

Perhaps even greater than the economic cost are the psychological and social costs to the individual who is incontinent of urine. Incontinence is seen as a major reason older people are placed in nursing homes. Furthermore, people who are incontinent may feel embarrassed and socially isolated. They may withdraw from participation in social activities and become depressed. Incontinence is associated with the development of other health problems such as skin breakdown, behavioral disturbances, and urinary tract infections.

Age-Related Changes
Affecting Incontinence

Although incontinence is more prevalent in the older population, it is not a normal aspect of aging. There are, however, a number of age-related changes that make the older person susceptible to developing incontinence. In older clients, the bladder capacity diminishes to about half that of young adults. The diminished ability of the kidneys to concentrate urine makes urinary frequency and nocturia (excessive urination at night) common problems for the older person. In addition, many older people experience sudden and unexpected contractions of the detrusor muscle (the smooth muscle that makes up the outside wall of the bladder), which cause an urgent need to void. Changes in the central and autonomic nervous systems of the older person cause a decreased ability to contract the external sphincter of the bladder, which further exacerbates urinary urgency. Many postmenopausal women experience thinning and weakening of the muscles of the pelvic floor and the urethra due to estrogen loss. In men, an enlarged prostate, often associated with aging, may lead to urinary retention, irritability of the detrusor muscle, and bladder spasms.

The urinary urgency that many older people experience often leads to incontinence in an institutional setting. When the older client cannot go to the toilet independently or as often as needed, as is the case in many hospitals and nursing homes, incontinence is likely to result. This is further exacerbated by the immobility that results from being ill or from needing medical interventions such as intravenous therapy. Warshaw et al. (1992) found that nearly half of 279 hospitalized clients over 70 years of age were incontinent or had indwelling urinary catheters. The authors contend that difficulties with mobility and summoning help contribute to the incontinence.

Types of Causes of Incontinence

For the nurse to intervene in the management of incontinence, it is important to understand the underlying causes of incontinence. Incontinence can be a result of a chronic problem, or it can be the result of an acute situation.

Acute Incontinence

Acute or transient incontinence is incontinence that occurs because of the presence of another medical problem and often resolves when the underlying illness is treated. The following mnemonic demonstrates the possible causes of acute incontinence (Stone & Chenitz, 1991):

D: Delirium
R: Restricted mobility, retention (acute)
 I: Infection, inflammation, impaction
P: Pharmaceutical, polyuria, psychological

Delirium is an acute confusional state that is brought on by an acute illness and that disrupts the physiological homeostasis in the older patient. In a delirious state, the patient is not aware of the need to void, nor does the person have the capability to get to the toilet.

Restricted mobility, as already discussed, is a common cause of incontinence in the elderly. Acute urinary retention is often caused by anticholinergic and narcotic medications and may result in overflow incontinence.

Urinary tract infection (UTI) causes frequency, urgency, and painful urination. This can lead to increased bladder contractions and incontinence. Many residents in long-term care have bacteria in their urine, a condition that is asymptomatic and does not require treatment. However, when bacteriuria is accompanied by urinary incontinence, the patient should be treated and the effect of the treatment on the incontinence noted.

It is important to remember that fecal impaction often obstructs the bladder outlet and may cause overflow urinary incontinence. In overflow urinary incontinence, the bladder retains urine, and when it reaches its capacity, the individual begins to drip or leak urine. In postmenopausal women, the changes that occur in the lining of the vagina and urethra because of lower levels of estrogen may cause inflammation and weakening of the pelvic floor, which can, in turn, cause incontinence.

Many drugs can cause urinary incontinence. The following is a list of drug groups that adversely affect the older person's ability to maintain continence:

Sedatives/hypnotics
Antipsychotics
Narcotics
Anticholinergics
Alpha-adrenergic blockers
Diuretics

Endocrine disorders that lead to hyperglycemia or hypercalcemia may cause urinary incontinence. Psychological causes that have been associated with urinary incontinence include depression and confusional states.

Nursing Implications. As nurses, it is important to understand that most bladder incontinence situations are transient and, very often, reversible. In most cases, acute or transient incontinence can be resolved with treatment of the underlying illness or with discontinuation of a causative drug. Incontinence should never be accepted without first ascertaining that the older client has been assessed for under-lying conditions and that treatment has been initiated.

Chronic Incontinence

There are four types of persistent or chronic incontinence. Incontinence is con-sidered persistent if it continues after reversible causes have been ruled out or treated. Persistent or chronic incontinence usually has a gradual onset, worsens over time, and occurs when there is a failure to either empty or store urine.

Urge Incontinence. Urge incontinence is the most common form of inconti-nence in the long-term care facility. It is closely associated with stroke and Alzheimer's disease. In this type of incontinence, the patient or resident feels the urge to go and then does not have enough time to get to the toilet before the urine is released.

Stress Incontinence. Stress incontinence occurs when a small amount of urine is released after there is a sudden increase in intra-abdominal pressure caused by coughing, sneezing, laughing, or lifting. This type of incontinence results when the bladder outlet sphincter is incompetent or weak. Stress incontinence is more com-mon in women and is often a result of damage to the pelvic muscles during child-birth.

Overflow Incontinence. Overflow incontinence is present in approximately 15% of nursing home patients (Newman, 1990). It is caused by bladder outlet ob-struction that results in impaired bladder emptying. When the bladder is not emp-tied sufficiently, the resident experiences frequent dribbling of urine.

Functional Incontinence. Functional incontinence results when the individ-ual is unable or unwilling to attend to toileting needs. In this situation, the bladder and urethra function normally, but cognitive, physical, psychological, or environmen-tal impairments make it difficult for the older person to get to the toilet. Inaccessible toilets, unavailable caregivers, depression, or inability to find the toilet are all possi-ble causes of functional incontinence.

Nursing Implications. Treatment of urinary incontinence is based on the un-derlying cause. Medication intervention may be used to treat infection, replace estro-gen, or stop abnormal bladder muscle contractions and tighten sphincter muscles. Surgical intervention is utilized to correct anatomical anomalies and remove ob-structions. Behavioral interventions require that the health-care professional pro-vide education and positive reinforcement to the client. At times, behavioral inter-ventions may be used in combination with medical or surgical interventions.

Behavioral Interventions. Behavioral interventions, which are most often provided by nursing personnel, are called training procedures and include:

Bladder training (retraining)
Habit training (timed voiding)
Prompted voiding
Pelvic muscle exercises

These techniques are most helpful with stress and urge incontinence.

Bladder retraining is used to restore the normal pattern of voiding by inhibiting or stimulating voiding. The goal is to lengthen the period of time between voidings. This is best done by instructing and assisting the individual to learn to suppress the urge to void in an attempt to increase the amount of urine the bladder can hold. This technique is used with individuals who are capable of understanding and remembering the instructions. Most bladder-retraining schedules begin with a schedule of toileting every 2 hours and gradually increase the amount of time between voidings.

Prompted voiding is different from bladder training in that the goal is not to increase bladder capacity but rather to teach the incontinent person to be aware of toileting needs and to request assistance from the caregiver. In this technique, the person is asked to try to use the toilet at regular intervals and is praised for maintaining continence and using the toilet. The schedule that is followed usually involves toileting on awakening, after meals, at bedtime, and, if awake, at night. More voiding times can be added if the individual's voiding schedule indicates that need. This intervention works well with moderately confused people.

Habit training works best with cognitively impaired or confused people and requires the caregiver to take the patient to the toilet at regular intervals. The toileting schedule may be every 2–4 hours, or the caregiver may toilet the individual on awakening, after meals, at bedtime, and at night, if awake.

Kegel's exercises are used to alleviate stress incontinence. The goal of such exercises is to strengthen the pelvic floor muscles. Patients who are taught Kegel's exercises must be cognitively intact and willing to participate in this exercise regimen.

Management of urinary incontinence is a difficult problem for the patient as well as the caregiver. Incontinence can have a severe negative impact on the individual's physical, psychological, and social well-being. In dealing with this disorder, nurses play a key role in both eduction and treatment. Incontinence is not a normal part of aging but is more prevalent in the aging population. Many forms of incontinence are reversible, and all attempts should be made to assess, treat, and resolve incontinence when it is present.

Constipation

Bowel functioning and the avoidance of constipation are common concerns for the older population. Many older people were raised during a time when anything but a daily bowel movement was considered abnormal. The concern regarding this problem is appropriate because numerous age-related changes in the gastrointestinal system make constipation more likely.

The older client is more likely to have an extended gastrointestinal transit time as a result of slower peristalsis. More water is removed from the stool when it is in the colon for longer periods of time. This causes the stool to become harder and more difficult to pass. Immobility, decreased exercise, and a lack of fiber and water in the diet are all common problems in the older population, and these factors tend to exacerbate the tendency to become constipated. Certain drugs also may lead to constipation and are as follows (Yakobowich, 1990):

Aluminum-containing antacids
Anticholinergics
Calcium carbonate
Iron salts
Laxatives (when abused)
Opiates
Phenothiazines
Sedatives
Tricyclic antidepressants
Diuretics
Calcium-channel blockers

Immobility is particularly problematic in the maintenance of regular bowel movements. Muscular atrophy, a loss of tone in the muscles of the intestine, and generalized weakness of the muscles necessary for the expulsive mechanism of evacuation occur during periods of immobilization. The overuse of laxatives also causes a loss of muscle tone in the bowel.

Immobility not only affects the physiological functioning of the gastrointestinal system but also prevents the individual from interacting efficiently with the environment to meet the needs of the body. Factors such as strange environments, disruption of the usual elimination patterns, being forced to defecate in an unnatural position in unnatural surroundings (as occurs with the use of a bedpan), and suppressing the urge to defecate because of inability to get to the toilet will inhibit normal defecation.

Nursing Interventions

Nursing interventions aimed at prevention of constipation should be focused on establishing a regular pattern of bowel elimination that is not associated with straining or discomfort. It is important for the older person's overall health to attempt to correct constipation without resorting to the use of laxatives. These interventions should include increasing physical activity, increasing water intake, increasing dietary fiber, and establishing a regular bowel routine. Regular exercise stimulates motility in the gut.

The client should be encouraged to take 1500 to 2000 mL of fluids daily unless this is contraindicated by other health problems. Dietary fiber also plays an important role in the avoidance of constipation. Fiber holds water, thus making the stool softer and bulkier, and speeds the passage of stool through the intestine. It can be difficult to increase fiber in the diet of the older person because of lifelong dietary preferences and poor dentition. It may be helpful to consult a dietician. Although prunes and prune juice are often used to combat constipation, they may not be the best choice. Prunes have only 2 g of fiber per prune, and prune juice has none. Furthermore, prunes mimic the action of cathartics, and there may be rebound constipation when the use of prunes is discontinued.

Assisting the patient to develop a regular bowel routine is an essential part of bowel maintenance, and one in which the nurse plays a pivotal role. In facilitating regular bowel routines, the nurse must assess how much, if any, assistance the patient requires in getting safely to the toilet. The use of bedpans should be avoided if at all possible, but when they are used, the patient should be in an upright position unless this position is contraindicated. The nurse also needs to ensure that regular toileting times are maintained and that privacy is provided during toileting time.

ALTERATION IN SKIN INTEGRITY: PRESSURE ULCERS

A pressure ulcer is defined as any lesion caused by unrelieved pressure that results in damage to the underlying tissue. Pressure ulcers are an extremely serious health problem that can lead to pain, extended hospital stays, and further complications from infection. In hospitals, the pressure ulcer rate has been estimated to be as high as 29.5%, and in nursing homes it is estimated to be 23%. Older persons are particularly at risk, with those over the age of 70 accounting for 71% of all patients with pressure ulcers. A mortality rate of approximately 60,000 deaths per year is associated with pressure ulcers. In nursing homes, 66% of those residents who develop a pressure ulcer die. It is estimated that patients with pressure ulcers require 50% more nursing care than those without. Because pressure ulcers are, for the most part, preventable, maintaining adequate skin integrity is a quality-of-care issue for all nurses. Even more important than knowing the various treatment modalities is knowing how pressure ulcers develop and becoming an expert in prevention techniques.

Risk Factors

Mechanical Risk Factors

Four mechanical factors contribute to the development of pressure ulcers are pressure, friction, shearing, and moisture.

PRESSURE

Pressure ulcers usually occur over bony prominences, where normal tissue is squeezed between the internal pressure of the bone and an external source of pressure or friction, such as the chair or the bed. External pressure that lasts long enough and is sufficient to decrease blood flow results in inadequate oxygenation and nutrition to the area and the development of a pressure sore. Immobility is the most important risk factor in the development of pressure sores. Pressure of high intensity that is left unchecked for more than 2 hours can result in irreversible tissue damage.

SHEARING

When the head of the bed is elevated more than 30 degrees and the person slides toward the foot of the bed, shearing occurs. In this situation, the skin over the sacrum does not move whereas the subcutaneous tissue and gluteal vessels are stretched. This results in rupture of the blood vessels. Subcutaneous fat, which lacks the ability to stretch, is particularly vulnerable to injury from shearing forces. Sores that develop on the sacrum, heels, and anterior tibial region are most probably a result of shearing. When shearing and pressure are both present, the amount of pressure necessary to cause tissue damage is half the amount that causes tissue damage when shearing is not present.

FRICTION AND MOISTURE

Friction occurs when the skin is moved across the sheets, such as when the patient is being pulled up rather than lifted up in the bed. The result of this motion is damage to the epidermis, which can lead to ulceration or a break in the skin. Moisture caused by perspiration or incontinence can increase the friction between the surface and the skin. Moisture can also cause maceration (softening of the skin), which weakens the skin and increases the risk of infection. In the presence of moisture resulting from urinary or fecal incontinence, the risk of pressure ulcer development on the sacrum and buttocks increases fivefold. Incontinence is a strong predictor of skin breakdown.

Physiological Risk Factors

In addition to mechanical forces, there are also factors that are inherent to the individual that increase the risk of skin breakdown.

AGING SKIN

Aging skin increases the likelihood of developing pressure ulcers because it is less resistant to the mechanical forces that can damage the skin. With advancing age, there is a decrease in the thickness of the cell layers of the epidermis, a flatten-

Aging skin increases the likelihood of developing complications because it is less resistant to the mechanical forces that can damage skin.

ing in the epidermal/dermal interface, and a loss of subcutaneous tissue. In turn, these changes cause impaired wound healing and decreased thermoregulation, and the skin becomes more fragile.

IMMOBILITY

Immobility, combined with the age-related changes of the skin, greatly increases the risk of pressure ulcer formation. Normally, spontaneous body movements that occur during sleep and throughout the day protect the skin from pressure. A number of situations, however, prevent the body from spontaneous movement. These include a physical disability, loss of sensation, the presence of pain, or the use of sedating drugs or anesthesia. The use of physical restrains also causes immobility.

MALNUTRITION

Another physiological factor that can lead to pressure ulcer formation is malnutrition. Deficiencies in zinc, iron, vitamin C, and protein adversely affect the health of the skin. The more severe the malnutrition, the more severe the pressure ulcer is. In patients who have had weight loss or who are underweight, it is important to check the albumin level of the blood. A serum albumin level below 3.3 g% indicates that nutritional intervention is necessary to prevent skin breakdown (Stone & Chenitz, 1991). Malnutrition and the subsequent weight loss lead to loss of muscle mass and subcutaneous tissue. This diminishes the body's protective padding and increases the pressure over the bony prominences.

Staging

Pressure ulcers are graded according to the degree of tissue damage. The staging of a pressure ulcer dictates the type of treatment to be implemented. Staging provides a means of describing an ulcer that allows for the ulcer to be monitored over time. The staging criteria that are most widely accepted have been recommended by the Agency for Health Care Policy Research (1992a), a federally supported agency, under the U.S. Department of Health and Human Services. The staging is as follows:

Stage I: Nonblanchable erythema of intact skin. (The skin is reddened, even in the absence of direct pressure.)

Stage II: Partial-thickness skin loss involving epidermis and/or dermis. The ulcer is superficial and presents clinically as an abrasion, blister, or shallow crater.

Stage III: Full-thickness skin loss involving damage to or necrosis of subcutaneous tissue that may extend down to, but not through, the underlying fascia (the fibrous membrane covering the muscles). The ulcer presents clinically as a deep crater with or without undermining (connecting) of adjacent tissue.

Stage IV: Full-thickness skin loss with extensive destruction, tissue necrosis, or damage to muscle, bone, or supporting structures (for example, tendon or joint capsule). Undermining and sinus tracts may also be associated with Stage IV pressure ulcers.

Prevention

Assessment of risk is a vital first step in prevention of pressure ulcers. If a patient is found to be at risk for developing pressure ulcers, then interventions to prevent skin breakdown can be initiated before an ulcer develops. A number of assessment tools are available. The Norton scale is probably the most well known and is the basis of subsequent assessment tools. Norton identified physical condition, mental condition, activity, mobility, and incontinence as risk factors to be assessed for skin breakdown. The Braden scale, another risk assessment tool, includes these factors but adds nutritional status as a factor and identifies levels of impairment for each factor.

Assessment should be done within the first 24 hours of admission to a hospital or nursing home and repeated 24–48 hours following admission. Ongoing assessment is necessary to prevent new skin breakdown. This should be done every 24–48 hours in the hospital, monthly in the nursing home, and whenever there is a change in the patient's condition. Once the patient is found to be at risk for alteration in skin integrity, preventive measures should be aimed at reducing pressure on bony prominences, preventing shear or friction, keeping skin clean and dry, and providing adequate nutrition and hydration.

To reduce pressure, the patient should be repositioned at least every 2 hours. This decreases the amount of time that pressure is exerted on any one body part. The appearance of reddened areas indicates that more frequent turning or other interventions may be indicated. When placing a patient on either side, a wedge should be placed behind the patient to prevent the individual from lying directly on the trochanter (the bony prominence located below the neck of the femur). Although at one time it was common practice to massage reddened areas over bony prominences, this is no longer the practice. To do so may exert pressure on the area and may cause further breakdown of the small capillaries in the area. In some cases, it may be necessary to utilize pressure-relieving devices, such as air-, water-, or gel-filled chair pads or mattresses, as well as foam heel protectors and mattresses. The use of egg-crate mattresses, although common, does not provide sufficient pressure relief to prevent pressure ulcers. Because immobility is a major factor in pressure and the formation of pressure ulcers, the reduction or reversal of immobility becomes an important preventive measure. Walking programs and passive and active range-of-motion exercises not only improve muscle strength and joint flexibility but are important in the prevention of skin breakdown as well.

To reduce friction, patients should be lifted and not pulled when repositioned. The use of a lift sheet or a turn sheet is essential to evenly distribute the patient's weight and avoid undue friction and stress on the skin. Shear can be reduced by decreasing the amount of time and frequency that the patient's head is elevated in the bed. When out of bed and in a chair, the patient should be repositioned at least every 2 hours and long-term sitting should be discouraged. While in the chair, the individual needs to be examined for appropriate posture and alignment because an inappropriate sitting posture can lead to pressure ulcers and increased shearing forces.

Although skin should be kept clean and dry to prevent pressure ulcers, older people do not need to be bathed daily. Excessive bathing and rubbing can be drying and damaging to the skin. Utilizing a mild cleansing agent that does not promote dryness and patting the skin dry are essentials of good skin care for the older person.

A diet that provides adequate nutrition and hydration and that meets the protein and vitamin requirements of the individual promotes skin integrity. A dietary consultation is needed in a patient who has skin breakdown and/or has an albumin level below 3.3 g%.

Treatment

Sometimes, despite vigilant nursing care, a pressure ulcer does develop. Often an underlying disease state can defeat attempts to prevent skin breakdown. The treatment of pressure ulcers is extremely individualized, and there is much controversy as to which treatments and skin care products to use. The technology and products for treatment of pressure ulcers are changing every day. Treatment is aimed at promoting a healing environment by providing adequate circulation and oxygenation to the impaired tissue, and maintaining a clean and dry wound area. Exudate should be removed as much as possible and infection should be treated with the appropriate antibiotic. Any necrotic tissue needs to be debrided or removed before treatment of the ulcer can proceed. This should be done only under the supervision of a registered nurse.

ALTERED NUTRITIONAL STATUS

Adequate nutrition is essential to the maintenance of health, prevention of disease, treatment of chronic illness, and recovery from acute illness. When the body is inadequately nourished, the individual is more likely to develop an illness and is less able to recover from illness. Caloric or protein malnutrition is present in 12%–50% of the older population.

To be adequately nourished, the body must have a sufficient intake of carbohydrates, fat, protein, vitamins, minerals, and water. Difficulty obtaining appropriate nutrition can be a result of lack of knowledge about good nutrition, inadequate income or means of obtaining the appropriate foods, lack of socialization (which may lead to disinterest or overindulgence in food), or housing that is not adequate for storing and preparing nutritionally sound meals. The older person's diet is often lacking in calcium, vitamin C, riboflavin, niacin, and iron. A nutritional deficiency of any essential nutrient can cause changes to the body that, if left unchecked, can lead to illness.

Risk Factors

Anorexia (loss of appetite) is a major cause of inadequate nutritional intake in the older population. Poor dentition, poorly fitting dentures, or the lack of dentures may make it difficult for the individual to chew; and a soft or puree diet may be unappetizing. Not only may diminished mobility make it difficult for the older person to obtain and prepare food, but a sedentary lifestyle may lead to a decreased appetite. Polypharmacy, a situation not uncommon to the elderly, can adversely affect appetite by altering taste sensation, impairing cognition and mood, or interfering with the absorption of nutrients. Other causes of anorexia in the older population may include the increased incidence of chronic illness, social isolation, depression, and unappetizing institutional foods.

Changes in the metabolism of the older person translate into changes in nutritional requirements of the body. With aging, there is a decreased metabolic rate. This means that the body requires fewer calories for maintenance. Decreased mobility and the loss of muscle mass associated with aging also suggest that older people may need to decrease their caloric consumption. However, the older person uses more energy than a younger person to do the same activities. Therefore, if the individual is active, there may actually be a need to increase the caloric intake. Furthermore, with aging, the body does not metabolize protein as efficiently, so the older person may need protein in the diet.

Maintaining adequate nutrition in patients who have a disease process poses a particular challenge to the nurse. Patients with advanced dementia may have weight loss even when there is an adequate intake of nutritional requirements. It is suspected that this weight loss may be due, in part, to the increased use of antibiotics in a population that tends to have a higher rate of infection. Neuroleptics, another commonly used class of drugs in the demented patient, may also cause a loss of appetite. It has been postulated that there may a disturbance in the metabolism of patients with advanced Alzheimer's disease, and this, too, may account for the unexplained weight loss in this population. The term, "failure to thrive," has been used to describe another entity associated with weight loss. Failure to thrive occurs when some elderly nursing home residents experience a gradual decline in physical and cognitive functioning associated with weight loss, withdrawing from food, withdrawing from human contact, and exhibiting signs of depression.

Assessment

Assessing the nutritional status of the older person can be a difficult task for the nurse. The recommended daily allowance (RDA) that is established by the National Academy of Science Research Council is one way of monitoring how well an individual is meeting nutritional requirements. It is important to realize, however, that the RDA does not consider the specific needs of the population over 65 years of age. Furthermore, additional nutrients that may be needed as a result of infection or chronic illness are not addressed by the RDA.

Further complicating the assessment for malnutrition are the changes of the aging body itself. Many of the physical manifestations of malnutrition are similar to changes that are associated with aging. These include dry, thin hair; dry, flaky skin; sunken eyes; dry oral mucosa; weight loss; and muscle weakness. Using skinfold measures to estimate percentage of body fat may not yield accurate information because mean body mass (muscle tissue) decreases with age. Probably the most reliable indicator of adequate nutritional intake is a normal serum albumin level (3.5–5.5 g%). Monitoring an individual's weight over time is also an appropriate means of recognizing alteration in nutritional status.

Nursing Implications. To reestablish adequate nutritional intake, healthcare providers should strive to maintain oral feedings, possibly with appropriate modifications. This may mean making the diet more palatable with foods that have different textures and flavors. Providing the individual's food favorites whenever possible is also a good approach. Asking the help of family to provide favorite foods for the patient may be necessary. Making sure that the older person has dentures and that they fit well, and then providing a diet that is appropriate for the individual's dental status, is imperative. Everyone responds well to meals that are served in an attractive manner and in an environment that is relaxed and pleasant. Nursing staff should strive for this kind of atmosphere during mealtime by not raising their voices and trying to keep noisy dietary carts out of the eating area. Eyeglasses help the resident to see the food on the tray, and hearing aids allow the resident to socialize with table-mates during mealtime. It is important that the nurse make sure that the individual has whatever assistive devices are needed to make the eating experience a more pleasant one.

If, despite these efforts, the patient's nutritional status does not improve, the nurse needs to consider other interventions. It may be necessary to offer more assistance with meals. The individual may need to be fed, to have containers opened, or may just need ongoing gentle encouragement throughout the meal to continue eating. Often, gently touching the arm or shoulder while encouraging feeding helps the older patient to attend to the task of taking in food. Touch is a caring behavior that indicates both value and respect for the person being touched. Older people often are not touched or hugged frequently and generally respond positively to the act of being touched. A nutritional supplement may also be needed.

The dietician should assist in deciding what, if any, supplements are needed. Liquid dietary supplements are best offered between meals so that the supplement is not substituted for the meal itself. The supplement can provide a large percentage of the RDA requirements but does not completely meet all dietary requirements.

Tube feedings and parenteral feedings can be used when all other attempts at oral feedings have failed. However, these methods have numerous complications. Striving to maintain adequate oral intake should be the goal of all nursing personnel. Adequate nutrition affects every aspect of the individual's health and well-being.

SLEEP PATTERN DISTURBANCES

Older people often complain of not getting enough sleep or not feeling well rested after sleeping. Indeed, sleep disturbances do increase with age. It is estimated that sleep pattern disturbances affect half of those over 65 years of age who live at home, and two-thirds of those living in institutions.

Normal Sleep Patterns

A review of normal sleep patterns is necessary to understand the changes in sleep patterns that tend to occur with aging. There are five stages to normal sleep. During stage I, the individual is just nodding off, can be easily awakened, and may still have some fleeting thoughts. During stage II, a deeper stage of relaxation occurs: some eye movement is noted through the lids; there may be some brief fragmented thoughts, and the individual can still be easily awakened. Stage III is the early stage of deep sleep. Temperature and heart rate are reduced and muscles are relaxed. The individual is more difficult to arouse. This leads to stage IV, the period of deep sleep and relaxation. This is the restorative stage of sleep, where all body functions are reduced and considerable stimulation is needed for the individual to wake up. About 45 minutes into the stage IV, the period of rapid eye movement (REM) begins. During this phase, vital signs increase and may be irregular, and the body is in an arousal state, with bursts of central nervous system activity. Dreams occur during REM sleep. It is a stage of sleep important for learning, memory, adaptation, and problem solving. It is considered the mentally restorative stage of sleep. Insufficient REM sleep can cause emotional dysfunction that may progress to psychoses. REM sleep occurs approximately every 90 minutes during the stage IV sleep.

Age-Related Changes in Sleep Patterns

In the course of aging, people tend, on average, to sleep less than 8 hours per night. The older person has an impaired capacity to maintain sleep and thus sleep tends to be marked by more frequent and prolonged awakenings during the night. In addition, stage IV and REM sleep diminish. In extreme old age, changes in cerebral blood flow and organic brain syndrome are also associated with a shortening of the REM stage of sleep.

The sleep patterns of older people can be disturbed by such factors as needing to void frequently during the night (nocturia) and changes in vision and hearing that cause incorrect perceptions of their immediate environment. These changes can lead to ineffective sleep or sleep deprivation. Sleep deprivation is marked by fatigue, tiredness, eye problems, muscle tremor, muscle weakness, diminished coordination and attention span, apathy, and depression.

Sleep Disorders

In addition to age-related changes in sleep patterns, there are sleep disorders that are common to the older population. Sleep apnea affects 20% of the older population. This is a medical condition in which breathing stops for 10 seconds or more, numerous times throughout the night. Sleep apnea is associated with high blood pressure, obesity, heart disease, and stroke. Death can result because of the effect on the cardiovascular and respiratory systems. The affected patient complains of excessive daytime sleepiness and constant interruption of sleep. Cessation of breathing for 10 or more seconds, followed by very loud snoring or choking, is the primary objective symptom of sleep apnea. It is often first discovered by the night-shift personnel when the patient is admitted to the hospital or nursing home. The treatment for sleep apnea is usually weight reduction, continuous positive airway pressure (CPAP), oxygen, and occasionally surgery. Continuous positive airway pressure is a technique that forces air down the nose, through the throat, and into the lungs; it is used during sleep for those who have been diagnosed with sleep apnea.

Sundown Syndrome

Sundown syndrome is another disorder that affects many older people. Sundown syndrome is defined as the appearance or exacerbation of symptoms of confusion associated with the late afternoon or evening hours. This syndrome is marked by behaviors such as agitation, restlessness, confusion, wandering, and screaming that occur usually in the evening hours (sundown). Little is known about this disorder, which is a tremendous management problem for caregivers. Risk factors for sundown syndrome seem to be impaired mental status, dehydration, being awakened frequently during the night for nursing care, and recent relocation either to a new room or to the institution.

Nursing Interventions

Sleeping medications, tranquilizers, and sedatives are commonly used to promote sleep but should be avoided at all costs. Sedatives and barbiturates that depress the central nervous system may lead to other problems by depressing vital body functions, lowering basal metabolic rate, decreasing blood pressure, and causing mental confusion. Sleeping medications decrease spontaneous body movements that may lead to skin breakdown. Most of the medications used to promote sleep are not efficiently metabolized by the aging body, and thus the patient may experience a hangover effect the next day. In addition, these drugs tend to cause blurred vision, dry mouth, and urinary retention. Since it is known that the aging client cannot sleep as long as the younger individual, it is unreasonable to put an individual to bed at 8 P.M. and expect that person to stay in bed until 7 A.M. the next day.

There is much the nurse can do to promote sleep without resorting to the use of medications. Meeting the individual's comfort needs by offering back rubs, snacks such as warm milk, assisting with toileting needs, providing socks or an extra blanket to increase body temperature (which may be diminished in the older person), repositioning, and alleviating pain are just a few of the nursing interventions that may reduce insomnia. If these interventions do not promote sleep, it is prudent to allow the patient to come out of the bed and perhaps sit for a while in a comfortable chair near the nurses" station. This may reassure the patient of the surroundings and prevent the individual from attempting to get out of bed unassisted, perhaps risking a fall. During the daytime, increased motor activities and time out of doors, if possible, have been found to promote sleep.

IATROGENESIS

Iatrogenic disorders can be defined as those disorders that the patient acquires as a result of receiving treatment by a physician, nurse, or other member of the health-care team. Iatrogenesis also can occur when the patient does not receive treatment when it is indicated or receives incorrect treatment. The older person often presents with numerous chronic conditions that require complex interventions, numerous medications, and increased exposure to the health-care system. This puts the older person at increased risk of suffering untoward effects of medical treatment. Iatrogenic disorders include those previously discussed in this chapter: immobility, falls, incontinence, malnutrition, pressure ulcers, and disturbances of the sleep-wake cycle.

Studies have found that 30%–40% of those over 65 years of age suffer from iatrogenic complications (Stone & Chenitz, 1991). Common causes of iatrogenesis in the hospital are misuse or overuse of drugs, prolonged immobilization, nosocomial (hospital-acquired) infections, and malnutrition and dehydration secondary to preparation for diagnostic tests. In the nursing home, common iatrogenic disorders include immobilization, adverse drug reactions, falls, pressure ulcers, and nosocomial infections.

Iatrogenic disorders often cause a vicious cycle in which one disorder quickly leads to another. For instance, consider the patient who is admitted to the hospital for abdominal discomfort. The patient is unable to sleep and is prescribed a sleeping pill. Having taken this medication, the person is groggy when getting out of bed and because of the diminished righting reflexes common with aging, the person sustains a fall. The staff, not wanting the patient to be hurt again, apply a restraint. The patient is now unable to get up and suffers from some of the adverse sequelae of immobility, such as incontinence, disorientation, and pressure ulcer formation. In time, the patient's muscles become deconditioned and the next time the patient is assisted out of bed, there is another fall, the person suffers a hip fracture, and the cycle continues. One can see what a high price is paid for the negative effects of medical and nursing interventions.

CONCLUSION

The health-care needs of the older person are multiple and complex. Health-care providers often are not educated in the normal aging process or the older person's response to illness and health-care interventions. As a result, the layperson as well as the health-care provider may believe that there is little that can be done to improve the health status of older adults. Not only is this not true, but this attitude can lead to a self-fulfilling prophecy in which older people are expected to be ill and to experience functional decline. In turn, assessment and interventions aimed at correcting the illness, promoting function, and averting a subsequent decline may not be initiated and the older person is likely to become more ill and more dependent on others. Licensed practical nurses can and should play a pivotal role in ensuring that the health-care needs of the older person are being met. They also need to be aware of the problems that besiege the older person as a result of medical interventions. It is important to know that iatrogenesis can be prevented. Many of the clinical problems that the older person faces, both in health and in illness, can be averted or alleviated with nursing interventions that are focused on improving and maintaining wellness and promoting function.

CASE STUDY

Mrs. S. is an 84-year-old widow who was admitted to the hospital following a right cerebrovascular accident (CVA). Her medical history includes hypertension, atrial fibrillation, and bilateral total hip replacements due to degenerative joint disease. Prior to the CVA and this hospitalization, she was living in her own apartment where she was quite social and able to meet her own needs except for shopping and heavy housecleaning. Her family did those things for her. When admitted to the hospital, she was found to have left-sided weakness and some speech problems, although she was understandable.

The family is planning to admit her to the nursing home; they do not know if she will be able to return to her apartment but are hopeful that she might be able to go to an assisted living apartment. The report given to the nursing home from the hospital includes the following facts:

- During her hospitalization she became incontinent. A Foley catheter was placed to control the urinary incontinence, but she subsequently developed a urinary tract infection, so the catheter was removed.
- She developed aspiration pneumonia, which the physician assumed was due to aspirating food because of a swallowing deficit from her stroke. Her diet was changed to puree, and she has had no further episodes of aspiration, although she is taking only about 30% of her diet.
- She has started physical therapy and has progressed from the parallel bars to short distances with a walker. She does not own a walker, so she has not walked on the unit, only in the therapy department.
- Mrs. S. has not spoken much during her hospitalization, although she follows simple directions. The nurse thinks she "might be a little confused at times."
- Her blood pressure is well controlled with diuretics.
- The family is very concerned that if she falls she may damage the hip replacements, and they have requested that she be restrained.

CASE STUDY
DISCUSSION

Examine the list of facts in the case study for iatrogenic problems. How would you prevent such problems? How would you deal with them?

CASE STUDY
SOLUTION

In this case study, there are a number of iatrogenic problems that arose and that the nursing staff should address. The report from the hospital notes that Mrs. S. was provided with a Foley catheter because she was incontinent. The question the nurse should be asking here is *why* is Mrs. S. incontinent. True, the incontinence can be a result of damage from the stroke, but until attempts are made to take the patient to the bathroom, one cannot be certain. It may be that Mrs. S., having had a stroke that affected her speech, could not tell the staff that she needed to go. She may have to go to the bathroom as soon as the urge presents itself. A prompted voiding schedule would be helpful to the nurses in beginning to assess whether this incontinence is reversible. A Foley catheter should not be the first intervention used in the presence of incontinence. In this case, the use of the catheter prolonged the hospitalization by causing a urinary tract infection.

Another possible iatrogenic problem may be aspiration pneumonia. In this case, iatrogenesis may be a result of something that should have been done that was not done. In a patient who has had a stroke and who has difficulty talking, one would want to consider the possibility of a swallowing deficit as well. Therefore, a patient such as Mrs. S. should never be left alone to eat, and the nursing staff should be assessing her during mealtime for any difficulty swallowing. If a difficulty is noted, a speech and swallowing consultation is warranted. Once the diet was changed to puree, Mrs. S. apparently had no further problems with swallowing but had a decreased nutritional intake. Again, the nurse needs to assess the patient to understand why the diet is not being taken. There may be a number of reasons: the patient may not like her diet, she may still be having difficulty swallowing and is afraid of choking again, and she may be depressed and without an appetite.

It is indeed a positive step that Mrs. S. has been started on physical therapy and is walking, but there is more that the nursing and therapy staffs can do to promote functional ambulation. Walking does not have to be done just in the therapy department. The therapist needs to lend a walker to Mrs. S. or to instruct the family to buy one for her so that ambulation can be done on the nursing unit. Therapy takes place for only about 1 hour a day. Walking the patient on the unit augments therapy, improves the patient's gait, helps her to regain her confidence in her functional ability, and prevents the negative effects of immobility.

The nurse reports that Mrs. S. might be a little confused; however, there is little here to support that conclusion or to suggest that confusion should be expected. From the report, Mrs. S. was not confused prior to her hospitalization. Therefore, if indeed she is confused, it may be related to the urinary tract infection, the pneumonia, the relocation to the hospital, or the depression from the stroke. The possibility of confusion should not deter the nurse in any way from pursuing a plan of care that focuses on promoting the highest level of functional ability for this patient.

The family requests that Mrs. S. be restrained to prevent injury to her hip replacements. Instead of a restraint, the staff needs to consider ways of preventing a fall so that the family will not feel a restraint is needed. Some possible fall prevention interventions might include helping the patient to understand her limitations, toileting the patient at regular intervals, promoting lower extremity strengthening through exercise, keeping the patient out of her room and within sight of the staff, and perhaps using an alarm if the patient is unpredictable in her attempts to get up. Because Mrs. S. is on diuretics, one would want to assess her for orthostatic hypotension as a possible fall risk factor. Honoring the family's request for a restraint may serve only to cause contractures, skin breakdown, a worsening of her urinary incontinence, depression, and general deconditioning related to immobility. The family needs to be educated to the dangers of using restraints. The use of restraints will not promote a positive outcome for this patient.

Study Questions

Please select the one best answer.

1. An example of an intrinsic risk factor for falls in the older person is:
   a. The use of diuretics
   b. Weakened muscles in the lower extremities
   c. Glaring lights in the hallway
   d. The use of a cane

2. To promote mobility in the older client the nurse would:
   a. Turn the patient every 2 hours
   b. Encourage the patient to cough and take deep breaths
   c. Ask the family to bring in the patient's walker from home
   d. Assume that the physical therapist is helping the patient to walk

3. The best way to promote urinary continence in the older person is to:
   a. Stop giving the diuretic because it causes the patient to have urinary urgency
   b. Obtain a urine specimen for culture and sensitivity
   c. Offer the bedpan every 2 hours
   d. Assist the patient to the toilet in the morning, after meals, and at bedtime

4. When seeing a reddened area on the patient's coccyx, the nurse would do all but one of the following interventions:
   a. Turn the patient every 2 hours
   b. Ask the doctor to order a medication to treat the skin
   c. Help the patient to the toilet more frequently
   d. Measure how much of the diet the patient is taking every day

5. Which of the following is not an example of an iatrogenic disorder?
   a. Falling because of dizziness after receiving mediation for pain relief
   b. Depression because of a stroke
   c. Incontinence because the patient could not find the bathroom
   d. Loss of weight because the patient cannot chew the food that is provided

References

Agency for Health Care Policy Research. (1992a). *Pressure ulcers in adults: Prediction and prevention. Clinical practice guidelines* (DHHS publication No. 92–0048). Rockville, MD: Department of Health and Human Services.

Agency for Health Care Policy Research. (1992b). *Urinary incontinence in adults. Clinical practice guidelines* (DHHS publication No. 92–0038). Rockville, MD: Department of Health and Human Services.

Brummel-Smith, K. (1990). Rehabilitation. In C. Cassel, D. Riesenberg, L. Sorensen, & J. Walsh (Eds.), *Geriatric medicine* (2nd ed.) (pp. 242–267). New York: Springer-Verlag.

Burrage, R. (1991). Physical assessment: Musculoskeletal and nervous system. In W. Chenitz, J. Stone, & S. Salisbury (Eds.), *Clinical gerontological nursing: A guide to advanced practice* (pp. 327–341). Philadelphia: W. B. Saunders.

Sattin, R. (1992). Falls among older persons: A public health perspective. *Annual Review of Public Health, 13,* 489.

Stone, J., & Chenitz, W. (1991). The problem of falls. In W. Chenitz, J. Stone, & S. Salisbury (Eds.), *Clinical gerontological nursing: A guide to advanced practice* (pp. 291–308). Philadelphia: W. B. Saunders.

Tinnetti, M. (1990). In C. Cassel, D. Riesenberg, L. Sorensen, & J. Walsh (Eds.), *Geriatric medicine* (2nd ed., pp. 528–538). New York: Springer-Verlag.

Yakobowich, M. (1990). Prescribe with care: The role of laxatives in the treatment of constipation. *Journal of Gerontological Nursing, 16*(4), 4–11.

Bibliography

Bender, P. (1992). Deceptive distress in the elderly. *American Journal of Nursing, 92,* 29.
   A description of the unusual way that older people present illness.

Braden, B., & Bryant, R. (1990). Innovations to prevent and treat pressure ulcers. *Geriatric Nursing, 11,* 182–186.
   This article will give the student a variety of approaches to pressure ulcer care and treatment.

Braun, J., & Lipson, S. (Eds.). (1992). *Toward a restraint-free environment.* Baltimore, MD: Health Professions Press.
   A comprehensive description of how to avoid the use of restraints when caring for the older patient.

Koroknay, V., Werner, P., Cohen-Mansfield, J., & Braun, J. (1995). Maintaining ambulation in the frail nursing home resident: A nursing administered walking program. *Journal of Gerontological Nursing, 21* (11), 18–24.
   This article describes the development of a walking program for frail nursing home residents.

Knapp, M. (1993). Night shift: The restorative care sleep specialists. *Journal of Gerontological Nursing, 19*(5), 38–42.
   Offers an excellent view of how the night nurse can make a real difference in the health of the older patient.

MacRae, P., Asplund, L., Schnelle, J., Ouslander, J., Abrahamse, A., & Morris, C. (1996). A walking program for nursing home residents: Effects on walk endurance, physical activity, mobility, and quality of life. *Journal of the American Geriatrics Society, 44* (2), 175–180.
   This article presents the positive outcomes resulting from a walking program in long-term care.

Penn, C., Lekan-Rutledge, D., Joers, A.M., Stolley, J., & Amhof, N. V. (1996). Assessment of urinary incontinence. *Journal of Gerontological Nursing, 22* (1), 8–19.
   This is an excellent resource for understanding and assessing the predisposing and age-related factors in urinary incontinence.

Rubenstein, L., Josephson, K., & Robbins, A. (1994). Falls in the nursing home. *Annals of Internal Medicine, 121,* 442–451.
   This article provides a thorough discussion of the causes of falls in elderly nursing home residents.

Urinary Incontinence Guideline Panel. (1996). *Managing acute and chronic urinary incontinence.* Quick reference guide for clinicians number 2, 1996 update. (AHCPR Publication No. 96–0686). Rockville, MD: Agency for Health Care Policy and Research, Public Health Service, U.S. Department of Health and Human Services.
   This publication presents the most recent guidelines for incontinence management.

Videotape

Newman, D. (1992). *Progress bowel and bladder rehabilitation program* [Videotape]. Philadelphia: Scott Health Care.
   An incontinence nurse specialist explains the various types of incontinence and offers a descriptive and user-friendly view of management strategies. An interactive video that will appeal to all levels of nursing staff. (Approximately 45 minutes).

Chapter

JEANNE ROBERTSON SAMTER

10

Psychological Assessment

Learning Objectives

After completing this chapter, the student will be able to:

1. Identify three cognitive functions.
2. Describe two benefits of using a standardized examination to screen for cognitive functioning.
3. Identify four uses of psychological assessments.
4. Describe the impact of depression on the mental status score.

INTRODUCTION

Psychological assessments are essential tools in identifying limitations and charting progress of residents/patients in all health-care settings. They provide the basis for determining how much of a return to normal an individual can expect to achieve. The end point of therapeutic interventions is the attainment of optimal functioning. Psychological assessments are important in any health-care setting, but especially where the focus is restorative care. Restorative goals include the maintenance of baseline functioning. For many nursing home residents this is a full-time pursuit.

Restorative care in its truest application requires a body-mind-spirit connection. Nurses practicing within this framework are concerned with the prevention of falls, incontinence, and immobility. These are physical indications that a resident is declining and that interventions are needed to maintain physical functioning. Behavioral indicators have received less prominence in terms of restorative care. Some examples are failure to eat and a decline in functional level, such as severe memory loss or confusion without a physiological basis.

Although one can expect a certain amount of decline in older people who have vascular and central nervous system (CNS) disease, it is important to identify the areas of decline and recognize when interventions are essential. Maintenance of mental health and cognitive functioning is as important to restorative care as is maintenance of physiological processes. Nurses working with the elderly need to understand basic concepts of mental health and cognitive function so that they can participate in the older person's care more effectively. Assessment tools provide a brief, methodical approach to noting changes commonly found in individuals with cerebrovascular diseases, delirium, and common dementia disorders.

MENTAL HEALTH

Over the years, clinicians in the field of mental health have tried to diagnose symptoms, traits, and patterns of behavior that identify disease. The view that identification and treatment of disease establish health is known as the medical model. The simplest definition of mental health, then, would be the absence of identifiable disease. A more positive approach is to define traits that describe the mentally healthy personality. Any definition of health, however, reflects the value judgments or mental health background of the individual defining the trait. Although some expert clinicians have tried to integrate the biological and psychosocial viewpoints into one theory, workers in the field of mental health have splintered into many groups. A number of theories and concepts have evolved to account for the way human beings relate to each other and for the way in which mind and feelings work within each person. Each of these theories approaches the individual in a different way.

Practitioners use terms that have been formulated by theorists to describe and discuss psychological problems. Words such as *id, ego,* and *superego* are used by therapists who base their practice on Sigmund Freud's theory. *Enmeshment* is a term used by some family therapists to describe interactions among family members that keep them dependent on each other. A therapist practicing within a Gestalt framework may focus on the feeling experience of an individual.

The current trend is to identify wellness in mental health. Although it is difficult to define wellness, some of its characteristics have been described by psychologists, nurses, and physicians. Some of these characteristics are:

- A clear meaning and purpose in life
- A strong reality orientation
- An ability to cope creatively with life's situations
- A capability for open, creative relationships

Mental health is not necessarily a product of good nurturing or of a life of positive experiences. There are individuals who function well in life (i.e., maintain a satisfying job and career, have a family, make a contribution to their community) despite poor nurturing and environmental handicaps. Most views of mental health now embody a continuum of health and illness. This continuum is dynamic rather than static. There are a number of situations that have an impact on the functioning of an individual. These situations include:

- The death of someone close
- Unemployment
- The birth of a child
- Relocation

Any individual, if sufficiently stressed, can demonstrate some signs of impairment. One theorist (Gilbert, 1992) refers to the continuum of functioning as a scale of differentiation. Individuals higher on this scale require more stressors to impair their functioning than individuals lower on this scale. These individuals choose a life course based on thought and conviction rather than on impulse and show an ability to stand by a belief that is different from that of a group to which they may belong.

It is important for nurses working in the field of gerontology to identify and promote positive mental health traits. Nurses can then reinforce healthy traits and interactions in older persons.

Cognition

Cognition is a mental activity concerned with processing information. It refers to a "broad range of mental behaviors, including awareness, thinking, reasoning and judgment" (Restak, 1988, p. 318). This process is very complex and involves a number of abilities or functions. Since it cannot be directly observed, many psychologists define cognition in terms of cognitive functions. There are a number of ways of conceptualizing the cognitive functions. One scientist's definition is perceiving, thinking, remembering, communicating, orienting, calculating, and problem solving. Other psychologists include awareness and orientation under perception and classify judgment, reasoning, and visual-spatial ability as cognitive processes.

Memory

In general, the more active people have been, the better their overall memory is as they age. A dysfunction in memory occurs in almost all of the cognitive disorders common in the elderly. Generally, psychologists refer to two categories of memory, short-term memory (STM) and long-term memory (LTM). The time interval for measuring STM is seconds, whereas for LTM it is minutes and beyond. Recently, there has been an interest in the study of very remote memory. Many elderly persons demonstrate excellent long-term recall, although this recall may be rooted more in a belief than in fact. This means that the stories they tell of their childhood or young adulthood are stories based on their belief systems rather than on what actually happened. This skill may be enchanting to staff and can be used effectively as a tool (i.e., reminiscence) to strengthen a resident's self-esteem.

Memory functions are extremely important to a person's ability to think. A deficit in STM means that a person is unable to recall some of today's events. A resident with severe impairment of STM experiences the routine of each day as a new experience. Such a resident is trapped in an endless cycle of requesting basic information about the environment from strangers, such as "Where is my room?"; "When do we eat?"

Memory impairment limits the ability of a person to form a new idea or relate one fact with another. It is nearly impossible for memory-impaired individuals to organize new information into categories. A place where one can put something (a pair of glasses) for sakekeeping may change several times a day. A never-ending search for an important item then becomes a ritual.

Screening for memory impairment is the most important part of any assessment for the elderly. The loss of STM is the first symptom of Alzheimer's disease. A stroke may also impair memory function, but in this case the type and extent of impairment depend on the location of the damage. Other STM deficits may be due to depression. Individuals suffering from depression are inattentive to their environment. They are often preoccupied or self-absorbed. A decline in STM, then, is an important finding on assessment and should prompt further investigation.

Reminiscence is an excellent tool to use to strengthen the resident's self-esteem.

Perception

Psychologists believe that all behavior depends on how a person sees the self, the situation one is in, and the interaction between these two. Behavior changes as an individual becomes aware of details in life surroundings. Learning, problem solving, remembering, and forgetting are all part of one's awareness of the environment. Effective communication with an older person depends on the nurse's ability to understand the perceptual world of that person. With such an understanding, the most bizarre behavior often becomes comprehensible.

The first phase of forming a perception is the ability to use the five senses to collect information about the environment. Frequently, in the elderly, there are real impairments in the sense organs. Approximately 70% of the visually impaired individuals in this country are 65 years of age or older. Hearing deficits are also prominent. Taste, touch, and smell sensitivity decline markedly with aging.

There is a feeling component to perception as well. Individuals take in information from the environment and form opinions about such information. Perceptions are normally evaluated against past experiences. A resident thus compares a meal eaten within the institutional setting with recollections of meals eaten with the person's own family. These recollections of past experiences are a part of forming perceptions.

Perceptual distortions are also known as hallucinations and delusional thinking. Although both may indicate a psychiatric illness in younger individuals, perceptual distortions are common in dementing illnesses. Impaired memory and a natural distrust of a strange environment exaggerate this tendency in the institutionalized elder.

Orientation

Orientation refers to a person's awareness of self in the context of a particular time and place. Tests for orientation determine whether patients know their names, where they are, and the approximate time of day. Sometimes the expression "oriented times three" is used to indicate that an individual's orientation to time, place, and person is correct. Assessment of orientation is covered on every mental status examination. This is important information because a disturbance in orientation is one of the most frequent symptoms of any brain disease. Awareness of time and place requires that individuals know where they are and can remember it. In this way, individuals keep in touch with ongoing history. Orientation depends on a person's ability to link each minute with the previous minute. Disorientation with respect to time is the first major confusion to occur as a result of dementia. Loss of a sense of place is likely to follow. Last, the person loses the ability to recognize other people and eventually cannot remember who he or she is.

Thinking

Every area of the brain is involved in the mental operation of thinking. The ancient Greeks believed that there were "higher" levels and "lower" levels of thinking, a distinction that is still relevant. Higher-level thinking includes the ability to form concepts and think in an abstract manner. Asking a patient to interpret a proverb tests the patient's ability to think abstractly. If a person interprets the proverb "a stitch in time saves nine" in a way that conveys that prompt attention to a problem prevents trouble in the future, the person's ability to abstract think is considered intact. A concrete interpretation adheres closely to the exact meaning of the phrase. Concrete thinking is a "lower" mental ability. Some areas of humor are based on concrete interpretation or literal translation of an abstract idea.

Thinking processes have a hierarchical order. The lower mental abilities are more enduring and less affected by brain injuries and disease processes. The higher levels of thinking tend to be more fragile. At first glance, interpreting proverbs may seem a bit removed from a person's ability to function in the real world. The use of good judgment, the ability to think abstractly, and the capacity to reason, however, are higher-level abilities that indicate the difference between independent and supervised living. These abilities to some extent can be determined by proverb interpretation. In general, tests for abstraction are not included as part of the short tests of mental function.

Communicating

The only vehicle for viewing thinking processes in an individual is communication. People understand human thought when it is reflected in language. It is important to assess language problems because they are common in cerebrovascular and dementing disorders. Assessment of communication patterns, word order, and the general sense of a sentence provide a window into the dementia process. This is especially true with the patient who has experienced a stroke. Sometimes patients who have had a stroke will have severe problems with communication. Small connecting words such as "if", "and", and "but" are missing. There are also several types of aphasia that impair an individual's ability to communicate.

Calculating

Calculating is a cognitive function that must be assessed carefully in terms of the person's intelligence and educational level. Poor performance may indicate dementia or delirium, anxiety, or depression. *Serial 7s* is one test that can determine a person's ability to calculate. The person is asked to subtract 7 from 100 and then to subtract 7 from that remainder, continuing 5 times. A nurse interviewed a moderately to severely impaired patient with Alzheimer's disease. Although the patient was completely disoriented with regard to time and place and could not recall the names of three objects even seconds after they were told to him, he performed magnificently with the serial 7 calculations. In seconds he completed the operation, then turned to the nurse, announcing proudly that mathematics was always his favorite subject. The patient had been a judge.

Problem Solving

Problem-solving skills are essential to an individual's ability to function in any environment. Even some very demented people can demonstrate aspects of problem-solving ability. Individuals in the early stages of Alzheimer's disease frequently make lists. Lists are coping devices that enable the recall of event sequences. When asked questions of orientation, some elders search for familiar cues in the environment. Examples of this behavior include the patient who was asked the date, spied a newspaper, then winked, and smiling broadly gave the correct answer. Another patient called to a nursing assistant passing by the door. When the nursing assistant entered the room, the patient asked her for the date and promptly relayed this information to the nurse interviewer.

A individual's environment is filled with a multitude of clues that facilitate orientation, aid a failing memory, and maintain a stable perceptual field. Use of these clues enables clients to maintain in communication with nurses, other patients, and families. Sometimes this communication is superficial and becomes a shell of social graces. Because a patient's environment is rich with problem-solving clues, room changes and unit changes should be made infrequently, and only after the most careful thought.

ASSESSMENT TOOLS AND HOW TO USE THEM

Mental status examinations are the most frequently used psychological assessments. Mental status assessment includes probing of the cognitive functions as well as level of consciousness. In selecting a tool, it is important to remember that examinations with brief instruments are generally better tolerated by the elderly. A short examination is much less tiring for an older person to sit through than a lengthy one. No brief instrument, however, is a perfect detector of cognitive impairment.

Screening tools initially may seem intimidating or cumbersome to use in clinical practice. Most tools are short and can be easily committed to memory after using them a few times. All of the following tests are easy to learn and administer: Pfeiffer's SPMSQ (Pfeiffer, 1975), Folstein's MMSE (Folstein, Folstein, & McHugh, 1975), Kahn's MSQ (Kahn, Goldfarb, Pollak, & Peck, 1960), Jacobs' CCSE (Jacobs, Bernhard, Delgado, & Strain, 1977), and Kiernan's NCSE (Kiernan, Mueller, Langston, & Vandyke, 1987). These scales are compared in Table 10.1 and are listed with a brief description in Box 10.1.

A very important factor to consider in the scoring of all tests is that test results are influenced by the educational level of the elder. An older person with a lack of a formal education can score several points lower than an older person with greater deficits but more education. Some of the mental status tests have a method of scoring to correct for education.

There are some important reasons for a nurse to gain skills in using assessment tools. A standardized test allows a nurse to collect pertinent information in a short period of time. The collection of this information is organized and methodical. The initial test establishes a baseline and allows for comparison of changes over time.

Memory

Assessing memory functions is the most important assessment in working with cognitively impaired residents. There are three steps in the memory process. Each step needs accurate assessment. The first step is reception (encoding), followed by storage

TABLE 10.1 MENTAL STATUS EXAMINATIONS

	NCSE	KAHN	SPMSQ	MMSE	CCSE
Level of consciousness (LOC)	X			X	X
Cognitive functions					
Remembering	X	X	X	X	X
Communicating	X			X	
Problem solving					
Perceiving					
Thinking	X				X
Orienting	X	X	X	X	X
Calculating	X	X	X	X	X
Corrects for education and culture		X	X		X
Number of questions	2 PG	10	10	30	30
Time required (minutes)	5–20	5	5	10	10

NCSE: Neurobehavioral Cognitive Status Exam
KAHN: Mental Status Questionnaire
SPMSQ: Short Portable Mental Status Questionnaire
MMSE: Mini–Mental Status Exam
CCSE: Cognitive Capacity Screening Exam
  The categories of cognitive function are developed from "The assessment of cognitive function in the elderly" by B. J. Gurland, 1987, *Clinical Geriatric Medicine, 3,* pp. 53–63.

(retention), and finally, retrieval (recall). Folstein's MMSE tests memory by asking the client to repeat after the nurse three times, for example, apple, ball, and lamp. The number of trials it takes for the client to recall the three items is noted. Immediate repetition enables the nurse to determine whether the client has heard the three words correctly. Once the client repeats them accurately, the nurse requests that the client remember them. In 5 minutes, the nurse asks again for the client to recall the three objects. Each item recalled is given a score of 1.

Orientation

All short mental status examinations include questions about orientation. Time orientation is tested by asking for the date (day, month, year, and day of the week) and the time of day. Because clients often become quite skilled in using clues from the environment, it is important to remove newspapers or calendars that may help them find the answer. The client can sometimes have an accurate sense of time passing, yet may not remember the exact date. The nurse may ask questions such as "How long has it been since you last saw me?" or "What was your last meal?"

    Assessment of orientation in place generally begins with questions about the name or location of the place in which the person is being examined. The nurse needs to find out whether patients know the kind of place they are in, for example, a nursing home or hospital. Short mental status examinations ask questions about the state, county, or country of residence. Many moderately to severely demented people are not able to recall places. It may be more functional to question a patient regarding the location of the bedroom or the dining room, for example, "Can you tell me where your room is?"

Box 10.1   BRIEF DESCRIPTION OF COMMON SCREENING TOOLS

The Mini-Mental Status Exam (MMSE) was developed by Folstein to be used with medical and psychiatric patients. Scores in the range of 9–12 indicate a high likelihood of dementia. Scores of 25 and over are considered normal.

The Short Portable Mental Status Questionnaire (SPMSQ) was developed by Pfeiffer. This test is a little quicker to administer than Folstein's MMSE. Questions of orientation and memory are addressed and there is one question concerning calculation. LOC is not assessed. An advantage over the MMSE, however, is that there are specific directions for scoring this test so as to correct for education and race. A test score of 8–10 indicates severe intellectual impairment; 5–7, moderate impairment; 3–4, mild impairment; 0–2, intact status.

The Mental Status Questionnaire (MSQ) was developed by Kahn. This questionnaire has two versions: one for the institutionalized elderly and the other for use with adults in the community. Five or more errors indicate severe impairment, 3–5 errors indicate some impairment, and fewer than 2 indicates no impairment.

The Cognitive Capacity Screening Exam (CCSE) was developed by Jacobs. This mental status questionnaire was adapted specifically to diagnose diffuse organic mental syndromes on busy medical wards. A score of less than 20 indicates diminished cognitive capacity.

The Neurobehavioral Cognitive Status Examination (NCSE) was developed by Kiernan for use with behaviorally disturbed adults in acute diagnostic units. This test differs from the others in that it has two separate scores. One score is given for LOC, orientation, and attention. Another score is given for language, construction, memory, calculations, and reasoning. The two separate scores enable clinicians to differentiate areas of impairment more clearly. This examination is two pages long, with directions to the clinician on how to administer it. It can be completed in 5 minutes by nonimpaired patients and by most patients with impairments in 20 minutes.

Level of Consciousness

The determination of a person's level of consciousness (LOC) is an important assessment to make in the event of delirium or a head injury. Folstein's MMSE is one tool that screens for LOC. It is important for the nurse to know the four levels of consciousness and to be able to define each in behavioral terms. The first level is *alert*, which means that the person is awake and responding in an appropriate manner. The next level is *lethargic*. A person is lethargic when the individual can be aroused and once aroused responds in an appropriate manner and with an orientation that is consistent. The third LOC is *stuporous*. If a person can be aroused but responds inappropriately when aroused and then returns to sleep when the stimulus is stopped, the person is stuporous. This response may be the initial phase of a delirium. *Comatose* is the fourth level. A person who is comatose does not respond to any stimulus except deep pain.

Delirium and the Mental Status Examination

Nurses sometimes have a difficult time recognizing delirium. Sudden onset is the most significant feature described by experts. Elderly individuals, however, may develop a delirium gradually, over the course of 2 or 3 days. One sign is a fluctuating level of consciousness. This can vary from mild confusion to stupor in an active delirium, which is frequently characterized by visual hallucinations. A nursing home resident was being assessed for delirium by the nurse. The resident, who was talking about snakes in her bed, suddenly stopped and turned to the nurse. "Your hands are very chapped," she said. "You should use gloves to do your housework. I always did." Then the resident returned to her delirious state.

Another feature of delirium is disorientation. One person may be mistaken for another. Sometimes a client imagines being at home or in another location. Other cognitive functions may become impaired. There also may be a disturbance in the sleep cycle. Many delirious elders are awake all night and then sleep during the day.

Validity and Reliability of Assessment Scales

Whenever a questionnaire is used in any clinical setting, psychologists are concerned about two questions: validity and reliability. Is the test question a valid question? For example, does the question really measure memory, or orientation, or thinking? Validity is determined by the agreement reached by a panel of individuals who are experts in the content of the particular test questions used. The more experts are involved in designing the process, the greater the validity of the test questions. Reliability is concerned with consistency. Will two nurses, each asking the same patient the same questions, get the same answers? When the answer to this question is "yes," the test questions are reliable. All standard mental status questionnaires considered in this chapter are valid and reliable instruments. They have been used by a variety of experts for a number of years with consistent results.

Because rating scales are designed to collect standard information about patients in a methodical way, nurses should review the methods of using the rating scales together. This practice ensures that information is gathered in the same way. One nurse can interview an elder while another nurse observes. Then they can reverse roles and compare the answers they received. Some experts recommend continuing this technique with 10 patients or until 80% of the ratings are the same.

WHEN TO ASSESS

Many hospitals and nursing homes use some sort of standard mental status examination to screen for gross impairments on admission. This is an excellent practice. Although some initial confusion, agitation, or depression is often seen in elders who are newly admitted, this practice, if consistently done, helps staff to get a baseline of the person's overall cognitive function. The assessment can be repeated if the patient demonstrates acute changes in behavior, mental status, or functional level; for example, if there is a decline in activities of daily living (ADLs). Although screening tools are not diagnostic, that is, they do not point out the exact nature of the problem, they do show, in a factual way, specific areas that have changed.

ASSESSMENT TECHNIQUES

Elderly clients generally remain cooperative unless they perceive the questions asked as challenging their mental competence. Catastrophic reactions such as screaming or leaving the room angry can be precipitated when a person is pushed to perform beyond the person's competency. A client's refusal to answer questions should be accepted. This information in itself is significant. Clients, aware of their cognitive impairments, may become defensive when their vulnerabilities are exposed. Attention to the following factors promotes the success of the psychological assessment.

Timing

The timing of an interview is an important factor in determining success. Regular staff, especially primary nursing assistants in the nursing home setting, are especially skilled in knowing the best time to interview a resident. Allowing a client to select a time may be the most effective way to gain cooperation.

Privacy

Privacy is very important. Questions that to caregivers may seem routine are often considered deeply revealing and very personal to clients. All interviews should be conducted in the person's room or a location that ensures confidentiality.

Elimination of Interruptions

Interruptions undermine the importance of psychological assessments. They negatively affect a person's attention span, and they distract the nurse from focusing on the client. Some interruptions are beyond the control of the nurse and occur regardless of the precautions taken. Reasonable efforts should be made to eliminate as many as possible, because they impact on the reliability and validity of the assessment.

Positive Introduction of the Assessment

Introducing the psychological assessment in a positive and respectful manner is useful. Describing the test as "a lot of silly questions" may prompt the response that "if they are so silly, why should I answer them?" Let the client know that the information gained from this assessment should help the nurses in planning and giving care.

WHAT TO DO WITH THE ASSESSMENT INFORMATION

All information obtained from the client must be used on the client's behalf. This information should be dated and appear in an accessible place on the chart with a notation that this document must remain on the chart. In general, assessment information is not updated unless a client demonstrates a behavioral problem or has a marked decline in functional level.

Applications in Clinical Practice

In the hospital or nursing home, psychological assessments may be used as one of the factors determining the unit assignment of a new patient/resident on admission. They contribute to the identification of the person's strengths and potentials. When used in conjunction with the patient's ability to perform ADLs, psychological assessments may point out the need for psychiatric evaluation. When a patient's mental functioning appears much lower than the score of a psychological assessment might indicate, a mental illness is suspected.

Psychological assessments can be used as a basis for care planning. This is especially important when a patient's social graces lead staff to the conclusion that the patient is functioning at a higher level than is the case. Many individuals with a dementing process learn strategies to cover for losses in cognition. They may rely upon list making, props in the environment, and social cues from others. Staff can sometimes make excessive demands on patients if they are unaware of cognitive deficits.

Psychological assessments can allow a broad determination of the effects of an intervention. For example, a person with sadness, who wishes to die, may be treated with an antidepressant. Effective treatment may enhance the abilities of depressed older persons to attend to their environment, thereby improving memory and perception. On the mental status examination, such patients may achieve higher scores in the area of recall. This information is useful to a consultant when a more extensive evaluation is considered necessary. It is helpful to be able to tell a consultant that a patient has dropped four points on Folstein's MMSE because the examination was conducted 6 months before. It is also useful to note the specific area of decline, for instance, the area of decline is in orientation to time and place or in immediate recall.

Clients vary greatly in symptom severity and the rate of progression. Although in the latter stages of dementia clients present very much the same regardless of disease process, the initial symptoms may clearly demonstrate one disease over another. For example, the initial symptom of Alzheimer's disease is the gradual progressive decline in the ability to learn new information. The most significant early symptom of Pick's disease is a change in personality (Albert, 1990).

Therefore, symptoms of dementia are a moving target that must be tracked. The tracking is done by frequent, well-recorded assessments. If an assessment tool has been used to establish a baseline in the early stages of the disease process, it may contribute to the diagnostic process.

OTHER ASSESSMENTS

Assessing Depression

Although recent research indicates that depression is no more prevalent in elderly people than it is in younger people, its manifestation is different and, therefore, difficult to identify. It is important for nurses to gain skill in the assessment of depression because of their focus on the quality of life for all people. There is a heavy emotional cost to depression that ultimately affects the immune system. This can lead to cancer and other physical illnesses as well as infections.

Depression, therefore, predicts the onset of disability almost as powerfully as disability predicts depression. Elderly individuals who are depressed are in a high-risk category for institutionalization because they are less motivated to care for their personal hygiene and nutrition. This increases their vulnerability to disease. Depressed individuals are frequently withdrawn and socially isolated, so that they have weak support systems. The path to a nursing home for these individuals is apt to be very short and direct.

It is a fact that people over the age of 65 are beginning to face some significant losses: economic, vocational, family supports, as well as friendships. Physical disabilities, however, are frequently viewed as the beginning of the end. "If you have your health, you have everything," one grandmother reports. The loss of health signals a life of dependency for most elderly individuals.

Generally, the most impressive feature of a depression is an unpleasant mood. To psychiatrists, the term *clinical depression* refers to a cluster of specific symptoms. These symptoms are clearly defined in a diagnostic manual called the *Diagnostic and Statistical Manual* (DSM-IV) (1994) and must be present for a specified duration. Depression may be chronic or acute, and the symptoms may vary in intensity as well.

Severe depression is thought to impair cognitive functioning at any age. Memory seems to be the function most influenced by a depressed mood, but there are many ways that memory can be affected. For example, information committed to memory when a person is depressed is likely to be biased. Other clinicians focus on the ability of the clients to attend to their environment as the indicator of a depression.

Methods for the identification of depression in the elderly are controversial. To date, there is no assessment scale that can be used to screen for depression in the institutionalized elderly. A resident's response to questions on baseline scales can provide useful information to psychiatric consultants. Because questions on the baseline scales are taken from the DSM-IV manual, nurses using scales should gain some familiarity with responses that indicate depression. Table 10.2 describes five scales used by clinicians as brief screening tools with the elderly. These scales include Zung's SDS (Zung, 1983), Yesavage's GDS (Yesavage et al., 1983), Hamilton's HRDS (Hamilton, 1967), Beck's BDI (Beck, Ward, & Mendelson, 1961), and Sunderland's DMAS (Sunderland et al., 1988).

TABLE 10.2 DEPRESSION SCALES					
Designed for Use:	**GDS**	**DMAS**	**SDS**	**HDRS**	**BDI**
1. As a self-rating scale	X		X		X
2. With the elderly	X				
3. With demented residents		X			
4. In measuring the intensity of depressive mood		X			
5. In screening for depression	X		X	X	X
6. With cognitively intact residents	X		X	X	X
7. Number of questions	30	24	22	17	27

GDS: Geriatric Depression Scale (Yesavage)
DMAS: Dementia Mood Assessment Scale (Sunderland)
SDS: Self-Rating Depression Scale (Zung)
HDRS: Hamilton's Depression Rating Scale
BDI: Beck's Depression Inventory

Assessing Pain

Chronic pain may leave a person totally fatigued and unable to participate properly in a restorative care program. In addition, some behavioral problems in the institutionalized elderly stem from ineffective pain management. A psychiatric evaluation may be requested for screaming or abusive behavior on the part of a resident of a nursing home. A failure to identify pain as a factor affecting behavior and function may result in poor medical management.

Pain in the elderly is frequently either over- or undertreated simply because it is difficult to assess. Some elderly people want every ache treated with a drug, whereas others maintain a stoic attitude: "Why bother? There is nothing that can be done, anyway." Often the elderly perceive pain differently. In fact some pain receptors may not be as acute as they were in the past. Medical journals document clinical cases describing "silent" myocardial infarctions or "painless" intra-abdominal emergencies. These cases may not, in fact, be silent or painless but may reflect an elder's denial of the gravity of pain indicative of acute medical conditions.

Some barriers to pain assessment are cognitive impairments, delirium, and dementia. People who have a dementia process or have had a stroke and became aphasic may be unable to give an accurate pain history. They may not be able to describe when the pain started or at what point in the day the pain becomes most severe. Most people describe the pain in the here and now.

A person in pain is often self-absorbed and inattentive to activities in the environment. Because pain frequently leads to depression, the mental status examination score may demonstrate a decline in recall.

Delirium may be one manifestation of an attempt to treat a person's pain. An assessment for delirium should be made whenever there is a change in the level of consciousness after the start of any new drug, particularly a pain medication. A sensitivity to medications that results in delirium makes pain management difficult.

Multiple chronic disease processes as well as acute diagnoses compound the difficulty. There may even be an acute exacerbation of a chronic problem. These multiple sources of pain make diagnosis difficult and pain management becomes a real challenge.

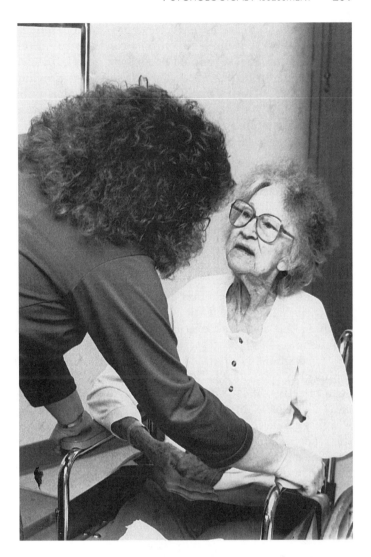

Pain assessment in the elderly is a demanding and necessary skill.

Myths of Pain

One of the myths regarding pain in the elderly is that pain is normal. As body systems begin to wear out, one might expect an increase in pain. Pain, at any age, however, is the most common symptom of a disease process and should be investigated and treated.

Another myth is that pain and sleep are incompatible. Nurses often disbelieve a patient's complaint of pain when they bring a pain pill and find the patient asleep. The wrong conclusion is drawn. It is believed that an individual really in pain could not possibly sleep. The exhaustive feature of pain, however, is seldom considered in the assessment process.

The last myth is that narcotic drugs are not safe in the elderly. Narcotics provide effective pain relief for some chronic conditions and terminal illnesses. These drugs should be used on a scheduled basis, for example, every 4 hours or every 6 hours. Use of a narcotic on an "as needed" basis does not provide effective pain management. Some nurses believe that narcotics dull an elderly person's level of consciousness. They fear that a client will not be able to benefit from the support of family or friends in the time remaining before death. Effective relief of pain actually promotes interaction, and the initial drowsiness soon wears off.

Methods of Assessment

Although pain is a highly subjective experience, there are two methods of assessing it. Simple observation from a nurse who knows the client well can be very effective. A grimace or clutch of the chest provides a vivid picture of pain. Assessment questions may follow these observations. The clinical practice guidelines (Carr & Jacox, 1992) for acute pain management identify the quantifiable measures of pain that should be considered in any assessment. These measures include the intensity of the pain, the duration of the pain, the quality of the pain, and the personal meaning this pain has to a resident. Also included is the impact on the resident's functioning.

Assessment tools are available. A good tool addresses a client's pain history and coping strategies for dealing with pain, as well as medications in the past that have been effective. It is important to ask questions that help to describe or define the pain. Noting the intensity and duration assists in providing an objective measure to a highly subjective experience. Simply asking "How is your pain today?" may prompt the response "Well, it is there."

The simplest method of pain assessment is the use of a pain intensity scale. The nurse can draw a line indicating that the far left (L) end of the line defines no pain and the fight (R) end represents the most pain the client has ever experienced. Clients can point to the place on this line which reflects their current pain level.

SUMMARY

Observations of a person's behavior and functional status are subjective and often inconsistently reported. It is difficult to get a clear idea of decline or progress over time without some objective measures. Psychological assessments and other assessment tools provide the means for collecting factual information about a client.

Brief mental status examinations universally identify assessments of memory and orientation as the two features that provide that most information about an individual's cognitive functions. Assessments help to establish a client's baseline functioning. They can be used to establish a diagnosis, plan care, and evaluate treatment efforts. Psychological assessments also enable the nurse to define problem areas in a more specific manner to consultants. Clients cooperate well with assessments if the nurse is sensitive to timing, respects the client's privacy, limits interruptions, and presents the assessment tool in a positive manner. Other assessments that can provide important information in planning care are those which assess depression and pain.

CONCLUSION

Many institutionalized elderly are all too aware of declining abilities. These losses have a dynamic impact on the self-concept. A life once vital and central to a young family now does not seem worth the effort to maintain. A lowered self-concept and diminished self-esteem complete the picture of physical decline. The process can become circular without the intervention of a caring and knowledgeable staff.

The performance level of most individuals improves in a supportive environment. Therefore, recognition and reinforcement, both of cognitive skills and abilities and of attributes of mental health, can positively affect restorative care efforts. Nurses who consistently identify strengths in a factual way are instrumental in improving the quality of life for their clients.

CASE STUDY

Ms. F. is 81 years old. She had a long career with the government that involved traveling all over the world. Although she never married, she is a devoted aunt and a vital member of her extended family. She is the youngest of three siblings. Her two older brothers live in New York and California. Despite the distance, the three communicate regularly through letters and telephone calls. Nieces and nephews are always attentive to Ms. F. She never spends a holiday alone.

The retirement years for Ms. F. became the highlight of her life. She continued her travels, sometimes with friends and at other times with a niece or nephew.

Only one problem seemed to dampen Ms. F.'s life. In her middle years, every once in a while (3–5 years), she became depressed, or "blue" as she describes it. Two episodes she "toughed out" on her own. Although she continued to function in her job, her appetite diminished. She woke up at 3:00 A.M. on most days and had no energy to do much of anything. In a couple of months, the blueness lifted, and she returned to the good life. These periods seemed to have no precipitating event. She saw a psychiatrist for the first time when she was 54 years old. He prescribed an antidepressant, nortriptyline (Pamelor). This medication was successful in treating the depression. After 6 months the medication and brief therapy were stopped. She did quite well in the following years.

When she was 78 years old, Ms. F. made the decision to come to a nursing home. Her family thought that she was having some minor problems with memory. Although she denied feeling depressed, she noticed a real decline in her energy level and ability to do for herself. She was placed on a unit with other residents who functioned independently. A niece came to help her decorate her room. Whatnots displayed unique treasures from a life of travel.

Based on this information, answer the following question:

1. With respect to the administration of the mental status examination, the charge nurse decided:
   a. Not to give the examination. It would be insulting to Ms. F. to be questioned in such a way.
   b. To check with Ms. F. regarding a good time to conduct some routine admission assessments, which would include the MMSE.
   c. That Ms. F. was doing so well there was no need for such a test.
   d. To ask the social worker to conduct this examination in a few weeks after the resident had adjusted better.

Ms. F. was a trim woman and her clothing was exquisite. From the start, the other residents seemed to respect her. Although she did not become a member of one of the unit cliques, there was no one who did not accept her and welcome her company when she sat down. Her admission MMSE score was 29/30. She was unable to recall one object after 5 minutes.

A few months after admission, some of the residents began to remark to the staff that Ms. F. was ignoring some of their efforts to engage her in a conversation. She started retreating to her room a little more. In general, she seemed more withdrawn. She favored a chair off to herself rather than an available seat in a group of other residents.

Based on this information, answer the following question:

2. The charge nurse was concerned. She went to visit Ms. F. in her room. The two problems the charge nurse was assessing in this interview were:
   a. Delirium and dementia
   b. Depression and dementia
   c. Depression and hearing loss
   d. Depression and possible delirium

Ms. F. was a little vain and disclosed to the charge nurse during this interview that her hearing was not what it used to be. "I don't want to wear a hearing aid," she said. The charge nurse convinced Ms. F. that a routine audiology appointment might be useful.

She was scheduled for a clinic appointment the following week. She had a great deal of wax buildup that was interfering with her hearing. When the wax was removed, her hearing improved, but the audiologist convinced her that a hearing aid would be most beneficial and told her, "It's an attractive device and can be made to fit your glasses." The persuading force was Ms. F.'s love for classical music. Clearly, she had not been able to enjoy her music with the hearing loss. She ordered a hearing aid.

The bad weather set in, holidays came and went, and Ms. F. holed up in her room "reading the paper." As spring approached and there were a few days of good weather, Ms. F. could not be dissuaded from staying in her room. When Ms. F. was weighed routinely, staff were horrified to note a 10-lb weight loss. In reviewing the minimum data set (MDS), the staff noted that she had lost a total of 15 lbs in 3 months.

Based on this information, answer the following question:

3. The charge nurse decided to conduct a mental status examination. Ms. F. agreed to being tested. The nurse noted that it took four repetitions of the objects for her to recall them. In 5 minutes she could not recall a single object. Since Ms. F. was well oriented, the nurses believed that:
   a. There was some dementia.
   b. She needed a battery for her hearing aid.
   c. She was depressed.
   d. A combination of a, b, and c.

The psychiatrist was called to assess Ms. F. He determined that she was depressed and recommended nortriptyline (Pamelor), an antidepressant. The primary physician prescribed Pamelor 25 mg every evening. After 3 weeks, the nurses reported that Ms. F. was smiling and seemed to be out of her room more. Her appetite was a little better; at least she ate a good breakfast. The primary physician conferred with the psychiatrist and increased the Pamelor to 50 mg daily. Six weeks later Ms. F. was on the porch enjoying lovely June days. She had been in the facility for a year. The charge nurse decided to repeat the mental status examination to determine whether there was marked improvement in her depression. Ms. F. was able to recall two out of the three objects. Her recall had improved. She was a little vague about the date; however, she knew the season, month, and year.

Based on this information, answer the following question:

4. The charge nurse wondered if:
   a. Ms. F. was just a little confused
   b. Ms. F. might have a disturbance in orientation related to a dementia process
   c. An adjustment in the antidepressant might be appropriate
   d. She should discourage Ms. F. from subscribing to a daily newspaper since it might be too tiring for her declining abilities

Toward the end of November Ms. F. slipped. Although she did not fall, she injured her back when she grabbed onto the support rail in her bathroom. The nurses noticed that she held on to the furniture and walls as she walked. She had x-rays, which revealed osteoporosis. The staff and primary physician discussed with her the idea of using a walker to get around. She agreed to try this and went to physical therapy (PT) for an evaluation and a walker. Two weeks later the resident was still complaining of pain. She stayed in her bed more and did not come out for meals. Aspirin was ordered for her pain. Staff came by to visit. A few more weeks passed. Answer the following questions about this situation:

5. Some of the staff believed that:
   a. The resident was exaggerating her problem to get more attention
   b. The resident was depressed because of the pain and decline in function
   c. The resident had more extensive physical problems than they realized
   d. That further assessment was needed to determine the factors behind the resident's decline

6. The charge nurse decided that the following assessment(s) would help staff understand the resident's decline:
   a. Pain history and physical assessment per physician
   b. GDS
   c. MMSE
   d. All of the above

The resident described the pain as severe, the worst she had ever experienced. The physician decided to hospitalize her for more tests. Hospital laboratory work showed dehydration. Magnetic resonance imaging (MRI) revealed that there was a disc pushing in on the spinal cord. The doctor ordered intravenous fluids and mepiridine (Demerol) to manage the pain. When the charge nurse stopped by the hospital to see Ms. F. on the way home from work, she was shocked to find that Ms. F. did not remember her and believed it was nighttime. She had no idea where she was and had no recall from one moment to the next. It was January, and she believed it was June.

Answer the following question regarding this situation:

7. The charge nurse realized that her resident:
   a. Was depressed
   b. Was in extensive pain
   c. Had not heard a word she had said
   d. Was delirious

During her hospital stay, Ms. F. was treated for gastrointestinal problems related to aspirin use and had back surgery that resulted in some postoperative complications. When Ms. F. returned to the nursing home, it was spring. She had a marked decline in her functional ability. She was now in a wheelchair and had been assigned to another unit. The staff from her original unit visited her to help her get adjusted. They focused on her abilities and her life of travel. They invited her to visit them and attend groups on the first floor. Ms. F. seemed very vague to them. The nurses felt sad and wondered whether Ms. F. would ever again be as bright and interested in her surroundings as she had been on their floor.

The MMSE was repeated. The nurses on the third floor realized from the MMSE that Ms. F.'s cognitive status had changed significantly. There were deficits in orientation and memory. Her ability to perform calculations, however, had not declined.

In a postadmission care conference, the staff identified Ms. F.'s patient care needs. Answer the following question about this determination:

8. They believed that they must implement all the following except:
   a. To assist the resident to accept her decline
   b. To assess her ability to move about and participate in a walking program
   c. To request a psychiatric evaluation
   d. To encourage her to participate in all unit activities

The resident slowly began to respond to the staff's plan of care. She was restarted on an antidepressant that had been stopped while she was in the hospital. She responded well to a walking program. Although she had lost some of her agility, she achieved some independence with a walker. Her dementia had advanced slightly, but she could and did participate in activities. It was decided that staff would continue to do an MMSE annually to monitor her progress.

CASE STUDY
SOLUTIONS

1. b
2. c
3. c
4. b
5. d
6. d
7. d
8. a

Study Questions

Please select the one best answer.

1. The health-care providers who are best qualified to conduct psychological assessments, such as Folstein's MMSE, are:
   a. Psychologists
   b. Nurses
   c. Social workers
   d. Psychiatrists

2. The social worker of a unit annually conducts an MMSE on all the residents. She informs you that Mrs. H.'s score in the area of orientation has dropped 2 points from last year. You suspect that the drop is due to:
   a. Delirium
   b. Arthritis
   c. Progression of dementia
   d. Depression

3. The activities department has alerted you to the fact that, recently, Mr. J. has not been interested in attending programs sponsored by their department. This morning he complained to you that he believes he is having problems with his memory. He did not eat breakfast and only picked at his lunch. He denies feeling depressed. You conduct an MMSE. There is a change in score from the admission MMSE conducted 3 months ago. His immediate recall of three objects on Folstein's MMSE has declined. You suspect:
   a. Delirium
   b. Progression of dementia
   c. A urinary tract infection
   d. Depression

4. Mrs. C. does not come out of her room for breakfast. The night shift staff report that the resident was up all night and that she has a fever. You go to Mrs. C. to see whether you can assist her. She seems to be asleep. When you touch her arm, she opens her eyes. She does not quite recognize you, her favorite nurse. She believes that it is bedtime and her main concern is that her husband (who has been dead for 20 years) is late, coming home from work. When you leave the room she returns to "sleep." Yesterday her MMSE score was 30/30. You know immediately that she is:
   a. Depressed
   b. Having a massive stroke
   c. Delirious
   d. Confused, due to dementia

5. Important considerations when conducting psychological assessments are:
   a. Timing
   b. Privacy and elimination of interruptions
   c. Positive introduction of the assessment
   d. All of the above

References

Albert, M. S. (1990). Neuropsychological testing. In C. K. Cassel, D. E. Riesenberg, L. B. Sorenson, & J. R. Walsh (Eds.), *Geriatric medicine* (Vol. 2, pp. 48–54). New York: Springer-Verlag.

Beck, A. T., Ward, C. H., & Mendelson, M. (1961). An inventory for measuring depression. *Archives of General Psychiatry, 4*(53), 561–571.

Carr, D. B., & Jacox, A. K. (1994). Acute pain management: Operative or medical procedures and trauma. In *Clinical geriatric medicine. Diagnostic and statistical manual of mental disorders* (4th ed.). Washington, DC: American Psychiatric Association.

Folstein, M. F., Folstein, S. E., & McHugh, P. R. (1975). Mini-mental status: A practice method for grading the cognitive state of patients for the clinician. *Journal of Psychiatric Research, 12,* 189.

Gilbert, R. M. (1992). *Extraordinary relationships: A new way of thinking about human interactions.* Minneapolis: Chronimed Publishing.

Gurland, B. J. (1987). The assessment of cognitive function in the elderly. *Clinical Geriatric Medicine, 3*(1), 53–63.

Hamilton, M. (1967). Development of a rating scale for primary depressive illness. *British Journal of Social and Clinical Psychology, 6,* 78–96.

Jacobs, J. W., Bernhard, M. R., Delgado, A., & Strain, J. J. (1977). Screening for organic mental syndromes in the medically ill. *Annals of Internal Medicine, 86,* 40.

Kahn, R., Goldfarb, A., Pollak, M., & Peck, A. (1960). Brief objective measures for the determination of mental status in the aged. *American Journal of Psychiatry, 117,* 326.

Kiernan, R. J., Mueller, J., Langston, J. W., & Vandyke, C. (1987). The neurobehavioral cognitive status examination: A brief but differential approach to cognitive assessment. *Annals of Internal Medicine, 107,* 481.

Pfeiffer, E. (1975). A short portable mental status questionnaire for the assessment of organic brain deficit in elderly patients. *Journal of American Geriatrics Society, 23,* 433.

Restak, R. M. (1988). *The mind.* New York: Bantam Books.

Squire, L. R. (1987). *Memory and brain.* New York: Oxford University Press.

Sunderland, T., Alterman, I. S., Yount, D., Hill, J. L., Tariot, P. N., Newhouse, P. A., Mueller, E. A., Mellow, A. M., & Cohen, R. M. (1988). A new scale for the assessment of depressed mood in demented patients. *American Journal of Psychiatry, 8,* 145.

Yesavage, J., Brink, T., Rose, T., Lum, O., Huang, O., Adey, V., & Leirer, V. (1983). Development and validation of a geriatric depression screening scale: A preliminary report. *Journal of Psychiatric Research, 17,* 37–49.

Zung, W. K. (1983). A self-rating depression scale. *Archives of General Psychiatry, 12,* 63–70.

Bibliography

American Medical Directors Association. (1996). *Depression: Clinical practice guideline.* Columbia, MD: AMDA.

> *This clinical practice guideline was developed for use by the interdisciplinary team in long-term care facilities. It was designed to facilitate decision making and was developed specifically to be used in conjunction with the Minimum Data Set (MDS) and the Resident Assessment Instrument (RAI).*

Billig, N. (1987). *Too old to be sad: Understanding depression in the elderly.* Lexington, MA: D. C. Heath & Co.

> *Writing in clear everyday language, Dr. Billig describes the signs and symptoms of depression and what to do for someone who is depressed.*

Carr, D. B., Jacox, A. K., et al. (1992). Acute Pain Management Guideline Panel. *Acute pain management: Operative or medical procedures and trauma. Clinical practice guideline* (AHCPR Publication No. 92–0032). Rockville, MD: Agency for Health Care Policy and Research, Public Health Service, U.S. Department of Health and Human Services.

> *The guideline reflects the state of knowledge, current at the time of publication, on effective and appropriate care.*

Gilbert, R. M. (1992). *Extraordinary relationships: A new way of thinking about human interactions.* Minneapolis: Chronimed Publishing.

> *It is useful to try to understand as much as possible about relationship patterns—in whatever arena they may occur. This book demonstrates precisely how to apply family systems theory to everyday life.*

Grabhorn, R. (1985). *Cognitivity: A creativity kit.* Indianapolis: Biodot International.

   A creativity kit played as a game. Designed to be a systematic yet pleasurable procedure. Based on the disciplines of the cognitive sciences. It allows the definitive knowledge of the logical left brain hemisphere to interchange and combine with the more fanciful imagery of the right brain hemisphere which, in turn, actually creates new ideas.

Hogstel, M. O., & Keen-Payne, R. (1996). *Practical guide to health assessment: Through the lifespan* (2nd ed.). St. Louis: Mosby-Year Book.

   This portable, practical clinical guide can be used when studying or performing health assessments in any clinical setting. Organized by body system, it contains a variety of guides and forms that can be applied in the clinical setting.

Kane, R. A., & Kane, R. L. (1981). *Assessing the elderly: A practical guide to measurement.* Lexington, MA: Lexington Books.

   Three of the mental status examinations and two of the depression scales highlighted in this chapter are replicated and compared. Emphasis is placed on regular and consistent use of assessment tools to describe improvement and decline.

Kulowicz, L. H., & NICHE Faculty. (1997). Nursing standard of practice protocol: Depression in elderly patients. *Geriatric Nursing, 18*(5), 192–200.

   This article combines a great amount of information into the development of nursing protocols related to depression and the elderly.

Chapter

COLLEEN BRILL

11

Common Clinical Problems: Psychological

Learning Objectives

After completing this chapter, the student will be able to:

1. Recognize three behaviors that may signal the presence of a psychological problem in an elderly person.
2. Explain how to use nursing interventions for clients with common psychological problems.
3. Discuss how to manage difficult behaviors of elderly persons.
4. Compare reality orientation, reminiscence, remotivation, resocialization, and validation techniques.
5. Select important information about psychological medications to include in client teaching.

INTRODUCTION

Psychological problems are disturbances in mental or emotional health that occur as a result of external or internal stimuli. These problems are usually assessed by examining thought patterns, behaviors, and emotions. Because psychological difficulties are not as obvious as some physical problems that can be diagnosed by laboratory tests, it may be difficult to diagnose and correctly treat elderly people with these problems.

Almost any psychological problem that can occur with other age groups can also occur with older adults. A few of the more common psychological problems that are found in clinical situations will be described in this chapter. A glossary of terms used in this chapter is presented in Box 11.1.

GENERAL GUIDELINES FOR COMMUNICATING WITH THE ELDERLY

It is helpful to review some basic principles for good communication, particularly as they relate to communicating with the elderly person with psychological disorders.

Box 11.1 GLOSSARY OF PSYCHOLOGICAL TERMS

Anxiety: generalized unpleasant feeling of apprehension.

Behavior modification: treatment method of changing behavior.

Bipolar affective disorder: psychological disease involving mood swings from mania to depression.

Delirium: sudden, reversible state of confusion.

Delusion: false, fixed idea or belief.

Disorientation: state of not knowing what day or time it is, or not knowing where one is.

Hallucination: false sensory impression, often seeing or hearing something that is not there.

Illusion: misperception of a real event or object.

Neurolinguistic programming: a way of communicating using neurological, behavioral, and speech patterns.

Neurotransmitter: chemical in the brain that carries electrical impulses to neurons.

Paranoia: way of thinking that systematically interprets others as being intentionally harmful.

Phobia: exaggerated fear of a particular object or class of objects.

Schizophrenia: psychological disease involving severe thought and perception disturbances.

Sensory deprivation: condition of decreased stimulation that can cause hallucinations, illusions, and disorientation.

Social support: emotional and physical assistance given by loved ones.

Somatization: extreme preoccupation with physical problems.

Values and Culture

How the nurse interacts with people who have emotional problems depends a lot on the values and culture of the nurse and the patient. What one person may see as normal may not be seen as normal by a person who has different values. If a nurse has been brought up to value touch as a way of communicating concern and a client perceives touching without permission as an invasion of privacy, this difference may have a negative influence on the communication process.

Nurses know that elderly people, as a group, come from a wide variety of backgrounds. Many are from cultures that are different from the cultures of the nurses who are their caregivers. A Hispanic resident may stand very close while talking to staff members. A staff member not aware of this cultural difference may interpret this as being intrusive. A Japanese client who values modesty may have difficulty talking openly about bowel and bladder problems, for example. If you recognize that you need more information about the cultural diversity of the people to whom you give care, there are several excellent textbooks available for independent study.

Prevention of Psychological Problems

In addition to the ideas for promoting wellness that were presented earlier in this book, there are some general guidelines for preventing psychological problems with elderly clients. Making an extra effort to assign the same staff members to an elderly person with a psychological problem may help to prevent a client from becoming emotionally upset. This is true both in the hospital and in the nursing home. A hospitalized patient may be assigned nine different nurses during a 3-day stay. The sheer number of names to remember is difficult, but it is especially difficult for the older client with a psychological problem because other factors, such as hallucinations, may interfere with the ability to accurately perceive information. Maintaining an environment with an elderly person's familiar belongings can be helpful to promote self-worth and prevent disorientation. This is an important point to remember during a period of change and at times of stress. In some facilities, elderly people are allowed to bring their own china cabinets and crystal to use on a small table in their rooms in the nursing home. This can make mealtime more pleasant and also remind the residents of valued social roles. Small objects and pictures can be placed near the older person during a hospitalization to prevent the disorientation that sometimes goes along with stressful changes during an illness. Playing taped music of familiar songs may be better than television viewing in preventing sensory deprivation of older persons in a critical care unit. These are just a few examples of simple nursing interventions that can be used to prevent psychological problems caused by stress in older adults.

Forming Relationships With People Who Have Psychological Problems

Every relationship has stages. During the beginning of a relationship, people are usually uncomfortable. As time goes on and trust is established, people enter a stage of the relationship that is comfortable and allows for more open exchanges. The last stage of a relationship involves termination. During this time, there also can be some nervousness about having to say good-bye. For people who have emotional problems and are older and for the nurses who work with them, problems can be prevented by understanding the normal stages of relationships.

Beginning a Relationship

People who have psychological problems may not be easy to get to know initially. They may have had problems starting relationships all their lives and forming a relationship with a new nurse might be difficult. Some people with mental illnesses have trouble trusting others and find it difficult to trust a new nurse or a new roommate in a hospital or long-term care facility. There are a few things that can be done to help make the beginning of a relationship more comfortable.

If the person with a psychological problem does not talk or becomes upset at first, do not take it personally. Remember that this person may be feeling uncomfortable and unsure of how you will react. The nurse can be creative in dealing with problems like this and needs to respond in a natural way. Some approaches to consider are using humor to diffuse tension or finding an interest of the client's, such as tying flies or crocheting, and asking more about it.

Important points to keep in mind are the need to establish trust and not to reject the patient. You may need to try saying to the patient, "It seems like you'd rather not talk right now. I'll come back in an hour and sit here (or at the desk, or at a table in the dining room) for five minutes, and if you'd like to talk just let me know." Be realistic about what you can and cannot do. Promising to do something and not following through is worse for someone who is mentally ill than it is for others, because of the difficulty many have with trusting people.

Some people with emotional problems have trouble trusting others. It is important to develop trust with such people.

Being patient is also very important. Like the nurse in the previous example, some nurses have had to be available for several days before seeing any results. When the results do come, and the nurse is able to communicate with someone, it can be a very rewarding experience.

Ending a Relationship

Nurses begin and end relationships with many people every day. Sometimes this happens in small ways, like taking a weekend off or going away for a conference or vacation. Sometimes it is more permanent, like discharging a client to another facility or to the home, changing jobs, or saying good-bye to a client who is dying. During this phase of a relationship, clients may sometimes do things very similar to the behaviors described in the section dealing with beginning a relationship.

If a nurse is going away for a while, clients may start demanding more attention by ringing the call light more frequently, by becoming angry or irritated by small things, or by not responding or talking. To prevent this from happening, it is best if the clients know as soon as possible when to expect the separation and to talk about it openly with the nurse. If a permanent separation is approaching, some kind of formal farewell, like a good-bye party, might be helpful. Taking pictures with clients and staff can also help ease the difficulty of a separation. If a client is being discharged home, do not always assume it is a joyous occasion. Sometimes the situation at home is worse than being in the nursing home or hospital. Even if a person is looking forward to going home, mixed feelings may exist about having to adjust again. It is not unusual for someone who is about ready to go home to suddenly become worse. If this happens, it may be a clue to you that the person is having problems with ending the present experience. If the nurse talks about this openly and starts by sharing feelings like "Things just aren't going to be the same around here without you, Mr. M.," the client may be more willing to talk about personal feelings.

Problem Behaviors

If a person with a psychological problem begins to display any unusual behaviors, it may be due to a number of different causes. Recent changes in relationships may contribute to increased wandering, shouting, and aggressive or withdrawn behaviors. These behaviors are not uncommon after a room or roommate change, or when getting used to new staff members. If the problem behaviors seem to be related to changes in relationships, then it might be helpful to find ways to help the person better adjust using some of the examples in this chapter.

COMMUNICATION SKILLS

The hallmark of nursing care for persons with psychological problems is the ability to communicate effectively. In addition to the listening skills described in this book in the chapter on management, there are other communication skills that can be used to make it easier to talk to older people with psychological problems. A few standard communication skills, concepts from neurolinguistic programming (Bandler, 1985), and validation (Feil, 1993), will be described in this section.

Neurolinguistic programming uses observation of a person's words and behaviors to help establish the best way of relating to that person. Validation, a communication approach for relating to disoriented elderly people, helps the disoriented express themselves. Sometimes communication with someone who is disoriented is blocked by the listener's need to have the disoriented person think or talk in a "logical" way. When the listener is able to put away that need to communicate in a "normal" way, that opens the possibility of communicating in other ways. When this happens the listener is able to understand and validate the disoriented person's experiences.

Empathy and Genuineness

Feeling with someone is using empathy. Trying to show that the nurse wants to understand someone helps communication. Empathy can be expressed by maintaining eye contact, using a caring tone of voice, listening closely to what someone says, and making statements such as "This must be difficult for you," or "It sounds like you are having a rough time right now." Using a tone of voice as if talking to a child keeps the nurse from using empathy and is not helpful in communicating with the elderly. Such comments as referring to the elderly person as "honey" or "dearie" are patronizing and, therefore, a hinderance to effective communication. Another example of patronizing behavior is referring to an elderly person in a report to another nurse as a "real cutie" or a "sweetheart."

It is important that the nurse be genuine when showing empathy. Being genuine means that nurses must truly represent themselves. Finding things you would really say to a patient is more important than saying the right thing from a book. The examples given here are no more than just examples. Nurses have to find their own style of communicating with others.

Listening

Listening to someone includes listening to feelings, words, and behaviors. Sometimes people with emotional problems may forget or confuse the facts or use words that do not make sense. When this happens, it is especially important to listen to feelings instead of trying to get the facts straight. If a resident is incomprehensible but is speaking loudly and has tearful eyes, you might respond by saying, "This is extremely frustrating for you."

Preferred Sense Words

All people relate to their surroundings through their senses. Most people respond more through one sense than through others. How a person talks will give an idea of which sense is that person's preferred sense. If Mrs. J. says, "I see what you mean. Look at this," she probably is a person who responds best to sight or visual words. Some people respond best to hearing or auditory words, and others respond best to words about feelings or movement. A list of commonly used visual, auditory, and

TABLE 11.1	COMMONLY USED PREFERRED SENSE WORDS	
Visual	**Auditory**	**Kinesthetic**
See	Listen	Feel
View	Hear	Grasp
Picture	Sound	Move
Look	Loud	Touch

kinesthetic words is included in Table 11.1. The nurse can use the person's preferred sense to establish rapport. For example, if a client says, "No one listens to me anymore," a response like "What would you like for me to listen to, Mr. J.?" will receive a better response than "What would you like me to see, Mr. J.?"

Nonverbal Communication

Using direct eye contact and a caring voice tone can help the communication process. Positioning the body at eye level and approaching an elderly person directly from the front also may help communication.

Touch

Touching is an important part of communicating with elderly people. Many people miss human contact and enjoy being touched. Some people with psychological problems may enjoy touch whereas others may not. A person with psychological problems may become frightened, withdrawn, or agitated if touched. When the nurse touches someone who has an emotional problem, it is a good idea to ask the person first if it would be all right. Saying, "Would it be okay if I gave you a hug?" might be a way of showing respect for the person. Some people who are very withdrawn may respond only to touch. Someone who has a severe loss of vision or hearing may respond only if the nurse moves very closely. Touch can be used to stimulate sensory memories as well. Different people respond to touch in different ways. A list of common responses to touch is found in Table 11.2. A person who talks about his mother or says, "Ma, ma, ma" repeatedly may respond well to stroking on the upper cheek.

Matching and Mirroring

Research has determined that it helps the communication process if a person can match or mirror another's behavior. Mirroring is doing exactly what the person is doing as if the person were looking into a mirror. Matching is using the same pattern or intensity of tone the person is using. This must be done in a respectful way and not as a way of making fun of the individual. If the nurse feels uncomfortable doing this, it is not genuine and does not help communication.

Matching and mirroring are nonverbal ways of helping someone know that you hear what they are saying. Matching of emotions can be done by labeling the emotion out loud, using the same intensity used by the client. Mrs. C. may pound her fist on the arm of her wheelchair and say "I hate them, I hate them, I hate them." Using

TABLE 11.2 COMMON RESPONSES OF DISORIENTED ELDERS TO TOUCH	
Remind Client of	**Touch Technique**
Mother	Palm of hand in a light circular motion on the upper cheek
Father	Finger tips, in a circular motion, medium pressure, on the back of the head
Spouse/lover	Hand under the ear lobe, curving along the chin, with both hands, a soft stroking motion downward along the jaw
Child	Cupped fingers on the back of the neck, with both hands, in a small circular motion
Brother/sister or good friend	Full hand on the shoulders and upper back by the shoulder blades; use full pressure in a rubbing movement
Animals/pets	Finger tips on the inside of the calf

Adapted from Feil, N. (1989). *Validation: The Feil method.* Cleveland, OH: Edward Feil Productions, p. 73, with permission.

matching and mirroring, the nurse would pound on the table with the same rhythm she is using and say "You're angry, you're angry, you're angry," using the same intensity of emotion.

Universal Symbols

A universal symbol is an object in the present that represents something important from the past. Sometimes these symbols increase in importance for people who develop disorientation as they grow older. The symbols can be something that has meaning to the client, such as a reminder of a hobby or life's work, or it can be a different type of symbol. A few typical symbols are listed in Table 11.3. An apron can be made with a large pocket in the front that can contain significant symbols. A farmer may fondle farm tools placed in the pocket of the apron and by doing this revive a memory of a time in the life he enjoyed. As he touches the tools, the nurse can encourage communication using these symbols of the person's previous life.

TABLE 11.3 UNIVERSAL SYMBOLS AND WHAT THEY CAN MEAN	
Symbol	**Possible Meaning**
Jewelry, clothing	Worth, identity
Shoe	Container, womb, male or female sex symbol
Purse	Female sex symbol, vagina, identity
Cane or fist	Penis, potency, power
Soft furniture	Safety, mother, home
Hard furniture	Father, God
Napkin, tissue	Earth, belonging, baby
Flat object	Identity
Food	Love, mother
Drink from a glass	Male power, potency
Any receptacle	Womb
Picking the nose	Sexual pleasure
Playing with feces	Early childhood pleasures

From Feil, N. (1989). *Validation: The Feil method.* Cleveland, OH: Edward Feil Productions, pp. 47–48, with permission.

Verbal Communication

Communication skills described in general nursing books also can be used successfully with the elderly. There are a few skills that are important to emphasize when working with the elderly who have psychological problems. Some skills are more helpful than others. The following discussion includes validation techniques, which are especially useful with the disoriented.

Open Questions

Verbal communication can be helpful by using open questions instead of closed questions. A closed question is a question that can be answered with a simple "yes" or "no." An open question tends to encourage the person to talk more. Open questions are asked using such words as "who," "what," "where," "when," and "how." "Why" questions are usually not very helpful, especially with someone who is disoriented. Some people with psychological problems may not be able to logically or rationally answer a "why" question. If a resident in a nursing home says she is looking for her mother, you may validate her by asking open questions like "What does your mother look like? What did you like to talk about with your mother? What did you and your mother do together?"

Vague Pronouns

If a person is not able to fill in the details with enough facts to be understood, try using vague or ambiguous pronouns to help foster communication. Sometimes people refer to all women as "she" and all men as "he." If the nurse becomes too concerned about accurate details, the opportunity to communicate may be lost. Instead of worrying about the facts, try to focus on the feelings. If a client says "She's all alone. She can't stay there," you can respond "You're worried about her. She's important to you."

Speaking Slowly

Many people who have emotional problems have slowed thought processes. When this is combined with normal aging changes, it is very important for the nurse to use slightly slower speech and wait a little longer for the patient to respond. Asking questions one at a time, instead of running several questions together, can also make it easier to talk to an older person with an emotional problem.

Giving Instructions

When giving directions, it is best to do so slowly, one step at a time. Individuals who are very disoriented may not be able to do any self-care unless prompted by very simple cues. Telling patients who are disoriented to brush their teeth may not get any results, but if you tell them to pick up the toothbrush, then pick up the toothpaste, then put the toothpaste on the brush, then put the brush in the mouth, and then brush up and down, they may be able to do more self-care than was thought possible at first.

Guided Choices

Some people may not respond to open questions as well as they do to guided choices. When asked "What would you like to do today?" someone with a psychological problem may not know how to respond. However, when given a choice between two activities, with choices given one at a time, the person may be able to respond. An example in this case might be "How would you like to go to singing time today? Would you rather go for a walk outside?"

Asking the Extreme

When someone who is disoriented is upset about something he or she thinks happened, ask questions about the extremes of the situation. What is the worst? What is the best? Imagine the opposite. . . . When is it better? When does it not happen? Suppose every night an elderly woman thinks some men are coming to attack her. The nurse might ask, "When do they usually come? When are they not there? What helps you feel safe? What doesn't help you very much?"

Communication skills are important tools to help the nurse work with people who have psychological problems. Sometimes the tools work well, whereas other times they do not work so well. Remember that nothing replaces the nurse's judgment in a given situation. The nurse selects what to do in each situation with each patient. No two people are alike, but it can be helpful to know a few of the basic skills so that they can be used with the common psychological problems discussed throughout this chapter.

GRIEVING AND DEPRESSION

Surviving losses is part of the aging process. An older person may lose relationships with people through death, retirement, relocation, or losing the ability to maintain contacts with friends and family due to physical problems. An elder also may suffer the loss of valued social roles, a home, financial security, vision, hearing, or other body functions. The grief process that occurs with the loss of a loved one also is associated with the losses listed here.

Dealing With Grief

It is helpful to keep in mind the stages of the grieving process—denial, anger, bargaining, depression, and acceptance—when dealing with losses. These stages do not always occur with every person. Some people who experience losses may become angry but not go through the other stages. As a nurse, it is important to accept the client's response to grief and not have a preconceived idea of how the client should respond.

A person can be helped to talk about grief by asking open-ended questions such as, "What did you do on your former job? When did you start working there? How did you get started working there?" if the person is grieving over the loss of a job. Asking open-ended questions about feelings also can help another to express grief. Sometimes it can be uncomfortable to hear a person talk about negative emotions like anger and sadness. Encouraging someone to express feelings and allowing expressions of anger or crying can help that person deal with feelings effectively. Saying something like, "How did you feel about that?" or "What upset you the most about that?" can encourage someone to talk about feelings. Telling someone who is sad and grieving, "Don't cry now, it will be all right" only gives false reassurance and tells the person to keep it inside. If emotions are not expressed, they tend to be expressed later in dysfunctional ways such as extreme anger, agitation, or withdrawal.

Depression

Because depression is a part of grieving and loss, it is a serious problem among the elderly. There may be other factors that also contribute to depression among the elderly. Most of the current theories about depression have a strong emphasis on neurobiological causes and take into account the fact that depression tends to run in families. Most researchers conclude that depression is linked to the amount of the neurotransmitters serotonin and norepinephrine present in the nerve synapses. Lower serotonin and norepinephrine levels seem to be associated with depression.

Factors within the body can deplete these substances, but external factors such as stress or decreased exposure to light also can influence the amounts of neurotransmitters. Try slumping your shoulders forward and keeping your head down on your chest. Think about something that makes you feel sad. Now sit up straight and hold your head high. Try thinking that same depressing thought. Chances are that you will find it very difficult to think about the depressing thought as you raise your head and sit upright. As they grow older, many people suffer from physical problems that may affect their ability to be upright and these physical problems can then influence the way the brain functions.

As health-care providers, nurses also know that regular exercise can help maintain a higher level of endorphins in clients' bodies. Endorphins are naturally produced morphinelike substances that help people feel better. If the ability to exercise is impaired, then the body and mind are affected, and depression may result. Getting exposure to sunlight also can affect some people by changing their mood. For the homebound elderly, this may be a problem. A poor diet also may contribute to the development of depression. Many older people have poor nutritional intake due to a variety of psychological and physical factors such as poor denture fit, cost of nutritious foods, changes in taste sensations, and eating alone. When the effects of the losses of aging are combined with those from physical risk factors, it is clear why many elderly people are depressed (Wilson & Kneisl, 1992). The good news is that most people who have depression can be helped by treatment. Medications that treat depression are very effective for most people.

The tricyclic antidepressants used to be widely prescribed and are still effective for many people. Major problems with using these antidepressants are side effects related to the cardiovascular system and problems with urinary retention. Many elderly persons have problems with heart disease and hypertension, and men may have prostatic hypertrophy. These problems can be contraindications for the use of these drugs. With the advent of serotonin-selective reuptake inhibitors (SSRIs) such as fluoxetine (Prozac), sertraline HCl (Zoloft), and paroxetine HCl (Paxil), safer treatment options are available for persons who have depression and other physical problems. Another antidepressant used very effectively with many elderly is bupropion (Wellbutrin). Wellbutrin must be monitored closely if there are any eating disturbances or if there is a concern over weight loss.

Medications are an important part of treating depression but are most successful when used in conjunction with other types of therapy. Individual therapy with a counselor trained to work with elderly clients can help the person develop coping skills for dealing with depression. Cognitive therapy is a type of therapy used by many mental health professionals with clients who are depressed.

Depression and Confusion in the Elderly

Assessing someone who is depressed is complicated by factors that occur as a result of normal aging. The previous chapter describes how to assess someone with depression, and how to use standard measures of depression. Some of the behaviors seen in those with depression may be very similar to behaviors seen with other problems common in older people. Individuals who are depressed may not care about their surroundings and begin to be disoriented and confused, as they draw inward. It can be very difficult to know whether the mental slowing and memory loss attributed to depression are actually changes commonly found in the early stages of dementia. Many elderly people who have depression are thought to have dementia and are not treated for their depression (Table 11.4).

Depression and Suicide

Assessing for the risk of suicide is essential for someone who is depressed. The suicide rate among the elderly is very high. It may not seem likely that an older person would have thoughts about suicide, but it happens. If a client says something like, "I just don't want to live anymore," the tendency may be to discount the person and say "Oh, you don't mean that" or "You'll feel better tomorrow, you're just having a bad day." If a person expresses a wish to die, makes funeral plans, has a major change in life, or begins to give away cherished possessions, be aware that these can be signs that the person may be planning suicide.

TABLE 11.4   DIFFERENCES BETWEEN DELIRIUM, DEMENTIA, AND DEPRESSION

	Delirium	Dementia	Depression
Onset	Rapid	Slow	Rapid
Duration	Short	Long	Short or long
Night symptoms	May worsen	Frequently worsen	Usually do not worsen
Cognitive functions	Variable	Stable	Variable
Physical causes	Common	None	Possible
Recent changes	Common	None or minimal	Common
Suicidal ideation	Rare	Rare	Common
Low self-esteem	Rare	Rare	Common
History of psychiatric symptoms	Not usually	Rare	Common
Mood	Labile	Labile	Depressed
Behavior	Labile	Labile	Slowed thought and motor processes

Asking people whether they are having thoughts about killing themselves is not "putting the thought into their heads." Many people are relieved to talk to someone about suicide if the nurse asks in a calm, matter-of-fact manner. Finding out whether the client has a plan, and what it is, is essential information. If a homebound client describes a hoard of potassium supplements or cardiac medications that are readily available, and if the person's conversation indicates a plan to take the medication after the nurse leaves, that is a situation requiring immediate action. Persons who say they do not want to live, but have not thought about how they would end their lives, are at a much lower risk for an immediate suicide attempt than those who have a plan. Many incidents of so-called "noncompliance" with medications are actually intentional attempts to overdose. If a client is having thoughts about suicide, listen carefully, intervene immediately if necessary, and refer the person for treatment.

Failure to Thrive

The term *failure to thrive* is most often applied to young children who do not grow and develop as expected. Some elders who are depressed also may have a failure to thrive or a giving-up complex (Haber, McMahon, Price-Hoskins, & Sideleau, 1992). This may be the case when the older person no longer makes an effort to continue with life, for instance, refuses to eat, refuses medications, or chooses to resist or refuse treatment for health problems.

Clinical Problems

A 72-year-old man finds no meaning in life and feels sad, especially in the winter.

Possible Solutions

1. Explore feelings by asking when his sadness started, when is it better, when is it worse.
2. Plan ways to decrease isolation in winter, such as attending church and senior lunch program when weather permits. Ensure telephone contact with support system when the weather is bad.

He has recently been told he must take insulin for diabetes and cries when talking about it.

1. Refer to diabetes nurse educator and diabetes support group.

DELIRIUM AND DEMENTIA

Because depression can cause some confusion and disorientation, it can be difficult to determine whether the older person has a problem with delirium, dementia, or depression (see Table 11.4). Many factors influence a person's ability to think clearly.

Emotional stress and change can cause anyone to have difficulty with remembering scheduled appointments or to be distracted easily from activities of daily living such as turning off the burner when cooking. Sometimes physical factors such as illness, insufficient oxygen, or high or low blood sugar levels may cause a person to behave in a very bizarre way. The person who has a problem with disorientation can be found in any setting. When a person becomes disoriented, caregivers may become resigned to the problem and consider this a normal part of the aging process. This is not usually correct. Clarification of the characteristics of delirium and dementia and the differences between them can provide guidance for how to intervene with the disoriented individual.

Delirium

The psychological problem of delirium refers to a situation in which a client has a fairly rapid change in behavior and thinking ability. Mental status changes that occur with this acute problem usually affect individuals' abilities to recall where they are, what day or time it is, or even what their own names are. Delirium may cause agitation or rapidly changing moods. Someone who is delirious commonly has an anxious facial expression. Short-term memory may or may not be intact. With delirium, the client pays little attention to surroundings or may respond slowly to new surroundings.

The client with delirium usually talks in a rambling way that does not make sense. The person may have difficulty staying awake or have increased activity and be awake all the time. Sensory and perceptual disorders such as hallucinations and delusions may be present, for example, the perception that the nurse holding a syringe has a knife or hearing a baby crying that is not there. Changes in thought content and process may also be present. Fixed ideas or beliefs may be evident, as well as disjointed or flighty thoughts.

Delirium can result from a variety of physiological causes and can be reversed. Malnutrition, electrolyte imbalances, infections, acid-base imbalances, changes in blood sugar, hypoxia, drug reactions, dehydration, and head trauma are a few of the common causes of delirium. It is important to determine what is causing the delirium because the sooner the problem can be treated, the sooner the delirium will clear.

When a client has a period of delirium it can be very upsetting for the family and nursing staff. Explaining what is happening to all those involved can help reduce stress and make it easier for everyone to handle the problem behaviors that occur.

Clinical Problems	Possible Solutions
A 75-year-old client who has just had surgery develops delirium, is agitated, and tries to pull out his nasogastric tube.	1. Check for physical causes. 2. Use elbow splints on the arms to prevent having to use restraints. 3. Ask a family member or a volunteer to sit with the client to prevent removal of the tube.
An 82-year-old woman who has just received meperidine thinks the nurse who enters the room with a stethoscope is going to hang her with a rope.	1. Stop meperidine use and notify physician. 2. If possible, remove the stethoscope and return later, when she is less agitated, to take her apical pulse. 3. If she is able to listen, explain that what is happening seems very real, but because of the medication, the stethoscope seems like something else.

Dementia

The syndrome of dementia is usually defined as the loss of intellectual abilities to the extent that it interferes with normal activities of daily living. Dementia is characterized by problems with cognitive ability, personality changes, memory impairment, decreased intellectual functioning, and changed judgment and mood.

Dementia usually occurs gradually, over a period of months or years, and is the result of some type of damage to the brain. This damage can be caused by neurological diseases such as Pick's or Huntington's disease, or can be the result of vascular problems such as multi-infarct dementia. The most common type of dementia is Alzheimer's disease. It is estimated that, in the future, dementia will outweigh heart disease and cancer as a major health problem.

Because dementia is such a significant concern, new approaches to dealing with this syndrome are being examined. Validation therapy is a way of communicating with disoriented elders (Feil, 1993). Validation means respecting the feelings of the person and confirming that from the individual's perspective, the experience is true.

This therapy is being used in many countries all over the world for people who are disoriented to decrease stress, promote self-esteem and communication, reduce chemical and physical restraint usage, and make it possible to sustain independent living for a longer period of time.

A brief introduction to validation techniques follows. More information on communication strategies is given later in this chapter. For those with a special interest in validation, additional resources are included in the bibliography.

Stages of Disorientation

Naomi Feil (1993) has described four stages of disorientation that occur with people who are "old-old" (over 80 years of age). These changes occur in people who have had fairly normal lives until they reach their 80s, when they begin to show signs of disorientation.

MALORIENTATION

Malorientation is the first stage of disorientation. People who are maloriented may initially appear as if nothing is wrong with them.

These people may be oriented as to where they are and who the President of the United States is but are beginning to forget information important for maintaining normal activities of daily living. They may try to cover up their memory loss by making up excuses. They do not like to be around people who are disoriented because they are threatened by their own memory loss. They deny their feelings and blame other people for their problems.

People who are maloriented respond best to open questions about facts, not feelings. It is important to hold onto acceptable social roles and rules for people who are maloriented. Encouraging someone who has been a teacher to lead the Pledge of Allegiance may be a way of helping maintain dignity and promoting self-esteem. Often the technique of using commonly preferred sense words assists this person to relate to the caregiver. It is best to listen to the maloriented person until you identify what the person's preferred sense is, and then address the person with words that represent that sense. For example, someone who often says "Oh, yes, I *see* what you mean" probably is a visual person and may respond to visual words better than to other choices (see Table 11.1).

TIME CONFUSION

As people become more disoriented, they withdraw more and more from the real world and retreat into their own inner world. During this stage, people lose a sense of real time and respond to an inner sense of time. Someone may think about the mother (who is dead) and because past time has fused with present time talks about her as if she was present.

Feeling a need to orient the time-confused person, a nurse might say something like "Your mother is dead; you can't go to see her." This only agitates and distresses the individual, who has no real need to stay in a painful present reality. Using the validation approach, the nurse would move close, use touch, and say "You miss your mother. What color eyes did she have? Blue or brown?" This is an effort to stimulate pleasant thoughts and memories for the client. There are several different methods of touching a person with dementia that are designed to evoke feelings about a loved one. For example, touching someone gently on the cheek stimulates the rooting reflex of an infant and generally reminds a person of mother. Refer to Table 11-2 to review common forms of touch.

REPETITIVE MOTION

If people with dementia continue to retreat from present reality, they may enter the stage of repetitive motion. During this stage, movements or sounds are repeated constantly. Usually speech is limited to single-syllable words, and eye contact is made only after someone touches and talks to the person. The use of touch with these people is very important. Individuals with repetitive motions are often ignored emotionally, with caregivers providing physical care only. Validation techniques of sustained eye contact, stroking, and touching can help reach people in this stage of disorientation and prevent the final stage, which is that of vegetation. When persons are in the repetitive motion stage, they often communicate through universal symbols. These people use objects to represent thoughts. A common example is carefully folding and holding or caressing a napkin, which could represent a baby. Other examples are given in Table 11.3.

VEGETATION

The final stage of disorientation and withdrawal is vegetation. In this stage very little movement or sound is noted. Eye contact is very rare. Using touch and familiar music can help reach a person in this stage.

Alzheimer's Disease

The most common type of dementia is Alzheimer's disease. The disease was first described in 1906 by a neurologist, who observed neurofibrillary tangles in an autopsy of the brain. Although there have been many advances regarding Alzheimer's disease over the years, the only way to conclusively diagnose Alzheimer's disease is autopsy. This means that Alzheimer's disease is usually diagnosed by first ruling out any other causes of delirium or dementia. When symptoms of dementia are present and no other organic disease causing behavioral and mental changes can be found, a diagnosis of Alzheimer's disease can be made. Many elderly persons with dementia syndromes are diagnosed as having Alzheimer's disease; some of these people have well-supported diagnoses and some do not. The estimates that 50% of all dementias are of the Alzheimer's type are probably due, in part, to the exclusionary nature of the diagnosis for Alzheimer's disease.

Alzheimer's disease is commonly found in persons over the age of 80 but can be found in persons as young as 30. Recent research findings indicate a strong correlation for increased incidence of Alzheimer's disease as people age. There also seems to be a significant correlation between both Down's syndrome and head trauma in relation to Alzheimer's disease. Much debate and controversy surround the role of aluminum in Alzheimer's disease. At this time, evidence exists both to support and to reject the idea that Alzheimer's disease is related to increased exposure to aluminum.

The disease is often described as having three stages. The early stage consists of mild forgetfulness that affects recent memory. Because of its similarity to normal aging changes, Alzheimer's disease may be difficult to diagnose in the early stage. The middle stage is characterized by cognitive, mood, and behavioral changes such as suspiciousness and agitation. The late stage of Alzheimer's disease consists of severe memory impairment, impaired mobility associated difficulty with activities of daily living, and deteriorating speech.

Some researchers are examining Alzheimer's disease on a continuum from the latent phase that occurs before symptoms are in evidence, through the malignant phase, when symptoms appear and diagnosis is made, to continued deterioration and eventual death. Research regarding Alzheimer's disease is progressing rapidly, leading to hope for new treatments in the near future. At least half a dozen drugs are currently being investigated for use in the management of dementia. The medication tacrine (Cognex) is at present being used with mixed success in the treatment of mild-to-moderate Alzheimer's disease. Because of the effects of this drug on the liver, it is necessary to make frequent checks of liver enzymes.

AGITATION

Agitation can occur as a result of physiological or psychological problems. Some people become agitated due to physical causes that result in delirium. Common psychological problems that can cause agitation are the manic phase of bipolar affective disorder, stress or anxiety, flashbacks from traumatic experiences, postabuse reactions, or dementia. When people become agitated, they also may become violent. Such violence can be directed toward themselves or others. Preventing agitation, and managing it once it occurs, can be accomplished by following a few simple principles. For example:

- Watch for signs of agitation. Some people show signs of increasing irritability before a severe problem occurs. Others may have sudden, explosive outbursts. Notice if someone is talking very loudly, pacing more or faster, or making threatening comments to staff or others. Before an actual outburst occurs, try to keep the person talking to you by using some of the communication skills discussed in this chapter. With many people who are agitated, simply matching their breathing patterns or tone of voice is calming. With most people who are agitated, it is best to step back about 4–6 feet while talking with them. With disoriented elderly people, the reverse may be true, especially if a sensory deficit is present. It may be more calming to move closer to maintain sustained eye contact and touch. This must be done cautiously to protect your own safety and that of others. If other clients or visitors may be harmed, move them out of the way.
- An important point to remember if a client becomes physically aggressive is that the thumb is the weakest point of the hand. If the client has a hold on you, the way to remove yourself is by rotating away from the thumb of the client's hand. For further information on intervention techniques, most psychiatric facilities provide training sessions that allow you to practice dealing with these behaviors in a way that minimizes harm to yourself and protects the patient.

Clinical Problem

A 78-year-old woman who is legally blind attempts to hit a staff member when she is being returned to bed.

Possible Solutions

1. Call resident by name.
2. Move close to her face and maintain eye contact.
3. Match her voice tone and breathing while talking to her.

Behavior modification is a type of intervention used to change behavior by giving positive feedback for desired behaviors and negative feedback for undesired behavior. These techniques are sometimes helpful when dealing with agitated behavior. Many elders do not respond to behavior modification very well, and other types of interventions, such as distracting or validating, need to be tried.

Clinical Problem

A 90-year-old resident makes loud whistling noises every night at 7 P.M. The staff enter her room and talk to her when she does this.

Possible Solutions

1. Close the door and ignore the behavior.
2. Enter her room at 6:30 P.M. and talk with her, giving positive reinforcement for not whistling.
3. Find something she likes to do and reward her with this for not whistling.

Patient Rights and Legal Responsibilities

The current standard of care in nursing homes and in mental health centers is that the patient has the right to the least restrictive form of treatment. Federal and state regulating agencies such as the Health Care Financing Administration (HCFA) have specific regulations protecting these rights. In most states, treatment can be done involuntarily only if a danger exists to the individual or to others. The length of time allowed for this type of treatment varies from state to state but is usually only a few days. If longer treatment is required and the client is unwilling to consent, then an application for guardianship may be made. This takes away the client's rights to make personal decisions and gives that to a guardian. This is a procedure that may be necessary for people with some types of mental illness, including dementia.

When agitated behaviors become severe, the nurse has to make a decision about how to handle the problem. Points that must be considered are the patient's right to the least restrictive treatment environment and the legal issues related to the use of chemical and physical restraints. If a client has an episode in which increased symptoms of bipolar affective disorder or schizophrenia are exhibited, an antipsychotic drug is likely to be more effective than for someone with dementia or delirium. Before giving a chemical restraint, it is necessary to try talking to the person as well as to use behavioral interventions. When all else fails, physical restraints may be necessary on rare occasions.

Violent Behavior

If a client starts to act violently, the nurse must remember to protect the people from their own behavior at all times. The nurse needs to call for help and, as a member of a team, then decide what the intervention should be.

Clinical Problem

Mrs. C. starts yelling and shouting, "Call the police, call the police."

Possible Solutions

1. Maintain eye contact, speak in a calm voice and call Mrs. C. by name.
2. Tell her to talk to you and say, "You're frightened of something."
3. Have another employee remove other clients from the room and decrease stimuli.

Sexual Acting Out

Acting out feelings of anxiety may take many forms. Sometimes elderly clients with dementia lose social controls and express sexual feelings very openly. Some people in the early stages of Alzheimer's disease have an increased desire for sexual activity. People with other types of psychological problems, such as bipolar affective disorder, demonstrate sexual feelings in ways that are not socially appropriate. Dealing with these behaviors is almost always difficult, no matter how experienced the nurse is.

Before deciding whether the sexual behavior is a problem, a few questions need to be asked. The staff need to consider whether their attitudes are the problem or whether it is the behavior itself. Another possibility to consider is whether the sexual acting out might be a way of expressing a need for affection and touch.

Clinical Situation

Mr. J. walks into the visitor's area, unzips his trousers, and begins to masturbate.

Possible Solutions

1. Notice any factors that seem to trigger the behavior in order to intervene before the behavior occurs.
2. Quietly lead him to his room.
3. Give affection and attention when he is not sexually acting out.

PARANOIA

Some people with emotional problems fear that other people are trying to hurt them. Such paranoid ideas are an indication of problems the person may have with trusting others. This can occur with dementia, schizophrenia, or other psychological problems. Many times people who are paranoid seem very convincing and logical. Developing trust is the most important thing to accomplish with someone who is paranoid. This can be best done by being consistent and reliable in all you do with the person. Do not make promises you cannot keep. If you say you will do something, follow-up with the paranoid person is especially important. It is particularly important to avoid putting medicines in food or drink without the paranoid client's knowledge.

Clinical Problem

A 70-year old man thinks the nurses are poisoning him.

Possible Solutions

1. Ask him if he feels this way all the time, or whether there are times when it is worse than others.
2. Ask him what would have to happen for him to feel safe eating the food here.
3. If necessary, bring in food from home or have the client open canned food for himself.

DEVELOPMENTAL DISABILITIES

Historically, people who had developmental disabilities did not live to old age. With advances in health care, more individuals who have developmental disabilities, such as Down's syndrome, are living longer. There is evidence that as individuals with Down's syndrome grow older, they are at high risk of developing Alzheimer's disease.

Individuals with developmental disabilities may have some of the problem behaviors that have been identified in this chapter. Principles for setting limits on behavior are the same for those with developmental disabilities as they are for those with any other problem:

- Recognize the person's feelings and encourage expression of them.
- State the limit clearly.
- Point out ways that behavior can be expressed within the limits and what is outside the limits.
- Allow the client to express anger at having limits placed on him or her.

Clinical Problems

A 67-year-old resident is throwing food at his roommate.

Possible Solutions

1. Tell him to stop throwing food and go to his room.
2. Tell him it is okay to be angry, but is it not okay for him to throw food.
3. Tell him that if he is angry he can tell someone.

SUBSTANCE ABUSE

Staff working with people who have chemical dependency problems recognize that there are a growing number of elders with substance abuse problems. Because many elders are treated for a wide variety of physical problems, sometimes they receive prescription drugs from several different sources. The availability of prescription drugs contributes to problems among the elderly of prescription drug abuse.

Alcoholism is another problem for many elders. Many of the same reasons people use substances to self-medicate (depression, losses, loneliness) in other stages of life are even more of a problem for the elderly. Because many of the memory lapses found with substance abuse are similar to those in the early stages of dementia, substance abuse may not be discovered for quite some time. Sometimes families have difficulty confronting older family members about substance abuse problems. The denial so characteristic of most substance abuse problems is especially difficult to break down with the elderly client. This then creates a problem with the treatment process. If a substance abuse problem is suspected, it is best to contact trained professionals to assist with interventions.

EATING DISORDERS

Often the reason for seeking health care is a problem with eating. Problems with eating can be due to physical factors, such as loss of taste sensation or poor denture fit, but many times eating difficulties are due to psychological problems. Anorexia can be a symptom of a psychological problem, such as depression, or it can be a problem in itself.

Compulsive resistance to eating or anorexia has historically been most commonly found in young women. More and more clinicians are now describing similar symptoms in the elderly. Eating or not eating can be used as a way of exhibiting controlling or resisting behaviors, especially in stressful situations. Compulsive overeating can also occur in the elderly, as can the binging and purging found in bulimia. Some elderly with psychological problems have phobias related to certain foods. Others may become paranoid about food believed to be poisoned or contaminated.

Regardless of the specific problem, treating someone who has an eating disorder may require tremendous amounts of creativity. Sometimes the only effective treatment is using a feeding tube until adequate weight gain is achieved. Behavior modification techniques, such as giving privileges for weight gain and withdrawing privileges for weight loss, may need to be planned by the health-care team or a psychiatric nurse specialist.

ACUTE PSYCHOLOGICAL PROBLEMS

Problems with emotions or behavior that require intensive treatment may occur. These problems can sometimes be dealt with by using outpatient visits by a nurse therapist. A psychiatric nurse specialist can also make regular home visits through a home-health agency. When it becomes impossible to continue home care, sometimes older people with psychological problems are placed in nursing homes, state mental hospitals, or acute care psychiatric units.

Nursing home residents with psychological problems may have acute problems that can be managed with consultation from a psychiatric nurse specialist. Agitated or violent behaviors may be helped by the expert advice of a qualified nurse specialist, who may make it possible to avoid hospitalization in an acute care psychiatric unit.

If an older client is hospitalized in an acute care psychiatric unit, there may be special issues to consider. Some units exclude these elders from group therapy because of behavior disruptions, physical problems, impaired thinking ability, or the response of the other clients. Even the most disoriented elder may have a rich wealth of experiences and wisdom that can improve the group's ability to problem solve. Elders can also benefit from the different viewpoints contributed by group members of various ages.

Consideration for the daily schedule and special interests of the older client make it important for nurses to individualize care. If an older person is accustomed to going to bed early and getting up early, unit schedules may need to be adapted. If a relaxation group is scheduled for 10:00 P.M. or earlier, individual sessions may need to be planned for the elderly person who retires early.

CHRONIC MENTAL ILLNESS

If a person has had a chronic mental illness, such as major depression or schizophrenia since youth, the person continues to have that illness as aging takes place. As with any type of chronic illness, there are times when the person seems better and times when the person seems worse.

Some unique factors affect the aging process of people with chronic mental illness. Sometimes, because of behaviors that are typical of their illnesses, people who have chronic mental illnesses do not have many resources. This may be because they have not been able to hold a job or have worn out existing support systems of family and friends. As caregiving parents or grandparents age and die, quite often no one is left to care for the aging mentally ill person.

The Homeless Chronically Mentally Ill

A large percentage of the homeless population are mentally ill. As they grow older, the homeless are less able to survive on the street and may be placed involuntarily in state mental hospitals or long-term care facilities. One of the problems for people with such illnesses may be an impaired ability to interact with others socially. The nurse cannot assume that such individuals will respond well to group activities, such as bingo games. Perhaps individual activities or outings with only one staff member might be a better plan. Respecting a person's individuality is an important maxim to keep in mind when caring for people with chronic mental illnesses.

Social Support and the Chronically Mentally Ill

Many individuals with chronic mental illness also have had problems with relationships throughout their lives. Sometimes the symptoms of their illnesses have been perceived as strange by others. For this reason, they may not have been able to form friendships or may have had difficulty with relationships. It is not unusual to find that someone who has a chronic mental illness is single or childless.

Family members may have been cut off from the person with chronic mental illness because of continuous problems with behavior over the years. Occasionally, family members have lost track of the person with chronic mental illness because that person moved from boarding home to state hospital and back out into the community again. Whatever the reason may be, many people who have chronic mental illness grow older without the support of friends and family. Nurses can make an effort to locate friends and family members of the mentally ill elder when possible. Someone who does not have support available from family or friends might be a good person to benefit from an adopt-a-grandparent program.

GROUPS FOR THE ELDERLY

Many older adults with psychological problems can benefit from group interactions. There are a few types of groups that have been used successfully with elderly clients.

Reminiscence

Based on memories of similar events or experiences, many elders can form bonds in groups. Stimulating memories of childhood or early adulthood can serve to improve feelings of self-worth and provide an opportunity to review their lives. Memories may stimulate laughter and happiness or other emotions and serve as a way of coping with present circumstances. Groups can be conducted around an important event, such as Pearl Harbor Day. Common, shared experiences, such as early school days, can be recalled to promote socialization and provide mental stimulation. Remi-

Many older adults with psychological problems can benefit from group interactions.

niscence also can be used individually as a means of helping people wrap up any unfinished business. A very structured form of reminiscence is the life review process. This process provides an opportunity for evaluation and integration of life experiences. People in the more advanced stages of disorientation are not able to benefit much from this type of therapy.

Remotivation

To improve interest in and quality of life, remotivation techniques can be used. The emphasis with remotivation is the use of real objects to stimulate senses and provide new motivation in life and the surrounding world. Pictures, plants, animals, or sounds can be used to encourage group interaction. Holidays, birthdays, or hobbies can be used to focus on remotivation for participating in the here and now. The focus is on factual information as opposed to exploration of feelings. These groups work best with those who have depression or early stages of disorientation.

Resocialization

Encouraging residents to assume social roles can stimulate feelings of increased self-esteem. The focus for this group is on social roles and not on problem solving. Discussion may occur about previous social gatherings and how people behaved during these events. The emphasis is on the present and discussion of factual information.

Group members are assigned roles, such as the greeter, or to serve each other refreshments. Feelings are not the focus of resocialization groups, which can be helpful for the mildly disoriented.

Reality Orientation

Helping residents become oriented to present reality is the goal of reality orientation. Constant reminders about the present, that is, where they are and what day it is, are given. Current events on the television or in the newspaper can be used as topics to stimulate discussions. The season of the year, holidays, and the weather are other topics to promote orientation to reality. These groups are focused on keeping people oriented to present reality and are not usually very effective with people who have more than mild disorientation.

Validation

Validation groups combine some of the other types of techniques with group problem solving and a focus on support. Members are assigned roles, sing familiar songs, serve each other refreshments, and reminisce about the past. Movement is encouraged during group activities. The group is presented with a problem to solve. Resolving losses and expressing feelings are emphasized. Validation groups are most effective for people who have moderate disorientation.

PSYCHOTROPIC MEDICATIONS

As with all medications, adaptation is necessary when using psychotropic medications with the elderly client. Teaching patients and their families about the reason for the medication, side effects, toxic effects, and what to do if a dose is missed, are all very important when psychotropic drugs are used with the elderly.

Many psychotropic drugs require a period of time—sometimes several weeks—before a therapeutic effect is achieved. This waiting period may be longer for some older clients. They may show more signs of toxicity at lower doses than usual because an impaired ability to excrete the drug results in a buildup in the bloodstream. Another possibility is that they may be more difficult to treat, because there are side effects due to the difference in distribution and excretion of drugs in the aging body.

Psychotropic medications work in the brain in a variety of ways. Most medications work by helping to change the level of neurotransmitters or chemicals in the brain. It is hoped that reestablishing a more normal balance will help the person have fewer psychological problems. Because these drugs work on the brain, it is important to use them only for psychological problems and not just because the resident has behaviors that irritate other people. Before any drugs are used to sedate a person with problem behaviors, all other types of nursing interventions need to be used along with documentation of the interventions.

A new drug has been used to successfully change the chemical balance in the brain for some people with schizophrenia. The drug clozapine (Clozaril) has been helpful for many people who have chronic schizophrenia.

Because of physical health problems, some medications used to treat mental health problems may be contraindicated or may require careful administration in the older client. For example, an elderly man who has prostate disease may, if given a tricyclic antidepressant, have extreme difficulty voiding.

A common side effect of many psychotropic drugs is constipation. When combined with normal aging changes, the constipation resulting from psychotropic medications can become a troublesome problem for the elderly client.

Orthostatic hypotension is a problem that results from many psychotropic drugs. Simple teaching techniques can help manage some of the postural blood pressure changes; however, many times these changes are severe enough to require that the medication be discontinued.

Clinical Problem	**Possible Solutions**
Mrs. N. usually walks well, but since starting on an antidepressant has fallen three times in the past week.	1. Check lying, sitting, and standing blood pressure. 2. If she has orthostatic hypotension, teach her to sit on the side of the bed for a few minutes before standing up slowly.

PHYSICAL AND MENTAL HEALTH

Because there is such a strong relationship between physical and mental health, many professionals feel that all diseases have both physical and emotional aspects. Some older people grew up in a time when it was frowned on to admit that mental illness existed, but it was more socially acceptable to have a physical problem. One grandmother described a time early in her marriage when she became so upset with her husband that she became "sick" and took to her bed for a week.

This expression of emotional problems through physical complaints is called *somatization*. Many times if a stressful situation is encountered, the person who uses somatization may develop a backache, headache, or stomachache to avoid dealing with problems. This does not mean the ache is "all in the head," but it may mean the person finds it easier or more acceptable to have a physical pain than an emotional one. For someone who has done this for 80 or 90 years of life, it may be difficult if not impossible, to change this way of coping. The nurse can help the patient learn to meet needs more directly by encouraging the person to talk about feelings openly.

CONCLUSION

The care of elderly people in all arenas of nursing is an opportunity to practice the art of nursing on its highest level. The skills and understanding that are needed to give meaningful care to the elderly with psychological problems are complex and require a personal and professional commitment to the needs of people as they age. If you feel a need for additional information on this complex subject, please refer to the materials listed at the end of the chapter.

Case Study

Mr. A. is an 80-year-old retired farmer. He lived with his wife on the farm until 1 year ago, when he became too ill for his wife to manage his care alone. At that time he became a resident of a nursing home in a nearby town. He has been forgetful for several years and now wanders the halls looking for his pickup truck. During the winter, he walked away from the nursing home and wandered for several hours. This resulted in frostbite on several fingers and toes. He becomes agitated when told he cannot go back to his home. What actions can be taken to assist Mr. A.?

Case Study
Solution

Working with the entire nursing staff, a plan is developed for using validation therapy with Mr. A. When he asks about his truck or home, the staff ask him questions such as, "What color is your truck?"; "What did you do with your truck?"; "Where did you go?"; "With whom?" Coveralls with a front pocket are obtained, and a small hammer and screwdriver are placed in his pocket. His toolbox is brought into his room. The staff have put him in charge of a small garden outside the nursing home. Individual sessions of validation are scheduled 20 minutes a day three times a week by the activities staff.

Over a 6-week period, the staff notice that Mr. A. spends quiet, productive time in the garden area. He carries his tool box with him most of the time but does not use its contents. He no longer leaves the building except to work in his garden. He is still forgetful.

Study Questions

Please select the one best answer.

1. The best intervention for an elderly resident of a nursing home who suffers from chronic mental illness is:
   a. To encourage him to lead a large group singing
   b. To plan one-on-one activities with staff and other residents
   c. To invite the resident to sit on the residents' council of the nursing home
   d. To have the resident join a weekly bingo group

2. An elderly homebound client taking medication for a psychological problem needs to know which of the following?
   a. If dizziness occurs, notify the nurse.
   b. It may take several weeks to get the desired effect.
   c. Report any changes in vision.
   d. All of the above.

3. Validation techniques are best described as:
   a. A way of helping someone resolve past experiences
   b. Helping someone find new meaning in growing older
   c. A reminder of a painful present reality
   d. Bringing someone from the past into the present world

4. When a hospitalized client suddenly becomes disoriented, the best intervention is which of the following?
   a. Ignore the client's feelings because they are a normal part of aging.
   b. Tell the client to cheer up because things are not so bad.
   c. Do not allow the client to talk about being sad because that makes it worse.
   d. Encourage the client to discuss feelings openly because it helps to talk about problems.

5. When teaching a client or the client's family about the use of psychotropic drugs, one of the most important concepts to teach is:
   a. The meaning of the different colors of the medications
   b. The stress psychotropic drugs put on the kidneys
   c. To anticipate the chronic light-headedness that most people experience
   d. Not to expect the full effect of the drug for several weeks

References

Bandler, R. (1985). *Using your brain for a change.* Moab, UT: Real People Press.
Feil, N. (1993). *Validation: The Feil method.* Cleveland, OH: Edward Feil Productions.
Haber, J., McMahon, A. L., Price-Hoskins, P. H., & Sideleau, B. F. (1992). *Psychiatric nursing* (4th ed.). St. Louis: Mosby-Year Book.
Wilson, H. S., & Kneisl, C. R. (1992). *Psychiatric nursing* (4th ed.). Redwood City, CA: Addison-Wesley Nursing.

Bibliography

Feil, N. (1993). *The validation breakthrough.* Baltimore: Health Professions Press.
   A book from Naomi Feil that provides an excellent, comprehensive view of validation therapy. Practical examples are included.
   Available from:
   Health Professions Press
   P.O. Box 10624
   Baltimore, MD 21285-0624
Hall, G. R. (1991). This hospitalized patient has Alzheimer's. *American Journal of Nursing, 91*(10), 45–50.
   A comprehensive continuing education program for management of Alzheimer's patients in acute care settings.
Rader, J. (1993). Modifying the environment to decrease use of restraints. *Journal of Gerontological Nursing, 17*(2), 9–13.
   An article that includes how-to information and creative approaches for decreasing restraint usage in long-term care.
Hogstel, M. (Ed.). (1995). *Geropsychiatric nursing* (2nd ed.). St. Louis: Mosby Year Book.
   This edited text contains practical and helpful information for dealing with mental health problems and the elderly.

Educational Support Material

Alzheimer's Association. National Alzheimer's Library and Resource Center.
919 North Michigan Avenue
Chicago, IL 60611-1676
1-800-272-3900
Lists of resources on many topics related to Alzheimer's and related diseases.

Brill, C., Castleton, M., & Hess, M. L. (1993). *Validation* [Computer-assisted instructional program].
Available from Edward Feil Productions, address below.
Program designed for use with IBM-compatible computers as an in-service program for lay persons or health-care providers. Contains basic information on validation therapy and case studies for practice in application.

Feil, N. (1978). *Looking for yesterday* [Videotape]. Cleveland, OH: Edward Feil Productions.
Edward Feil Productions
4614 Prospect Avenue
Cleveland, OH 44103
Several videotapes are available from this source. This video provides an introduction to the problem of dementia. Neurolinguistic applications are explained, and comparisons between validation and reality orientation are demonstrated.

Chapter

SISTER ROSE THERESE BAHR and KATHLEEN R. CULLITON

12

Restorative Care

Learning Objectives

After completing this chapter, the student will be able to:

1. Define rehabilitation and restorative nursing in a holistic framework of nursing.
2. Identify the clinical implications of restorative care in walking programs, continence training, and feeding/self-help programs.

INTRODUCTION

Nurses strive to promote an older adult's health. Generally, nursing care involves assisting older adults to overcome the symptoms of an acute health problem or the worsening of a chronic condition. Nurses use medications, treatments, and referrals to help the individual overcome physical, psychological, social, and spiritual illness. In the acute-care setting, nurses assist older adults through the crisis of illness and discharge them back into the community to their homes or a supportive living environment. The goal of nursing care to assist the older adults back to health, and allow them to return to their homes. Assessment of their general health and ability to meet their personal needs are considerations during the discharge process. There are times an older adult is no longer physically or emotionally able to safely return to his or her home.

The purpose of this chapter is to present an overview of gerontological nursing concepts based on rehabilitative and restorative care. Both rehabilitative and restorative nursing care surpass the traditional custodial approach that has prevailed in the care of older adults in hospitals, nursing homes, and homes prior to the initiation of the 1990 Omnibus Budget Reconciliation Act (OBRA) regulations. Data collection for residents in nursing homes is done on the minimum data set (MDS) (see Chapter 4) and emphasizes restorative care of older adults as a major priority of care.

Demographically, America is graying. Along with the aging process comes increased disability for many elderly persons. It has been statistically projected that 40% of all disabled persons in America presently are 65 years old or older. As the aging population increases, nurses are called on to provide rehabilitative and restorative care to more and more older people as they enter health-care facilities.

UNDERSTANDING REHABILITATION AND RESTORATIVE CONCEPTS

Rehabilitation is the process of teaching and training individuals to achieve their highest level of independent function. People are most familiar with rehabilitation programs for spinal cord injuries. Rehabilitative care is a multidisciplinary care model. Physical therapists, occupational therapists, speech therapists, dieticians, respiratory therapists, recreation therapists, social workers, psychologists, nurses, and rehabilitation physicians are all members of rehabilitation care teams. Rehabilitation is initiated after an extensive assessment of an individual's physical, emotional, spiritual, and functional assets and liabilities. Assessment information is reviewed along with the resources available to assist the individual to develop a rehabilitative plan. Often, there is no reason for an individual to need all available services. Then the team is restructured to include the necessary health-care team members. This team works with individuals and their families to develop rehabilitative goals and to decide the best way to work toward these goals. Selecting a short-term or long-term living environment is one of the first choices that a rehabilitation team must make. Every care environment has the potential to be a place for rehabilitation. The limiting factors often are not enough family support, environmental safety, insurance reimbursement, and access to the rehabilitation team. An older adult who had a total hip replacement may want to go home, but home has an upstairs bathroom and there is no one available to prepare meals. These factors present a problem. A young man may be recovering well from knee surgery and want to have intensive inpatient therapy, but his insurance company does not approve the cost. An elderly woman may want to go to her rural community hospital for rehabilitation after a stroke, but the services that she needs are not available in that community. The rehabilitation team works with the older adult to help the person access support services and find the most appropriate environment for the rehabilitation process.

Restorative nursing care is related to rehabilitation. It has the same goal—to assist older people to reach their highest functional ability. The major difference is the intense involvement of the whole health-care team. Because of the direct involvement of therapies and other health-care professionals, rehabilitation is an expensive service. Restorative care is initiated after an older person has reached the rehabilitative goal or has not demonstrated any further improvement. The whole health-care team is involved in designing restorative care plans but is not directly involved in the implementation. For example, an older person who is in a rehabilitation program after a stroke would have the benefits of a physical therapist to learn exercise, safe walking, and transferring techniques. The older adult continues to need assistance with exercises and walking, but a nurse or a nursing assistant encourages the person to do as much as possible independently and assists him or her, if necessary.

Rehabilitation provides individuals with intensive short-term strengthening and retraining while restorative care continues the process over time. It is unfortunate when an older adult has a major health crisis and goes through intensive therapy and training only to move to an environment where everything is done for him or her, and the benefits of the therapy are lost. Examples of restorative programs are ambulation, personal care, feeding, and toileting. The challenge for the nursing team is to continue to promote high levels of independent function. It is faster to transfer a patient into a wheelchair and push the person to the dining room for breakfast but that is not promoting independence. Restorative care demands that the nursing staff assist the older adult to walk to the dining room. Unfortunately, this same concept of needing to hurry is associated with high incidences of incontinence. It is often perceived as faster to change an older adult's briefs and bedclothes than to anticipate the need for voiding and then walk the person to the bathroom.

The same principle applies to eating and personal care. Have you ever watched someone struggle to put on a shirt over a paralyzed arm? Watching that struggle is uncomfortable because the nurses know they could help that person get the shirt on faster and without as much stress and strain. It is very difficult to watch someone try to eat independently and see the stress and frustration that can occur. Yet, that older person deserves the right to feel the satisfaction of accomplishing a task or meeting a personal goal.

The concepts of rehabilitation and restorative care are critical to promoting an older adult's optimal level of function. The focus of rehabilitative and restorative care is to maximize the abilities and functions of older adults to ensure the highest level of independence and quality of life. Rehabilitation and restorative care are not isolated treatments with limited application. They embody a broad set of principles to incorporate into every facet of nursing care in all settings.

Within the context of the interdisciplinary team (IDT) effort and after clinical conferences with the team to determine what plan is to be designed, licensed practical nurses (LPNs) working cooperatively with the registered nurse (RN) prepare the goals and the nursing care plan. In this capacity, the nurse's role becomes one of practitioner, educator, counselor, case manager, researcher, and consultant (Fraley, 1992).

THE NURSES' ROLES

Bedside Caregiver

As caregivers, LPNs provide direct care to older adults until the skills necessary for self-care have been developed by the individual. Nurses need to give older adults positive reinforcement, encouragement, hope, and an opportunity to develop and utilize both their physical and social skills (Hanlon & Sharkey, 1989).

Educator

When serving in the role of educator, nurses provide older people and their families with information related to the disability, and its treatment and management. Included in the education plan should be health measures to obtain and retain function and to prevent further disability (Bopp & Lubkin, 1990). The nurse must realize that effective outcomes are more likely to come when older adults and their families are included in the process of determining the goals of rehabilitation/restoration of function and treatment. It is important for older adults and the family or other caregivers to recognize they are responsible for the decisions made and actions that result from those decisions. That is a predominant principle of rehabilitative and restorative care (Zejdlik, 1983).

Counselor

As counselors, nurses assist elderly people to describe, analyze, and respond to the current situation that makes rehabilitation or restorative care necessary. Counseling is the process of helping people solve and effectively cope with their problems. Counseling disabled people and their families is an ongoing progress that requires supportive behaviors from the entire IDT. LPNs, on establishing trust and rapport with the older adult and the family, need to focus on assisting them to deal with their grief over the losses imposed by the older person's current disability. The opportunity to express personal feelings assists the elderly person in developing coping skills related to the event of trauma that made rehabilitation/restoration therapy necessary. The LPN should counsel the disabled, elderly persons and their families in healthy ways to respond to the feelings of loss, frustration, and anger they generally feel. To express and deal with such feelings with each other as a family assists in maintaining positive relationships between the family members and the older person.

Advocate

When assuming the role of advocate, LPNs use their influence and power as health professionals to bring about necessary changes for both the patient and the family's well-being so that rehabilitation and restorative care can have the maximum effect. Such interventions aid the older adult and the family members in obtaining necessary community-based services that maintain older disabled adults as fully functioning, independent individuals, within the constraints of the limitations imposed by the disability. Such interventions may include the use of assistive or adaptive devices like crutches, a walker, a plate guard, and a padded spoon.

Case Manager

Generally an RN is the case manager for disabled clients. However, in some situations the LPN is asked to serve in that role. The case manager role places the nurse as a central figure working with the total health-care team throughout the entire episode of illness. The major focus for a case manager is to resolve actual problems and prevent potential problems for the aging person. The treatment plan, once agreed on by the IDT, is under the supervision of the licensed nurses (RNs and LPNs) working in conjunction with each older adult and family. Once the plan is agreed on, a contract is entered into by the individual, family members, and the nurse so that the plan can be implemented with clear communication to each person involved. This management may take place in a hospital or nursing home and continue into the community where home-based care is provided.

Researcher

Many LPNs work in conjunction with RNs and a qualified nurse researcher to gather data on the rehabilitation and restorative care of older adults. Many questions remain unanswered regarding rehabilitative and restorative care of older adults in a number of areas. Each area provides a rich arena for research. Some of the research interests are:

- The management of behavioral symptoms
- Feelings about placing disabled family members outside the home and into an institution for care on a permanent basis
- Barriers that prevent the use of respite and day-care services
- Accurate measures of caregiver burden
- Effective coping strategies used by caregivers
- Types of educational and support programs needed to assist caregivers
- Services needed to individualize care at different stages of an illness or injury

All of these clinical questions need to be raised when older individuals suffer a traumatic episode and require nursing care. The nurse is responsible for raising questions regarding the specific needs of older individuals and seeking systematic answers through research. A research approach helps to build a body of knowledge regarding rehabilitation and restorative care.

GOALS OF REHABILITATION AND RESTORATIVE CARE

A goal is defined as a written statement of desired behavioral outcomes from which steps or strategies may be designed to achieve that desired end. Goals provide direction. They are the measuring tool for an effective plan of care. For example, "I will buy a car today" is a statement of the desired outcome. A defined series of steps needs to be taken prior to the accomplishment of that goal such as establishing a means to pay for the car, deciding what type of car one wants to buy, finding out the selling price of cars at various car dealers, checking on insurance, and so forth.

From the time of injury or disability, the efforts of all health-care professionals involved in the older adult's care are to be focused on the ultimate goal: *the highest level of personal independence possible within the limitations imposed by the injury*. In setting goals, licensed practical nurses assess the patient to determine what assets of mind, body, and spirit are present that will aid in the accomplishment of the goal. For instance, can the person ambulate sufficiently to make trips to the bathroom, dining room, and physical therapy department? The LPN might ask a number of questions:

- Is the person able to communicate needs verbally?
- Can the person feed himself or herself?
- What are the goals of the older adult?

The information derived from the assessment is important in determining realistic and achievable goals for each individual. For lifelong quality of living, the components of a successful rehabilitation and restorative program must include the following goals, which should be individualized toward increasing the function and performance of the individual:

- Independence and self-care
- Mobility
- Involvement in activities—social, civic, family, church, and recreation
- Fulfillment of life's goals
- Holistic approach to living with a disability

The LPN must be knowledgeable in evaluating the current holistic status of the older adult for the goals of rehabilitation and restorative care to be individualized and focused on the improvement of function and performance. For older adults, major changes in three areas are critical to the success of a rehabilitation and restorative care program. Changes must be noted in physical, functional, and psychological status. Each of these areas can greatly affect the ability of the older adult to carry out the goals identified in the plan of care.

Physical Changes Affecting Restorative Care

A number of physical changes may be present when an older adult sustains an injury or trauma necessitating rehabilitation. Existing health problems must be considered in planning rehabilitative and restorative care.

- *Musculoskeletal* changes due to old fractures, osteoporosis, arthritis, osteoarthritis, muscular dystrophy, or loss of strength in arms and legs can create mobility difficulties. Such situations can occur because of muscle atrophy, decreased bone mass, loss of subcutaneous fat, and decreased flexibility of the joints and limbs.
- *Cardiovascular* changes due to diminished cardiac output, irregular heart rate, and increased blood pressure readings can result in diminished circulation that does not bring sufficient oxygen to the body. Such conditions often cause a lack of activity because of fatigue. Cardiac changes may be the result of thickening of heart valves, thickening of blood vessels, or delayed response to stress.
- *Respiratory* changes related to diminished respiratory rates can create ventilation challenges for the older person and may be caused by long-standing asthma, obstructive lung disease, emphysema, tuberculosis, upper respiratory illnesses, limited rib cage expansion, atrophy of respiratory muscles, decreased arterial oxygen tension, decreased vital capacity, and diminished cough.
- *Renal and digestive tract* changes create elimination difficulties that may impair the proper implementation of a restorative program. These changes may include decreased peristalsis of the intestinal tract that results in constipation or diarrhea, decreased intestinal enzyme levels that reduce the ability to properly digest foods, diminished glomerular filtration in the kidney, and decreased bladder capacity resulting in incontinence or retention of residual urine. The latter may create edematous lower limbs that make it difficult for the older person to ambulate in a comfortable manner.
- *Consciousness and mental status* changes may result in short-term memory loss, slower thought processing, and increased pain threshold.
- *Perceptual* changes may be demonstrated by loss of visual acuity, diminished hearing, decreased sense of taste, lower sensitivity to touch, and decreased proprioception (spatial sensitivity).

Functional Changes Affecting Rehabilitative and Restorative Care

Changes in function in older adults may result from the impact of social and environmental situations. These changes can include:

- Inability to negotiate stairs in the home
- Functional implications of acute and/or chronic disease processes
- Physical factors such as limited range of motion, strength, and endurance
- Inability to consume sufficient nutrients to maintain optimum health
- Inability to cook food, clean a home, or complete the laundry and other critical chores

These functional changes need to be assessed by a nurse so that the realistic goals can be established.

Psychological Changes Affecting Rehabilitative and Restorative Care

The psychological status of an older adult is a critical component of any rehabilitation and restorative care program. When the older person enjoys psychological well-being, there is a strong motivation to work toward the highest possible level of function. When elderly people feel needed and wanted by family, friends, and associates, they generally possess self-esteem and a positive self-image, which are two critical factors in developing a high degree of motivation to proceed with the restorative care program.

DEVELOPING GOALS FOR REHABILITATIVE AND RESTORATIVE CARE

When developing goals for rehabilitative and restorative care, LPNs need to complete a full nursing assessment under the guidance of a registered professional nurse. The nursing assessment should include a complete database with the following elements:

- Nursing history that includes the older adult's past medical conditions, psychological impairments, hospitalizations, and previous injuries (See Chapter 8)
- Physical assessment of all bodily systems (See Chapter 8)
- Functional assessment to check for functional ability and mobility (See Chapter 8)
- Mental status and psychological parameters that may be present, e.g., depression, anxiety (See Chapter 10)
- A spiritual assessment to determine any spiritual needs or deficits that may be a deterrent to good rehabilitation progress

Following the assessment, the LPN and RN work together as a team to analyze the data and prioritize rehabilitative and restorative goals for the patient. The following principles of holistic nursing care should be the guidelines for identifying such goals:

- When the older adult enters the hospital or nursing facility, rehabilitation must begin immediately.
- Proper body alignment is to be maintained at all times.
- Pressure ulcers are to be prevented on all body parts.
- Rehabilitation is to be implemented concurrently with the illness, whether chronic or acute, temporary or permanent, disabling or nondisabling.
- All joints must be kept free through proper exercise/range of motion.
- Convalescence is a gradual process and may extend over a considerable period for the older person.
- Nurses must understand the patient's self-concept and feelings of dependency and isolation if they exist.
- The time period for rehabilitation depends on the person's psychological acceptance of the condition.

- People born with disabilities usually have less difficulty accepting their condition than those who acquire disabilities later in life.
- More severe emotional reactions are produced when accidents are traumatic.
- Loss and its meaning vary with every person.
- Any personality problems that may be exhibited are generally the result of the person's personality characteristics before disability.
- The usual initial reactions to physical injury are shock, fear, disbelief, and anxiety.
- Periods of grief are produced when loss of any physical ability is experienced.
- Depression, anger, and denial may be present.
- Values are examined and limitations put in perspective over time.
- Time is essential for acceptance.
- The family needs emotional support and comfort during the acute phase of the trauma/illness.
- All information possible should be given to the family and older adult, including information about resources for rehabilitation services and economic assistance.
- The nurse or social worker should be familiar with community agencies that can help.

IMPLEMENTATION OF GOALS IN REHABILITATIVE AND RESTORATIVE CARE

Goal 1: Maintenance of Joint Function

The implementation of planned care for elderly people suggests that a holistic approach is to be adopted. The major concern in implementing care is the prevention of deformities through passive exercises that keep joints moveable, promote venous return and lymphatic flow, and help prevent excessive demineralization of bones. This goal and care are dependent on the physician's orders that identify the extent of the exercise program to be implemented. By means of a thorough assessment of the physical condition of the older adult, and the specific illness and prognosis for recovery, nurses assume responsibility for the passive exercise program. Such a program may include range-of-motion activities, where each joint is put through the normal activities of which it is capable, that is, supine, prone, lateral, medial, anterior, and posterior positions. This approach maintains the wellness capability of the joints and reduces the complication of contractures, strictures, and the limitation of activity. By implementing passive range of motion, nurses are assisting the injured person to resume independence of function and perform at optimal levels.

Goal 2: Active Exercise

Another group of interventions is designed to improve function and performance. This group of interventions can be referred to as *active exercise*. Active exercise entails transferring from bed to chair, walking and ambulating with assistive devices, proper use of crutches, knowledge of how to maneuver the wheelchair, hand-eye coordination, and the use of assistive devices that promote independent of living in a normal manner. In each of these activities, nurses, in the role of teacher, help to motivate the person to be as active in personal care as possible.

Goal 3: Bladder Continence

In some situations, it is necessary for the LPN to initiate bladder-training programs. Achievement of continence avoids the use of indwelling catheters. Bladder training aids in reducing the chance for urinary tract infections and increases self-esteem. Retraining is based on the development of clear patterns of communication between staff, the older adult, and the family regarding the schedule for toileting (usually every 2 hours). It is necessary for the bladder to be emptied at set times throughout the day. Limiting fluids after 6:00 P.M. so that the bladder can retain urine throughout the night is another strategy. At times, periodic catheterization may be employed to develop reflex emptying when sensation for voiding is diminished or absent.

Goal 4: Bowel Continence

In addition to bladder training, it is important to employ bowel-training techniques if they are needed. Bowel training requires the establishment of a routine for emptying the bowel daily. This occurs most normally in the morning approximately 20 minutes after breakfast. The intake of breakfast stimulates the duodenocolic reflex, which assists in bowel elimination. A diet consisting of whole-grain breads, cereals, fresh fruits, fluids, and whole bran, along with increased fluid intake is helpful in providing both the bulk and fluid needed for effective bowel training. This approach also reduces the complication of constipation in the older adult. If constipation does occur, it may be necessary to provide medication to soften the stool and allow the bowel contents to move into the lower colon area for elimination. It also is helpful in bowel-training programs to request that the older adult assume the squatting position to facilitate bowel elimination. This is not always possible. Rectal suppositories are useful when initiating a bowel-training program. Enemas are rarely used as part of a bowel-training program.

Goal 5: Appropriate Sexual Expression

The implementation of a holistic plan of care means that the LPN must be aware of the older adult's sexual needs. It is important to implement nursing care that allows each person to meet personal sexual needs. This means building in time during the rehabilitation and restorative care process for partners to have privacy. It also can include offering the sense of touch by holding hands with the elderly in appropriate ways and, when given permission, for squeezing the shoulder or forearm with a firm but gentle touch.

Goal 6: Psychosocial and Spiritual Well-Being

It is extremely important to include interventions that address the psychosocial and spiritual needs of older adults. Communication, increased self-concept and self-esteem, treating the person with dignity and respect, as well as meeting spiritual needs are essential to holistic nursing care. Examples could include uninterrupted time to pray, arrangements for visits from the local clergy, and allowing religious artifacts in the room.

In implementing rehabilitation and restorative care, nurses follow the plan of care outlined by the interdisciplinary team from the database of information collected during the admission assessment and periodically throughout the course of the care. The nurse must be alert to changes that need to be made in the plan of care.

The implementation of care measures should focus on previous coping skills of the older adult. It is important that older adults become partners in the care regimen by sharing knowledge and adaptability. The goals are established by the older adult, the family, and the nurse as a member of the IDT based on the assessment data. When the goal is stated in specific, measurable terms, then evaluation of the progress and outcome of care is easily measured. The terms of the goal are to be put in the framework of self-care and self-responsibility.

ASSESSMENT OF GOALS

Goals are assessed at intervals—sometimes daily, sometimes weekly, sometimes monthly—depending on the goal to be accomplished. When the goals have been stated in observable, measurable terms, then the assessment of their achievement is relatively easy. In the course of the disease or traumatic injury, in-depth documentation is extremely important for noting the progress of the person. A systematic approach to fulfill all the stated goals assures the patient, family and health-care team that a holistic approach has been incorporated into the older adult's care. This approach reassures both the older adult and the nurse that custodial care will be avoided and rehabilitation and restorative nursing from a holistic perspective is in place.

Goals Specific to the Elderly

Restorative nursing goals specific to older adults include:

- Improvement of function
- Delay of deterioration
- Accommodation to dysfunction
- Comfort in the dying process

Improvement of Function

Functionality is defined as the ability to continue to live one's preferred lifestyle without disruption. To put that concept into different terms, it means that each older

Goal assessment on a daily or weekly basis is essential to good care.

adult can live independently, do activities of daily living (ADLs) and instrumental ADLs (IADLs), be mobile, and have self-care ability. To live independently suggests that there is no need for physical assistance or supervision from another person.

To improve function, it is necessary to take into account the impact of the older person's social and environmental situation, functional implications of acute or chronic disease processes, and the physical factors that may influence function. By combining these factors, a picture of the capability of older adults to live and function should emerge for the health-care team, including the LPN.

Range of motion is a series of exercises performed on a regular basis to preserve the function of the joints and muscles. It is extremely important that this maintenance function be performed correctly and on a schedule so that no deterioration of the physical status of the person occurs. The nurse does this activity or instructs another health team member to carry out this procedure correctly under the direction of a physical therapist.

Improving the strength of the muscles necessitates that some resistance be exerted so that the muscle works hard to maintain or improve its function. This is often accomplished through the use of weights or by pushing against an object to provide resistance. The actual testing of the muscle strength and endurance is done by the physical therapist, and a plan of exercise is identified. This plan must be carried out meticulously so that every muscle and its function is duly exercised, and strength and endurance are improved.

Mobility is identified in various stages, depending on the type of injury or disease present in the older adult. Usually the progression is from bed mobility, through transfer activities, to wheelchair or ambulatory locomotion. Transfer includes getting from bed to chair and back to bed, on and off a toilet, and in and out of a bathtub or car. These activities involve standing, sitting, pivoting, turning, or side-slide movement (sliding from bed to chair using a transfer board). To promote function in mobility involves locomotion or moving from one point to another. Older adults may need to use a wheelchair, so the ability to propel and maneuver the wheelchair is important. Wheelchair use involves the development of arm strength with the use of weights or other forms of strength building. Other assistive devices such as crutches, braces, and splints may be needed to assist in locomotion. To help the individual reach optimal function, instruction needs to be given regarding the best approaches to maintaining balance and endurance as well as in the use of devices to prevent falls.

When the goal is to improve function, there is a positive outcome orientation. For example, if the nursing diagnosis is stated:

- Body image disturbance, self-esteem disturbance related to function limitations, role and lifestyle change

Then the goal should be written:

- The older adult will verbalize positive statements about self.
- The older adult will identify and demonstrate appropriate strategies to deal with functional limitations.

Some of these strategies could be the ability to handle buttons and zippers, to tie shoelaces, and to put on underwear. If the older adult is unable to perform these functions, then devices such as long-handled reachers, button hooks, and elastic shoelaces may allow the person to perform more independently.

In helping older people retain functional ability and avoid deterioration, it is important to be cognizant of the disease processes that may interfere with their ability to achieve independent living. Such limiting problems most often involve cardiorespiratory, neurological, or musculoskeletal systems. Many of these conditions may impose significant functional limitations on the person. All of these factors are to be kept in mind when implementing goals for rehabilitative and restorative care for the elderly. Dedication to the restorative care plan helps older people to keep motivated and to engage in the purposeful and varied activities that promote function and performance.

Delay of Deterioration

A primary goal of rehabilitative and restorative nursing is the delay of deterioration in all functional aspects. For example, if on admission and during the course of treatment bouts of depression are noted, this should be documented in terms of the behaviors exhibited as well as their frequency and duration. The RN is to be notified and a psychiatric consult requested if it is determined to be appropriate for the individual older adult. Depression signals initial deterioration of motivation. Helping the person to maintain a spirit of hopefulness is one way to assist in the delay of deterioration.

Another approach to ensure delay of deterioration is to make certain that the nursing care plan calls for exercise of all mobile bodily parts, that is, legs, arms, fingers, toes, neck, hips, and knees. Movement of all of these joints is essential in the maintenance of a healthy state. No nurse should ever allow a contracture to occur. Use of pillows, a footboard to prevent foot drop, and resting splints for wrists and fingers aids in proper alignment of the body to maintain function and delay deterioration. Properly aligned and supported body parts assume their natural posture and position. As noted earlier, passive range of motion for all joints can delay deterioration to a great extent. However, caution must be exercised. If care is not used in moving the joints, soft tissue injury can result from undue stretching of the muscles and joints; this could cause additional injury and slow the rate of recovery or cause great pain when the person becomes active once again.

Another priority concern is the prevention of pressure ulcers. Excellent skin care should be a daily part of nursing care for all patients. This is especially important for elderly people who have impaired nutritional status. Pressure ulcers may develop over any bony prominence as well as on the occiput, ear parts, sacrum, and greater trochanter. Special devices to cushion these parts need to be used as a preventive measure and include special pillows, donuts, and gauze dressings, as well as special mattresses (egg crate, circulating water, or air). Turning the patient every 2 hours is the best preventive measure that can be taken to ensure skin integrity. When turning the patient, the support of limbs and back for good body alignment is essential to keep weakened muscles from further deterioration.

Cognitively impaired elderly are in need of individualized nursing care. These people need as much sensory stimulation as possible to maintain their contact with reality. Putting the person in a position where others can be seen as well as the radio and TV can help stimulate cognitive functions and lessen the possibility of further deterioration.

To delay deterioration, older adults should participate in out-of-bed activities as soon as they have achieved a medically stable condition. First they should dangle their feet for several minutes to gain a sense of balance. Once this activity is tolerated, the nurse should help the older adult to stand by the side of the bed with whatever assistive device needed, for example, a walker or cane. Finally, the person should be assisted to walk to a chair and sit with proper support for up to 15 minutes at a time. Nurses are essential for providing the appropriate encouragement for the individual.

Accommodation to Dysfunction

The goal of helping elderly people to accommodate to dysfunction requires a great deal of motivation on the part of the nurse. It is essential for the LPN to listen attentively and actively to the personal fears, hopes, thoughts, feelings, and values that are expressed by the person who is adjusting to the deficits left by an accident, in-

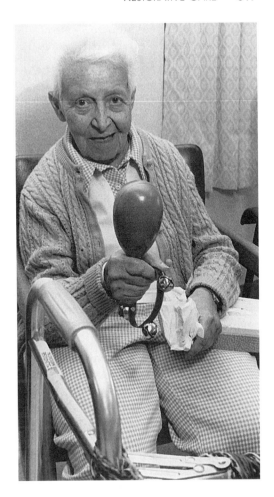

Holistic wellness occurs when the psychological self-image of a person incorporates his limitations in a healthy and acceptable image.

jury, or stroke. Nurses should be aware that a rehabilitation program is primarily a learning and training process. Each person must have the ability to absorb new information on how to use personal potential and how to practice new skills. For example, if a person has sustained an injury that created a drop-foot gait, the individual must learn to accommodate walking by lifting the foot intentionally so that it remains flat as weight is shifted from one side of the body to the next. This requires major concentration until the old adage "practice makes perfect" becomes second nature to the walker. The nurse's role is to continue to encourage the person to keep working for the highest outcome possible.

Holistic wellness occurs for the restorative care patient when:

- The psychological self-image of the person incorporates personal limitations into a healthy and acceptable image
- Social activities and interactions with friends and family continue to be a major part of the person's life

• The person exhibits acceptance of the new lifestyle with joy, peace, and gratitude for the remaining strengths of his or her personhood

These are the elements to be found when the goal of accommodation to dysfunction is achieved. As the grief and sense of loss diminish, a healthier view of life strikes older people so that life once again is worth living for them.

Comfort in the Dying Process

It has been noted that 75% of deaths in older people suffering from trauma were caused by falls, thermal injury, and motor vehicle accidents. Falls, for both elderly men and women, are the leading cause of death. Falls constitute approximately 50% of all fatalities. The most common injuries are associated with fractures of the hip, femur, proximal humerus, Colles' fracture of the wrist, and head injuries. In deaths in people 65 years of age and older, 25% are from motor vehicle accidents. As the population continues to age, this percentage of deaths and injuries will undoubtedly increase. Death from thermal injury accounts for approximately 8% of all accidental deaths in those 65 years of age and older. These injuries include burns and inhalation injuries, electrical injury, and contacts with sources of heat. The most commonly reported types of thermal injuries include scalds, flame burns, and contact with hot objects.

Restorative nursing may include providing comfort measures and palliative care to those elderly who, because of severe injury and trauma, are in the process of dying. Palliative care means providing the care requested by the elderly person in terms of advance directives and a living will. The individual's decisions are to be honored by the nurse and family members. It may be that the older adult has requested that no food or water be given after it has been determined that no benefits will be derived from such comfort measures. Life-sustaining technologies such as intravenous solutions of water and saline or use of a respirator also may be requested to be terminated if no positive outcome is predictable. All of these wishes are to be followed using the Code of Ethics for Nurses.

Nurses are to be supportive of dying elderly patients and their family members. Nurses must be accountable to the dying person for decisions that have been made and facilitate their implementation. All decisions are to be carried out in a humane and compassionate manner. The dying process is a precious approach to the end of one's life. Nurses are to approach with reverence the body, mind, and spirit of the older person who moves into the terminal state of life. The nurse should attend the dying person with dignity, respect, and appreciation for personal uniqueness.

CLINICAL IMPLICATIONS OF REHABILITATIVE AND RESTORATIVE CARE

Using the framework of the restorative care principles and guidelines cited earlier, four clinical rehabilitative programs for older adults are outlined. These programs include:

• Walking or ambulation programs
• Bladder and bowel continence training

- Feeding and self-feeding programs
- Self-care—ADL programs

Walking Programs

Mobility is critical to optimal functioning for older people. To be mobile means that the individual will enjoy the satisfaction of independence in living. Nurses play a key role in providing motivation for a walking program. Depending on the type of assistive device needed by the older adult to aid in gait control, the nurse follows the directions given by the RN, physician, and/or the physical therapist. A key point is that excellent foot care is critical to maintaining a walking program. Also, properly fitting shoes are important to establish proper posture while walking.

The older adult may need braces or crutches to walk in a way that is beneficial. Leg and back braces are devices that are used to support body weight, limit involuntary movements, or prevent and correct deformities. Crutches are devices that may be necessary to help the person learn to walk again in a normal manner. Crutches may be used on a temporary or permanent basis, depending on the type of injury sustained during the trauma.

For successful crutch walking, it is important to strengthen the muscle groups used in this activity. This should begin as soon as the physician feels that the older adult has recovered sufficiently to consider walking. Strengthening exercises should be provided while the patient is still confined to bed. These exercises include the muscles of the arms, shoulders, chest, and back. Before ambulation, the older adult should be taught how to move from the bed to the chair and should be capable of performing this movement without assistance. Older people who need assistance to learn to stand, balance themselves, and ambulate again sometimes experience difficulty. This makes patience on the part of the nurse an important quality.

Important points in crutch walking include correct measurements for crutches so they will have a proper fit. It is important that they have heavy rubber tips to prevent the crutch from sliding. The crutches need to be moved in a rhythmical way that propels the person forward. Finally, the crutches should have padding on the underarm piece so weight is not placed on the radial nerve. The handhold on the crutches may have padding to reduce irritation there as well. The nurse should emphasize good posture for the person who is crutch walking; the head should be held high and the pelvis should be kept over the feet for excellent balance. Crutch walking is best taught in several short lessons to reduce fatigue in the older adult. When ambulation begins, it is important to have an attendant both in front and in back of the person to provide stability and to reduce anxiety about possible falls.

There are several types of gaits that may be used in crutch walking, depending on the type of injury and the physician's orders. These types are:

- *Four-point gait:* The patient bears weight on both feet and has four-point contact with the floor (both crutches and both feet).
- *Two-point gait:* There are two points of contact with the floor (crutches only).
- *Swing-to gait:* Crutches are placed ahead of the person and, with weight on the crutches, the body swings through to the crutches.
- *Three-point gait:* Partial weight bearing is permitted.

As the older adult practices the walking program outlined, the person should master sufficient ADLs to be independent. This independence includes being able to get up and down steps and in and out of cars. It is important for nurses to be very familiar with all assistive devices used in walking programs.

Walking programs also are initiated for those without assistive devices. It is recognized that walking for the older adult is an excellent physical fitness activity. It provides cardiovascular fitness as well as aerobic exercise. Walking for 20–30 minutes, three times a week, has been supported by research as a way to maintain good physical fitness and conditioning. Walking should be a lifelong program to promote wellness and joy in living.

Continence Training

A second major clinical challenge is maintenance of bladder and bowel continence in the traumatized, disabled older adult. The older adult who is the recipient of good nursing care should not experience urinary or bowel incontinence. The use of an indwelling catheter is not effective bladder management. This is because urinary infection can result within 24 hours of catheter insertion. Catheter insertion also lowers the self-esteem and self-concept of the person trying to regain control of a traumatized life.

Bladder retraining is generally successful when a regular time schedule is established for emptying the bladder. Retraining of the bladder takes patience on the part of both the older adult and the nurse. A similar program for bowel training should be initiated soon after admission. As noted earlier, increase of fiber and fluid and a regular toileting regimen promote bowel elimination on a regular schedule. If constipation does occur, stool softeners are the treatment of choice to resolve this problem.

Feeding and Self-Feeding Programs

The clinical challenge of maintaining nutrition adequate for tissue repair and health demands a high level of skill on the part of the LPN. In the early stages of rehabilitative and restorative nursing, the older adult may need to be fed through a nasogastric tube. A specially formulated feeding prepared to caloric specifications is fed through the tube on a regular basis. The tube should be patent, and sufficient fluid should be used to keep it clear and unclogged. After each feeding, flush the tube with 30 mL of water.

As the older adult progresses in recovery, there may be a need to be on a feeding program where manual assistance by the LPN or aide is needed until the person has sufficient strength for self-feeding. Older adults should be fed at regular mealtimes, and snacks also should be provided. Promoting the older person to a self-feeding program is a definite sign of progress. Encouragement is to be given by the nurse so that the older adult consumes sufficient calories to have adequate nutrition to meet the energy demands of rehabilitation.

Self-Promoting Behaviors and ADLs

Independence in personal care is a definite challenge for older adults with disabilities that affect their range of motion, mobility, strength, coordination, and dexterity. It is important that members of the nursing care team allow older adults to have time to independently perform aspects of their own care. Occupational therapists can provide assistive equipment that makes self-care easier. Built-up handles for tooth brushes and hair brushes are easier for older adults to hold. A chair in the tub or shower may allow a weak individual to be able to bathe independently. Lowered sinks, counters, and mirrors might allow a wheelchair bound person to sit up to the sink to wash and perform other personal care. Specially designed sleeves with long handles and long-handled shoe horns allow older people who are unable to bend over to put on their own socks and shoes. Clothing with Velcro fasteners is easier to fasten and unfasten when dressing. Adjustments in the care environment and education of all of the personal care staff is essential to the success of self-care–ADL programs.

SUMMARY

This chapter provides an overview of the principles that govern rehabilitation and restorative nursing practices for LPNs who care for older adults in various settings. Through appreciation of the uniqueness of older adults and their special needs, rehabilitative and restorative nursing care can help them achieve optimal functioning to live life to the fullest.

CASE STUDY

At the age of 60, Mr. A. suffered a severe, incapacitating stroke on the left side of his body. Mr. A. and his wife had planned to retire in 5 years and travel. The stroke created major difficulties regarding the couple's anticipated retirement. While hospitalized, Mr. A. developed a drop-foot condition that interfered with his rehabilitative program. He became despondent over his condition and refused to participate in the walking program.

CASE STUDY
DISCUSSION

As the LPN responsible for Mr. A.'s care, you need to do an assessment of his holistic needs. What are the priorities of care?

CASE STUDY
SOLUTION

1. Mr. A. needs assurance from the health professionals, nurses, and therapists that he will gain sufficient strength to walk with the aid of a walker and eventually to walk independently.
2. The LPN and Mr. A. contract to carry out the walking/exercise program on a daily basis to correct the drop-foot problem.
3. By setting goals, Mr. A. perceives his condition in a more positive light and is encouraged by his progress.
4. The LPN is also concerned about Mr. A's despondency. She documents Mr. A.'s behavior and informs the registered nurse about his psychological state. Together the nurses talk with Mr. A. about his depression and seek his approval to obtain a psychiatric consultation. This problem is then referred to the mental health professional.
5. The LPN arranges for Mr. A. and his wife to become participants in a clinical conference where the rehabilitative team reviews Mr. A.'s case and allows him to make informed decisions on how to proceed on discharge. This may include referral to various social agencies that could assist him in obtaining medical equipment for home use, receiving nursing care in the home if his wife feels unable to take care of Mr. A., and seeking social security/pension payments if Mr. A. believes he can no longer work.
6. Mr. A. is encouraged to eat nutritious meals so that his tissue can repair. He needs sufficient energy from his nutritional intake to properly do his exercises and walking program.

7. Activities are scheduled for him so that he can regain his social skills and interact with people without embarrassment and hesitation. Mr. A. was discharged from the hospital within 2 weeks of the incident, feeling that he once again was in charge of his life and that life was worth living. He could also see that the goals he and his wife had established for retirement could indeed be accomplished. Mr. A. learned to live with his disability and, because of good nursing care, the quality of his life was not diminished.

Study Questions

Please select the one best answer.

1. The aim of rehabilitation for older adults is to:
   a. Engage in limited ADLs
   b. Deny function and performance that existed prior to the incident
   c. Keep food and fluids at a level so that energy and strength are minimized
   d. Restore an individual to his former function and environmental status

2. Which of the following directives *most closely* coincides with the desired goals of a successful geriatric rehabilitation program?
   a. Keep physical changes at a minimum and promote self-esteem.
   b. Promote independence and self-care, along with mobility and a holistic approach to living with the disability.
   c. Promote involvement in limited activities and range-of-motion exercises.
   d. Promote the fulfillment of patient's life's goals in spite of mobility problems.

3. Principles of rehabilitation include the *most important* step in nursing care, which is:
   a. Doing passive range of motion
   b. Understanding the patient's self-concept and encouraging feelings of dependency
   c. Beginning rehabilitation immediately on the patient's admission
   d. Giving selective information to the family

4. Rehabilitation goals specific to older adults include:
   a. Range-of-motion exercises, transfer skills from bed to chair, dependency on enema usage
   b. Improvement of function, delay of deterioration, development of codependent behavior
   c. Accommodation to dysfunction, comfort in the dying process, accommodation to an indwelling catheter
   d. Delay of deterioration, improvement of function, accommodation to dysfunction, comfort in the dying process

5. In continence training for bladder control, the nurse should:
   a. Increase fluids, especially during the evening hours, and toilet the patient every 4 hours
   b. Restrict fluids during the nighttime hours and toilet the patient at his or her request
   c. Increase fluids during the daytime hours and toilet the patient every 1000 mL
   d. Increase fluids during the daytime hours and toilet the patient every 2 hours

References

Bopp, A., & Lubkin, I. M. (1990). Teaching. In I. M. Lubkin (Ed.), *Chronic illness: Impact and implications* (2nd ed. pp. 528–547). St. Louis: C. V. Mosby.

Fraley, A. M. (1992). *Nursing and the disabled across the life span* (pp. 207–226). Boston: Jones & Bartlett.

Hanlan, D., & Sharkey, E. L. (1989). Professional practice of rehabilitative nursing. In S. Dittmer (Ed.), *Rehabilitation nursing: Process and application* (pp. 321–338). St. Louis: C. V. Mosby.

Zejdlik, C. M. (1983). Patient and family health education. In C. M. Zejdlik (Ed.), *Management of spinal cord injury* (pp. 219–226). Montery, CA: Wadsworth.

Bibliography

Gress, L. D., & Bahr, R. T. (1984). *The aging person: A holistic perspective.* St. Louis: C. V. Mosby.
This text places major emphasis on the personhood of the older adult as a unique individual. An excellent discussion of holistic nursing care.

Hogstel, M. O. (1993). *Nursing care of the older adult* (Vol. 3). New York: John Wiley & Sons.
An excellent treatise on care of older adults with special attention to restorative nursing care.

Sankar, A. (1991). *Dying at home.* Baltimore: The Johns Hopkins University Press.
An excellent and practical guidebook on the experiences of caring for a person dying at home. Useful for caregivers of the dying family member.

Videotapes

A Perspective of Hope [Videotape]. Boston: Fanlight Productions (30 minutes).
This video presents a positive but realistic view of nursing on the frontiers of change in nursing homes. It shares the stories of the nursing homes that participated in the Robert Wood Johnson Teaching/Nursing Home Projects.

Survivors [Videotape]. Boston: Fanlight Productions (28 minutes).
Excellent video portraying the problems of growing old with a disability. Includes a discussion of nursing care in, and out of, health-care facilities.

Chapter

PAMELA E. HUGIE

13

Pharmacology and Its Significance for Elderly Clients

Learning Objectives

After completing this chapter, the student will be able to:

1. Identify physiological changes of aging that affect pharmacotherapeutics in the elderly.
2. Identify sensory changes of aging that affect pharmacotherapeutics in the elderly.
3. Identify psychological changes of aging that affect pharmacotherapeutics in the elderly.
4. Identify polypharmacy problems in elderly persons and nursing interventions to compensate for them.
5. Develop a nursing care plan to synthesize interventions to assist elderly persons to maintain proper pharmacotherapeutics.

INTRODUCTION

One of the biggest advances in medical care has been the discovery and rediscovery of plants and chemical compounds that formulate drugs. Drugs are prescribed to manage and sometimes even cure physical and mental illnesses. Ancient civilizations used a variety of herbs and other plant and mineral substances to ward off, prevent, and treat physical and mental problems. Many modern drugs used in western medicine practice have a long history of effectiveness in healing. Some medicines that are prescribed today were originally discovered and used by diverse medical practitioners and healers from other cultures. Quality medical care and medications are responsible for increasing life expectancy of the population. A dilemma of western medicine is the heavy dependence on the use of medications for managing and treating diseases. Many patients do not consider that a medical treatment is complete unless they receive a prescription for a drug. This can be a serious issue for older adults. This chapter examines issues related to drug use and older adults. Some basic terms related to drug use are:

Pharmacology—The study of medications.

Pharmacotherapeutics—The use of medications to treat diseases. The benefit of a medication (desired effect) is weighed against the unwanted and dangerous effects (side effects) to measure the appropriate use of any medication.

Pharmacodynamics—The effect of specific medications at the site of action. Pharmacokinetics, half-life, protein binding, disease processes, and aging affect pharmacodynamics.

Pharmacokinetics—The study of how a medication moves into and through the body, and how it is excreted from the body. The processes of absorption, distribution, metabolism and excretion, are impacted by aging and diseases and influence the pharmacodynamics of any drug.

Half-life—The time required for half the medication to be excreted or inactivated by the body.

Protein binding—Binding properties of proteins. Proteins in the blood stream are binding sites for many drugs. The portion of a drug that is bound to a protein is inactive (only a free drug is available to have a desired effect). Two drugs that are both highly protein bound compete for protein binding sites. This significantly increases the level of free drug in the blood stream (drug molecules that were bound to the protein and have been released). The significant increase has an impact on the effects and adverse effects of the drug.

Adverse drug reactions (ADR)—Unwanted effects or side effects of a medication. Related to changes in pharmacokinetics, dosage amounts, timing of doses, and interactions of medications with other medications or foods

AGING CHANGES THAT AFFECT PHARMACOTHERAPEUTICS

Changes in Vision

Changes in vision can have a serious impact on the safe use of medications by older adults. As individuals age, they experience increased difficulty distinguishing colors,

Visual deficits often are a source of concern with medication management of the elderly.

especially blue and green because of the hardening and yellowing of the lens in their eyes. This yellowing often makes it difficult to differentiate shades of blue, purple, brown, and green, yet older people can see bright yellow, red, and black more clearly. Many older adults have difficulty distinguishing individual pills by color. When older patients are instructed to take the "pink pill in the morning and the blue one at night," they may make errors.

Reading small print is also a challenge for many older adults. Elders often have trouble reading the label on drug bottles because of the small print. Attaching a large print tag to a bottle and having a magnifying glass by drug bottles can help an older person read the medication bottle label and avoid medication errors. Using a medication box or mediplanner is a good idea for many elderly individuals. Medication boxes are filled with the person's ordered medication. For each time during the day that the older person has to take a medication, the box has a separate compartment. Usually, the box is filled for a week at a time, and the days of the week and times of medication doses are clearly marked in large, bold, raised initials, and symbols. Family members and friends can be taught to assist the elderly person to prepare the medication box for a week at a time.

Sensitivity to glare is another visual challenge for aging eyes. Shiny surfaces like plastic tape over medication labels can be difficult for older people to read. Portions of instructions written on paper that has been laminated may be missed or difficult to read because of reflecting glare. Labels for drug bottles should be printed on paper that is not shiny. Medication instructions should be in bold, large print on white or yellow paper to ensure that they can be read.

Decreased Hearing Acuity

Hearing changes (decrease in clarity of higher decibel sounds) increase the possibility that an older person may be unable to hear and understand instructions. Often, out of habit, older adults may nod their heads or state that they understand instructions even if they did not hear all the instructions. Asking them to repeat or demonstrate instructions are excellent ways to ensure that the instructions have been heard. Using large print instructions and following them when giving verbal instructions also help the older person. Many people with hearing difficulties develop lip-reading skills. Make sure that the older adult can see your mouth while you are giving instructions. Wearing lipstick if you are female, and speaking slowly and intentionally rather than louder enhance an older person's ability to read lips. Throughout the time that you, the nurse, are giving verbal instructions, stop and ask older people whether they have any questions. Clarify information and have them restate and demonstrate the teaching that is occurring.

Decreased Taste Acuity

With age, older adults experience changes in taste. It is most obvious in foods. A common complaint is that food is bland or has no taste. Changes in recognizing tastes and flavors result from changes in the taste buds and often in the sense of smell. The ability to differentiate medications by taste is inhibited, and the potential for unknowingly taking nonmedications or caustic poisons increases. Encourage older adults to throw away old prescription bottles and not to use them for storing household cleaning products and other poisons that may be mistaken for medications.

Changes in Touch and Dexterity

Older adults experience decreased touch sensitivity as they age. This can be worsened with decreased circulation and peripheral nerve deterioration in the hands and feet. Arthritic joint changes can combine with decreased touch to seriously decrease strength, which can make it difficult to open modern packages. Childproof lids that require a person to push down and turn at the same time to open them are very difficult for older people to open. Individual drug doses in plastic bubbles that require the plastic to be torn or the backing to be ripped off also are difficult to open. Pharmacists use alternative packaging for older adults if the older person requests it. Flip-top lids can replace the hard-to-twist childproof lids. Bubble-packed medications can be cut out of the packaging and placed in a pill bottle or a pill box.

Cognitive Changes

With increasing age, older adults may have changes in their thought patterns. It is important for the nurse to question what has caused the thought pattern changes. Are the causes pathological, drug-induced, or the result of aging?

Many elders have trouble remembering whether they have taken their medications. Multiple drugs with varying dosages administered at different hours often create confusion.

Many elders are uninformed about how the body functions and the influence of drugs on bodily functions. These subjects were not taught in school when many of these clients received their formal education. Many may be embarrassed to discuss these issues with a health-care professional of the opposite sex.

The technical language that health-care professionals frequently use can be difficult for elderly people to understand. They are often unwilling to ask questions. Many older adults do not want to seem "stupid" or "senile." Many elders state that they trust the doctor or nurse to do what is right. Some older adults report feeling a sense of awe that interferes with their communication with their physician.

Compliance Factors

Often individuals do not correctly follow their drug regimen. This can be intentional or be the result of poor understanding. If older adults do not understand how a drug works or do not like the effect of a drug, they may make mistakes in administering their medications. Common problems are taking doses at the wrong time and altering the dosage amounts.

Forgetting to take medications is a routine compliance issue. When giving elderly people medication instructions, ask them to describe a typical day. Instructions to take a medication everyday before breakfast may encourage compliance, rather than instructing them to take the drug at 8:00 A.M., especially if they sleep until noon or are up at five in the morning. Studies have demonstrated that more medication doses are forgotten when a drug is dosed frequently during the day rather than once a day. Simplified dosing schedules that consider the older adult's daily routine and the use of medications that are dosed only once a day can help the patient to avoid forgetting to take medications.

Drugs are taken for the chemical effect that they have on the body. Unfortunately, unwanted effects or side effects are common for many medications. Individuals often choose to alter the dosages or quit taking an ordered medication because of these side effects. One of the most common side effects that older adults complain of is upset stomach. This often is caused by the medication's dissolving in the stomach and irritating the stomach lining. Stomach irritation can be lessened by instructing the older adult to take the medication with food. If the medication needs to be taken on an empty stomach, encourage them to take at least 8 oz (one cup) of water with the medication. This washes the medication through the stomach faster and hopefully lessens stomach irritation. Encourage your patients to talk about uncomfortable side effects of their medications. Often by simply changing the timing of a medication dosage (from morning to bedtime dosing), unwanted or bothersome side effects may decrease significantly.

It is not uncommon for people to simply stop taking a medication. News in the media and advice from neighbors or friends may make older people uncomfortable with specific drugs or even fearful off the drug's long-term effects on their body. Encourage them to discuss these concerns. Unfortunately, people who are not accurately following prescribed drug regimens are reluctant to tell their doctor. Not following orders could be interpreted as questioning the doctor's skill and knowledge, and most older people do not want to be disrespectful. Many older adults manipulate drug routines to fit their beliefs about personal medication needs. Encourage an open dialogue about medications. Allow the expression of concerns or questions. Review magazines and newspapers that older people read to keep informed regarding potential questions and concerns they may have regarding their medications.

Polypharmacy and Chronic Health Changes

A good rule to follow for pharmacotherapeutics in the elderly is that the smallest number of drugs should be prescribed at the lowest possible dose. Two thirds of physician office visits by elderly clients result in the prescription of one or more new drugs. Of these prescriptions, 50% will not have the desired therapeutic action for various reasons that range from too high or too low a dosage to not getting the prescription filled. Studies have shown that many physicians who prescribe for elderly patients do not make adjustments in dosages although the need for such adjustments related to age have been clearly established. Many physicians are not educated on dosage adjustment for the elderly. Most drugs are not tested for their effects on the elderly. Studies on drug dosing, effects, and side effects are done most commonly with healthy middle-aged adults; then these results are applied mistakenly to drug use for older adults. Such practices can lead to unanticipated drug effects and misdiagnosed drug side effects.

Among the elderly, 85% suffer with at least one chronic disease. People with chronic health problems frequently have several drugs prescribed for each problem. The result, for older adults, often is complex, multiple drug medication regimens. This complexity is compounded when the older individual has multiple physicians prescribing medications. Pharmacists are skilled at identifying potential drug interactions, but their effectiveness depends on awareness of the total medication regimen. If an older person uses more than one pharmacy, a pharmacist cannot be aware of other drugs the individual is taking. Increased numbers of medications and varied dosing schedules can lead to mistakes in taking medications and serious drug interactions, or compounded drug side effects. For example, an older adult with Alzheimer's disease may have periods of agitated behavior. A tranquilizer may be prescribed to decrease the agitation. Unfortunately, the tranquilizer has a sedating effect that can increase drowsiness and make the older adult at a higher risk for immobility and falls. This can lead to joint pain and pain associated with injuries that may require pain medications that can further increase immobility related to drowsiness and increased risk of falls. Using drugs to treat disease symptoms and using other drugs to treat the side effects of such drugs can lead to severe adverse drug effects of polypharmacy. Drug holidays and assessment of drug regimens to simplify them are important steps in avoiding adverse effects of polypharmacy.

Complex prescription routines are not the only cause of polypharmacy. Many elderly individuals take multiple nonprescription medications, such as laxatives, herbs, vitamins, and other home remedies. These widely available, over-the-counter (OTC) medications may interfere with prescribed medications, leading to adverse drug reactions.

Older adults are significantly more prone to have undesirable drug reactions than younger adults. This potential increases in direct proportion to the number of medications being taken. Studies have shown that the potential for adverse drug reactions is 100% when an older adult is taking eight or more drugs a day. Common symptoms of adverse drug reactions or drug toxicity are changes in mood or behavior, restlessness, confusion, irritability, anxiety, insomnia, and hallucinations suggestive of mental deterioration. Many of these symptoms can be confused with acute brain problems, while the adverse drug reaction may go unrecognized. More medications may be prescribed to treat the symptoms of adverse drug reactions and the cycle of problems continues.

Financial Concerns

Medications are expensive. Sometimes older adults self-prescribe rather than pay money for an office visit and a prescription. The end result of this behavior is the use of limited financial resources on OTC, self-prescribed medication that may or may not be beneficial. Elderly clients spend three times more on nonprescription drugs than the general public.

Many elderly patients experience nutritional changes related to decreased financial resources. This may mean a decreased consumption of protein, resulting in decreased serum protein levels and decreased drug binding ability. An increased use of alcohol, with resulting liver damage, may increase the metabolism time of the drug so it circulates longer in the body.

The cost of physician office visits and getting prescriptions filled may be difficult for the aged client to manage. Some patients never get their prescriptions filled. Some save their prescriptions until they can get to the pharmacist with money (this may result in not taking the medications for a month or more). Some patients choose over-the-counter medications for relief of the same symptoms as the prescribed drug and never get the prescription filled. Some patients "save" their drugs by taking only one dose a day instead of two so the medication will last longer. Some patients take the medications until the symptoms decrease and then put the rest away for "later." Some patients share "over-the-fence" medications and health information with their friends and neighbors to save the money of an office visit or prescription filling. For homebound patients, filling a prescription may necessitate the added expense of hiring someone to deliver the prescription, or of driving them to the pharmacy and back home.

PHARMACOKINETICS

Physiological changes related to normal aging and various disease processes affect the pharmacokinetics of many medications. When an individual takes a medication, there are certain expected events that assist the medication to get to the intended site of action or effect. Medications in pill form are usually formulated to break down in the stomach acid or the small intestine. The dissolved medication is then absorbed in the stomach or small intestine. If the individual has had a part of the stomach removed or has a low concentration of stomach acid, the pill may not be dissolved enough to be absorbed as expected. A good blood supply is necessary for the distribution of medication. Diminished blood supply to or from an area of the body alters the effective distribution of the medication. Most medications are metabolized by the liver. Liver disease or changes in the blood circulation to the liver change the expected metabolism of a medication. Excretion is the last step in pharmacokinetics. The kidneys have a major role in the excretion of most medications. Kidney disease or decreased blood flow to the kidneys can seriously change the intended excretion of medications. The following information is a discussion of the specific pharmacokinetic concerns for older adults.

Decreased Absorption

The overall effect of aging changes in the elderly is decreased absorption. A major complaint by many older individuals is changes in gastrointestinal (GI) motility, with resultant diarrhea or constipation. Drugs are absorbed poorly if they travel through the intestines at a rapid rate. Chronic diarrhea and overuse of laxatives move a medication through the intestines at a rapid rate and decrease the time that the drug is in contact with the intestinal wall to be absorbed. Drugs are also absorbed poorly if the intestine is impacted with stool, as in constipation.

Changes in the gastrointestinal tract probably interfere with normal absorption of medications. Older adults often have changes in the quality and quantity of digestive enzymes that are important for dissolving and transforming medications into a form that can be absorbed through the intestine. Gastric pH becomes less acidic and there is an overall decrease in the number of absorbing cells in the intestinal mucosa. The smooth muscle tone and motor activity of the gastrointestinal tract decline with advancing age. These changes, along with slowed intestinal motility, decreased intestinal blood flow, and slowed gastric emptying time serve to further decrease potential drug adsorption. Atherosclerotic changes reduce the flow of blood to the major organs, resulting in slower disintegration of solid dosage forms such as tablets. Because of the changes in GI motility, drugs that are manufactured for normal adult GI motility are not suited to the slower geriatric bowel. Some drugs may be absorbed in lesser amounts; for example, acidic drugs are ionized to a greater extent, resulting in decreased absorption. Acetylsalicylic acid (aspirin), for example, is more ionized in the elderly since their secretion of stomach acid is decreased. Aspirin, therefore, may have decreased absorption in the geriatric client. Some drugs may be absorbed in greater amounts. For example, drugs that are absorbed from the intestines are more thoroughly absorbed if they remain in contact with the intestinal wall for longer periods of time.

Distribution

Drug distribution is greatly altered in the elderly. As people age, the body mass becomes leaner, with decreased parenchymal tissue and increased fat content. Increased fat results in increased absorption of fat-soluble drugs. This results in decreased activity and prolonged effects for such drugs. Examples of drugs showing this effect are hypnotics, sedatives, fat-soluble vitamins, and heparin.

Changes in the cardiovascular system of the aged may result in delayed arrival of the medication at the target receptors, slow release of the drug from the storage tissue, and slowed excretion of the drug. Decreased blood flow to the specific target tissue may result in decreased drug distribution.

Elderly people have decreased plasma protein concentrations. Plasma protein is an important factor in drug binding in the serum. Most drug dosages are set for patients with normal plasma protein levels. If the patient has less plasma protein, more of the drug is free (i.e., unbound to the protein) and, therefore, free to act on the receptors and cause its effect. Warfarin (Coumadin), for example, is 90% bound in the average adult. Its dosage is regulated because 90% of it is bound to protein and will not be available to the patient. If the patient is elderly and has half the normal adult protein level, a normal dose of warfarin can overdose the patient. Some researchers believe that with aging, the number and nature of drug receptors in the body change. This could result in a decreased or increased response to a normal dosage of medication.

Another factor influencing drug distribution is the chronically dehydrated state that many older adults experience. Decreased fluid consumption frequently results in a lower blood volume; this in turn reduces the amount of the drugs and decreases distribution in the blood.

Metabolism

The elderly client experiences a decrease in the rates of overall metabolism, microsomal metabolism of the drug, and hepatic biotransformation of the drug, as well as a decline in the body's ability to transform active drugs into inactive drugs. The overall effect of these changes is that the drug remains for a longer time in an active form in the geriatric patient. Some drugs may remain in the body twice as long as in the younger adult.

Excretion

The altered filtration and decreased plasma volume that occur with dehydration commonly found in the elderly change the excretion of medications. Age-related renal changes result in slower excretion of the drug. Slowed excretion keeps drugs in the body longer and can lead to drug toxicity. Decreased respiratory and vital capacity, with increased carbon dioxide retention, results in decreased excretion of those drugs normally excreted by respiration, for example, anesthetics. Decreased and changed excretion results in an overall increased pharmacological effect of medications on the elderly.

The overall effect of aging changes in the geriatric patient is increased pharmacological effect. Although less medication is absorbed, it stays longer in the body and remains in circulation for a longer time.

PHARMACOLOGY PROBLEMS

Pharmacology in the elderly is frequently identified as a "can of worms." Problems include misuse, overuse, underuse, erratic use, and contraindicated use of drugs. Misuse phenomena include incorrect dosing, sharing of "over-the-fence" medications between neighbors and friends, and use of the same medications for a variety of purposes. Incorrect dosing involves physicians who prescribe dosages based on guidelines for mature adults. As an individual ages, the dosage requirements for most medications decrease. Many medications given in normal adult doses to the elderly result in overdose.

"Over-the-fence" medications appear in scenarios where "Aunt Matilda" has a pill that worked for her shoulder pain and a friend with shoulder pain then calls her to borrow some of the pills that helped Aunt Matilda. The friend may seem to benefit by not having to pay for and make a physician's office visit; Aunt Matilda may feel good about helping another person; but in actuality the drug may not help or may indeed be detrimental to Aunt Matilda's friend. Another aspect of misuse occurs when a drug is taken for a variety of symptoms. "Well, this pill works for my upset stomach; it will probably work for my diarrhea."

Overuse may result from the theory that if one pill works well, then two pills will work better. Patients may feel that if they feel better with a vitamin supplement, two vitamin supplements will be even better. This behavior may actually poison the aged person's system.

In underuse problems, the patient takes less medication than prescribed to "save" pills or money if finances are a problem. Many elderly patients are on fixed and limited incomes, the cost of medication is high, and medication is sometimes too expensive for the patient to afford. Erratic use frequently occurs with short-term memory loss or forgetfulness; for example, a patient may forget to take medications for a day or two.

Contraindicated use can apply in a number of situations. For example, most elderly patients receive several drugs from several physicians. They also may have the prescriptions filled at several pharmacies. The end result is that the elderly population is at a much greater risk for drug interactions, allergic reactions, and problems with polypharmacy (taking multiple medications).

Specific Drug Problems with the Elderly

If all medications were carefully monitored and taken properly, and if the dosage were regulated and accompanied with instructions, the elderly client would still be at greater risk than a younger adult for drug-specific problems due to aging changes in drug absorption, metabolism, and excretion. For example, if the elderly client were prescribed the proper dosage of digoxin, understood the medication regimen, and were in full compliance, the person would still be at a higher risk for complications to develop. The elderly person experiences more side effects and difficulties.

Table 13.1 identifies categories of drugs that may precipitate side effects and adverse effects in the elderly. It is important that the nurse be aware of the possibility of potential problems and monitor for them. Another specific drug problem is the use of OTC medications by the elderly. Antacids, laxatives, alcohol, and home remedies frequently interfere with the proper functioning of medication.

Antacid Abuse

Antacids are consumed in large amounts by the elderly. Physically, a decreased amount of gastric acid has been documented with aging; paradoxically, however, antacid use usually increases with age. The antacids may be used by the elderly for

TABLE 13.1 SPECIFIC DRUG PROBLEMS WITH THE ELDERLY

Effect	Drugs
Drugs that cause dry mouth	Analgesics, anticholinergics, antidiarrheals, antilipemics, antiemetics, antipsychotics, antiulcer medications, muscle relaxants, antihistamines, antiparkinson medications, antihypertensives
Drugs that promote gastroesophageal reflux	Anticholinergics, beta-blockers, diazepam, dopamine, theophylline
Drugs associated with ulcer formation	Adrenocorticotropic hormones, aspirin, indomethacin, iron, histamine, phenacetin, potassium
Drugs that alter absorption of nutrients	Colchicine, neomycin, cholestyramine, antacids, tricyclic antidepressants, carafate
Drugs that promote constipation	Aluminum- and calcium-containing antacids, narcotic analgesics, anticholinergics, diuretics, iron, tricyclic antidepressants
Drugs that may promote diarrhea	Analgesics, anti-inflammatory agents, antacids, antiulcer medications, antibiotics, antihypertensive medications, asthma drugs, cardiovascular drugs, diuretics, iron
Drugs that may promote hepatic damage	Acetaminophen (Tylenol), analgesics, anesthetics, antibiotics (especially penicillin and sulfa), antineoplastics, cardiovascular drugs, oral hypoglycemics, steroids
Drugs that may cause excessive depression	Antihistamines, antipsychotics, anxiolytics, cardiac glycosides, narcotics, sedative/hypnotics
Drugs that may cause dysrhythmias	Antidepressants, cardiac glycosides, phenytoin
Drugs that may damage the kidneys	Aminoglycosides, antibiotics, colchicine
Drugs that may precipitate electrolyte imbalances	Corticosteroids, diuretics
Drugs that may precipitate blood dyscrasias	Antineoplastics, antipsychotics

symptoms of chest pain. Early angina attacks may be considered heartburn and treated with antacids. Other pathological processes may also be perceived as heartburn. This behavior can result in lack of care for serious health problems. Many antacids are high in sodium content. Excessive use of antacids can increase the severity of cardiovascular and renal disease, exacerbate hypertension, and result in increased fluid load for the aged body. Antacids are notorious for altering the motility of the gut, with resulting diarrhea or constipation. Both of these factors result in changes in the pharmacokinetics of the medication regimen.

Laxative Abuse

Another class of drugs abused by the elderly is laxatives. Laxatives may be taken once, twice, or more times a day. Some geriatric patients forget that they have had a bowel movement and take more laxatives to facilitate another bowel movement. Although there is no consistent alteration in frequency of bowel movements with advancing age, the ingestion of laxatives increases significantly.

Laxative abuse may result in actual damage to the intestinal mucosa. The ascending colon is often the site for this damage and may dilate and shorten, losing its typical muscular features, so that there is decreased absorption of other medications (and nutrients) that are administered orally. Laxatives also inhibit the absorption of medications from the intestine; thus, there are decreased levels of drug available and frequently decreased therapeutic effect. Laxatives also result in fluid and electrolyte imbalances that may exacerbate cardiovascular or renal problems. The patient who is a frequent abuser of laxatives should be assisted to develop other bowel training methods. Psychological intervention may even be necessary.

Alcohol Abuse

Alcohol abuse is a social and a health problem in many elderly people. It is the primary drug of abuse worldwide. Alcohol abuse interferes with pharmacotherapeutics and also frequently results in altered nutritional status. This may be seen in decreased serum protein levels (as discussed earlier in this chapter), decreased protein binding, and resultant overdosing of patients. Acid-base balance and fluid and electrolyte levels are adversely affected by alcohol abuse. Changes in these two homeostatic mechanisms result in changes in the pharmacotherapeutic effects of the medication regimen.

Alcohol impairs thinking, judgment, and psychomotor coordination, all of which may lead to decreased medication compliance. Alcohol increases or decreases the effects of several other drugs, and other drugs often increase or decrease the effects of alcohol. Alcohol is a central nervous system depressant that potentiates other central nervous system depressants, particularly barbiturates. When taken concurrently, these two drugs may result in central nervous system depression, coma, and death.

Alcohol has a vasodilating effect and, consequently, increases the hypotensive effects of most antihypertensive drugs. The effect of alcohol on oral anticoagulants varies. Alcohol intake decreases the effects of the anticoagulants until liver damage occurs, at which point the anticoagulant effects are increased.

Use of home remedies frequently interferes with pharmacotherapeutics. Some home remedies have actual benefits, some have only psychological benefits, and some are actually detrimental. For example, the use of bicarbonate of soda for "acid stomach" is detrimental and may result in serious acid-base imbalance. The ingredients of the home remedy need to be evaluated. The nurse must evaluate the frequency of use and the possible interactions.

NURSING CARE OF THE ELDERLY RECEIVING MEDICATIONS

When managing care of elderly persons receiving medications, the nurse should follow the nursing process as taught in Chapter 4 of this book. The five-stage nursing process consists of assessment, diagnosis, planning, implementation, and evaluation.

Assessment

Prior to administration of medication, a thorough assessment of the geriatric patient should be completed. A thorough health history is extremely important. Ask the patient about past diseases, illness, or symptoms and how they were handled. Inquire about the person's current health status. The history must include past use of drugs, present uses of drugs, prescribed drugs, OTC drugs, over-the-fence drugs, and street drugs. Specifically ask about use of laxatives and antacids. Assess the patient's allergies. Clarify stated allergies. Did the allergic reaction cause the patient to have difficulty breathing? Hives? Nausea? Vomiting?

Assess the patient's social support network and home environment. Is the patient able to get prescriptions filled? Are there family or friends to help with medication compliance? Assess the patient's cognitive skills. Is the person confused or disoriented? Is this problem transitory? Is the patient capable of understanding any teaching that occurs? Is depression present?

Assess the patient's sensory status. Is vision impaired? Is hearing impaired? Is the patient strong enough to open pill bottles? Assess the patient's current understanding of therapies and medication regimen. Does the individual understand the drugs, dosage, side effects, and/or adverse effects of current medications?

Assess compliance. Does the patient take medications at the proper time? For what reasons would the patient miss a medication? Does the patient have someone to provide transportation to the doctor's office or the pharmacy?

A thorough physical examination must be performed. Watch the patient for nutrition and fluid status. Is the patient thin and emaciated? Dehydrated? Is the patient's serum protein level low? This may necessitate a reduction in some drug dosages. Is the patient obese? If so, the person may require increased dosages of fat-soluble vitamins and medications.

Diagnosis

Many nursing diagnoses are applicable to the elderly person undergoing medication therapy. Some applicable diagnoses include:

- Altered health maintenance related to insufficient teaching
- Ineffective management of therapeutic regimen related to lack of motivation
- Noncompliance related to lack of financial resources
- Noncompliance related to inability to open bottles

Planning

To promote responsible medication habits in older adults, nurses must help them become informed medication consumers. Because many elderly patients remain in acute-care settings for only a very limited time, discharge planning and teaching must begin on admission.

Before beginning any teaching session, some preparations are important. Choose an environment with good lighting and minimal environmental distractions. Make sure that the patient who has glasses and hearing aids is wearing them. Prepare visual aids and reading materials with strong colors and large print.

Plan the teaching session to be only 15–20 minutes long. Speak clearly and slowly. Use a low-pitched voice (some elders have difficulty hearing a higher pitch). Always face the patient when speaking.

Whenever possible, relate the learning to prior life experiences. For example, when teaching about the thyroid drug methimazole, help the patient identify personal health problems before seeking medical treatment and relate those symptoms to how the person will feel if the medication is "too low." Tie administration times for medications to the person's daily schedule. If the patient eats oatmeal every morning without fail, the morning dose of digoxin can be associated with the oatmeal breakfast.

Treat the patient as mature and capable of understanding. Do not be patronizing in your teaching approach. Teach a family member, friend, or neighbor at the same time. Have the patient teach the other person and observe the knowledge integration. Provide sufficient time for review, questions, and return demonstrations.

Consider the need for assistive devices. Medication boxes come in a multitude of styles with individual slots for different days and times. Consider the need for non-childproof caps. Medication containers can be color coded and accompanied by a wall chart with the color coding system shown. Teach the patient to turn bottles upside down once the medication is taken. Allow the patient to be responsible for taking personal medication the last few days in the hospital. The nurse should monitor these actions and review any areas of knowledge deficit.

Encourage the patient to carry a list of medications (including prescription and nonprescription drugs) at all times. Another family member should carry the same list as well. The patient should be encouraged to share the list with all physicians and pharmacists prior to receiving or filling any new prescriptions. Patients should be encouraged to locate a pharmacy they like and fill all prescriptions there. On all admissions to the hospital, the nurse should review all medications and refer incompatibilities to the physician or pharmacist.

Implementation

In administering medications to the elderly, several strategies are important. When administering medications by mouth, be aware of the medication form. Time-release capsules (e.g., theophylline, cold capsules) should not be opened or crushed and mixed with food. Should the patient be unable to swallow the capsule, contact the physician or pharmacist for a liquid form. Enteric-coated capsules should not be crushed or dissolved. Disruption of the enteric coating allows gastric acid to come into contact with the medication and inactivate it. Offer the most important medication first. Give the patient enough fluid so the medication gets to the stomach.

Parenteral injections should be given into the dorsogluteal or ventrogluteal sites. The deltoid muscle should be avoided because in most elderly patients it has lost much of its mass. The vastus lateralis muscle should be avoided due to decreased muscle mass and decreased circulation. Avoid injections into edematous areas that have decreased circulation.

Intravenous therapy needs to be closely monitored in elderly people since most elderly people operate in a slightly dehydrated state. Fluid overload is especially critical in the person who may have underlying cardiac and renal disease that would be exacerbated by excess fluid.

Some patients may experience visual changes with changes in a medication regimen. Recommend that the client not change prescription eyewear until the medication regimen is established.

Evaluation

Evaluation, the final step in the nursing process, is critical in administering medication for the geriatric client. Evaluate the patient's learning curve by doing a return demonstration teaching session. Ask questions that the patient may encounter in the home setting. Allow the patient to ask questions of you.

Evaluation of compliance is based primarily on patient and family report. Ask the patient if all medications are being taken, then clarify as to how and when the medications are being consumed. Ask about the occurrence of side effects. If expected side effects do not occur, the nurse should wonder whether the medication is being taken. Blood levels (if available for a given medication) should be evaluated to see if the levels are commensurate with the patient's report. Monitor the elderly adult's laboratory results to determine kidney and liver function. Ask the patient for a personal evaluation of how the new medication is working. Does it help? What concerns does the patient have?

The outcome of a successful medication plan can be evaluated by the following criteria:

- The elderly patient's ability to solve problems related to polypharmacy
- Communication of adverse reactions
- Adherence to regimen

CONCLUSION

Pharmacology in the elderly is a complex issue. The nursing care of the elderly client must include attention to the details of the client's medication regimen. The nurse needs to be familiar with the aging changes that affect pharmacotherapeutics, including pharmacokinetic changes, sensory changes, psychological changes, problems of polypharmacy, chronic health changes, and financial changes. It is important that the nurse understand the drugs likely to be misused and be aware of specific drugs of misuse with the elderly, namely antacids, laxatives, alcohol, and home remedies.

The nurse needs to be able to implement the nursing process on behalf of patients to assist them to develop into well-informed medication consumers. The ability to teach regarding medication administration and to evaluate the impact of medications on the elderly person are critical skills for the nurse to have.

CASE STUDY

Mr. W., 74 years of age, lives at home alone. He does fairly well on his own. He has difficulty seeing but can read soup can labels. He has arthritis in his hands and opens cans with an electric opener.

Mr. Wyatt's drug history includes:

- Digoxin 0.4 mg p.o. q.d.
- Hydrochlorothiazide 50 mg p.o. b.i.d.
- Potassium supplement daily
- Propranolol 40 mg t.i.d.

Note: p.o. = orally; q.d. = daily; b.i.d. = twice daily; t.i.d. = three times a day.

Mr. W. denies any use of street drugs and states that he "doesn't believe in that stuff." When asked about other medications, he states that he uses Mylanta "several times a day, just one tablespoon full," and Ex-Lax every day for a bowel movement. He also takes a small blue-and-white capsule that his brother gave him because it helps his brother's arthritis. He takes that capsule "once or twice, maybe three or four times a week."

Mr. W. is currently complaining of weakness, dizziness, and occasional chest pains that he treats with Mylanta. His feet and hands seem to be swelling a lot lately.

Mr. W.'s neighbor called the home health-care agency where you work and requested that a home visit be made because Mr. W. seems to be getting thinner and thinner. The agency assigns you to go visit. You find Mr. W. sitting on the porch with his feet propped up and half asleep.

CASE STUDY
DISCUSSION

1. What is the first step in your home visit?
2. What nursing diagnoses may apply to Mr. W. at this time?
3. While looking at his brother's blue-and-white capsule, you discover the word "indomethacin" on the side. What is your best course of action regarding this over-the-fence drug?
4. Mr. W. is wondering why his feet are swelling and he is feeling weak and dizzy. What drug interactions could be causing these symptoms?
5. What role does the Ex-Lax play in Mr. W.'s pharmacotherapeutics?
6. What referrals does the nurse need to make?
7. What should the nurse do to assist Mr. W. to become compliant?

CASE STUDY
SOLUTION

1. Introduce yourself, explain why you have come, and begin a complete assessment. The history, drug history, and physical assessment need to be

completed. View Mr. W.'s environment. Ask about support services, friends, family, neighbors. Explore nutritional status and assess what food is available for Mr. W. Assess eyesight. Can he read drug labels? Assess compliance. Does he know when and how to take the medications?

2. Knowledge deficit related to medication regimen

   Noncompliance related to lack of understanding
   Ineffective management of therapeutic regimen
   Sensory deficit related to diminished visual acuity

3. Although indomethacin is a nonnarcotic analgesic and nonsteroidal anti-inflammatory drug, it has not been prescribed for Mr. W. Identify his feelings about the medication. Does it seem to help his arthritis? Does he have side effects with the drug? Explain to the patient why it is important not to use this drug unless prescribed by the physician. Identify interactions of indomethacin with other prescribed medications (decreases the effectiveness of diuretics and antihypertensive therapy, increases gastric irritation, increases serum levels and risk of toxicity from digoxin). Stress the importance of not taking drugs unless prescribed by the physician. Offer to make an appointment for him to see his physician and ask for a prescription for a medication to relieve arthritis pain.

4. Increased sodium intake from use of Mylanta could result in peripheral edema. Use of indomethacin could decrease the effect of the hydrochlorothiazide and propranolol, thereby increasing body fluid volume. With increased body fluid volume the heart could be working harder, increasing myocardial oxygen demand and causing angina.

5. Ex-Lax facilitates movement through the gut, thereby decreasing absorption of all the other medications; it probably contributes to fluid and electrolyte imbalance.

6. Refer to the physician for evaluation of chest pain (if this resembles cardiac angina, consider emergency referral) or to social services for necessary social support. Call on family members for assistance with medications and transportation, and suggest Meals-on-Wheels.

7. Set up a scheduling plan. Draw a calendar with medications depicted. Teach the patient to take medications at specific times each day. Encourage discontinuance of Ex-Lax, Mylanta, and indomethacin. Build on the knowledge that he already has. Relate medications to events in Mr. W.'s lifestyle. If he seems unable to manage medications on his own, ask the physician for a referral for home-health nurses to administer medications as needed.

Study Questions

Please select the one best answer.

1. Considering the pharmacokinetics in the elderly patient, which of the following statements is true?
   a. Overall absorption in the elderly is decreased.
   b. Overall distribution in the elderly is enhanced.
   c. There is an increase in receptors with aging.
   d. Excretion in the elderly is facilitated, resulting in a shorter duration of drug action.

2. Which of the following factors would influence compliance the most in the elderly client on a fixed income?
   a. Dietary habits
   b. Cost of filling prescriptions
   c. Body fat to lean muscle weight ratio
   d. Family support

3. Mrs. M., age 82, lives at home alone. Her daughter visits once a day and helps her bathe. Mrs. M. cooks her own meals and works in her home and yard. Which of the following factors could place Mrs. M. at risk of making a medication error?
   a. Multiple medications
   b. Visual changes
   c. Different schedules for different drugs
   d. All of the above

4. Mrs. M.'s daughter reports that she seems to take laxatives two or three times per day. What effect would laxative abuse have on the other medications Mrs. M. is taking?
   a. Increased absorption due to clearance of the GI tract
   b. Increased absorption due to facilitation of medication through the GI tract
   c. Decreased absorption due to increased gut motility
   d. Decreased distribution due to increased fluid consumption

5. Mrs. M. seems to have difficulty remembering whether or not she has taken her pills. Which of the following would assist her in this endeavor?
   a. Medication pill boxes with compartments
   b. Turning the bottles upside down
   c. Color coding the medications with a check-off list
   d. All of the above.

Bibliography

Ali, N. (1992). Promoting safe use of multiple medications by elderly persons. *Geriatric Nursing, 13*(2), 39–42.
   Use of the nursing process to promote safe medication use in the elderly.
Gray, M. (1990). Polypharmacy in the elderly: Implication for nursing. *Orthopedic Nursing, 9,* 49–54.
   Discusses the terms, prevalence, and problems of polypharmacy in the elderly.
Hahn, K., & Wietor, G. (1992). Helpful tools for medication screenings. *Geriatric Nursing, 13*(3), 160–166.
   An excellent screening tool for medication drug histories in the elderly.
Williams, S., & DiPalma, J. (1992). Medication-induced digestive system injury in the elderly. *Geriatric Nursing, 13*(1), 39–40.
   Discusses the effects of medication on the digestive system of the elderly and interventions to alleviate those effects.

Chapter

YVONNE A. SEHY

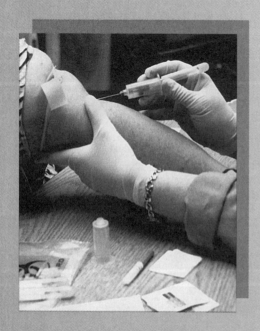

14

Laboratory Values and the Elderly

Learning Objectives

After completing this chapter, the student will be able to:

1. Identify laboratory tests that are important indicators of health and disease in the elderly.
2. Apply an understanding of laboratory tests to the health of elderly persons.
3. Identify at least three reference resources for understanding laboratory values.
4. Identify medications that have an influence on laboratory tests for elderly people.
5. Describe nursing actions appropriate for abnormal laboratory values.

INTRODUCTION

Among the tools for health and illness measurement are laboratory tests. A battery of laboratory tests is done on admission to a hospital or nursing home and, for the elderly, they also are done often when visiting the physician.

As a licensed practical nurse (LPN) you have studied laboratory values and their meaning in your medical and surgical nursing classes. The purpose of this chapter is not to repeat that information; instead it is to provide a ready reference of significant tests for elderly people along with specific and pertinent information that relates to the elderly.

MEANING OF LABORATORY VALUES IN THE ELDERLY

Laboratory tests are a routine part of the health examination for all people. For many tests, the normal ranges are different for elderly people than for the people under 65 years of age. For others, there is no change with age. Also, elderly people may have greater deviations from normal laboratory indicators when under stress, and their return to normal is often slower. Conditions such as anemia, electrolyte imbalances, and infections are common in the elderly. They can be discovered and treatment can be monitored through the use of laboratory tests. The diagnosis and treatment of these conditions result in substantial improvement in health, even in elderly individuals with multiple health problems.

Relationship to Clinical Status

You, as the LPN, need to remember that all laboratory findings must be evaluated in relation to the individual's total clinical situation. The elderly person's gender, dietary pattern, activity level, use of tobacco and alcohol, current medications, and aggressive medical and nursing interventions can alter laboratory findings. Laboratory values should never be considered in isolation, especially when dealing with the often frail elderly person seen in clinical settings. For example, abnormal laboratory values may indicate a physiological stressor such as dehydration or medication side effect rather than illness. It is essential that you consider all facets of the individual's health and habits when you review the laboratory results.

Routine Laboratory Evaluations

A routine laboratory evaluation generally consists of the following:

- Complete blood cell count
- Serum glucose
- Serum creatinine level
- Serum electrolytes
- Thyroid function tests
- Urinalysis
- Stool guaiac test

It is important to remember that behind every laboratory procedure there is a human being who is anxious about the procedure itself or the results of the procedure.

Other specific laboratory tests not part of the routine evaluation may be ordered to help diagnose illness and disease. They include:

- Chest x-rays for those with symptoms or at risk of pulmonary disease.
- Tuberculosis testing, which is recommended for individuals in group living situations or at risk for exposure.
- Baseline electrocardiograms, which should be done in all elderly patients and repeated when there is suspicion of heart rate or rhythm changes, or myocardial infarction.

This chapter includes discussion of the most common laboratory tests ordered and their meaning for the elderly. The values shown in boxed text are normal reference values from *Harrison's Principles of Internal Medicine* (Wilson, 1991), unless otherwise indicated. As an LPN, you must refer to the reference intervals used by the clinical laboratory where you work for the most precise reference ranges.

COMMON SCREENING TESTS

There are three common screening tests that should be performed on elderly clients. The physician may request additional tests, but these three are those most commonly used for general screening and are important for you to know.

Tuberculin Skin Test

Tuberculin Skin Test	
Negative result	<10 mm of induration

General Information

The tuberculin skin test, using purified protein derivative (PPD), is the screening method of choice for the detection of tuberculosis. Unfortunately, as many as 25% of elderly people who are clinically ill with tuberculosis show no reaction (<10 mm of induration) to intradermal injections of 5 U of tuberculin.

Some elderly people, who show no initial reaction to the test, respond after the test is repeated 1 week later. The majority of people who react positively to the test have no clinical evidence of infection. Nursing home residents, whose risk of infection is five times greater than that of nonresidents, should be screened with a tuberculin skin test on admission and annually thereafter. Although the incidence of infection is low and treatment with isoniazid is known to be effective, congregate living poses the risk of epidemic infection.

Nursing Implications

Because anergy (lack of reaction to specific antigens) is common in old people, some clinicians recommend that all purified protein derivatives should be placed with appropriate intradermal technique and should be done annually.

Urinalysis

Urinalysis	
Appearance	Clear yellow/straw
Specific gravity	1.005–1.020
pH	4.5–8.0

General Information

The normal urine should test negative for glucose, ketones, blood, bilirubin, lupus erymathosus, protein nitrates, and calculi in the elderly, though traces of protein may be present. There may be between 0 and 3 red blood cells, 0 and 4 white blood cells, a few epithelial cells, and a few crystals per high-power field on microscopic examination. Elderly people commonly have the presence of 0–3 hyaline casts on low-power field. In addition, between 10% and 50% of older people have asymptomatic bacteriuria.

Nursing Implications

- Usually a midstream, clean-catch specimen is requested. For this, the urinary meatus is cleansed with soap and water or a mild cleaning solution, voiding is initiated, then a sample is collected in midstream to allow clearing of contamination from outside the urinary meatus.
- First morning and fasting urine specimens are collected when the individual awakes and can provide the most concentrated urine of the day. Analytic values for protein, nitrite, fasting urine glucose, and urinary sediment are highest at that time.
- The 24-hour urine specimen measures the average excretion for substances eliminated in variable amounts during the day.
- Urine specimens should be sent to the laboratory within 10 minutes or refrigerated to prevent growth of bacteria as well as to prevent the bacteria from utilizing the glucose.

A urinary tract infection is a specific illness that is common in the elderly. The highest incidence of reported urinary tract infections is in long-term care facilities. This occurs because the urinary tract pathogens often become resistant to antibiotics in nursing homes.

1. Typical symptoms are:

    Frequency
    Burning
    Hematuria

2. In an older person, the only symptoms exhibited may be:

    Nocturia
    Incontinence
    Confusion
    Anorexia
    Lethargy

Stool for Occult Blood

Stool for Occult Blood	
Negative result	Absence of test color

General Information

Gastrointestinal bleeding is common in older people, especially those taking aspirin-containing medications and nonsteroidal anti-inflammatory agents. Up to 2.5 mL of blood per day normally appears in the stool. Hemorrhoids and colorectal cancer are the most common causes of minor bleeding in the elderly.

Abnormal bleeding from the gastrointestinal tract may be either occult (hidden) or obvious by observation. Minor bleeding may be accompanied by a decrease in the

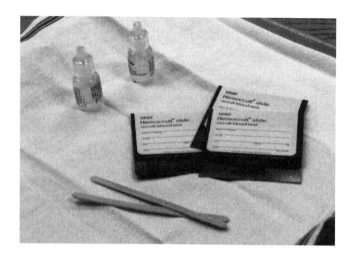

All laboratory procedures require the proper equipment and care of the specimen. This is the equipment necessary to test a stool specimen for occult blood.

hemoglobin and hematocrit, as well as by symptoms of fatigue and weakness. The fecal occult blood test is useful in screening for colorectal cancer.

Nursing Implications

- There are various tests for fecal occult blood, all requiring the contact of a reagent with a stool specimen.
- A positive test result, indicated by color (usually blue), occurs when there is more than the normal amount of gastrointestinal (GI) blood loss.
- Recommendations are to test at least three stool specimens and to sample from at least two areas of each stool.
- Instruct the patient to avoid red meats, vitamin C intake, iron supplements, and aspirin for 2–3 days before and during stool testing, to avoid invalidating the results.

Check the manufacturer's directions for other restrictions.

HEMATOLOGIC INDICATORS

In addition to the three common screening tests, hematologic tests are routinely done on all clients.

Complete Blood Count

The complete blood count includes red blood cell (RBC) count, hemoglobin, hematocrit, RBC indices, white blood cell (WBC) count, platelets, and frequently, but not always, a differential. Values for the complete blood count do not change with age.

Red Blood Cell Count

Men	$5.4 \pm 0.9 \times 10^{12}$/L
Women	$4.8 \pm 0.6 \times 10^{12}$/L

General Information

The RBC count is used to compute and support other hematological tests to diagnose anemia, polycythemia, and other bone marrow abnormalities.

1. Decreased RBC count may indicate:

   Anemia
   Fluid overload
   Kidney problems
   Bone marrow invasion of other cells or tumors
   Recent hemorrhage
   Chronic illness and autoimmune diseases

2. Increased RBC count may be caused by:
   Polycythemia
   Dehydration
   Hypoxia
   Congestive heart failure
   Impaired pulmonary ventilation
   Abnormal hemoglobin

Hemoglobin

Men	14–18 g/dL
Women	12–16 g/dL

General Information

Normal hemoglobin levels are maintained throughout life in healthy individuals. Hemoglobin concentration in whole blood correlates closely with the RBC count.

1. Increased hemoglobin levels may be caused by:

   Polycythemia
   Dehydration

2. Decreased hemoglobin levels may be caused by:

   Anemia
   Recent hemorrhage
   Fluid retention causing hemodilution
   Kidney disease

Hematocrit	
Men	47.0 ± 5.0%
Women	42.0 ± 5.0%

General Information

Hematocrit measures the percentage by volume of packed RBC in whole blood.

1. Decreased hematocrit levels may be caused by:

   Anemia
   Hemodilution
   Bone marrow disease
   Kidney disease

2. Increased hematocrit may be caused by:

   Polycythemia
   Significant volume depletion with an associated increased blood urea nitrogen (BUN) and creatinine.

Red Blood Cell Indices	
MCV	90 ± 7 fL
MCH	29 ± 2 pg
MCHC	34 ± 2%

General Information

Red blood cell indices—mean corpuscular volume (MCV), mean corpuscular hemoglobin (MCH), and mean corpuscular hemoglobin concentration (MCHC)—aid in the diagnosis and classification of anemias by providing information about the size, hemoglobin concentration, and hemoglobin weight of an average RBC.

White Blood Cell Count
$4.5–11.0 \times 10^9$/L

General Information

The WBC count is also known as the leukocyte count. It is used to identify infectious or inflammatory processes, to evaluate the need for further tests, and to monitor response to chemotherapy or radiation therapy. There is a decrease in the WBC count with age due to a reduction in lymphocyte counts. This results in fewer lymphocytes to resist infection.

1. Decreased WBC count (leukopenia) may be caused by:

   Bone marrow depression, due to primary disease (leukemia, myeloma, and other tumors)
   Reactions to antineoplastics or other toxins
   Viral infections (influenza, infectious hepatitis)
   Sepsis
   Radiation treatments
   Drug use, including phenytoin, nonsteroidal anti-inflammatories, and metronidazole

2. Increased WBC count (leukocytosis) may be caused by:

   Infection
   Inflammation
   Tissue necrosis
   Leukemia
   Excessive exercise
   Stress

In the elderly, infection may not be accompanied by a normal increase in the number of WBC (leukocytes), so that a WBC differential is required to detect and diagnose disease.

White Blood Cell Differential

Neutrophils 1.8–7.7	$\times 10^9$/L or 30%–60%
Eosinophils 0–0.45	$\times 10^9$/L or 1%–4%
Basophils 0–0.20	$\times 10^9$/L or 0%–0.5%
Lymphocytes 1.0–4.8	$\times 10^9$/L or 25%–35%
Monocytes 0–0.8	$\times 10^9$/L or 1%–4.0%

General Information

The WBC differential is used to determine the severity of an infection, detect allergic reactions and parasitic infections, identify various leukemias, and assess the individual's capacity to resist and overcome infection.

Five types of WBCs are classified in the normal differential:

- Neutrophils
- Eosinophils
- Basophils
- Lymphocytes
- Monocytes

The absolute number of each type of WBC is obtained by multiplying the percentage of each type of WBC found in a sample of peripheral blood by the total WBC count.

Platelet Count	130,000–400,000/mL

General Information

Platelets, also called thrombocytes, are necessary for formation of the aggregate or plug necessary for clot formation and hemostasis. Platelets also supply phospholipids for the process of coagulation in the thromboplastin generation pathway. When the platelet count is below 50,000/mm^3, spontaneous bleeding may occur.

1. Decreased platelet count (thrombocytopenia) may be caused by:
   Bone marrow disease
   Folic acid or vitamin B_{12} deficiency
   Disseminated intravascular coagulation
   Drugs (antineoplastics, furosemide, indomethacin, penicillin, phenytoin, quinidine sulfate, salicylates, sulfonamides, thiazides, tricyclic antidepressants, and others)
   Destruction due to immune disorders, radiation, or mechanical injury
   Disseminated intravascular coagulation
2. Increased platelet count (thrombocytosis) may be caused by:
   Iron deficiency anemia
   Hemorrhage
   Splenectomy
   Polycythemia vera
   Malignancies
   High altitudes
   Persistent cold temperature
   Strenuous exercise

Coagulation

Prothrombin Time (PT)	
Normal	9.5–11.8 s (control ± 1s)
Therapeutic	1.5–2.0 times normal control

General Information

Anticoagulation therapy is indicated in many conditions, such as pulmonary embolus, deep vein thrombosis, chronic atrial fibrillation, and heart valve prosthesis. Warfarin (Coumadin) is used in oral anticoagulation therapy. PT is an indirect measure of prothrombin and an overall evaluation of these extrinsic coagulation factors. The PT is determined before initiation of warfarin therapy and then daily until maintenance dosage is established. Thereafter, PT determinations may be made at 1–4-week intervals, depending on the stability of the patient's therapeutic level.

Nursing Implications

- Risk of serious hemorrhage is high in elderly anticoagulated patients over age 70, especially those at risk for falls.
- Many drugs have a potentiating or inhibiting effect on warfarin, so that all medications being taken by an individual taking warfarin must be reviewed. Diets high in vitamin K should be encouraged.

Activated Partial Thromboplastin Time (APTT)

Normal	25–36 s
Therapeutic	1.5–2.5 times normal control

General Information

APTT evaluates all the clotting factors of the intrinsic pathway, except for two, by measuring the time required for formation of a fibrin clot. The APTT is used to monitor heparin anticoagulation therapy aimed at increasing the APTT to a therapeutic range. The APTT is more sensitive and is often used in place of the PTT.

Nursing Implications

- If PT or APTT values are higher than the therapeutic range, or if bleeding or signs of bleeding such as hematuria, black tarry stools, hematemesis, bruising and petechiae, epistasis, hemoptysis, continuous abdominal or head pain, faintness, or dizziness occur, withhold the anticoagulant dose and notify the physician immediately.
- Periodic urinalyses as well as stool guaiac and liver function tests are carried out to detect hemorrhage or liver dysfunction.

BLOOD CHEMISTRY INDICATORS

Blood Glucose

Blood Glucose, Plasma

Fasting:	
Normal	75–115 mg/dL
Diabetes mellitus	140 mg/dL on at least 2 occasions
Two hours after eating:	
Normal	140 mg/dL
Impaired glucose tolerance	140–200 mg/dL
Diabetes mellitus	>200 mg/dL on at least two occasions

General Information

In the elderly, the exact definition of abnormal glucose tolerance is unclear. Using the National Diabetes Data Group and the World Health Organization diagnostic criteria, diabetes mellitus is present when the fasting (12–14-hour fast) plasma glucose is over 140 mg/dL on two separate occasions or over 200 mg/dL 2 hours after oral glucose administration.

A number of drugs and conditions affect plasma glucose levels.

1. Decreased blood plasma glucose (hypoglycemia) is indicated by:

   Plasma blood glucose values below 100 mg/dL
   Weakness
   Restlessness
   Hunger
   Nervousness
   Sweating
   Rapidly decreasing mental alertness in the elderly without the common
   symptoms listed above

2. Decreased plasma glucose levels may be caused by:

   Beta-blockers
   Ethanol
   Clofibrate
   Monoamine oxidase inhibitors
   Strenuous exercise
   Failure to refrigerate the blood sample and analyze it within a few hours of
   collection

3. Increased blood plasma glucose (hyperglycemia) is indicated by:

   Plasma glucose levels, which usually exceed 600 mg/dL. Plasma glucose
   above 160–180 mg/dL is the average renal threshold resulting in glyco-
   suria in older persons.
   Lack of symptoms.
   Urinary frequency.
   Dehydration.
   Weakness.

4. Elevation of plasma glucose levels may be caused by:

   Chlorthalidone
   Thiazide diuretics
   Furosemide
   Oral contraceptives
   Benzodiazepines
   Phenytoin
   Phenothiazines
   Lithium
   Epinephrine
   Nicotinic acid
   Corticosteroids
   Recent illness or infection

If undected, worsening hyperglycemia results in alterations in mental status and hyperosmolar coma in the elderly patient with noninsulin dependent diabetes mellitus (NIDDM).

Electrolytes

Normal values for electrolytes are the same for the young and old. Numerous conditions, medications, and dietary factors influence electrolyte values. Common electrolyte-related causes of weakness in the elderly are hypernatremia (high sodium), hyponatremia (low sodium), and hypokalemia (low potassium).

Sodium, Serum	136–145 meq/L

General Information

The elderly are at increased risk of serum sodium imbalance. Decreased sodium levels promote water excretion and increased levels promote retention, primarily through stimulation or depression of aldosterone secretion. Loss of body water causes concentration of serum sodium (hypernatremia), whereas an increase in body water causes dilution of serum sodium (hyponatremia). Sodium also plays a role in acid-base balance, chloride and potassium levels, and neuromuscular function.

Hyponatremia

A sodium concentration of less than 136 mEq/L occurs when there is an excess of water in relation to total sodium.

1. Symptoms may be absent or there may be:

   Fatigue
   Headache
   Restlessness
   Decreased skin turgor
   Nausea
   Muscle cramps and tremors
   Disorientation
   Confusion
   Coma
   Seizures
   Death

2. Conditions causing hyponatremia include:

   Vomiting
   Diarrhea
   Renal disorders
   Diuretics

Congestive heart failure
Cirrhosis
Overhydration
Adrenal insufficiency
Use of nutritional support formulas without additional sodium
Syndrome of inappropriate antidiuretic hormone secretion (SIADH) associated with numerous drugs and diseases

Hypernatremia

A sodium concentration greater than 146 mEq/L is a result of a deficit of body water relative to total sodium content and is usually caused by dehydration.

1. Symptoms include:

    Weakness
    Thirst
    Restlessness
    Dry, sticky mucous membranes
    Flushed skin
    Oliguria
    Diminished reflexes

2. Conditions contributing to hypernatremia include:

    Inadequate fluid intake
    Diarrhea
    Polyuria associated with diabetes mellitus
    Diuretics
    Increased insensible water loss from fever and tachypnea

3. Conditions causing hypernatremia include:

    Hypertension
    Dyspnea
    Edema
    Kidney disease due to a lack of response to ADH

4. Conditions causing excess sodium concentration are:

    Increased dietary intake
    Aldosteronism
    Intravenous infusion of normal saline for treatment of fluid loss or shock

Potassium, Serum	3.5–5.0 mEq/L

General Information

Potassium maintains cellular osmotic equilibrium and helps regulate muscle activity by maintaining electrical conduction within the cardiac and skeletal muscles.

Potassium also helps regulate acid-base balance, enzyme activity, and kidney function. Potassium deficiency develops rapidly because the body has no effective way to conserve potassium.

1. Signs and symptoms commonly seen with hypokalemia (decreased serum potassium levels) include:

   Mental confusion
   Rapid, weak, irregular pulse
   Hypotension
   Anorexia
   Decreased reflexes
   Muscle weakness
   Paresthesia

2. Hypokalemia is caused by:

   Diuretics
   Diarrhea
   Vomiting
   Renal tubular acidosis
   Malnutrition
   Urinary potassium losses associated with glycosuria and ketonuria, and with hyperaldosteronism

3. Signs and symptoms of hyperkalemia (increased serum potassium) are:

   Weakness
   Malaise
   Nausea
   Diarrhea
   Muscle irritability
   Oliguria
   Bradycardia

4. Hyperkalemia is caused by:

   Renal failure
   Cell damage from burns
   Injuries
   Chemotherapy
   Acidosis
   Addison's disease
   Diabetes mellitus

5. Several drugs may increase serum potassium levels, including:

   Spironolactone
   Triamterene
   Nonsteroidal anti-inflammatories (NSAIDs)
   Beta-blockers
   Angiotension converting enzyme inhibitors (ACE inhibitors)
   Penicillin G
   Amphotericin B

Methicillin
Tetracycline

Calcium, Plasma	9–10.5 mg/dL

General Information

Calcium absorption becomes less efficient in both men and women with age. Dietary calcium is associated with the loss of bone that begins in the 40s. Calcium helps regulate and promote neuromuscular and enzyme activity, skeletal development, and blood coagulation. Parathyroid hormone, vitamin D, calcitonin, and adrenal steroids control calcium blood levels. Almost all of the body's calcium is stored in the bones and teeth. Serum calcium varies inversely with the body's phosphorus level. The body requires ingestion of about 1 g per day of dietary calcium, because calcium is excreted in the urine and feces.

1. Signs and symptoms of hypocalcemia include:

    Circumoral and peripheral numbness and tingling
    Muscle twitching
    Facial muscle spasm
    Muscle cramping
    Seizures
    Dysrhythmias

2. The causes of hypocalcemia include:

    Insufficient activity of the parathyroid glands
    Hypomagnesemia
    Hyperphosphatemia due to renal failure
    Laxatives
    Chemotherapy
    Corticosteroids
    Malabsorption
    Acute pancreatitis
    Alkalosis osteomalacia
    Diarrhea
    Rickets (vitamin D deficiency)

3. Signs and symptoms of hypercalcemia are:

    Hypertension
    Bone pain
    Muscle hypotonicity
    Nausea
    Vomiting
    Dehydration
    Mental confusion
    Coma
    Cardiac arrest

4. The causes of hypercalcemia are:

> Hyperparathyroidism
> Thiazide diuretics
> Cancer
> Addison's disease
> Hyperthyroidism
> Paget's disease
> Immobilization
> Excessive vitamin D intake
> Calcium-containing antacids
> Androgens
> Progestins and/or estrogens
> Lithium carbonate

Phosphate Serum	3–4.5 mg/dL

General Information

Phosphate helps regulate calcium levels, carbohydrate and lipid metabolism, and acid-base balance. Adequate levels of vitamin D are necessary for absorption of phosphates from the intestine. About 85% of the body's phosphate is found in bone. Calcium and phosphate have a reciprocal relationship. The kidneys regulate phosphate excretion to maintain a balance with serum calcium.

Chloride, Serum	98–106 mEq/L

General Information

Chloride interacts with sodium to maintain the osmotic pressure of the blood. Chloride is important in maintaining the acid-base balance in the body and varies inversely with the bicarbonate level. Low chloride levels are usually seen with low sodium and potassium levels.

End Products of Metabolism

Blood Urea Nitrogen, Serum	10–20 mg/dL

General Information

BUN is the chief end product of protein metabolism. The BUN level reflects protein intake, liver function, and kidney excretory capacity. The normal BUN value remains unchanged with age. Since protein intake is often low in the elderly, BUN values may be normal even with impaired renal function. Elevation of BUN levels without serum creatinine elevation suggests dehydration.

There are usually no signs or symptoms of an increased blood urea nitrogen level other than those associated with dehydration or other underlying renal disease. Likewise, with decreased BUN levels the signs and symptoms are those of the underlying condition.

1. Increased BUN levels occur with:

   Renal disease
   Reduced renal blood flow
   Urinary tract obstruction
   Increased protein catabolism (starvation, burns)
   Drugs such as aminoglycosides, amphotericin B, and methicillin

2. Decreased BUN levels occur with:

   Severe liver failure
   Malnutrition
   Overhydration
   Chloramphenicol use

Creatinine, Serum	<1.5 mg/dL

General Information

Creatinine values also are unchanged with age. Yet, since lean body mass declines with age, the total daily production of creatinine also declines, staying below 1.2 mg/dL. This causes an overestimate of renal function in the elderly based on static measurements of serum creatinine.

Creatinine clearance declines by almost 10% per decade after 40 years of age and is a more reliable indicator of kidney function than the BUN and serum creatinine values. In the elderly, creatinine clearance is important for determining the dosage for drugs that are cleared by the kidney to avoid drug toxicity. Creatinine clearance (mL/min) is defined as a ratio. For men, the formula is:

$$\frac{[140 - \text{age (yr)}] \times \text{body weight (kg)}}{\text{serum creatinine (mg/dL)} \times 72}$$

For women, multiply the result from the above formula by 0.85.

Increase in serum creatinine may be caused by:

- Renal disease
- Diabetic acidosis
- Starvation
- Muscle disease
- Hyperthyroidism
- Use of ascorbic acid

- Barbiturates
- Diuretics

A high serum creatinine level indicating renal failure may be associated with nonspecific symptoms such as weight loss and weakness. Since creatinine is easily excreted by the kidneys, with minimal tubular reabsorption, serum creatinine levels are directly related to the glomerular filtration rate (GFR).

Bilirubin, Serum	
Total	0.3–1.0 mg/dL
Direct	0.1–0.3 mg/dL
Indirect	0.2–0.7 mg/dL

General Information

Bilirubin is the major product of hemoglobin breakdown and is excreted as a pigment in bile. The excretion of bilirubin is dependent on the normal production and destruction of RBCs and a functional hepatobiliary system, where bilirubin is conjugated and excreted. The direct bilirubin value increases with the obstruction of the flow of bile through the biliary system since this causes uptake of direct bilirubin into the circulation. Levodopa may cause false increases in bilirubin.

Uric Acid, Serum	
Men	2.5–8.0 mg/dL
Women	1.5–6.0 mg/dL

General Information

Uric acid, the major end metabolite of dietary and endogenous purines, is excreted through the kidneys. Cell breakdown and catabolism of nucleic acids, excessive production and destruction of cells, and inability to excrete uric acid are causes of hyperuricemia. An increase in serum uric acid is found in a variety of conditions including gout, impaired renal function, congestive heart failure, hemolytic anemia, polycythemia, neoplasms, and psoriasis.

Serum uric acid levels above 8 mg/dL in men and 6 mg/dL in women are often associated with symptoms of gout. Gout is an acute inflammation of a joint, commonly the metatarsophalangeal joint of the great toe, caused by uric acid crystal accumulation.

Causes of increased serum uric acid levels include:

- Loop diuretics
- Thiazides
- Starvation

- A high-purine diet
- Stress
- Alcohol abuse
- Chemotherapy

Levodopa, acetaminophen, ascorbic acid, and phenacetin may cause false elevations in uric acid levels.

Liver Function Tests

Most liver function tests remain unchanged in the elderly. The alkaline phosphatase level is frequently elevated in the old. Total alkaline phosphatase may rise due to Paget's disease, bone fracture, trauma, or osteoporosis. For clients taking tacrine (Cognex) for Alzheimer's disease, liver function tests are very important.

ALT (SGPT) (alanine aminotransferase, alanine transaminase) or (serum glutamic-pyruvic transaminase)	0–35 U/L

General Information

Alanine aminotransferase, an enzyme necessary for tissue energy production, is present predominantly in the liver. It is also present in the kidney, heart, and skeletal muscles and is a relatively specific indicator of acute liver cell damage.

Elevated ALT levels are caused by:

- Liver disease
- Different medications
- Cholecystitis
- Intrahepatic cholestasis
- Pancreatitis
- Hepatic congestion due to heart failure
- Acute myocardial infarction
- Trauma
- Lead ingestion
- Carbon tetrachloride exposure

Falsely elevated ALT levels are caused by the use of barbiturates and narcotic analgesics.

AST (SGOT) (aspartate aminotransferase, aspartate (transaminase) or (serum glutamic-oxaloacetic transaminase)	0–35 U/L

General Information

Aspartate aminotransferase is an enzyme found in cells of the liver, heart, muscles, kidneys, pancreas, and RBCs. Serum levels are highest during acute cellular damage and decrease during tissue repair. The AST level is useful in monitoring the progress of myocardial infarction and acute liver disease.

Elevations are found in:

- Myocardial infarction
- Liver disease
- Extensive surgery
- Hemolytic anemia
- Pulmonary emboli
- Delirium tremens
- Diseases of the brain, muscle, pancreas, spleen, and lungs

General Information

Alkaline phosphatase is an enzyme active in bone calcification and in lipid and metabolite transport. Serum alkaline phosphatase levels are sensitive to biliary obstruction by space-occupying hepatic lesions, such as tumors or abscesses, and to metabolic bone disease. Alkaline phosphatase isoenzymes may be identified to differentiate hepatic and skeletal diseases.

Increases in alkaline phosphatase are found in:

- Gallbladder disease associated with obstruction
- Paget's disease
- Bone metastasis
- Hyperparathyroidism
- Liver disease
- Osteomalacia

LDH, Serum (lactic dehydrogenase)	200–450 U/mL 60–100 U/mL

General Information

Lactic dehydrogenase is most useful in diagnosing myocardial infarction but also is elevated in hepatic disease, pulmonary infarction, and anemias. It is present in almost all body tissues. Five tissue-specific isoenzymes may be measured: of these, lactate dehydrogenase (LDH_4) and LDH_5 are found in the liver and the skeletal muscles. Elevated LDH values are diagnostic in hepatitis, active cirrhosis, and hepatic congestion.

NUTRITIONAL INDICATORS

The elderly require and consume fewer total calories per day than younger adults. Carbohydrate intake may increase slightly (40% of total calories), whereas fat and protein intakes generally decline in older people. Lean body mass and total body protein decrease, whereas the percentage of body fat increases with age.

It is critical that you, as an LPN, recognize that the elderly are often at risk for malnutrition. This is due to conditions such as decreased mobility, cognitive and sensory deficits, chewing and swallowing difficulties, and loss of appetite due to medications, illness, or the environment. The increased occurrence of wounds, infection, and dehydration creates additional nutritional demands on the elderly, yet the most significant causes of poor nutrition in older people are poverty and chronic illness.

Because of these physiological and societal factors, it is important to have baseline laboratory values for several indices of nutritional status and to understand their significance:

* Total serum proteins measures visceral protein stores.
* Serum albumin is the most widely used indicator of protein status.
* Serum transferrin is an indicator of protein stores.
* Serum cholesterol indicates lipid mass.
* Serum creatinine indicates lean body mass.

The hemoglobin, hematocrit, and lymphocyte count included in the complete blood count (CBC) reflect the body's ability to transport nutrients and resist disease. Other common nutritional indicators are iron and micronutrients such as vitamins and minerals.

Nutritional deficiencies are often identified only when an associated problem such as weight loss, poor wound healing, or weakness occurs. Treating an underlying cause such as medication use or an illness may correct the deficiency. Otherwise, an increased dietary intake of the nutrient, or vitamin and mineral supplements, may be indicated.

Protein Indicators

Total Serum Protein	5.5–8.0 g/dL

General Information

The major blood proteins are serum albumin and the globulins, which together equal the total serum protein value. The measurement of total protein is performed by protein electrophoresis and aids in the diagnosis of protein deficiency, blood dyscrasias, and hepatic, gastrointestinal, renal, and neoplastic diseases.

1. Symptoms commonly seen with low serum protein values are:
    Dermatitis
    Hair thinning

Muscle wasting
Weakness
Poor wound healing

2. Total protein values are increased with:

Dehydration
Diabetic acidosis
Infections
Multiple myeloma
Monocytic leukemia
Chronic alcoholism
Chronic inflammatory disease

3. Common causes are:

Edema
Tissue breakdown
Poor wound healing

4. Total protein values decrease with:

Malnutrition
Hepatic disease
Renal disease
Gastrointestinal disease
Hodgkin's disease
Trauma such as burns, hemorrhage, and shock
Hyperthyroidism
Congestive heart failure

Albumin, Serum	3.5–5.5 g/dL

General Information

Albumin values of less than 3.5 g/dL indicate protein malnutrition and are accompanied by an increased incidence of morbidity and mortality. Albumin maintains oncotic pressure and transports substances such as bilirubin, fatty acids, hormones, and drugs that are insoluble in water.

1. Albumin is increased only in multiple myeloma.
2. Albumin is decreased in:

Malnutrition
Liver and renal disease
Collagen diseases
Rheumatoid arthritis
Metastatic carcinoma
Hyperthyroidism

Essential hypertension
The use of cytotoxic agents

Globulins, Serum	2.0–3.0 g/dL

General Information

The four types of globulins identified by protein electrophoresis are found in differing quantities in various conditions. Alpha$_1$, alpha$_2$, and beta-globulin are carrier proteins that transport lipids, hormones, and metals through the blood. Gamma globulin is an important component of the immune system.

Globulins are increased in:

- Tuberculosis
- Chronic syphilis
- Subacute bacterial endocarditis
- Myocardial infarction
- Multiple myeloma
- Collagen diseases
- Rheumatoid arthritis
- Diabetes mellitus
- Hodgkin's disease

Nursing Implications

Because a consistent relationship between protein intake and serum albumin levels has not been established, a high-protein diet is not advised except for individuals with evidence of protein calorie malnutrition. Protein allowance is the same for older people as for younger ones: 0.8 g/kg body weight. Protein should provide at least 12% of total calories for the healthy older person. The proteins from animal sources such as beef, poultry, fish, and dairy products are the most complete, whereas complementary vegetable proteins have less biological value. Some patients may need nutritional supplementation through oral, enteral, or parenteral routes if malnutrition is severe.

Iron Indicators

Iron, Serum	
Men	80–180 µg/dL
Women	60–160 µg/dL

General Information

Iron appears in the plasma bound to the glycoprotein transferrin. Iron is essential in the production and function of hemoglobin as well as other compounds. Dietary iron is absorbed by the intestine and distributed in the body for synthesis, storage, and transport. The body has no mechanism for eliminating excessive iron; therefore total body and bone marrow iron stores increase with advancing age, although serum iron may be depleted. Serum iron values should be interpreted together with the total iron binding capacity (TIBC) and the serum ferritin. It may be necessary to seek bone marrow and liver biopsy as well as iron absorption or excretion studies to obtain a definitive diagnosis in iron-related disease. A decrease in serum iron with an increased TIBC occurs in iron deficiency anemia, which is most commonly caused in the elderly by gastrointestinal blood loss or malabsorption.

Ferritin, Serum	15–200 ng/mL

General Information

Ferritin is an iron-storage protein. Serum ferritin level indicates the amount of available iron stored in the body. It is measured to distinguish between iron deficiency (decreased ferritin level) and chronic infection or inflammation (increased or normal ferritin level).

1. Serum ferritin is increased in:

   Hepatic disease
   Iron overload
   Leukemia
   Hodgkin's disease
   Chronic renal disease
   Hemolytic anemias
   Acute or chronic infection and inflammation

2. Ferritin is decreased in chronic iron deficiency.

Total Iron-Binding Capacity (transferrin), Serum	250–460 μg/dL

Total iron-binding capacity decreases with age and reflects the transferrin content of the serum. Transferrin, a beta-globulin protein, transports circulating iron that is stored in various forms in the bone marrow, liver, and spleen. In protein-energy malnutrition, the TIBC is less than 250 mg/dL (see discussion under serum iron above).

Lipoproteins

Total Plasma Cholesterol	
Desired	<200 mg/dL
Borderline	200–239 mg/dL
High	240 mg/dL

High-Density Lipoprotein (HDL) Cholesterol	
Desired	>35

Low-Density Lipoprotein (LDL) Cholesterol	
Desired	130 mg/dL
Borderline	130–159 mg/dL
High	160 mg/dL
Triglycerides	160 mg/dL

General Information

Blood lipid and lipoprotein cholesterol levels that are influenced by heredity, diet, and obesity are directly related to atherosclerotic heart disease in the elderly. HDL cholesterol, LDL cholesterol, and a decreased level of plasma triglycerides are all associated with decreased incidence of coronary heart disease.

In women, the increase in plasma total cholesterol with age is due primarily to an increase in LDL cholesterol. HDL cholesterol increases slightly in men over 65 years of age but decreases in women of the same age. The risk for coronary heart disease in the elderly gradually increases without intervening therapy.

Both total cholesterol and HDL cholesterol should be measured in screening tests for the elderly. The findings of a high initial cholesterol value should be followed by two subsequent evaluations because there may be significant daily variations in values. Older persons may have a total cholesterol of less than 200–240 mg/dL but have elevated LDL cholesterol and decreased HDL cholesterol and so have an increased risk of coronary heart disease. Conversely, the HDL cholesterol may be high, accounting for a total cholesterol level greater than 200 mg/dL, so that there is a reduced risk for coronary heart disease. Total cholesterol and HDL cholesterol may be obtained from nonfasting blood samples. Triglyceride levels are only accurate after a 12-hour fast. LDL cholesterol levels may be calculated after the total cholesterol, HDL cholesterol, and triglycerides are known.

Lipid abnormalities are often familial, but secondary causes are common in the elderly. They include:

- Diets high in saturated fat or cholesterol
- Excessive alcohol intake
- Estrogen supplements
- Thiazide diuretics
- Beta-blockers
- Smoking
- Uncontrolled diabetes
- Hypothyroidism
- Uremia
- Corticosteroid use
- Sedentary lifestyle
- Morbid obesity

Cholesterol levels less than 120–156 mg/dL have been associated with increased mortality in nursing home residents. Cholesterol is decreased in:

- Malnutrition
- Hyperthyroidism
- Chronic obstructive pulmonary disease

Nursing Implications for Lipid Abnormalities

- Weight control
- Increased physical activity
- Restriction of alcohol
- Cessation of smoking
- Restriction of dietary fat

Dietary restriction must be made cautiously since maintaining adequate calorie and protein intake is a major concern among the elderly. Drug therapy to control lipid levels may be beneficial in older persons with known coronary heart disease or high risk of disease.

DRUG MONITORING AND TOXICOLOGY

Drug monitoring is important when the margin of safety between therapeutic and toxic blood levels is narrow. Drug blood levels are useful guides in maintaining therapeutic levels as well as in identifying toxic levels of drugs. Not all drugs have a known therapeutic blood level even though toxic levels have been identified. Some drugs, such as amphetamines, are monitored through urine testing. The elderly metabolize and eliminate drugs more slowly than mature adults, a fact that heightens the importance of drug monitoring.

Three commonly monitored drugs—digoxin, theophylline, and phenytoin—are discussed, because they require close observation from you, the nurse. Numerous

TABLE 14.1 **COMMONLY MONITORED DRUGS**

Alcohol
ethanol
isopropanol (rubbing alcohol)
methanol (antifreeze)

Amphetamines (urine testing)
amphetamine
dextroamphetamine
methamphetamine (Desoxyn)
phenmetrazine (Preludin)

Antiarrhythmics
disopyramide (norpace)
lidocaine (Xylocaine)
procainamide (Pronestyl)
propranolol (Inderal)
quinidine (Quinaglute, etc.)
verapamil (Calan, Isoptin)

Antibiotics
amikacin (Amikin)
gentamicin (Garamycin)
kanamycin (Kantex)
netilmicin (Netromycin)
tobramycin (Nebcin)

Anticonvulsants
cabamazepine (Tegretol)
ethosuximide (Zarontin)
phenobarbital (Luminal)
phenytoin (Dilantin)
primidone (Mysoline)

Antidepressants
amitriptyline
nortriptyline (Pamelor, Aventyl)
desipramine (Norpramin)
doxepin (Sinequan, etc.)
imipramine (Tofranil)
lithium (Lithobid)

Barbiturates and Hypnotics
amobarbital (Amytal)
glutethimide (Doriden)
pentobarbital (Nembutal)
phenobarbital (Luminal)
secobarbital (Seconal)

Bronchodilators
aminophylline
theophylline (Theo-Dur, etc.)

Cardiac Glycosides
digitoxin (Crystodigin)
digoxin (Lanoxin)

Hemoglobin Derivatives
carboxyhemoglobin (Hg = CO)
methemoglobin
sulfhemoglobin

Nonnarcotic Analgesics
acetaminophen (Tylenol, etc.)
salicylates (aspirin)

Phenothiazines
chlorpromazine (Thorazine)
prochlorperzine (Compazine)
thioridazine (Mellaril)
trifluoperazine (Stelazine)

classes of drugs are commonly checked for therapeutic or toxic levels. Please review the list in Table 14.1. Refer to a basic laboratory manual for specific drug therapeutic and toxic values.

Digoxin

digoxin (Lanoxin) level, serum

Therapeutic	0.5–20 ng/mL
Toxic	2.5 ng/mL

General Information

Digoxin, used in the treatment of congestive heart failure and cardiac arrhythmias, has a prolonged half-life in the elderly because of its reduced renal clearance. Serum digoxin level has a narrow therapeutic range and despite the availability of tests for serum drug levels, digitalis toxicity is relatively common in the elderly.

The most common side effects of digitalis toxicity are:

- Visual changes
- Headache
- Nausea and vomiting
- Weakness and fatigue

Weakness and fatigue are sometimes the only indicators of digitalis toxicity in elderly people.

Quinidine significantly increases the serum level of digoxin. Consequently, the digoxin dose must be reduced when both of these drugs are prescribed. Also, a change from tablet to elixir preparation of digoxin increases the absorption and serum level, so that the digoxin dose again needs to be reduced. Both low-serum potassium level and high-serum calcium level increase the risk of serious arrhythmias in persons on digoxin therapy.

Nursing Implications for Digoxin Blood Levels

- Draw blood samples for determining serum digoxin levels at least 5–6 hours after the daily dose, and preferably just before the next scheduled daily dose.
- Check the apical pulse for 1 full minute.
- Suspect digitalis toxicity when there is a sudden change in heart rhythm or pulse (especially a decrease).
- Withhold the medication and report to the patient's physician when there is a sudden change in pulse or rhythm.
- Monitor the serum potassium level, especially if the patient is taking diuretics.

Theophylline

theophylline, serum	
Therapeutic	10–20 μg/mL
Toxic	20 μg/mL

General Information

Theophylline, a bronchodilator, may or may not be associated with improved respiratory effort on spirometry testing. Nevertheless, theophylline improves mucocilliary clearance of the lungs and may improve myocardial contractility, stimulate respirations, and act as a mild diuretic.

Wide variations in the rate and extent of absorption and rate of metabolism for theophylline result in peak-to-trough fluctuations in serum concentrations and subsequent subtherapeutic or toxic responses.

1. Indications of possible toxicity include:

   Anorexia
   Abdominal discomfort
   Nausea
   Vomiting
   Dizziness
   Shakiness
   Restlessness
   Irritability
   Palpitations
   Tachycardia
   Hypotension
   Heart arrhythmias and seizures

2. Dizziness is a common side effect at the initiation of theophylline use in the elderly.

3. Elimination of the drug is reduced in persons with:

   Heart failure
   Kidney or liver dysfunction
   Alcoholism
   Fever

4. Smoking and phenytoin increase the elimination of theophylline so that an increase in dosage is required. The macrolide antibiotics (e.g., erythromycin), as well as others, may increase serum theophylline levels and cause toxicity.

Nursing Implications

- Regular monitoring of serum concentrations of theophylline is necessary to determine therapeutic dosage.
- The serum level must be checked when signs or symptoms of toxicity develop or when medications affecting serum levels are added or discontinued.

Phenytoin

phenytoin (Dilantin), serum

Therapeutic	10–20 μg/mL
Toxic	30 μg/mL

General Information

Phenytoin, an anticonvulsant that also has antiarrhythmic properties, is metabolized by the liver and excreted in the bile and partially by the kidneys. Phenytoin unfortunately has a number of potentially serious adverse reactions and side effects that necessitate monitoring of several parameters, including liver, kidney, thyroid, and hematological functioning.

1. Potential adverse reactions and side effects are:

> Drowsiness
> Mental confusion
> Tremors
> Bradycardia
> Hypotension
> Photophobia
> Blurred vision
> Nausea
> Vomiting
> Epigastric pain
> Abnormal blood counts
> Fever
> Skin eruptions
> Pneumonitis

2. Acute kidney or liver dysfunction results in toxic drug levels.
3. Decreased phenytoin serum levels may result from:

> Chronic alcohol abuse
> Antacids
> Antihistamines
> Antineoplastics
> Barbiturates
> Excess of folic acid
> Rifampin

4. Increased serum levels may result from:

> Acute intake of alcohol
> Anticoagulants
> Aminosalicylic acid
> Benzodiazepines
> Cimetidine
> Dexamethasone
> Estrogens
> Isoniazid
> Methylphenidate
> Phenothiazines
> Salicylates
> Sulfonamides
> Phenylbutazone

Nursing Implications

- Liver and thyroid function tests, blood counts, and urinalysis are recommended prior to initiation of therapy, at monthly intervals during early therapy, and at regular intervals thereafter.
- Lower doses are given to geriatric patients and those with liver or kidney impairment.
- When phenytoin is given intravenously, vital signs and cardiac function must be monitored closely.
- Serum concentrations of magnesium, folic acid, vitamin D, and vitamin K may be decreased with phenytoin therapy and should be monitored.
- Symptoms of low serum magnesium may mimic those of phenytoin toxicity.

SUMMARY

The use and interpretation of laboratory values are important in substantiating clinical judgment and providing comprehensive health assessment in the elderly. Physiological changes in older persons, presence of disease, use of medications, variance in diets, and even exercise affect laboratory values. It is, therefore, necessary to monitor changes in an individual's laboratory values as well as to compare an individual's values with those of other older persons in similar situations.

Understanding laboratory values in the elderly is a continuing endeavor for all health-care practitioners. It is important to consistently refer to comprehensive laboratory manuals and individual laboratory reference intervals used in a particular locality, as well as to specialized geriatric references. As new information becomes available, the interpretation of laboratory data will become more useful in determining care for elderly people.

CASE STUDY

Mr. K. is an 85-year-old resident of a small, independent group home where he has been caring for himself, but sharing provided meals with the other residents. He underwent a transurethral resection of the prostate 4 years ago for benign prostatic hypertrophy. He has been treated for heart irregularity and congestive heart failure in the past. Today he is being admitted to your intermediate care facility by his daughter because of several recent falls. Mr. K. reports that he has been nauseated and has not been eating well for the past few days. He also complains of wetting before reaching the restroom and blames this on his slow movement due to severe degenerative arthritis of his joints. Medications include:

- furosemide (Lasix) 40 mg in the morning
- digoxin 0.125 mg in the morning
- ibuprofen (Motrin) 600 mg twice a day
- acetaminophen (Tylenol) 500 mg every 4 hours as needed

On physical assessment you find the following:

- Height 5 ft 10 in
- Weight 135 lb
- Blood pressure sitting 120/70 and pulse irregular at 80/min
- Blood pressure standing 90/60 and pulse irregular at 90/min
- Respirations 20/min and unlabored
- Temperature 98.8°F (36°C)
- Lungs are clear
- Skin is warm and dry, with dry mucous membranes

Laboratory values available are:

- Potassium 3.2 mEq/L
- Sodium 132 mEq/L
- Chloride 106 mEq/L
- BUN 30 mg/dL
- Creatinine 1.4 mg/dL
- Glucose 130 mg/dL
- Urinalysis 3–5 WBCs, 0–3 RBCs, positive bacteria, specific gravity 1.022

CASE STUDY
DISCUSSION

1. What problems have you identified based on the resident's history and physical assessment?
2. What other laboratory tests would be helpful?
3. What nursing actions will you take immediately?

CASE STUDY
SOLUTIONS

1. Underweight with risk of malnutrition
   Heart arrhythmia with possible orthostatic hypotension
   Probable urinary tract infection with urinary incontinence
   Anorexia and nausea possibly related to medications or urinary tract infection
   Recurrent falls with several possible causes, including weakness due to decreased food and fluid intake, hypokalemia and hyponatremia, difficulty ambulating due to degenerative arthritis, orthostatic hypotension due to dehydration, and infection

2. Complete blood count to assess for anemia and infection
   Digoxin level to check for toxicity as a cause of anorexia and nausea
   Urine culture and sensitivity to identify and quantify the urine bacteria and determine antibiotic sensitivity
   Total protein to evaluate nutritional status

3. Safety measures to prevent falls, such as having the patient call for assistance before getting up to go to the restroom. Advise the patient to change positions slowly from lying to sitting, then from sitting to standing. Consider a bedside commode since the patient has urinary incontinence and difficulty ambulating.
   Provide fluids and simple, easily digested foods in frequent small amounts. If nausea occurs, notify the physician.
   Withhold digoxin until the level value is obtained. Report to the physician.
   Withhold the Lasix since the resident is dehydrated and has hypokalemia and hyponatremia, probably as a result of the diuretic. Report to the physician.
   Check any stools for occult blood since ibuprofen (a nonsteroidal anti-inflammatory) is often the cause of gastrointestinal bleeding. If the CBC indicates an iron deficiency anemia, the physician will probably discontinue this medication. Acetaminophen tylenol may be used on a regular schedule to control arthritic pain.

Study Questions

Please select the one best answer.

1. All laboratory test results for the elderly should be:
   a. Evaluated against younger clients
   b. Evaluated against the other older clients on the unit
   c. Evaluated against the client's total clinical situation
   d. Evaluated against the client's CBC results

2. With tuberculosis on the increase among the elderly, it is critical for the LPN to know that:
   a. Tuberculosis (TB) skin tests are inaccurate on people over the age of 65
   b. When there is no initial reaction to the TB skin test on elderly clients, it should be given again 1 week later
   c. It is unnecessary and expensive to do TB screening on nursing home residents
   d. Isoniazid is not an effective TB drug of choice for the elderly

3. The PT test is a measure of the overall coagulation factors. The risk of serious hemorrhage is high in the elderly when:
   a. Warfarin is used
   b. Medication reviews on all medications are done
   c. PTs are drawn daily until the therapeutic dose is determined
   d. They are at risk for falls and subsequent bleeding

4. Potassium deficiency develops:
   a. Slowly in the elderly
   b. In the kidneys
   c. Rapidly because there is no way to conserve it
   d. Only when using diuretics

5. Every elderly person with a low-serum albumin level should be:
   a. Put on a high-protein diet
   b. Put on bedrest
   c. Put on a diet of 12% complete proteins
   d. Put on vitamin supplements

References

Ford, R. D. (1987). *Diagnostic tests handbook.* Springhouse, PA: Springhouse Corporation.
Wilson, J. D. (1991). *Harrison's principles of internal medicine, vol. 2.* New York: McGraw Hill.

Bibliography

Alford, D. M. (1991). Tips on promoting food and fluid intake in the elderly. *Journal of Gerontological Nursing, 17*(11), 44.
   Because good nutritional intake is essential to obtaining normal readings of laboratory values, this article supplies information on how to effectively promote an adequate intake.
Melillo, K. D. (1993). Interpretation of abnormal laboratory values in older adults. *Journal of Gerontological Nursing, 19*(1), 39.
Melillo, K. D. (1993). Interpretation of abnormal laboratory values in older adults: Part II. *Journal of Gerontological Nursing, 19*(2), 35.
   These sequential articles give succinct and pertinent information on reading laboratory values in the elderly.

Appendix A

LIVING WILL INSTRUCTION GUIDE

INTRODUCTION

This packet contains a legal document that protects your right to refuse medical treatment you do not want, or to request treatment you do want, in the event you lose the ability to make decisions yourself.

The *Choice In Dying Living Will* has been created to protect your constitutional right to state your wishes about medical care in the event that you develop an irreversible condition that prevents you from making your own medical decisions. The Living Will becomes effective if you become terminally ill, permanently unconscious, or minimally conscious due to brain damage and will never regain the ability to make decisions.

> Note: This document will be legally binding only if the person completing it is a competent adult (at least 18 years old).

CHOICE IN DYING LIVING WILL

How Do I Make My Living Will Legal?

Choice In Dying recommends that you sign your Living Will in the presence of two adult witnesses. Your witnesses should not be:

- Related to you by blood or marriage
- Beneficiaries of your estate
- Your health care provider or an employee of your health care provider, or
- Your appointed health care agent or proxy

> Note: You do not need to notarize your Living Will.

Can I Add Personal Instructions to My Living Will?

Yes. You can add personal instructions in the part of the document called "Other Directions." For example, if there are any specific forms of treatment that you wish to refuse that are not already listed on the document, you may list them here. Also, you can add instructions such as, "I do not want to be placed in a nursing home," or "I want to die at home."

If you have appointed a health care agent, it is a good idea to write a statement such as, "Any questions about how to interpret or when to apply my Living Will are to be decided by my agent."

> It is important to learn about the kinds of life-sustaining treatment you might receive. Consult your doctor or order the Choice In Dying pamphlet, "Medical Treatments and Your Living Will."

(Reproduced with permission from Choice in Dying, Inc.)

What if I Change My Mind?

You may revoke your Living Will at any time by:

- Executing a new Living Will
- Tearing, burning, or otherwise destroying your document, or
- Notifying your doctor orally or in writing of your intent to revoke your document

WHAT TO DO AFTER YOU HAVE COMPLETED YOUR DOCUMENT

1. *Your Choice In Dying Living Will* is an important legal document. Keep the original signed document in a secure but accessible place. Do not put the original form in a safe deposit box or any other security box that would keep others from having access to it.
2. Give photocopies (xerox copies) of the signed original to your health care agent and alternate, to your doctor(s), family, close friends, clergy, and anyone else who might become involved in your health care. If you enter a nursing home or hospital, have a xerox copy of your document placed in your medical records.
3. Be sure to talk to your doctor(s), clergy, and family and friends about your wishes concerning medical treatment. Discuss your wishes with them often, particularly if your medical condition changes.
4. If you want to make changes to your document after it has been signed and witnessed, you must complete a new document.
5. Remember, you can always revoke your *Choice In Dying Living Will*.

ANSWERS TO CHAPTER STUDY QUESTIONS

Chapter 1	1. b	2. a	3. a	4. d	5. b
Chapter 2	1. c	2. a	3. a	4. b	5. c
Chapter 3	1. c	2. d	3. a	4. d	5. b
Chapter 4	1. b	2. c	3. c	4. d	5. a
Chapter 5	1. a	2. d	3. b	4. c	5. a
Chapter 6	1. d	2. c	3. a	4. d	5. d
Chapter 7	1. c	2. a	3. b	4. d	5. b
Chapter 8	1. b	2. c	3. c	4. d	5. d
Chapter 9	1. b	2. c	3. d	4. d	5. b
Chapter 10	1. d	2. c	3. d	4. c	5. d
Chapter 11	1. b	2. d	3. a	4. d	5. d
Chapter 12	1. d	2. b	3. c	4. d	5. d
Chapter 13	1. a	2. b	3. d	4. c	5. d
Chapter 14	1. c	2. b	3. d	4. c	5. c

Index

Note: Page numbers followed by "f" indicate figures; page numbers followed by "t" indicate tables; and page numbers followed by "b" indicate boxed material.